THOMAS F. TORRANCE

An Intellectual Biography

THOMAS F. TORRANCE

An Intellectual Biography

ALISTER E. McGRATH

t&t clark

Published by T&T Clark International
A Continuum imprint

The Tower Building,
11 York Road,
London, SE1 7NX

80 Maiden Lane,
Suite 704
New York, NY 10038

Copyright © T&T Clark Ltd, 1999

All rights reserved. No part of this publication may be reproduced,
stored in a retrieval system, or transmitted in any form or by any means,
electronic, mechanical, photocopying, recording or otherwise,
without the prior permission of T&T Clark Ltd.

First published 1999
Paperback edition 2006
Reprinted 2006

ISBN 0 567 08683 6 (hardback)
ISBN 0567 03085 7 (paperback)

British Library Cataloguing-in-Publication Data
A catalogue record for this book is available from the British Library

Typeset by Waverley Typesetters, Galashiels

Contents

PART TWO
THE CONTOURS OF A SCIENTIFIC THEOLOGY

Photographs and Maps

Maps

Introduction

THOMAS FORSYTH TORRANCE is widely regarded, particularly outside Great Britain, as the most significant British academic theologian of the twentieth century, and is especially noted for his ground-breaking contribution to the study of the relationship of Christian theology and the natural sciences. He is unquestionably one of the most prolific of theological writers: by the time of his retirement in 1979, Torrance had authored, edited or translated more than 360 pieces; since his retirement, he has added more than 250 further items to this already impressive list. The most senior member of the nearest thing to a 'theological dynasty' that Great Britain has ever produced, Torrance has produced a massive theological *oeuvre* covering a wide range of topics, particularly the seminally important field of science and Christian theology. While prophets are perhaps always doomed to be without honour in their own country, it is clear that many inside and outside Scotland are finding Torrance to be a major stimulus to their own thought. The rapidly increasing number of doctoral theses devoted to an analysis of aspects of his thought is a telling indication of his long-term significance.

Every reader likes to know why a particular book was written. I had been aware of Torrance's work for some years, having made extensive use of some of his writings in relation to a number of projects on which I was engaged over the period 1980–92. It was, however, from 1992 that I began to appreciate more fully the depth of Torrance's thought, and the immense erudition which lay behind it. My initial research work was in the field of molecular biology, and it had always been my intention to focus my attention on the complex and exciting field of the interaction of science and religion. In 1992, I was finally able to begin this work in earnest. It has to be said, in the nicest possible way, that this is a field which largely remains the preserve of amateurs, particularly theologians who clearly do not feel that the lack of any first-hand laboratory experience or any fundamental understanding of the methods and norms of the natural sciences should inhibit them from contributing to the debate.

It was thus with a certain mingled sense of wariness and weariness that I turned to work my way through Torrance's substantial contributions to the field. This evaporated after reading the first chapter of *Theological Science*. It was immediately clear that Torrance knew what he was talking about, and was able to forge connections between science and Christian theology which were serious, informed and important. Torrance's writings were, quite simply, of landmark significance. As I wrestled with the broad issues with which I was confronted in the dialogue between science and religion,[1] I found myself constantly returning with increasing appreciation to Torrance's sustained intellectual engagement with the issues. It seemed that Torrance was one of the few – indeed, perhaps even the only – writer to appreciate the fundamental importance of *methodological* issues in relation to this dialogue. Indeed, it seemed entirely possible that this appreciation rested on the fact that Torrance knew enough about the history of theological method and the philosophy of science – including the ability to handle original sources in the original languages – to make connections which others simply were not competent to identify.

Having completed this major study of the intellectual foundations of dialogue between Christian theology and the natural sciences, it had been my intention to proceed immediately to a detailed engagement with the issue of 'the science of theology'. Given Torrance's importance to this subject, it was clearly essential to engage with his contribution in the area as a prolegomenon to attempting to make an original contribution to the field. Such was the intrinsic merit of Torrance's position that I initially played around with the idea of working on a major article, dealing with the presuppositions and consequences of his approach, before going on to publish my own contributions to the field.

Yet it soon became clear that Torrance's landmark contribution to this crucial area of modern theology could not be seen in isolation. One of the most striking characteristics of Torrance's theology is its internal coherence, in that each of its various elements is linked to others, on which it depends and which it, in turn, supports. As I developed my interest in Torrance, it

---

[1] See Alister E. McGrath, *The Foundations of Dialogue in Science and Religion*. Oxford: Blackwell, 1998.

became clear that I would need to explore the origins and development of the fundamental themes of Torrance's theology. Given Torrance's major role in shaping Barth-reception in the English language world, and his significance in relation to Scottish theological education and the Church of Scotland, it became clear that a much more ambitious project was appropriate – an intellectual biography of Torrance, exploring his theological development and assessing his significance.

The use of the term 'intellectual biography' is deliberate and considered. Torrance is primarily to be regarded as a man of ideas, someone who has a passion for the life of the mind as it is encountered by the reality of God. The decision to focus on Torrance as a man of ideas inevitably means paying correspondingly less attention to issues which might concern a traditional biography – such as family life and personal relationships with others in the academy and church. During his time as Professor of Dogmatics at Edinburgh and Moderator of the General Assembly of the Church of Scotland, Torrance inevitably became involved in the occasionally Byzantine politics of the University and Church. Those matters are unquestionably of considerable intrinsic interest; they belong, however, to another work, and have only been touched on in the present volume.

Although the primary concern of this work is to explore the development and nature of Torrance's understanding of the relation of the natural sciences and Christian theology, it is hoped that it will also serve as an introduction to the main themes of Torrance's theology and stimulate further research on that theology. In order to facilitate the latter, it provides two essential resources for any such undertaking – a total bibliography of Torrance's published writings and a detailed account of his life and aspects of his intellectual development. Although this work makes extensive use of Torrance's published works, it also draws to a significant extent upon Torrance's personal correspondence, sermons and autobiographical memoirs, of which virtually none have been published, and particularly unpublished texts of lectures from Torrance's periods at Auburn Theological Seminary (1938–9) and New College, Edinburgh (1952–79).

It will be clear from even a cursory reading of this book that Torrance demands a more detailed and thorough analysis than is possible in the pages of this work. This initial work may be regarded as a clearing of the ground for such more detailed engagement with his theology on my part; it is my hope that it may also encourage further engagement on the part of others, who will find in Torrance a theologian who repays careful study.

It will be obvious that it is impossible to do justice to the thought of as prolific and wide-ranging a writer as Torrance within a volume of this size, particularly when substantial sections of the text have deliberately been dedicated to biographical and bibliographical material. The analysis of Torrance's theology which will be found within these pages is intended to demonstrate the coherence and significance of Torrance's conception of 'scientific theology'. It is intended to follow this intellectual biography with a more detailed collection of studies of Torrance's thought, focusing on issues such as the regulative and foundational function of the *homoousion*, and the concept of 'kataphysic' theology.

I acknowledge with gratitude the most generous assistance of others in preparing this work. I owe particular thanks to Professor Torrance himself, who made his unpublished writings freely available to me, and was most generous in clarifying aspects of his career and intellectual development. Dr Iain Torrance proved an invaluable source of information, and traced family correspondence which cast light on important aspects of his father's career. I also gladly acknowledge the assistance of Dr Sebastian Rehmann, who tracked down even the most obscure publications relating to Torrance, and to the John Templeton Foundation for a grant to cover the costs of researching this work. Finally, I thank Wycliffe Hall, Oxford, for a period of sabbatical leave which allowed research for this work to be completed.

ALISTER E. MCGRATH
Oxford

PART ONE

The Emergence of a Scientific Theologian

CHAPTER I

Childhood:
Sichuan, China: 1913–27

I T is rare for the great events of history to fit neatly into numerical categories. Many would argue that the nineteenth century should not be mechanically defined as the period 1801–1900. Its origins could be said to lie in the aftermath of the French Revolution of 1789, which ushered in a new period of political and social change and development within western Europe. Similarly, the culture of the nineteenth century cannot be thought of as having undergone any radical change around 1900, so that one could speak of the 'ending of the nineteenth century'. If any event may be regarded as possessing that significance, it is the outbreak of the First World War in 1914. It is thus no cause for surprise that studies of nineteenth century political, social and intellectual history tend to focus on the period 1789–1914. In terms of its distinctive identity, the twentieth century may be said to have begun in August 1914.

That century would see significant new trends develop in every aspect of western culture, especially in the realm of ideas. Although the publication of Oswald Spengler's (1880–1936) *Decline of the West* in 1918 – which drew heavily upon the degenerative theories of Max Nordau (1849–1923) and Cesare Lombroso (1836–1909) – is probably the most celebrated sign of this shift in culture, others soon followed. On 29 May 1919, observation of a solar eclipse confirmed two of the three crucial predictions of Albert Einstein's special theory of relativity. The third was subsequently confirmed in 1923. The concept of a 'relativistic universe' appeared to be as revolutionary to the twentieth century as the Newtonian mechanical universe was to the eighteenth, calling existing human understandings of the world into question. On 23 June 1919, Marcel Proust (1871–1922) published *A l'ombre des jeunes filles*, a radical literary experiment with subliminal sexual emotions and disjointed time. J. B. Bury (1861–1927) poured scorn upon the idea of continuous development of human culture, civilization and ideas in his *Idea of Progress*, published in 1920. In that same year, the ideas of Sigmund Freud suddenly broke free of their captivity within specialized medical and psychiatric circles with the founding of the first psychiatric polyclinic at Berlin, and the launching of the *International Journal of Psycho-Analysis*. James Joyce's (1882–1941) *Ulysses* appeared in 1922, shocking the literary world, and causing the Anglo-American literary critic and writer T. S. Eliot (1888–1965) to remark that it 'destroyed the whole world of the nineteenth century'.

In the world of Christian theology, the First World War ushered in a similar period of reconsideration, often of a very radical nature. The settled assumptions of the forms of Christian theology which had achieved dominance within western European Protestantism were widely seen to have been rendered questionable by the events leading up to the war. Although it is clear that Protestant theology was affected to varying extents in different regions of Europe, the effects of the war were particularly marked within Germany.

The tradition of theologizing associated with F. D. E. Schleiermacher, A. B. Ritschl and Adolf von Harnack had gradually gained the ascendancy within German Protestantism. 'Liberal Protestantism', as it was generally known, was widely seen as embodying the religious and cultural values of modern Germany.[1] On the evening of 4 August 1914, shortly after the outbreak of the First World War, Adolf von Harnack drafted an appeal on behalf of the Kaiser to his people in support of the war effort. Shortly afterwards, he added his name to those of ninety-two other intellectuals, including theologians of the stature of Adolf Deissman, Wilhelm Herrmann, Adolf Schlatter, Friedrich Naumann and Reinhold Seeberg. For some more critical observers, this 'manifesto of the intellectuals' seemed to mark the end of the credibility of the theology which it represented.[2]

One such critic was Karl Barth. In his later recollection of his reactions to the support given by the theological establishment to the war policies of the Kaiser, Barth indicated his conviction that the theological tradition

[1] See Wolfgang Huber, 'Evangelische Theologie und Kirche beim Ausbruch des Ersten Weltkriegs', *Studien zur Friedensforschung* 4 (1970), 148–215.

[2] Wilfried Härle, 'Der Aufruf der 93 Intellektuellen und Karl Barths Bruch mit der liberalen Theologie', *Zeitschrift für Theologie und Kirche* 72 (1975), 207–24.

to which he belonged had demonstrated itself to be bankrupt. It was time to begin again.

> For me personally, one day in the beginning of August of that year stands out as a black day, on which ninety-three German intellectuals, among whom I was horrified to discover almost all of my hitherto revered theological teachers, published a profession of support for the war policy of Kaiser Wilhelm II and his counsellors. Amazed by their attitude, I realised that I could no longer follow their ethics and dogmatics, or their understandings of the Bible and history, and that the theology of the nineteenth century no longer had any future for me.[3]

In 1919, after years of wrestling with his conscience and biblical texts, Barth published the work which was to establish his reputation and signal the development of a significant new element in European theology. His commentary on Romans represented a sharp prophetic attack upon the liberal Protestant theology he had once held. This work, written while a pastor in the Swiss village of Safenwil, is prophetic in tone, stressing the utter inability of humanity to discover or conceptualize God unaided, and the radical failure of human culture to mirror or image God.

Barth's Romans commentary, particularly in its second edition (1921), marked the injection of a new theological trajectory into western European Protestantism, particularly in Germany and Switzerland. Although it was some time before either the nature or full significance of this new theological current would be apparent within English-language theology, the unquestioned benefit of hindsight allows us to note that the foundations of a theological revolution had been laid.

If the twentieth century can be said to have begun properly in 1914, Thomas Forsyth Torrance was born on its eve. The subject of our narrative would himself have a major role to play in the reshaping of western theology in the twentieth century, not least in relation to the reception and development of the theological agenda of Karl Barth. Yet Torrance was not born into the world of a Europe which was about to be plunged into war. His origins lie half a world away, in a remote inland region of China in which a small group of western missionaries were struggling against all the odds to establish Christian churches in the region. To understand Torrance's deep-rooted love and concern for missionary work and the nation and people of China, we must tell the story of how his father, Thomas Torrance senior, came to be in that region in the first place.

---

[3] Karl Barth, *Evangelische Theologie im 19. Jahrhundert.* Zürich: Zollikon, 1957, 6.

Thomas Torrance Senior: missionary in Chengdu

Thomas Torrance (1871–1959) was born on 12 March 1871 of farming stock in the parish of Shotts, in Lanarkshire, Scotland, about halfway between the two great cities of Glasgow and Edinburgh. While still a teenager, Torrance found himself drawn to the idea of becoming a missionary overseas. David Livingstone, the great pioneer of British missionary activity in the nineteenth century, came from the neighbouring parish of Bothwell, and had a profound influence on the young Torrance's vision for his future. Torrance's parents, however, were hostile to the idea of missionary work abroad. While they were perfectly happy to support him in studies which would lead to ministry in the Church of Scotland, they were not prepared to back him financially for work overseas on the mission fields.

Undaunted, Torrance determined to support himself. Several years' work at a cousin's drapery store in Hamilton were enough to allow him to raise the money to study theology at Hulme Cliff College (a missionary training college at Calver, twelve miles south-west of Sheffield). Having spent the years 1892–4 at Hulme Cliff College, Torrance went on to complete his training at Livingstone College, London (1894–5), which had been established primarily to provide training for the medical missionaries of the period. In 1895, he was sent to China by the China Inland Mission, arriving in Shanghai on 1 January 1896.

The China Inland Mission stood virtually alone among missionary societies at this time, in that it recognized the need for its missionaries to be taught Mandarin in schools especially established for this purpose. Other missionary societies provided their workers with language manuals and advice from native speakers. After a period of language study, Torrance was sent to the city of Chengdu, the capital city of Sichuan (Szechuan) province.[4] At that time, the China Inland Mission maintained eleven mission stations in that province, the most important of which was in Chengdu itself.

It was not an easy time to be a foreign Protestant missionary in China. The western powers gained major footholds in China as a consequence of the Opium War (1839–42). Under the Treaty of Nanjing (1842), China was forced to make major concessions to Britain, including the granting of 'extraterritoriality' (that is, exemption from Chinese laws) to British nationals. This proved to be the first of a number of 'unequal

---

[4] Throughout this work, we shall mostly use the Pin-Yin Romanization method, introduced in 1958, which has now generally displaced the older Wades–Giles method. The older Romanized forms are noted in brackets after the first occurrence of the term.

Tao Ran Shi. Thomas Torrance outside the Mission House in Chengdu, wearing traditional Chinese dress, c. 1900. Although many missionary societies had abandoned any requirement that their staff should wear Chinese dress, the China Inland Mission retained the practice for some time.

treaties' imposed upon China by western powers, which led to growing western influence in the region. During the period 1861–94, the 'Self-Strengthening Movement', championed by Qing dynasty scholars and officials such as Li Hongzhang (1823–1901) and Zuo Zongtang (1812–85), attempted to achieve a confluence of western technology with traditional Chinese culture. Western missionaries were generally welcomed, not least on account of their perceived potential as educationalists. Missionary schools came to develop throughout the region. Yet local resistance was often ferocious. In Chengdu, serious disturbances broke out in May 1895, the year before Torrance's arrival, during which several missionary buildings were destroyed.

The new initiatives of the 'Self-Strengthening Movement' were not, however, accompanied by much-needed political change. In many ways, China remained locked in its past. Impressed by the programme of modernization which had taken place in neighbouring Japan, the Qing emperor Guangxu (1875–1908) ordered a series of reforms which were intended to bring about rapid social and institutional change. In part, these were precipitated by China's disastrous defeat by Japan in the Sino–Japanese War of 1895. The 'Hundred Days' Reform' (11 June – 21 September 1898) were fiercely resisted by the conservative ruling elite, headed by the Empress Dowager Ci Xi, who overthrew Guangxu on 21 September and reverted to more traditional modes of government.

One aspect of this conservative backlash proved to be of particular importance to Christian missionaries throughout China: the new conservative elite gave covert support to the anti-foreign and anti-Christian movement of secret societies which came to be known as 'the Boxers' (from the older name of the group, *Yihequan*, best translated as 'Righteousness and Harmony Fists'). In 1900, Boxer bands were active throughout north China. Foreign Christian missionaries were particularly at risk, as were any buildings associated with Christianity. Chinese Christians were massacred in many areas.[5] Such was the scale of the action that foreign concessions in Beijing and Tianjin were besieged on 13 June 1900, eventually provoking an armed intervention by the western powers. At this point, the Qing court formally took command of the Boxer forces, and led a coordinated programme of resistance to the western relief army. Tianjin fell to the invaders on 14 July, and Beijing on 14 August. The Peace Protocol imposed upon the Qing court on 7 September marked a final humiliation for the dynasty.

Torrance survived the violence and turbulence of the Boxer revolt, and was able to spend much of the decade 1901–10 in building up the Christian presence in the Chengdu region. He was based in the town of Pi Xian (Pishien), about fifteen miles north-west of Chengdu. The period 1901–14 is widely regarded as marking the high-water mark of Christian missionary work in China. However, Torrance found himself somewhat

[5] The Boxers referred to Christian missionaries as 'Primary Hairy Men', and to Chinese Christians as 'Secondary Hairy Men'. All 'Hairy Men' were seen as legitimate targets for liquidation.

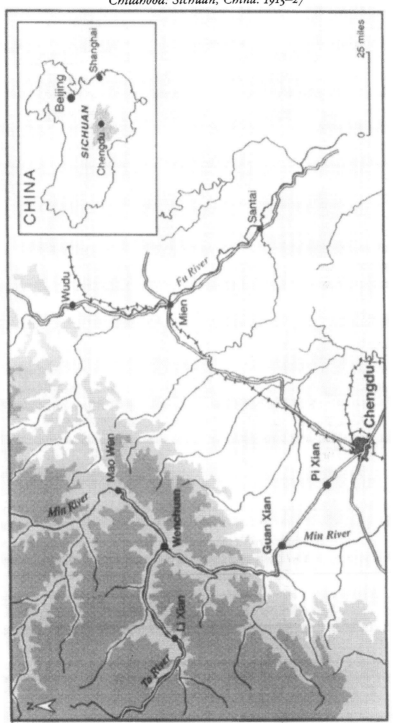

Map of China, showing Sichuan province and sites of particular importance to Torrance's early period.

ill at ease with developments for most of this period. It is clear that
Torrance gradually became increasingly dissatisfied with the policies of
the China Inland Mission, which he regarded as failing to ensure the
education and development of Chinese Christians. These disagreements
with the senior members of the Mission (especially Joshua Vale) eventually
led to Torrance severing his relationship with the Mission in 1910, and
returning to Scotland.[6]

However, this rupture did not end Torrance's association with missionary work in China, nor even with the city of Chengdu. At the Edinburgh
International Missionary Conference, held at New College in 1910, Dr
John Hykes, head of the American Bible Society mission in Shanghai,
persuaded Torrance to take over the Sichuan agency of the Society, based
in Chengdu. Torrance had already worked alongside friends in the
American Bible Society in the Chengdu region, and had some familiarity
and sympathy with their methods. He returned to Chengdu that same
year, and set up house in the American Bible Society premises in the heart
of the Old City.

Marriage and early family life

On 1 August 1911, Torrance married Annie Elizabeth Sharpe, an Anglican
who worked in Guan Xian (Guanshien), situated at the north-western
edge of the great Red Plain in Quan County, about thirty miles north-
west of Chengdu. Annie had been sent to Sichuan province in 1907 by
the China Inland Mission, for which Torrance had once worked in the
same region. They set up house at San Dow Guia, before moving to Wu
Chi Tong Tang in 1917. They would remain in this second house until the
family returned to Scotland in 1927. Annie threw herself into the work of
the American Bible Society in Chengdu. The work went well in Sichuan,
reflecting a generally upbeat mood within the Society as a whole. As John
Hykes commented, their problems had once focused on how to increase
the sales of Bibles; now their problem was how to limit the huge demand
for Bibles among the Chinese population.[7]

Yet even by 1911, it was clear that China was poised to undergo massive
changes, with major implications for the future of Christianity in the
region, and for foreign missionaries in particular. For many educated

[6] The papers relating to this disagreement are held as the Thomas Torrance Papers, Record
Group No. 16, Special Collections, Yale Divinity School Library, as part of the China Records
Project. See Joan R. Duffy and Martha Lund Smalley, *Guide to the Thomas Torrance Papers*. New
Haven: Yale University Library, Divinity Library Special Collections, 1996.

[7] See *Annual Report*. New York: American Bible Society, 1913, 349.

Thomas and Annie Torrance seated outside the house at San Dow Guia in 1915 with their children (left to right) Grace, Mary and Tom.

Chinese, the failure of the Boxer revolt and the humiliation of the Qing court pointed to the need to sweep away the old order altogether. An existing model lay to hand in Japan, which had succeeded in establishing a new social order, loosely based on western models, a generation earlier. Sun Zhongshan (Sun Yat-Sen) (1866–1925) was born in the city of Zhongshan, but was educated in Honolulu, where he became a Christian in 1883. In 1905 Sun founded the Tongmeng Hui ('United League') in Tokyo, attracting considerable support from Chinese students. Sun's 'Three Principles of the People' called for the overthrow of the Manchus, the ending of foreign influence in China, and the introduction of a popularly elected republican government. The death of Ci Xi in 1908 removed the most formidable obstacle to this programme. The last Qing emperor Pu Yi (1906–67) was a mere infant, incapable of holding Manchu power together. Instability inevitably led to insurrection.

Revolt first broke out among disaffected army units on 10 October 1911 in Wuchang, the capital of Hubei province. News of the revolt spread quickly, and led to risings throughout the region by Tongmeng Hui members. By the end of November, fifteen of the twenty-four provinces had declared their independence of the Qing empire. Sun returned to China the following month, and was proclaimed the provisional president of the new Chinese republic in Nanjing on 1 January 1912. However, Sun had failed to realize the power of the imperial army, and its pivotal role in both bringing about the revolution and defending it against possible foreign intervention. Sun had little option but to defer to Yuan Shikai, the commander-in-chief of the imperial army. On 12 February 1912, Pu Yi – the last emperor of China – abdicated. Yuan Shikai was sworn in as the president of the Republic of China on 10 March. A new era in Chinese history had begun, with the old order having been swept away.

Any hopes that the birthpangs of this new era would be brief soon evaporated. It became clear that civil war was a real possibility. In August 1912, alarmed at the growing despotism of Yuan Shikai, Song Jiaoren (1882–1913) founded the Guomindang (Kuomintang) or 'National Peoples' Party', a coalition of political groupings opposed to Yuan. In the elections of February 1913, the Guomindang won an overall majority. Yuan arranged for the assassination of Song in March. Hostility towards Yuan grew. Seven southern provinces staged an abortive rebellion against him during the summer of 1913. Following the suppression of this revolt, a cowed parliament elected Yuan president of the Republic of China in October. The Guomindang was declared to be an illegal organization the following month, and its members were evicted from parliament. Yuan died of natural causes in June 1916. One of his last acts was to attempt to revive the monarchy. By then, China was descending into anarchy, with warlords establishing control of key regions, including Beijing.

It was into this complex and rapidly changing situation that Thomas Forsyth Torrance was born, the second of six children. Mary Monlin, the first of the Torrance children, was born at Shanghai on 10 May 1912. Following the Sun Zhongshan revolt of the autumn of 1911, the British consulate requested all women and children living in Chengdu to leave for Shanghai. Annie Torrance, along with many other missionary wives, departed in December, travelling down the rivers Min and Yangtze by sampans to Chungking. They were then able to gain passage by steamer along the Yangtze to Shanghai by way of Ichang. Before long, the political situation had stabilized, and Torrance was able to travel to Shanghai and bring his wife and daughter back to Chengdu. The remainder of the children were born in Chengdu: Thomas ('Tom') Forsyth

(30 August 1913); Grace Brownlee (7 January 1915); Margaret Ramsay (30 September 1917); James Bruce (3 February 1923); and David Wishart (22 June 1924).

Thomas Forsyth was named after his great grandfather, Thomas Forsyth Torrance. He recalls that he grew up in a family environment in which the Christian faith was an assured and central reality of life:

> Through my missionary parents I was imbued from my earliest days with a vivid belief in God. Belief in God was so natural that I could no more doubt the existence of God than the existence of my parents or the world around me. I cannot remember ever having had any doubts about God. Moreover, as long as I can recall my religious outlook was essentially biblical and evangelical, and indeed evangelistic. I used to read three chapters of the Bible every day and five on Sundays which meant reading through the whole Bible each year. My father who could repeat by heart the Psalms and some of the books of the New Testament (the Epistle to the Romans, for example) encouraged us children to memorise many passages of the Holy Scriptures which I greatly appreciated later in life. Family prayers led by my father on his knees and the evangelical hymns he taught us to sing nourished our spiritual understanding and growth in faith. I can still repeat in Chinese, 'Jesus loves me, this I know; for the Bible tells me so.' I was deeply conscious of the task to which my parents had been called by God to preach the Gospel to heathen people and win them for Christ. This orientation to mission was built into the fabric of my mind, and has never faded – by its essential nature Christian theology has always had for me an evangelistic thrust.[8]

Throughout his childhood in China (1920–7), Torrance attended a school established by Canadian missionaries (generally referred to simply as 'the Canadian School') at Lan Tai Tze, on the campus of the West China Union University. This university was established by missionaries in 1910 on a sixty-acre site close to the East Gate of Chengdu.[9] The university brought together four major missionary groups: American Baptists, English Quakers, Canadian Methodists and Methodist Episcopalians. There was a degree of tension within the faculty of this university between liberal and conservative approaches to Christianity, reflecting similar

---

[8] 'Itinerarium mentis in Deum', autobiographical memoir, 1.

[9] An important primary source relating to this institution at this time is the Daniel S. and Jane Balderston Dye Papers, Record Group No. 22, Special Collections, Yale Divinity School Library, as part of the China Records Project. See Nathan H. Price and Martha Lund Smalley, *Guide to the Daniel S. and Jane Balderston Dye Papers.* New Haven: Yale University Library, Divinity Library Special Collections, 1992. The buildings in question are still in existence: the missionary university is now the West China University of Medical Sciences, with the 'Canadian School' as its Institute of Public Health.

The Canadian School, Chengdu.

tensions within western Protestantism as a whole. Torrance's family were firmly aligned with the more robustly conservative approach. By 1914, the student body of the campus had reached 258; a medical school was added in 1916.[10] By British standards, the education Torrance received was inadequate. Yet it was enough to allow him to dream of entering the University of Edinburgh when the time came, to prepare himself for missionary work in Tibet.

Torrance senior found himself fascinated by the Xiang (Ch'iang) people of the upper Min valley beyond Guan Xian. During the summer, the heat in Chengdu made it inclement for Europeans. In addition to the sweltering heat of the plains, they had to contend with the threat of malaria, cholera and dysentery (Chengdu had no proper sewage system at this time). The Torrance family would take to the hills for this period, during which Torrance senior spent his time on evangelistic visits to the Xiang people. The first such visit can be dated to 1916, with the first Xiang church being established in the main village of Tong Men Wai, Long Qi Xiang, situated in a lateral valley running up into the highlands from the To river into the heart of the Min Shan mountain range. Initially,

---

[10] For example, see *China Mission Year Book*. Shanghai: Christian Literature Society, 1915, 188–96; *China Mission Year Book*. Shanghai: Christian Literature Society, 1916, 253.

Annie Torrance outside the house at Wu Chi Tong Tang in 1917 with (left to right) Tom, Grace and Mary.

the church met in a local house, before a permanent building was erected. This church ('Fu Yin Tang') was built at the mouth of the valley of the Tong Men stream, at the point where it joins the To River. Torrance used to call the Tong Men valley 'The Glen', as it reminded him of parts of his native Scotland. In turn, Torrance himself was known as 'Tao Ran Shi' by the local peoples.[11] The church was destroyed in 1935 by retreating communist soldiers, who massacred the local pastors and their sons.

Torrance went on to establish more churches in Wenchuan county near the confluence of the Min and To rivers and beyond, in what were then the borderlands between China and Tibet, including Songpan. Torrance came to the view that the Xiang tribes were of Semitic origin, and developed a theory according to which they were the remnants of an ancient emigration from the Middle East before the Han kingdom was established in Chengdu. He noted in particular their strongly monotheistic religious beliefs, their sacrificial system, and especially their 'sacred rods with serpents entwined'. For Torrance, the ethnic distinctiveness of the Xiang peoples, and particularly their independence of Tibetan and Chinese religious beliefs, pointed to an evident connection

---

[11] Thomas F. Torrance was known as 'Tao Sheng De'.

with the religion of ancient Israel.[12] This theory did not find wide acceptance at this time; indeed, it is likely that considerably more attention was paid to his reports concerning the presence of pandas in the Songpan region, which are widely credited as the first reliable western reports of this remarkable animal.[13]

In 1920, the Torrance family returned to the United Kingdom on a period of furlough. After travelling to Shanghai by river, the family boarded a ship for the western Canadian port of Vancouver, British Columbia. After a train journey across Canada, they boarded a ship for England. The family returned to Torrance's family home in Shotts, Lanarkshire, before returning to Sichuan in 1921. Yet, soon afterwards, events were set in motion which would have major repercussions for Christian missionaries in the region in general, and eventually lead the Torrances to return to Scotland in some haste.

Political instability: the decision to leave China

While the Torrance family continued their work in Sichuan, political developments were proceeding apace. In 1919, Sun Zhongshan reestablished the Guomindang to counter the influence of the northern warlord government in Beijing. Frustrated by an apparent lack of success in attracting support from the west, he turned instead to the Soviet Union in 1921. This put the Soviet Union in a potentially difficult position, as their preferred option was to support the nascent Chinese Communist Party. However, the membership of the Communist Party was only about 300 at this stage, whereas the Guomindang counted 150,000 members. The Soviets decided to hedge their bets, and support both groups, instructing the Communist Party to support the Guomindang, at least for the time being. One of Sun's lieutenants, Jiang Jieshi (Chiang Kai-Shek) (1887–1975) was sent to Moscow for seven months' military and political study.

---

[12] His first account of these theories appeared in a thirty-six-page illustrated pamphlet entitled *The History, Customs and Religion of the Ch'iang: An Aboriginal People of West China*. Shanghai: Shanghai Mercury, 1920. Torrance set these views out more fully in a work written after his retirement at the end of 1934: *China's First Missionaries: Ancient 'Israelites'*. London: Thynne & Co., 1937. A new edition of this work was published by Thomas F. Torrance in 1988.

[13] Torrance was elected a Fellow of the Royal Geographical Society, in recognition of his research into various aspects of the history and geography of the western Sichuan region. In addition to his early reports on the pandas, he drew attention to the 'Black Pottery' of the Min Valley, now recognized as among the oldest in China. See Te Kun Cheng, *An Introduction to Szechuan Pottery*. Chengdu: West China Union University Museum, 1945.

The Guomindang–CCP coalition established its military headquarters at Guangzhou, and in the summer of 1925 launched a military expedition against the northern warlords. Growing tension between left- and right-wing factions within the coalition, evident from March 1926, led to a split within the movement. By early 1927, China was in chaos. The warlord government remained in place in Beijing; the left-wing Guomindang and communist groups established a stronghold at Wuhan; and the right-wing Guomindang regime was based at Nanjing. The tensions which developed during this period would eventually lead to the rise and final triumph of the Chinese Communist Party under Mao Zedong (Mao Tse-tung) (1893–1976). The 'Long March' would not begin until October 1934; in 1927, however, there was little indication that the communists would gain the ascendancy. The 1927 'Autumn Harvest Rising' in Hunan province, led by Mao, proved abortive.

Despite these differences between the members of the Guomindang–CCP coalition, it maintained a consistently anti-western and anti-Christian stance. This was exacerbated by the Shanghai incident of 30 May 1925, in which British troops opened fire on unarmed students, leading to growing anti-western feeling and hostility towards foreign missionaries. There is evidence that the incident and its aftermath led to growing tension between indigenous Chinese Christians and western missionaries, with many of the former believing that the latter were discrediting the gospel in the eyes of the Chinese people on account of their western origins. Although the term was not used, the subject of indigenization was under discussion as never before.

At this stage, most Christian missionaries were based in the coastal regions of China, in the great cities such as Shanghai. Relatively few were to be found in the inner regions, such as Sichuan. Increasingly, these missionaries felt beleaguered. Banditry and general hostility towards missionaries was increasingly leading to violent attacks against mission personnel and buildings. In January and February 1924, several missions in Sichuan were looted, and a member of the China Inland Mission wounded. On 7 June 1926, a female member of the Canadian Methodist Mission was murdered in Chengdu. About the same time, two Church Missionary Society missionaries were killed at a mission station close to the city.[14] Yet the incident which most provoked the fear of western missionaries took place on 24 March 1927 at Nanjing. Guomindang troops murdered Dr J. E. Williams, Vice-President of Nanjing University,

---

[14] Graham Watt, the son of one of these murdered missionaries, studied medicine at Edinburgh around the same time as Torrance was a student at the university.

in front of his home. Shock waves spread throughout the expatriate missionary community. To most, it seemed that there was only one solution, at least in the short term – withdrawal. By July 1927, it is estimated that only 500 out of an original 8,000 missionaries remained in the interior regions.[15]

In the spring of 1927, all women and children were ordered to leave Chengdu for the coast. Annie Torrance and her children travelled down-river by sampan to Chungking, where they came under the protection of the Royal Navy. They were loaded, along with other missionary families, onto a steamer which took them, under small-arms fire, to Ichang. Here, they changed ship and sailed to Hankow, where they boarded another steamer bound for Shanghai. After a wait of several weeks, they were joined by Torrance senior. The entire family then boarded the SS *City of Calcutta*, owned by the Ellerman and Bucknol Line, for the seven-week voyage to England via the Suez Canal.

So Torrance prepared to journey to Scotland. A new phase in his life was about to open.

---

[15] Figures based on *Chinese Recorder*, 58 (1927), 359.

CHAPTER 2

Education:
Scotland and Beyond, 1927–38

THE Torrance family returned to a Scotland in the depths of an economic recession. The Depression of the late 1920s had hit Scotland hard. Like most missionary families, the Torrances had little in the way of financial resources, making the acquisition of a house a serious difficulty. However, Torrance senior had an uncle who was the manager of the Beardmore Steel Works at Mossend, Bellshill, in Lanarkshire. Located in the south-west of Scotland, Lanarkshire is by far its most populous county, including the great city of Glasgow, and contained much of Scotland's heavy industry at this time. Torrance's uncle was able to find them a council house, which allowed them to settle down in the region, and plan for the future.

It was a time of considerable difficulty for the family. In addition to facing economic hardship – it was by no means easy to support a family of six children on a limited income during the Depression – the family had to confront the issue of their future. Thomas Torrance senior was convinced that he should return to Sichuan, and continue his work, this time with the American Bible Society. It was becoming clear that a degree of political stability was returning to the region, and Torrance believed that it was right for him to finish his ministry. There can be no doubt that he was right in this perception. By the end of 1927, the Guomindang government was firmly established in Nanjing. It would remain in power for a decade. The new period of political stability saw a marked lessening in hostility towards Christianity. Jiang Jieshi himself converted to Christianity in 1930, and believed that it was possible to achieve a working

The Torrance family in Scotland, 1927. The photograph was taken shortly before Thomas Torrance senior returned to Chengdu for his final period of service. From left to right: at back: Mary and Grace Torrance; middle row (seated): Annie; Margaret; Thomas senior; Tom Torrance; front row (standing): David and James Torrance.

compromise between traditional Confucian values and those of Protestantism. It was to prove a period in which Christian missionaries would have a new lease of life before the region was again plunged into turmoil through the triumph of Mao Zedong's Red Army.

Torrance senior therefore returned to China in 1928, leaving Annie to bring up the family. The family, who were by now settled in a more comfortable house than that which they had initially had on their return to Scotland, attended a local Baptist church, finding its theological position more acceptable than that of the local kirk. Torrance threw himself into his studies at Bellshill Academy, founded in 1898,[1] during the

---

[1] Torrance would subsequently undertake a Moderatorial Visit to the Academy in 1976, and deliver a sermon at the Academy on the occasion of its centenary on 7 June 1998.

Map of Scotland, showing locations of importance to Torrance's career.

years 1927–31. He wanted to enter Christian ministry and become a missionary, and thus concentrated his attention on those academic subjects he believed would help prepare him for this goal. To the annoyance of his mathematics teacher, Torrance chose to focus on Latin and Greek, finally taking his 'Highers' in English, History, Latin, Greek and Mathematics, and going on to the University of Edinburgh.

It had always been clear to Torrance that Edinburgh was his university of preference. Even during his period in China, he had heard Edinburgh spoken of in admiring tones. There were, of course, other possibilities. His mother, who was English, had thoughts of his going to the University of Durham, one of the older English universities located relatively close to Scotland. There was also the suggestion of considering Oxford or Cambridge. By the end of his time as a schoolboy, however, Torrance was quite clear as to what he wanted to do: he would study classics at Edinburgh, and then go on to New College to study divinity in preparation for the ordained ministry of the Church of Scotland.

When it became clear that Torrance intended to be a student at Edinburgh, the entire family moved to the city in 1931, settling in an apartment in Warrender Park Road in its Marchmont district. The family moved again in 1934 to a nearby house at 12 Chalmers Crescent. One of the reasons for the move was the need for a larger house in anticipation of the final return of Torrance senior from Sichuan at that time.

The continuing financial strictures confronting the family had a significant impact on Torrance's studies at Edinburgh. He had chosen to specialize in Classical Languages and Philosophy. The honours degree in this subject would have taken five years. With three sisters and two brothers to educate, the Torrance parents felt that they simply could not afford the luxury of an honours degree for their eldest son. Accordingly, Torrance enrolled for the ordinary degree, which would take three years, intending to proceed from there to study theology in the Faculty of Divinity for a further three years. At this time, the Scottish universities were the virtually undisputed masters of British theology, with Edinburgh as the jewel in Scotland's theological crown. Edinburgh was probably unsurpassed in terms of the quality of its philosophical and theological teachers during this period, and offered Torrance an outstanding environment in which to forge his thinking.

Edinburgh: the Faculty of Arts, 1931–4

Torrance's studies in the Faculty of Arts of the University of Edinburgh began in October 1931. It was to prove a challenging and exciting, even exhilarating, experience, exposing Torrance to both classical and contemporary debates. Torrance studied metaphysics under Norman Kemp Smith, with particular reference to the thought of Locke, Berkeley and Hume, while also attending lectures from Kemp Smith on Descartes and Kant. At first, the students used his abridged edition of Immanuel Kant's *Critique of Pure Reason*, graduating later on to the full text and Kemp Smith's celebrated commentary on it. Kemp Smith himself propounded a critical idealism, the general lines of which were set out more fully in his *Prolegomena to an Idealist Theory of Knowledge*. His lectures on David Hume were published in an expanded form in *The Philosophy of David Hume* in 1941 (which Torrance subsequently was asked to review). At this point, Torrance was particularly impressed by Kemp Smith's account of Hume's concept of 'natural belief', and recalls vividly the day when Kemp Smith handed him a copy of David Hume's *Dialogues Concerning Natural Religion*, with the words 'this will destroy a lot of bad theology'!

Torrance studied moral philosophy under Alfred Edward Taylor. Particular emphasis was placed on Mill, Bentham, Butler (of whom Taylor was particularly fond) and Kant, using Kant's *Critique of Practical Reason* and his *Introduction to the Metaphysic of Ethics*. A. E. Taylor also lectured on the Pre-Socratics, Plato and Aristotle. His teaching on Plato was particularly memorable as set out in *Plato, the Man and His Work* of 1926 – which later led Torrance to give careful attention to his outstanding *Commentary on Plato's Timaeus*. While Plato's idealism seemed to Torrance to have a dash of realism, Taylor's realism seemed equally to have a dash of idealism. Torrance's natural realist slant – which is clearly set out in his mature theology – was reinforced by Taylor's critical stress on 'the given', which he found impressively expounded in his Gifford Lectures, *The Faith of a Moralist*, published in 1930. It was Taylor who first directed Torrance's attention to 'the naturalistic fallacy', with reference to David Hume and G. E. Moore – that is, the fallacious argument from what is natural or what is the case to what *ought to be*, or the defining of ethical values from non-ethical premises. While appreciating Hume's critique of the way of reasoning from what we are naturally inclined to do to what we are obliged to do, or Kant's critique of the Aristotelian attempt to pass from 'the is' to 'the ought', Torrance found that he was nevertheless convinced of an ontological ground for moral obligation. It seemed to him that, if morality has no ultimate ground in God, it is ultimately subjective and relative. For Torrance, an intrinsic distinction obtained between what is right and what is wrong, and between the true and the false.

Torrance's interests also extended to the philosophy of science. At that time, the University of Edinburgh required students to take one science subject for an ordinary degree. At this time, Torrance was friendly with a fellow 'missionary kid' from China, Wreford Watson (later Professor of Geography at Edinburgh), who persuaded him to study geography to meet this requirement. The philosophical importance of the natural sciences seemed clear to Torrance, and he found this attitude reinforced by his philosophical teachers at Edinburgh. Kemp Smith and Taylor were both deeply aware of the philosophical relevance of recent work in mathematics and physics, and their bearing upon philosophical as well as scientific method. Kemp Smith pressed his students to study Max Planck's work *Where Is Science Going?* (published in English in 1933) and J. W. Dunne, *An Experiment with Time* (1927), while also commending some works by Sir James Jeans and Arthur Eddington. Taylor (who regarded Hume as 'on the side of the angels') used to refer to Hume's statement that science is 'founded on faith as much as Holy Religion', and clearly took into account recent developments in relativity and quantum theory in his teaching. He was known for his mathematical competence which his concern with Plato spurred him to develop. Yet even at this early stage, Torrance found his theology forcing him to interact with his understanding of the sciences:

> I was unable to keep my young theological convictions about the created or contingent nature of the universe out of the consideration. I could not think of the structures of this world as necessary or deterministic, for the living God could have and might have created a very different world characterised by different rational relations. The rational forms of the world as we know it derive from its creation out of nothing, which we may understand, therefore, only *a posteriori* through empirical inquiry and not through *a priori* reasoning.[2]

Although Torrance did not begin the formal study of theology until he entered New College in October 1934, it is clear that his theological development proceeded apace at this earlier stage in his studies. For example, Torrance read F. D. E. Schleiermacher's *Christian Faith* at this stage in his career, and found himself disappointed by what seemed to him to be its lack of a 'scientific' structure. He developed an interest in the early church, taking a class in ecclesiastical history under J. H. S. Burleigh, for which he was required to write a substantial piece on Augustine's *Confessions*. In particular, Torrance found himself giving careful thought to the question of the nature of revelation, and particularly its relation to Scripture and Jesus Christ:

---

[2] Torrance, 'Itinerarium mentis in Deum', 6.

So far as my view of Holy Scripture was concerned, I had been brought up to believe in its verbal inspiration, but my mother had taught me to have an objective and not a subjective understanding of the Word of God. This did not lessen but rather deepened my sense of the divine authority and verbal inspiration of the Bible which mediated to us the Gospel of salvation. She taught us to adopt a Christ-centred approach to the Holy Scriptures, for Christ was the Word of God made flesh. In him Word and Person are one, and it is therefore in terms of the living personal Word of God incarnate in Christ that we are to hear God addressing us in the Bible. My epistemological realism did not detract from that fact, but it did lead me to object to a crudely funda-mentalist and objectivist understanding of the Scriptures and to mechanistic and rationalistic concepts and propositions in theology, as it had done in my understanding of the laws of nature brought to light and given human formalisation in natural science. I could not think of the book of nature or of the Bible, albeit in different ways, as a transcription, far less a codification, of the mind of God, so that for one to think scientifically or theologically was necessarily to think the thoughts of God after him. That would be to impose upon nature rigid logico-deterministic patterns and to project on to God the kind of logico-causal relations which appeared to obtain in this world. A deeper, more dynamic and personal, yet objective way, was needed in relating God to nature and in relating the Word of God to the Holy Scriptures. That is what I hoped to find in the Faculty of Divinity, which indeed H. R. Mackintosh and Karl Barth helped me to do. After I entered New College my dear mother wisely gave me a copy of Barth's *Credo* to help me. Hence I found myself in conflict not only with the rationalistic liberalism of some of my teachers, but with the rather rationalistic and fundamentalistic way of interpreting the Bible being advocated in Inter-Varsity Fellowship circles together with a rather deterministic Calvinism which was then mistakenly being imported into the thinking of the Christian Unions.[3]

Torrance was, as this passage indicates, heavily involved in student Christian activities as an undergraduate, not least through his work in the Edinburgh University Evangelical Association, which had been founded in 1922. Both the City and University of Edinburgh had been deeply affected by the evangelistic work of Dwight L. Moody in 1874, and by Henry Drummond (who went on to initiate Christian Unions in Scottish universities). The university mission led in January 1885 by Stanley P. Smith and C. T. Studd consolidated this impact, and led to the emergence of a distinctively evangelical group within the university student body, from which the Evangelical Association would emerge in February 1922. During Torrance's undergraduate years, including his time as President of

[3] Torrance, 'Itinerarium mentis in Deum', 9.

the Evangelical Association, there was no chaplain associated with the University of Edinburgh, and the Association offered both pastoral support and theological teaching to its members. In addition, it was engaged in the active promotion of evangelistic work throughout Scotland.[4] However, there was tension within the student evangelical world at this time over a number of issues. One, alluded to in the passage by Torrance cited above, concerned the scope of the work of Christ: against the view that Christ died for all people (Torrance's position), others argued that Christ died only for the elect.

Torrance has always regarded himself as an evangelical with a strong commitment to the importance of preaching the gospel, and did not – and does not – regard the theological and political debates and tensions within evangelicalism as prejudicing this fact. The history of evangelicalism in the United Kingdom and the United States is frequently dominated by debates over who is in and who is out, not to mention who has the right to draw those somewhat contested boundaries in the first place. In 1953 the London-based Inter-Varsity Fellowship 'disaffiliated' the Edinburgh University Christian Union (the successor to the Evangelical Association) on account of its perceived Barthian leanings, which had been encouraged – it was argued – by Torrance himself.[5] At this early stage, however, Torrance was heavily engaged in student evangelistic work, which he saw as his natural vocation. It also shaped his future hopes, which focused on evangelism in some shape or form, suited both to the needs of the church and his own personal abilities. During his undergraduate period, Torrance's vision of his future was strongly linked with the expectation of continuing the missionary work of his father.

Late in 1934, Thomas Torrance senior retired from missionary work in China, and returned to live with his family in Edinburgh. The news which filtered back to him from China was not good. The advances made by the communist armies of Mao Zedong meant that Christianity was increasingly coming under persecution. The causes of this were twofold. In the first place, Christianity was seen as western, and was thus often viewed as a symbol of western oppression. This factor had been particularly significant in the earlier Boxer revolt. More seriously, however, the somewhat crude Marxist–Leninist philosophy which lay behind Mao Zedong's campaign laid down that religion was the enemy of the proletariat, and

---

[4] See D. Johnson, *Contending for the Faith: A History of the Evangelical Movement in the Universities and Colleges.* Leicester: Inter-Varsity Press, 1979, 103–8.

[5] D. W. Bebbington, *Evangelicalism in Modern Britain.* London: Unwin Hyman, 1989, 255.

Thomas F. Torrance, pictured in 1934, on the occasion of receiving his MA in classical languages and philosophy from the University of Edinburgh.

was therefore to be eliminated. Christianity would therefore suffer particularly during the period of communist rule, both on account of its nature as a religion and its perceived status as a western phenomenon. The churches in Sichuan province were no exception. By the end of 1935, all but one of the churches established in the upper Min and To valleys had been destroyed. Torrance was heartbroken by this news. It seemed that his life's work was being undone.

It was, however, news concerning one church in particular which was to prove especially poignant. One of Torrance's major achievements had been to establish a church in Tong Men Wai. This church was destroyed, along with others by Mao Zedong's soldiers in 1935; its pastor and many leading Christians (most known to Torrance personally) were massacred. However, a Chinese lieutenant-general, who was wise enough to keep his Christian beliefs strictly to himself, had been obliged to travel to Canada for medical attention. He had brought with him an item which had been saved from the destruction at Tong Men Wai, a copy of the New Testament which had been buried for safe keeping, along with a letter from Huang Taiqing, one of the few survivors of the massacre, relating what had happened. On the front page of the New Testament, the following words had been inscribed:

> This book was hidden in a cave among the rocks during the period of Communist oppression in the 24th year of the Republic of China (1935). Written by the Christian Church of Tong Men Wai in Li-Fan Prefecture in memorial of this event.

It might have seemed that Torrance's work had been completely in vain; however, those who had asked for the New Testament to be sent to Torrance did so in the belief that it was a symbol of resurrection, and that it held the promise of the future resurrection of the Xiang church. For Torrance senior, that promise never seemed to be fulfilled. What little news that they could obtain concerning the situation was bleak. Torrance senior died in 1959, a year which is now known to have marked renewed persecution of Chinese Christians.

The question of the future of the churches which his father had established, along with a general concern for the wellbeing and future of Christianity in China, would continue to trouble Torrance, and impact on his reflections on his own future. Our attention now turns to a formative period in his life, when he began to engage in detail with the intricacies of systematic theology at New College as he studied for the Bachelor of Divinity degree. It would be one of the most intellectually exciting and challenging periods of his life.

The Faculty of Divinity: New College, 1934–7

The Bachelor of Divinity can be thought of as comparable to a modern North American Master of Divinity – a professional graduate qualification, equipping its holder for Christian ministry. At this time, four Scottish universities offered the Bachelor of Divinity – Aberdeen, Edinburgh, Glasgow and St Andrews. Although the Bachelor of Divinity was treated as an undergraduate degree, it was a degree that was only open to graduates (sometimes referred to as a 'second first degree'). Torrance chose to study at Edinburgh, believing that the Faculty of Theology at New College was unsurpassed, especially in the area of Christian dogmatics.

The origins of New College are to be traced back to the controversy within the Church of Scotland in 1843 which led to the creation of the Free Church of Scotland. After a complex period of development, New College finally merged with the Faculty of Divinity of the University of Edinburgh in 1935. The background to this merger is to be found in the 1929 Union of the United Free Church of Scotland with the established Church of Scotland.[6] The result was that New College was no longer to be seen purely as a church institution, but as a faculty of the University.

Two figures at New College would exercise a lasting positive influence on Torrance. The leading systematic theologian at New College was Hugh Ross Mackintosh (1870–1936), who was appointed to the Chair of Systematic Theology in 1904, having previously been Minister of Beechgrove Church, Aberdeen (1901–3). Torrance was present at New College for the final lectures of Mackintosh's career. Mackintosh established his reputation through *The Doctrine of the Person of Christ* (1912), which would remain a set text for Edinburgh divinity students until the 1970s. For the young Torrance, Mackintosh was the leading representative of evangelical theology. Mackintosh insisted that student sermons should be expository and evangelistic – 'preaching for a verdict', as he would put it. The atoning love of God was to be given central place. To speak of Christianity without mentioning the atonement, he argued, was as inept as a sentence without a verb.[7]

Mackintosh envisaged a close link between theology and mission, arguing that a theology which failed to sustain and encourage a missionary

---

[6] For details, see D. F. Wright and G. B. Badcock (eds), *Disruption to Diversity: Edinburgh Divinity 1846–1996*. Edinburgh: T&T Clark, 1996.

[7] See H. R. Mackintosh, *The Heart of the Gospel and the Preacher*. Stirling: Drummond Tract Depot, 1913.

Professor Hugh Ross Mackintosh, New College, Edinburgh.

or evangelistic attitude was not a theology worthy of the name. He often posed a simple question as a litmus test to some theological account of a doctrine: 'How would that be received and understood on the mission field?' Torrance, who took detailed notes of Mackintosh's lectures during the year 1935–6, recalls his emphasis upon the centrality of Jesus Christ to a doctrine of revelation and salvation:

> H. R. Mackintosh used to press home to us again and again the perfect oneness of Jesus Christ with the innermost being of the Father. He used to refer with great awe to 'one of the best accredited parts of the tradition Jesus is recorded to have said: "No one knoweth the Son, save the Father; neither doth anyone know the Father save the Son, and he to whomsoever the Son willeth to reveal him"' (Matthew 11.27). I have never been able to forget Mackintosh's aphorisms which he varied again and again, 'When I look into the Face of Jesus, and see there the very face of God, I know that I have not seen that face elsewhere and cannot see that face elsehow.' 'And secretly, in the hour of meditation, when we try to look into God's face, still it is the face of Christ that comes up before us.' 'What Jesus was on earth God is for ever.' Mackintosh felt very strongly that what is ultimately at stake for us today as it was in Nicene times, is the cardinal truth of the Deity of Christ, the incarnate Son of God.[8]

Torrance's detailed notes of Mackintosh's dogmatics lectures – which take up nearly one hundred pages of closely-written text – are themselves a remarkable testimony to the high esteem in which Torrance held Mackintosh. He took no such detailed notes for any other lecture series or lecturer. The notes are heavily annotated at points, indicating a significant level of interaction with the ideas being explored by Mackintosh. There is no doubt that Mackintosh set out before his students a vision of Christian dogmatics as the core and foundation of every aspect of Christian life and thought, which opened Torrance's eyes to the potential importance and relevance of the subject.[9] Mackintosh's clear concern to relate theology and mission would have a powerful impact upon Torrance, and opened the way to a new understanding of his future as a missionary. Might not that missionary focus be linked with that of theological education?

[8] Torrance, 'Itinerarium mentis in Deum', 17. For this emphasis in Mackintosh's published writings, see H. R. Mackintosh, *The Doctrine of the Person of Jesus Christ*. Edinburgh: T&T Clark, 1912, 30. For further discussion of these points, see T. F. Torrance, 'Hugh Ross Mackintosh: Theologian of the Cross', *Scottish Bulletin of Evangelical Theology* 5 (1987), 160–73; R. R. Redman, 'H. R. Mackintosh's Contribution to Christology and Soteriology in the Twentieth Century', *Scottish Journal of Theology* 41 (1988), 517–34; R. R. Redman, 'Participatio Christi: H. R. Mackintosh's Theology of the Unio Mystica', *Scottish Journal of Theology* 49 (1996), 201–22.

[9] This is particularly clear in the early sections of the notes, dealing with the nature of dogmatics. Torrance, 'Dogmatics', unpublished manuscript, 1–2.

Mackintosh had studied at Marburg under the influence of Wilhelm Herrmann. This exposure to the German liberal Protestant tradition encouraged him to engage directly with its leading representatives, such as F. D. E. Schleiermacher and A. B. Ritschl. Mackintosh collaborated with A. B. Macaulay in the translation of the final volume of Ritschl's *Christian Doctrine of Justification and Reconciliation* (1900). Along with J. S. Stewart, Mackintosh was responsible for the translation into English of Schleiermacher's *The Christian Faith* (1928). Yet even in the preface to this work – which remains the standard English translation to this day – Mackintosh noted that 'a formidable attack' was being mounted on Schleiermacher's ideas 'by a new and active school of thought in Germany'[10] – a clear reference to the ideas of Karl Barth, which were then being widely discussed in German-language circles.

In one sense, Mackintosh cannot be regarded as the leading exponent of Barthianism in the United Kingdom. It is generally agreed that this distinction must be conceded to John McConnachie (1875–1948), Minister of St John's, Dundee.[11] Like Mackintosh, McConnachie had studied at Marburg under Wilhelm Herrmann, and had become familiar with the liberal Protestant tradition – including its weaknesses. McConnachie's first major published study of Barth's significance appeared in 1926,[12] and was followed by a series of works commending at least some aspects of Barth's theology, most notably its emphasis upon the priority of revelation. Interestingly, McConnachie cites Mackintosh's earlier work *The Doctrine of the Person of Christ* as following in the tradition of Ritschl and Herrmann.[13] Nevertheless, it is clear that Mackintosh had read Barth, and was undergoing a change in his evaluation of his significance.[14] As early as 1926, Mackintosh had signalled his awareness of the importance of Barth.[15] However, his full exposition of the substance of Barth's theology would have to wait until his Croall Lectures – published posthumously as *Types of Modern Theology, Schleiermacher to Barth* – which he delivered in New College and planned to repeat to his senior class each year. Torrance

[10] H. R. Mackintosh and J. S. Stewart (eds), *The Christian Faith*. Edinburgh: T&T Clark, 1928, v.

[11] J. McPake, 'John McConnachie as the Original Advocate of Karl Barth in Scotland: The Primacy of Revelation', *Scottish Bulletin of Evangelical Theology* 14 (1996), 101–14.

[12] J. McConnachie, 'The Teaching of Karl Barth: A New Positive Movement in German Theology', *Hibbert Journal* 25 (1926–7), 385–400.

[13] J. McConnachie, *The Significance of Karl Barth*. London: Hodder & Stoughton, 1931, 120–2.

[14] J. W. Leitch, *A Theology of Transition: H. R. Mackintosh as an Approach to Karl Barth*. London: Nisbet, 1952.

[15] H. R. Mackintosh, 'Leaders of Theological Thought: Karl Barth', *Expository Times* 39 (1928), 536–40.

looked forward to hearing these lectures in his final year (1936–7), and was devastated when Mackintosh died suddenly, without having seen the lectures through to publication.

Part of the excitement which Torrance experienced during his first two years at New College related to the clear shifts which were taking place in Mackintosh's thinking. It seemed clear to Torrance that he was gradually shedding the last vestiges of Ritschlianism in his thought, and that this process of transition could actually be discerned within his lectures. It is, of course, questionable whether it is proper to refer to Mackintosh as 'Ritschlian' in any meaningful sense of the term; nevertheless, it is clear that some kind of transition was taking place within his mind which involved a significant distancing from ideas which would generally be regarded as 'Ritschlian' in nature. Mackintosh often gave his students handouts at lectures, summarizing various points of importance – and at several critical junctures during the academic year 1935–6 would ask his students to delete passages, generally of a Ritschlian nature. Torrance recalls those lectures, and the impact which they made on his students.

> The struggle going on in Mackintosh's deeply sensitive mind was very evident in his teaching, especially I felt in his lectures on sin, when he would ask us to cross out paragraph after paragraph in the summaries of his lectures which he used to hand out to us. He had already revised them several years before he taught us in 1936, but he was still unhappy with them. Thus, for example, he altered 'religion' and 'religious' to 'faith' and 'believing', in view of the fact that our relation to Christ in faith and life becomes 'religious' only through his mediation of the forgiving and saving grace of God when through the Spirit we are brought into such an intimate relation to Christ as our Lord and Saviour that we 'share Christ's own faith in God'. Trust in God and trust in Jesus present themselves together and impress themselves on us. In spite of these changes, however, Mackintosh remained troubled and dissatisfied with his synopses. It was not that his basic theological convictions were changing, but he felt that clearer and more incisive expression of them was needed in respect of what he called 'the metaphysical Reality of Christ' both as true God and as true Man. We students were aware of being in the throes of a deep theological revolution which promised to lead the Church out of the spiritual doldrums that had come over it after the first world war and to set it back firmly on the basis of the Word of God, and some of us were concerned to further it as much as possible.[16]

Torrance was also influenced by another professor of theology at New College. Daniel Lamont, who lectured in apologetic and pastoral theology,

---

[16] Torrance, 'Itinerarium mentis in Deum', 21.

had earlier been a physicist and served for a while as an assistant to Lord Kelvin in Glasgow. In 1934 he had published *Christ in the World of Thought*, which Torrance greatly appreciated on account of the manner in which he sought to think out evangelical and Christological truth in relation to modern science. Lamont also introduced Torrance to the thought of Karl Heim of Tübingen, some of whose works had by then been translated by Edgar Dickie. Torrance read these with much appreciation, but was critical of Karl Heim's Kantian presuppositions. Years later Torrance would become a member of the 'Karl Heim Gesellschaft', and contributed to its magazine, *Evangelium und Wissenschaft*. Torrance's interest in science was stimulated to no small extent by Lamont, who made him enthusiastic to clarify the scientific structure of Christian Dogmatics. While this would remain a future development, it is clear that the foundations for much of Torrance's later thinking in this critically important area were laid in place in Edinburgh by 1936.

If Torrance found himself increasingly drawn to the ideas being developed by Mackintosh and Lamont, he found himself correspondingly critical of those associated with John Baillie (1886–1960), who succeeded W. P. Paterson at Edinburgh in 1934. Baillie, along with his brother Donald M. Baillie (1887–1954), is widely regarded as among the more important Scottish theologians of the mid-twentieth century.[17] Baillie had held a chair of theology at Auburn Theological Seminary in New York (1919–27), before moving on to chairs in theology at Toronto (1927–30) and Union Theological Seminary, New York (1930–4). While Torrance had considerable personal respect for Baillie, not least in relation to his writings on prayer,[18] he regarded the hostility of both Baillie brothers to Karl Barth to be fundamentally misplaced. That Baillie was familiar with at least something of Barth's theology is beyond dispute. Indeed, while at Union Theological Seminary (1930–4), Baillie indicated that, while he could not in any way be called a 'Barthian', he nevertheless believed that Barth's ideas should be taken with great seriousness.[19]

Torrance himself believed that the hostility of both Baillies to Barth could be traced to what may be called their 'philosophical reason' which had been moulded in their undergraduate studies under Andrew Seth, Kemp Smith's predecessor in Edinburgh University (who took the name Pringle-Pattison on coming into an inheritance near Selkirk, in the

---

[17] See David A. S. Fergusson (ed.), *Christ, Church and Society: Essays on John Baillie and Donald Baillie*. Edinburgh: T&T Clark, 1993.

[18] See T. F. Torrance, 'John Baillie at Prayer', in Fergusson, *Christ, Church and Society*, 253–62.

[19] See J. Baillie, 'Some Reflections on the Changing Theological Scene', *Union Seminary Quarterly Review* 12 (1957), 4–5.

Professor Daniel Lamont, New College, Edinburgh.

Scottish Borders), and under his brother James Seth, the Professor of Moral Philosophy, predecessor to A. E. Taylor. They both acted as assistants to James Seth, one after another. Torrance's perception of their approach was that:

> critical metaphysics and moral philosophy enabled them to move away from the narrow Calvinism of their upbringing, and helped them in their struggles for faith, but in some ways it accentuated the powerful moral element in the Westminster Catechisms. Their doubting minds took refuge in the moral claims thrust upon the human soul, and made them very sympathetic to the doubts of morally upright people who did not go to Church. They sensed more morality and belief in what they called 'honest doubt' than often appeared. On the other hand, their philosophical and moral reason made them resent Barth's rejection of natural theology which they interpreted in the light of Ritschl's questioning of the integrity and reliability of the human reason. Thus John Baillie failed to understand the critical thrust of Barth's famous pamphlet entitled *Nein!* (later published in English, along with Brunner's rebuttal *Natur und Gnade*, in *Natural Theology*, to which Baillie wrote a brief Introduction). In it Barth was concerned to rebut the poisonous handling in Nazi Germany of the idea that divine grace does not do away with nature (i.e. German blood and soil) but perfects and completes it. Moreover, Baillie failed to appreciate Barth's 'scientific starting-point' (as he called it), from the resurrection, which involved a sublimation (*Aufhebung*) not the abolition (*Aufhebung*) of rational thought, that is to say its lifting up on to a higher level through its coordination with faith – reason, as Barth understood it, is to be understood and employed in relation to its proper object in every field of knowledge.[20]

Perhaps something of this tension can be seen in an incident which is recorded as taking place between Barth and Baillie at the University of St Andrews in 1930. Baillie was reported as asking Barth whether the goodness of God had any resemblance to the goodness of man. Barth replied that there was no resemblance whatsoever. Baillie grimly replied: 'That is a statement to which I can ascribe no meaning whatsoever.' The incident was followed by an uncomfortable silence.[21]

Torrance attended lectures by Baillie during the academic year 1934-5, and found them puzzling. The lectures followed the general lines of Baillie's 1929 book *The Interpretation of Religion*.[22] Baillie argued that the

---

[20] Torrance, 'Itinerarium mentis in Deum', 16.

[21] Details in David A. S. Fergusson, 'John Baillie: Orthodox Liberal', in Fergusson, *Christ, Church and Society*, 123–53, 144, n. 50.

[22] J. Baillie, *The Interpretation of Religion*. Edinburgh: T&T Clark, 1929. For a discussion of this work, see Fergusson, 'John Baillie: Orthodox Liberal', 128–32. Similar themes are developed (in a rather tired manner, in my judgement) in Baillie's inaugural lecture at Union Theological Seminary in 1930: see J. Baillie, 'The Logic of Religion', *Alumni Bulletin of Union Theological Seminary 3* (1930), 6–16.

task of the theologian is to locate the origin of religious impulses within individuals and communities, and to examine its structures and effects. The approach in question can be thought of as broadly phenomenological, reflecting both the philosophy of Kant and the theology of the tradition exemplified by Schleiermacher, Ritschl and Herrmann. Torrance thought the approach outdated, failing to respond either to new insights in epistemology linked with the natural sciences, or the new emphasis upon revelation linked with the Barthian school. He believed that he could discern a deep-seated epistemological dualism behind Baillie's thinking, deriving from nineteenth-century philosophy of religion:

> On the one hand in Kantian fashion he sought first to establish a method of inquiry apart from the subject-matter of his inquiry, and on the other hand he worked out a theory of religion from its roots in the human soul and the moral claims of God upon it, without really taking divine revelation into account. I found this epistemologically untenable, not least in the light of the overthrow by general relativity of a dualist Kantian approach to knowledge, of which we learned from Lamont, and also found its rather stand-off relation to divine revelation theologically unacceptable – it certainly conflicted very sharply with the primary place given to revelation by Lamont in *Christ and the World of Thought* and by Mackintosh in *Immortality and the Future, The Originality of the Christian Message, The Divine Initiative, The Doctrine of the Person of Jesus Christ, Some Aspects of Christian Belief, The Christian Apprehension of God*, or *Types of Modern Theology*! I recall an occasion in one of his lectures when Professor Mackintosh, after referring to John Baillie's *Interpretation of Religion*, paused to say, 'But, gentlemen, is that really religion?' His own exhaustive study of Hegelian philosophy of religion convinced him that it is impossible for man to gain knowledge of God 'by digging into himself'.[23]

Torrance was of the view that Baillie was unprepared for the growing receptivity towards Barth among students and faculty at Edinburgh, and that their critical reaction to his earlier viewpoints led to discernible modifications to his thought. For example, Baillie's 1939 work *Our Knowledge of God* clearly takes a more positive view of both Barth and Brunner, and seems to reflect a degree of sympathy with the lines of interpretation set out in Mackintosh's Croall Lectures.

There is no doubt that Barth was a growing influence at Edinburgh. Mackintosh's death in 1936 might have robbed the faculty of someone sympathetic to Barth; the appointment of Professor G. T. Thomson (1887–1958) as Mackintosh's successor in the chair of dogmatics brought the translator of the first half-volume of Karl Barth's *Church Dogmatics* to

---

[23] Torrance, 'Itinerarium mentis in Deum'. 14.

Edinburgh. Yet Barth's influence was by no means limited to those faculty members who taught systematic theology. Norman Walker Porteous (1898–), who was called to Edinburgh in 1934 to succeed Adam Cleghorn Welch as Professor of Old Testament Literature, Language and Theology, had encountered Barth while undertaking Old Testament research at Münster in the 1920s. Porteous was fond of describing himself as the 'first English-speaking student of Karl Barth'. Torrance recalls Porteous' lectures exploring Old Testament theology in terms of the dialectic within Israel between God's self-revelation and nature religions (as exemplified in the Canaanite cults), a framework whose contours could easily be discerned as Barthian.

There could be no doubt that Barth's ideas were likely to have a major impact on Scottish theology; indeed, studies of Barth-reception in Great Britain indicate unequivocally that Barth was most enthusiastically and actively received in Scotland.[24] Through a series of publishing coincidences, 1936 saw some of Barth's influential early works appearing in English. *Credo: A Presentation of the Chief Problems of Dogmatics with Reference to the Apostles' Creed* was published in that year by Hodder & Stoughton, the London publishing house which had also published *The Word of God and the Word of Man* in 1928. *God in Action: Theological Addresses* was published in 1936 by T&T Clark, who had already published *Come Holy Spirit* (a collection of sermons by Barth and his colleague Eduard Thurneysen) in 1934. The second edition of the *Römerbrief* was translated by E. C. Hoskyns, and appeared in 1933.[25] The most important event in relation to British Barth-reception was the appearance of the first half-volume of the *Church Dogmatics*, translated by Thomson. Mackintosh asked his students to study this work, and it became a subject of considerable debate in the Common Room and the New College Theological Society. At this time, Torrance made his way through a work which had appeared a few years earlier – F. W. Camfield's *Revelation and the Holy Spirit: An Essay in Barthian Theology* (1933). During the academic year 1936–7, two visiting students further stimulated interest in and discussion of the Barthian theology. These were Dorothy Thurneysen (daughter of Eduard) and Marie-Louise Martin (a student of Barth's, who went on to be a missionary in the Congo and in Botswana).

Those who had hoped that translations of further sections of the *Church Dogmatics* would follow were disappointed; Thomson's next major

[24] See J. McConnachie, 'Der Einfluss Karl Barths in Schottland und England' in E. Wolf (ed.), *Theologische Aufsätze*. Munich: Kaiser Verlag, 1936, 529–70.

[25] Karl Barth, *The Epistle to the Romans*. London: Oxford University Press, 1933.

translation project was Heinrich Heppe's *Reformed Dogmatics* (which, admittedly, included a preface by Karl Barth).[26] Inevitably, the question arose as to what might happen in relation to the translation of the remainder of the *Church Dogmatics*. Some also raised questions concerning the quality of Thomson's translation of the first half-volume. But who would undertake to coordinate such a massive enterprise?

There could be no doubt in Torrance's mind that first-hand acquaintance with Barth's theology was going to be a major part of his theological education; this would demand a full working knowledge of the German language, which he did not yet possess. Yet other matters were also on his mind. While studying arts earlier, he had become increasingly interested in the history and thought of the early church. He had noticed a reference in the Divinity Calendar to a 'John Stuart Blackie travelling fellowship in Classical, Septuagintal, and Hellenistic Greek', which would allow him to travel in the Middle East, and gain a first-hand experience of the region. He was successful in winning this Fellowship, and began to make arrangements for his visit. In preparation for this, Torrance took a class in 'Colloquial Arabic', believing that this would enable him to travel widely in Arab countries and become more familiar with Semitic modes of thought and speech.

The Middle East: the Blackie Fellowship, 1936

The Blackie Fellowship was nominally awarded for a period of one year. However, Torrance was only given leave of absence from New College for six months, due to pressure of examinations. He therefore determined to make the most of the opportunities which the Fellowship afforded. William A. Curtis, Principal of New College, asked Torrance to 'shepherd' a group of New College students who were paying a short visit to the Holy Land as part of their studies. Torrance and a group of students (including Alan Brash, David Currie, James S. McEwen, William Meiklejohn, James Mackenzie, William Gardiner Scott and Ronald Gregor Smith) sailed out together on the SS *Mongolia* of the Peninsular & Orient Line, landing at Port Said in Egypt. A group of Egyptian hotel agents boarded the liner at Port Said, and inquired what hotel had been booked for them in Cairo. Upon being told that it was the Hotel Bristol, the agents informed them that it had been closed. Many of the group were alarmed, and wanted Torrance to reserve rooms in another hotel

[26] H. Heppe, *Reformed Dogmatics, Set Out and Illustrated from the Sources.* London: George Allen & Unwin, 1950.

immediately. Torrance inclined to the view that they were probably simply touting for business, and led the group on to Cairo, where their rooms proved to be ready for them at the Hotel Bristol.

Torrance saw the Blackie Fellowship as offering him the possibility of getting to know the Middle East in a manner that would otherwise have been impossible. After touring some of the great sites of Egypt, he went on to Jerusalem, spending Holy Week in the city. As is the case with most Christian visitors to the Holy Land, he found the experience brought a new depth and quality to his reading of the New Testament. An American missionary from the Transjordan offered Torrance (along with James S. McEwen and William Meiklejohn) transport in his car to the far side of the Jordan, where they toured the region around Jericho and beyond the Jordan River. The three students eventually made their way around most of the notable sites in the region, exploring Amman, Petra and the Dead Sea.

Torrance found himself generally welcomed by the Arabs living in the region, occasionally being treated with an unusual deference. It subsequently emerged that this reflected the fact that his name sounded like 'Lawrence' (T. E. Lawrence, often known as 'Lawrence of Arabia', who had been a strong supporter of Arab nationalism in the First World War). On learning that he was 'Torrance', they exclaimed: 'Ah! The *hakim* (doctor) from Tiberias!' – a reference to David Watt Torrance (1862–1923), who was a cousin of Torrance's father. Torrance had established a hospital at Tiberias in 1894, and had gained a virtually legendary reputation in the region on account of his work among poor Arab communities.[27]

On learning of this family connection, relations became considerably warmer. However, his situation was not entirely secure. It was a tense political situation, with increasing local resentment against the British occupying force. The Grand Mufti Husseini had just come back to Jerusalem from visiting Hitler and was spreading around anti-Jewish propaganda, which looked likely to provoke an Arab revolt. The great bulk of the British troops in the Middle East at this time were stationed in Egypt, with only small detachments in Palestine. A force of heavily armed Cameron Highlanders was stationed near the Jaffa Gate, under the command of Major Pringle-Pattison (the son of Professor Pringle-Pattison, Norman Kemp Smith's predecessor in Edinburgh) in the hope of containing any outbreak of violence.

[27] See W. P. Livingstone, *A Galilee Doctor, Being a Sketch of the Career of Dr D. W. Torrance of Tiberias*. London: Hodder & Stoughton, 1923.

The situation eventually became so dangerous that the Inspector General of Police, R. G. B. Spicer, hurriedly recruited a force of some seventy able-bodied 'volunteers', including Jim McEwen, Willie Meiklejohn, John Ross and Torrance himself. They were each given a police arm-band, a whistle, and a rifle with twelve rounds, and were put under the command of an Inspector of Special Constabulary. Torrance's first assignment was to guard a Shell Oil installation and an oil dump overlooking a timber yard, a coal yard and the housing complex near St Andrew's Hospice and Church. After a few days, Torrance was put in charge of a three-man patrol assigned to guard Barclay's Bank.

After several weeks of continuous duty, Torrance was relieved of his duties, so that he could travel to the north of the region, and continue his studies in Syria and Lebanon. Permission for this was readily granted. The volunteers were all asked to leave a note of their home address at the office of the High Commissioner. In recognition of the help they had given, they were subsequently awarded the General Service medal with clasp 'Palestine'. This came in useful later, when Torrance served during the Second World War with the Church of Scotland Huts and Canteens, in that the troops regarded him as an 'old soldier', well acquainted with King's Regulations.

Torrance then proceeded north by car to Galilee. This allowed him to explore Bethlehem and Nazareth, before moving on to the Lebanon and Syria. From there, he headed to Iraq, exploring the excavations which had been undertaken at 'Ur of the Chaldees' by Sir Leonard Woolley. He then proceeded to Basra, in the south of Iraq. At that time, the Iraqi Air Force was undertaking bombing raids against the 'Marsh Arabs' who inhabited the region, and who had risen against the Baghdad government. Torrance arrived at Basra while it was under martial law. He was arrested under suspicion of being a spy, and at one point was sentenced to death by hanging. Fortunately, he succeeded in persuading the military authorities that he was not a British spy (although his brief period of military service in Jerusalem proved a little awkward at this point); he was merely a theological student at Edinburgh University. Eventually, Torrance was escorted to the railway station, and placed on a train for Baghdad, from where he proceeded to Damascus.

From Syria, Torrance went initially to Istanbul, then to Athens, where he attempted to master modern Greek. He finally returned home via Rome, reaching Scotland in time for the examinations that summer. His final year at Edinburgh was not to be what he had hoped for; while he was in Damascus, he had learned of the death of H. R. Mackintosh. This news shocked and distressed him, not least because he had been looking forward to attending Mackintosh's lectures in his final year. Having chosen to specialize in dogmatics, Torrance had been eagerly anticipating being able to spend an entire year being taught virtually exclusively by Mackintosh. Now that would never happen.

Finally, Torrance went forward to his final examinations for the Bachelor of Divinity at Edinburgh. His specialization was to be systematic theology. Torrance attempted to persuade the Faculty of Divinity to allow him to be examined both in systematic theology *and* the language, literature and theology of the New Testament. The request was politely but firmly declined by William A. Curtis (1876–1961), who had been Dean of the Faculty of Theology and Principal of New College since 1935. The examination arrangements were complex enough without having Torrance muddle things still further. In the end, Torrance graduated *summa cum laude*.

What next? Torrance had been licensed by the Presbytery of Edinburgh as a Probationer of the Church of Scotland, and it was clear that ordination into that church lay ahead. Although still convinced of the importance of missionary work, Torrance's years at New College had led to the gradual emergence of a new vision of his calling. Mackintosh had shown Torrance that theology could indeed serve the church and its evangelistic ministry. Under his influence, Torrance came to think in terms of his future lying in a 'theological ministry in the service of the gospel'.

His examination success opened a door to him. He was awarded the Aitken Fellowship, which would allow him to travel to undertake postgraduate research at a location of his choice. Where should he go to study? There could only be one answer. He made the necessary arrangements to go to Basel, and sit at the feet of Karl Barth.

Basel: the encounter with Barth, 1937–8

The award of the Aitken Fellowship came late in the day, and Torrance's travelling and accommodation arrangements had to be made in some haste. First, he had to arrange for somewhere to stay in Basel. Through his friendship with Eduard Thurneysen's daughter, Torrance was able to secure a place at the Theologisches Alumneum, an ancient theological student house at Hebelstrasse 17. Thurneysen expressed his anxieties about the place: it was, in his view, 'rather primitive'. However, it provided Torrance with the *pied-à-terre* which he needed.

More seriously, however, he needed to acquire a good knowledge of the German language. Torrance travelled to Berlin for this purpose, but found that he was too late to secure a place at either the Deutsches Institut für

Ausländer or the Hegelhaus. However, he was found accommodation with Frau Jochmann, the widow of a German academic, who lived at Hohenzollerndamm 209, and took in foreign students as lodgers, and was provided with a *Lehrerin*, who was a former employee of the German Embassy in London, as a personal language tutor. 1937 was not the best of times for a British national to be resident in Berlin, and Torrance found himself having to make regular visits to the Police Headquarters to have his passport inspected. Torrance found the Nazification of German culture as ridiculous as it was oppressive, and began to get himself into trouble. Wandering down Berlin's Unter den Linden, he was greeted with a 'Heil Hitler!' from everyone he passed. Irritated by this, he responded to one such greeting with 'Heil deinen Grossmutter!'; fortunately, he was able to slip away before anyone could react.

Leaving Berlin, Torrance moved to Marburg, where many Scottish theological students (including H. R. Mackintosh) had cut their theological teeth. He was able to secure lodging at Marbacherweg 23 with the Heintzmann family, who were close friends of Principal William A. Curtis of New College, and had housed Edinburgh students in the past. Although the Heintzmann family spoke English, conversation was restricted to German to help Torrance master the language. At this point, Torrance worked his way through the original German edition of Barth's *Credo*, and began to wrestle with both the language and theology of the *Church Dogmatics*. After Marburg, Torrance spent a few days at Heidelberg, before travelling south to Basel, arriving at the Theologisches Alumneum a few days before the new semester was due to begin. Thurneysen (whom Torrance nicknamed 'McTurnip') had been right about the Alumneum; it was as primitive as he had feared. There was no heating in the bedrooms, and Torrance found he had often to break the ice in the water jug in his bedroom in the mornings in order to wash and shave. After the first semester, Torrance decided that he had had enough, and managed to find much more satisfactory lodgings nearby in a large house, in which he frequently entertained musicians who were students of Adolph Busch and Rudolf Serkin.

Barth's seminar for the academic year 1937–8 consisted of about fifty students. He was in the habit of selecting a smaller group for a more intimate seminar (the Sozietät), which would meet once a week in his home. The selection process involved the translation of a Latin text (which Barth read out to the class, and required them to transcribe as well as translate), and an examination on the topic 'Who is the Holy Spirit?'. Torrance chose to respond to this by exploring the Augustinian concept of *communio quaedam consubstantialis*, which Barth deployed in the first

Karl Barth lecturing at the University of Basel, 1937.

half-volume of the *Church Dogmatics*. Torrance found the Latin oral examination difficult, on account of Barth's highly idiosyncratic Latin pronunciation. Barth stopped Torrance in the street the day after the examination, and congratulated him on the piece. He also telephoned Eduard Thurneysen to inform him how pleased he was with 'der Schottlander'. On the basis of the examination, Barth selected just over a dozen students as members of the Sozietät. Torrance was one of them; his Edinburgh colleague James McEwan was not.

There is no doubt that Torrance regarded Barth as a theological master. He found himself immensely impressed by the manner in which he conducted both the seminar and the smaller Sozietät. He was also impressed by the respect in which Barth held his opponents, present and past. The seminar room in the old university building contained a bust of Schleiermacher. On one occasion, a student mischievously rouged up the bust. Barth was angered by the matter – the only occasion on which Torrance recalls seeing Barth angry. Though he disagreed with Schleiermacher, Barth declared, he was a great Reformed theologian, and was to be treated with respect.

Although Torrance would attend other lectures – for example, Heinrich Barth (Karl's younger brother) on Aristotle's metaphysics, Karl Ludwig Schmidt on the New Testament and Walter Eichrodt on the Old Testament – it is clear that Karl Barth was the main intellectual luminary in the Basel firmament for him. Yet this does not mean that Torrance was an uncritical admirer of Barth. At an early stage in his Basel period, Torrance began to have reservations about some aspects of Barth's theology, especially in relation to his apparent lack of emphasis upon mission or evangelism (so characteristic of Mackintosh).[28] Although Torrance would later revise this judgement (citing the strongly evangelistic tone of the final series of sermons delivered to prisoners in Basel prison, published in 1959 as *Der Gefangenen Befreiung!*, and Barth's strong support for his son Christoph undertaking missionary work in Indonesia), there were others who would make similar criticisms of Barth's theology elsewhere.

Barth's dogmatics lectures were given on four occasions each week, and were later published as *Church Dogmatics* II/1. The seminar met once a week in the afternoon in the Rheinsprung, exploring the teaching of the First Vatican Council on natural theology. The Sozietät met once a week, in the evening at Barth's own house; the text prescribed for study was a classic text of Reformed Orthodoxy – Wollebius' *Compendium Theologiae*. Torrance also managed to acquire a copy of the second half-volume of the *Dogmatics*, and spent much of his spare time at Basel wrestling with its ideas, especially Barth's discussion of 'The Incarnation of the Word' and 'The Outpouring of the Holy Spirit'.[29]

When Barth asked Torrance what he would like to do by way of a thesis, Torrance responded with the suggestion that he would like to write on the scientific structure of Christian dogmatics. To his astonishment

---

[28] See his letter to his sister Grace, 26 October 1937, where he comments that Barth 'lacks the Missionary note and the evangelistic note rather sadly. I can't quite make it out.'

[29] *Church Dogmatics* 13 vols. Edinburgh: T&T Clark, 1956–75, I/2, 1–454.

and chagrin, Barth replied immediately that he was far too young to do anything of the sort. The 24-year old Torrance would have to find some other project at this stage. Torrance then mentioned his growing interest in Greek patristic theology, which prompted Barth to suggest that he write on 'the doctrine of grace in the second-century fathers'.

The library facilities at Basel were excellent. The main university library was conveniently close to his lodgings, allowing Torrance ready access to the works which he needed. By the end of the academic year, he had accumulated a substantial amount of material, and was convinced that a significant work would result. Torrance left Basel at the end of the second Semester, fully intending to return the following academic year in order to complete his dissertation.

Torrance's time in Basel was immensely stimulating. It had offered him precisely the kind of intellectual stimulation – both linguistic and theological – that he had longed for. By the end of his year in Basel, Torrance's theological lodestars were firmly established in his intellectual firmament. Athanasius, Mackintosh, Calvin and Barth would act as *foci* for his theological reflection.[30] In addition, his dissertation was going well, and would be completed the following year. He would then have to face the *Rigorosum*, the major doctoral examination typical of German and Swiss theological faculties.

Yet Torrance's career was about to take an unexpected turn, on account of events in upstate New York. Torrance had begun to rethink his future in terms of sustaining, supporting and guiding the church in its evangelistic and missionary work through a career in theological education. Events were unfolding which would equip him for such a career more thoroughly than he might have dared to hope.

---

[30] See the interview published in 1990: 'Thomas Torrance', in Michael Bauman (ed.), *Roundtable: Discussions with European Theologians*. Grand Rapids, MI: Baker Book House, 1990, 111–12.

CHAPTER 3

America: Auburn Theological Seminary, 1938–9

TORRANCE had returned to Edinburgh early in the summer of 1938 after his year's postgraduate study in Basel under Karl Barth, and was looking forward to returning to Basel to complete his work on the apostolic fathers, and imbibing more of the heady theological elixir which saturated Barth's seminars. He was therefore somewhat disconcerted when, on his return to Edinburgh, Professor John Baillie set out a counter-proposal. Torrance, he declared, was needed to teach at Auburn Theological Seminary, a Presbyterian seminary in upstate New York.[1]

The background to this invitation needs explanation. In 1919, Baillie had married Florence Jewel (a descendant of the noted Elizabethan bishop John Jewel), and emigrated to New York state to take up the Chair of Christian Theology at Auburn Seminary. Baillie's wife – who was always known and addressed as 'Jewel' – had developed tuberculosis, and spent much of the period 1923–30 in various sanatoria. Baillie had remained at Auburn until 1927, when he moved to Canada to take up the Chair of Systematic Theology at Emmanuel College, Toronto, which was now an ecumenical college within the newly formed United Church of Canada. Baillie had kept in touch with many colleagues in North America after his return to take up the Edinburgh Chair in 1934, and had now been contacted by President Reed of Auburn Seminary with an urgent request for help.

---

[1] For the background to this institution, see Robert H. Nichols, *Presbyterianism in New York State*. Philadelphia: Westminster Press, 1963.

Auburn itself was associated with the 'New School' Presbyterianism, which had its origins in a controversy of 1837 over the role of the Westminster Confession of Faith.[2] The 'New School', was especially associated with the north-eastern states. By the 1920s, the Seminary was firmly associated with the more liberal traditions emerging within American Presbyterianism. Robert Hastings Nichols, a professor at the Seminary, had drafted a document which eventually became known as the 'Auburn Affirmation'.[3] This document affirmed the importance of 'liberty of thought and teaching', and signalled a willingness on the part of its signatories to distance themselves from the traditional teachings of the Reformed tradition. There is no doubt that Auburn was seen by many as being in the vanguard of the liberal counter-offensive against fundamentalism.

During the 1930s, the liberal position was represented at Auburn by its professor of Theology, John C. Bennett,[4] who had acquired a considerable reputation as something of a theological *enfant terrible*. In 1938, it was suddenly announced that Bennett would be leaving Auburn in something of a hurry to take up a position in the Pacific School of Religion in California. Rumours abounded over the cause of his sudden departure. According to one such rumour, an angry wealthy donor had cancelled her promise of nearly half a million much-needed dollars to the Seminary as a result of Bennett's public pronouncements. At any rate, whatever the reasons for his rapid departure, someone had to be found to take his place – quickly. Dr Reed, the President of the Seminary, appealed to John Baillie for help in finding a replacement. It was necessary that this person could teach systematic theology.

Baillie did not particularly care for Torrance's theology, which he knew to have been shaped by H. R. Mackintosh and Karl Barth; he nevertheless had high regard for Torrance as a person and a theologian. It seemed to him that Torrance might well be a suitable short-term replacement for Bennett. Torrance thought otherwise, at least initially. He wanted to return to Basel for further study with Barth, and to complete his dissertation on 'the doctrine of grace in the apostolic fathers'. However, Baillie put considerable pressure on him, and sang the praises of Auburn to such an extent that Torrance finally agreed. It was something that he never regretted.

---

[2] George M. Marsden, *The Evangelical Mind and the New School Presbyterian Experience*. New Haven: Yale University Press, 1970.

[3] Bradley J. Longfield, *The Presbyterian Controversy: Fundamentalists, Modernists and Moderates*. Oxford: Oxford University Press, 1991, 77–103.

[4] William R. Hutchinson, *The Modernist Impulse in American Protestantism*. Oxford: Oxford University Press, 1986, 186.

Baillie duly relayed this welcome news to Reed, omitting to mention Torrance's tender age, and possibly also omitting any reference to the considerable theological differences which existed between Torrance and Bennett. Inevitably, Reed formed the impression that a more senior person would be coming to Auburn. Unaware of this misapprehension, Torrance bought a typewriter and set sail on the Cunard flagship *Queen Mary* for New York. He had to teach himself how to type, and at the same time prepare some lectures with which to begin at Auburn that semester. His teaching load would be substantial, including virtually every aspect of Christian theology. Having written nothing of any substance on which he could base his lectures, he had no option but to spend the boat trip preparing for the opening lectures, and hope that he could somehow keep writing lectures in such a way that he could stay at least one step ahead of the students. Torrance's memories of the outward trip are blurred, and focus mostly on sitting on deck with his typewriter, hammering out what he hoped would be acceptable lectures.

President Reed had written to Torrance, arranging to meet him at the New York dock. When Torrance disembarked from the liner, he duly looked out for someone to approach him. There was nobody to be seen. Gradually, the milling crowd of passengers dispersed, leaving Torrance virtually alone in the dock. Finally, he was approached by Reed, who had been looking for a rather older person and had not expected someone so young. Reed had to return to Auburn almost immediately, so checked Torrance into the Yale Club in New York City to stay for a day or so, and made arrangements for him to travel by train as soon as possible to Auburn. When he arrived a few days later, President and Mrs Reed settled him into the rooms that had been prepared for him in the Dormitory. These struck Torrance as being very pleasant, being equipped with gas lighting and central heating, and all the conveniences Torrance needed. In due course he was taken round the Seminary, the chapel, the library, the dining hall, and the room in which he would lecture, and introduced to his new colleagues.

Baillie had also written to Weir Stewart, a governor of the Seminary, whom he knew from his own days at Auburn, asking him to look out for Torrance. Stewart struck Torrance as a delightful Scottish-American, full of humour and kindness. He was an industrialist, not a minister but a keen churchman, and was at that time the Moderator of the Auburn Presbytery. His home, located in Grover Street, not far from the Seminary, was thrown open to Torrance, and became a real home from home for him throughout his time at Auburn. He used to spend Sunday evenings with the family; they also allowed him to borrow their car during the

Torrance and Harry Mason at Auburn Theological Seminary, New York State, 1939.

Christmas vacation to meet up with some fellow former students of the Canadian School at Chengdu, who had settled in Toronto. Torrance also struck up a friendship with Harry Mason, Professor of Fine Arts in Religion, including music, who encouraged him to learn Italian, and Professor Robert Nichols, the Professor of Church History, whose son Jim, then at Yale, Torrance met again years later as a professor in Princeton Theological Seminary. By then, Jim had become an authority on the Mercersberg Theology of Schaff and Nevin.

Torrance had to work very hard to prepare his lectures and get them ready for delivery the next day. He found that he was regularly thinking and writing late into the night, often into the early hours of the next morning. Sometimes he would leave the Seminary round about midnight and visit a local diner run by an Italian family, and drink copious quantities of coffee to keep himself awake as he worked. Auburn itself had resources for this preparatory work which proved invaluable to him, particularly its library. Torrance found and studied the collected works of Jonathan Edwards (whom Norman Kemp Smith, Torrance's old Professor of Metaphysics at Edinburgh, regarded as the ablest American thinker). Kemp Smith had himself studied the writings of Jonathan Edwards, when he was Professor of Philosophy in Princeton before returning to Edinburgh.

The Auburn Lectures on theology

The lectures which Torrance so painstakingly typed out have been preserved in their entirety, typed out in full on $8\frac{1}{2}"\times 11"$ paper. They offer us a fascinating insight into Torrance's thinking at this early stage in his career. For Torrance, the Auburn Lectures are 'eggshells', a reference to Barth's comments on his earlier philosophical and theological ideas in Münster and Göttingen, which he regarded as merely preparing the ground for the *Church Dogmatics*. The Auburn Lectures represent a considered, measured and informed statement of a basic Christian orthodoxy, tempered at points by a Barthian emphasis, yet making surprisingly little in the way of explicit reference to Barth. For example, in the major section of the lectures dealing with 'The Doctrine of Christ' (occupying more than 350 pages of typewritten text), we find Torrance adopting both a structural framework and a theological perspective which corresponds broadly to that found in both Mackintosh's 1912 classic *The Doctrine of the Person of Christ* and Peter Taylor Forsyth's *Person and Place of Jesus Christ* (1909). Indeed, the 'Preface' to the lectures on 'The Doctrine of Christ' consists of two terse sentences, making Torrance's admiration for Mackintosh abundantly clear:

It is my conviction that the Person of Christ has too often been studied without close attention to His Work. Cf. H[ugh] R[oss] M[ackintosh]: 'In point of fact it is at the Cross that the full meaning of "God in Christ" has broken on the human mind.'[5]

Barth is cited appreciatively, along with a variety of writers from Martin Luther to Karl Adam, but is rarely given pride of place. The points at which Torrance's use of Barth are most marked are to be found in his treatment of the doctrine of the Trinity and the doctrine of revelation – issues to which we shall return when we consider Torrance's early relationship to Barth (see pp. 134–7).

In his lectures on Christology, Torrance followed many of the lines set out with such skill by Mackintosh at Edinburgh. His lectures mounted a vigorous and sustained attack on the entire liberal Protestant approach to the person of Jesus, from Schleiermacher through to Herrmann. Two passages may be noted, which illustrate this point very clearly. The first is from a lecture on 'The Apostolic Testimony to Christ' which critiques experientially based Christologies:

> The apostolic faith and testimony to Christ was not founded on an investigation of the self-consciousness of Christ – rather, where we do have that self-consciousness indicated in the Gospels, it is written after the full development of faith, and with a view to corroborating it . . .The attempt to build up a Christology upon a psychological analysis of Christ's self-consciousness – for what else is the approach of modern Christology than that? – cannot stand, as it was not one used until modern times.[6]

Torrance develops this point further during a lecture dealing with 'The Significance of Christ for Faith':

> The significance of Christ for faith is simply that Christ is the object of faith, the One in whom we believe; as such He has absolute religious significance – that is the essence of Christianity. Christ stands in the focus of true religion, and in laying hold of him we lay hold of God in a personal and immediate way. Another way of putting the same thing is to say that in Jesus Christ we are confronted with the Word of God, not a word about God, or a word that is later seen to be from God, but the Word who *is* God Himself speaking.
>
> A very significant fact in the New Testament witness we have just considered is the principle that *what* God reveals in Christ and the *manner* of that revelation cannot be separated for one moment . . . What God communicates in Christ is not something separate from Himself, but Himself, His own eternal

---

[5] Torrance, 'The Doctrine of Christ', unpublished typescript, 1.
[6] Torrance, 'Doctrine of Christ', 76.

person. The Word is the fact of Christ understood together with the meaning, the word is a fact-in-interpretation, self-interpretation. As such it is self-authenticating, its own authority, grounded in itself along without external legitimation.[7]

The points which Torrance makes in these passages are very similar – both theologically and verbally – to those enunciated by Mackintosh in his later period.[8] However, Torrance was no acolyte of the great Edinburgh dogmatician. At a number of points of importance, he engages in a respectful yet explicit criticism of Mackintosh. For example, he calls into question Mackintosh's argument that the sonship of Christ can be approached as a consequence of the revelation of the Fatherhood of God; and he also suggests that Mackintosh fell victim to the characteristic Ritschlian mistake of arguing that the significance of Christ could be determined from the impression which he made upon his followers.[9]

At this point in his career, Torrance appears to have agreed with Barth concerning the impropriety of 'natural theology'. He considers this issue at several points, particularly in his discussion of the nature and scope of revelation, and the doctrine of the Trinity. The fundamental point stressed by Torrance is that sin has so corrupted the human mind that it cannot recognize revelation for what it truly is. '[God] cannot be known to man directly because He is Creator, nor can He be known indirectly through nature because our eyes are corrupted by sin'.[10]

> Sin means therefore a barrier between God and man; it means that God and therefore the knowledge of Him is removed out of human reach; it means too that man left to himself has been delivered over to a reprobate mind.[11]

We shall return to this matter later, as it represents a point at which Torrance later felt the need to develop Barth's thinking in a slightly different direction.

---

[7] Torrance, 'Doctrine of Christ', 102.

[8] Torrance retained his notes of Mackintosh's dogmatics lectures of 1935–6, and it is possible to trace the points made in the above passage to Mackintosh's lectures. For example, in Torrance's notes to Mackintosh's lecture 'The Gospel and History', delivered at New College on 6 February 1936, we find a major section entitled 'Jesus is self-authenticating'. Similarly, in Torrance's notes of Mackintosh's lecture 'God in Christ: Christ's Relation to Faith', we find the following opening underlined sentence: 'Christian faith takes Jesus as the object of religious faith'; immediately followed by (again, underlined) 'In laying hold of Christ we lay hold of God personally ... Jesus stands in the focus of religion'.

[9] Torrance, 'Doctrine of Christ', 103. It may be noted that these views would be more representative of Mackintosh in his earlier period, prior to the First World War.

[10] Torrance, 'The Christian Doctrine of God', unpublished typescript, 99.

[11] Torrance, 'The Christian Doctrine of Revelation', unpublished typescript, 38.

It soon became clear to Torrance that the material which he was presenting in his lectures was considerably more evangelical and certainly more theological than the students had been used to.[12] Torrance's theology, reflecting his missionary background and the emphases of Mackintosh, led him to stress the importance of conversion and discipleship. Auburn, however, was a progressive 'New School' institution within the Presbyterian Church, and tended to be aligned with more liberal or progressive ways of thinking – ways for which Torrance had little sympathy. In the early weeks of his lecturing, Torrance sensed that a degree of tension was in the process of developing, when what he was saying conflicted either with what students had been taught or what they wanted to believe.

Torrance's evangelistic zeal was grounded on a strong theological, and particularly Christological foundation, with a strong commitment to the doctrine of the atonement as a central theological theme. It seemed clear to Torrance that a theology which failed to make the atoning death of Christ central was not worthy of the name 'Christian'. This view was certainly not what the students had heard from John Bennett, nor was it what many wished to hear in any case. Torrance recalls one case in particular:

One day a student called Harold Estes came into my rooms in the Dormitory to discuss an essay he had written on the atonement. He was a very gentle kindly person. In it he had spoken of the death of Christ simply as a demonstration of the love of God. He had been expounding something like what was known as a 'moral influence theory' of the atonement favoured by liberal thinkers but theologically quite inadequate, as H. R. Mackintosh had shown us in Edinburgh. To help Harold I showed him a reproduction which I had of Grünewald's famous painting of the Crucifixion, at Colmar, which is incredibly starkly vivid. I also showed him some of the enlargements of the painting, reproduced in a book I had with me, which focused on the fearfully lacerated flesh of Jesus which he suffered from the flagellation with thorns inflicted on him by the soldiers, deep wounds now blackened by the sun. Harold shrank back in horror at what he saw. I said to him: 'Harold, you have written about that as a picture of the love of God. It is certainly a picture of the fearful sin and hatred of mankind, but if you can tell me WHY Jesus was crucified, WHY he endured such unbelievable pain and anguish, then you will be able to say something of the real meaning of the atonement, and about why

---

[12] Professor George Newlands (Glasgow University) kindly drew my attention to an unpublished letter of 1939 from a faculty member at Auburn Theological Seminary to John Baillie, which bears out this perception: 'We enjoyed having Tommy Torrance here this year. Tom is youthful. He is inclined to be a bit dogmatic. Still, he is a fine chap, and everyone likes him and enjoys him.'

the crucifixion of Jesus was and is indeed a revelation of the love of God – Christ was crucified like that FOR our sakes, to save us from sin and judgment. The meaning of the atoning death of Christ is expressed in that word FOR – Jesus died for you and for me, and for all people. It is only in the light of that FOR that the death of Jesus is a picture of the love of God. And what a wonderful picture it is of the infinite love of God who so loved us that 'he did not spare his only Son but freely delivered up for us all, that we might be saved.' What I had been unable to say in words alone, could be conveyed with the help of that famous painting: 'Behold the Lamb of God who takes away the sin of the world!' It was with that in mind that I gave a lecture to the students on theology and art.[13]

Torrance experienced particular difficulty with one student who objected strongly to belief in the divinity of Christ, and to the cost of discipleship which acceptance of Christ as the incarnate Son of God involved. The student in question stormed into Torrance's room after a lecture, and made it clear to him that he was very angry over the matter. Torrance recalls saying to him: 'Paul, the very fact that you are so angry indicates that it is not that you cannot believe in the Deity of Christ, but that you don't *want* to.' At this, the student left abruptly and disappeared for three days. Then he returned, knocked at the door, and asked Torrance to go out to have a meal with him. They found a quiet restaurant where they could talk. The student looked 'ghastly' to Torrance; it turned out that this was because he had not slept for three days and nights. Torrance, however, felt that he looked at peace. Leaning across the table, the student told Torrance:

> You are right. If Jesus Christ is not the Son of God, I can do what I like, follow his teaching or not as I choose. But if he really is God, then I have no alternative, but to follow him and obey him.

As Torrance recalls, there was no doubt that Paul had given his heart to the Lord and was at peace.

For Torrance, the event illustrated in a particularly vivid way what it really means and costs to believe in Jesus Christ as one's Lord and Saviour. The young man was wholly transformed, and really understood the nature of Christian belief, and the cost of discipleship. Torrance subsequently used the incident to his students at Edinburgh in order to show them what belief in Jesus Christ as the crucified and risen Lord and Saviour really involved.

---

[13] Torrance, 'Memories of Auburn 1938–39', unpublished typescript. See 'In hoc signo vinces', *Presbyter* 3, 2 (1945), 13–20 (16.S).

It will be clear that Torrance ended up lecturing on a remarkably broad range of subjects, going far beyond the limited realms of 'theology' in the strict sense of that term. Throughout the two semesters, he offered courses on divine revelation and the distinctive nature of grace and the character of theological thought, which involved lectures on theology and philosophy, theology and psychology, and especially on theology and science. In the field of Christian doctrine, he lectured on the knowledge of God with special reference to the teaching of the Old and New Testaments, comparing the traditional or current doctrine of God with Christ's own teaching about God. He followed this up with courses on the classical doctrine of God with special attention to the doctrine of the Trinity. He also lectured on the Holy Spirit, and expounded the doctrines of the Church and the Sacraments. Side by side with all this he also offered lectures on prayer, the Christian life, the Christian message to the non-Christian world, and on theology and art. It will be clear that Torrance set out a grand vision of theology as the source and inspiration for the Christian life, at both the individual and corporate level. We shall explore one series of lectures he delivered at this time – on the theme of theology and the natural sciences – in detail at a later stage.

Looking back on this time, Torrance felt himself to have benefited enormously, both theologically and spiritually from that year in Auburn.[14] It forced him to prepare courses on the whole body of systematic theology, and to think out his own theological convictions very carefully, and find the best way of expressing biblical and theological truth to people living in the modern world. He also came to realize how difficult it is for many people to grasp the significance and face the challenge of the Christian gospel. He learned an immense amount about people that year; it was with that deepening understanding of the cost of faith and discipleship that he also learned something of how to be a theological teacher. That ability had been noted by others in the United States, as developments in 1939 would indicate.

Where next? Chicago and Princeton

Torrance's lectures attracted attention beyond Auburn. Other Presbyterian schools in the region began to express interest in hiring him. He was invited to lecture at McCormick Theological Seminary in Chicago.

---

[14] Auburn Theological Seminary no longer exists as a separate institution. It moved into New York in 1939, and became the Presbyterian wing of Union Theological Seminary. Auburn Hall, erected within the Union quadrangle in 1950, is perhaps the most tangible reminder of the institution at which Torrance taught.

Knowing that such lecture invitations are often preludes to discussions about employment at such seminaries, Torrance felt that he ought to nail his colours to the mast. He lectured for an hour on the doctrine of grace. President Stone of McCormick Seminary eventually closed the meeting by inviting all present to join in singing 'When I survey the wondrous cross'. Emil Brunner, who was then lecturing at Princeton, had visited the Seminary campus three weeks earlier; Torrance's lecture caused by far the greater rumpus within the seminary community.

Nevertheless, President Stone informed Torrance that it was his intention to recommend that the Board of Directors appoint Torrance as professor of systematic theology at the Seminary. He suggested that they think in terms of a probationary period of one year, to allow both Torrance and the Seminary to evaluate each other, followed by appointment at the rank of assistant professor, and promotion to full professor within two years. The Board meeting took place at the end of April 1938, and led to a formal offer to Torrance. Nevertheless, Torrance declined the offer, believing that something more interesting might come out of Princeton. In the end, this intuition proved correct, although the initiative in question came from the University, not the Theological Seminary.

Princeton University was then engaged in establishing a department of religion, the first of its kind in an American University, in which, it was planned, theology would be taught within the Faculty of Arts on an 'objective basis' and in a 'dispassionate way'. Torrance suspects (but cannot prove) that this may have been behind an invitation which he received from President John Mackay (a fellow schoolmate of John and Donald Baillie at Inverness Academy) to visit Princeton Theological Seminary toward the end of the summer semester of 1939. Torrance was asked to meet three professors of Princeton University, headed by the philosopher Theodore Green (who had received his Ph.D. from Edinburgh). They explained their proposal, and asked Torrance whether he would be interested in it. Green stressed that they wanted theology taught not on a confessional or church basis, but in a dispassionate way as one of the liberal arts, rather than as in a theological seminary. He added that there must not be any proselytising!

Torrance responded by declaring that he would be interested in teaching theology *as a science*. When he was asked to elaborate on this statement, Torrance explained his developing views on the matter: that in a rigorous science, 'we think not as we choose to think, but as we are compelled to think in accordance with the nature of the object, and thus in manners which are governed by the objective grounds on which the science rests'. The rigorous nature of scientific questioning could be applied equally well to Christian theology. Torrance, who disliked talk of 'dispassionate' approaches to theology, added that he could not guarantee that no one would be converted through the lectures, believing that this would lessen their interest in him as a potential candidate for the position. Two other candidates were being interviewed for the position, and Torrance did not expect the matter to go further.

To his astonishment, they decided to appoint him, and told him so the next day. However, other factors were now beginning to intrude into the perceptions of European academics in North America. Two or three days later Torrance was taking a walk with Emil Brunner on the campus of the Institute for Advanced Studies, when they began to discuss the alarming news coming in from Europe. It was now June 1939, and there was a growing consensus that war would break out soon. Torrance told Brunner that he did not think he could stay in the United States if war broke out in Europe. Brunner turned to him, and said: 'I think you and I ought to return before the submarines start.' That was good enough for Torrance. He made up his mind at once to return to Europe, and duly reported to Princeton University that he would have to withdraw from the appointment.

Looking back on his career, Torrance points to this decision not to accept the offer at Princeton as one of the two most difficult and significant decisions of his career. Nevertheless, he believed it to have been right and inevitable. His place was in Scotland, to which he would return. War was looming; but Scotland was where he belonged.

CHAPTER 4

Parish and Wartime Service, 1940–50

ON his return to Scotland from the United States, Torrance requested to join the British Army as a chaplain. War had not yet broken out, although it was widely agreed that it was only a matter of time before it did so. To his surprise, Torrance was told that it would be at least two years before he could join up. So what could he do in the meantime? Returning to Basel to complete his dissertation was now unthinkable, although its completion remained a matter of priority for Torrance. An alternative was to continue work on the project, but in another location, this time within the United Kingdom. Torrance thus went to Oxford.

Oriel College, Oxford, 1939–40

In the autumn of 1939, Torrance registered as a postgraduate student at Oriel College. Marcus Niebuhr Todd, the Vice-Provost of the College, supervised his work, and was especially helpful in relation to the detailed philological work on the Greek term *charis*. Todd, an expert on Greek archaeological inscriptions, proved an invaluable guide to Torrance. In the end, the philological work would not find its way into the dissertation to anything like the extent that Torrance had originally planned; his Basel advisor, Karl Ludwig Schmidt, insisted upon it being drastically pruned.

While at Oxford, Torrance became heavily involved in student Christian life, playing a major role in the mission organized by the Oxford Inter-Collegiate Christian Union, although he also became involved in the work of the rival Student Christian Movement.[1] During his time at Oxford, he attended St Columba's Presbyterian Church, close to Oriel College; fellow attendees included both the Provost (W. D. Ross) and Vice-Provost of Oriel College. Academically, it was a remarkably stimulating time. Although wartime restrictions were beginning to have a major effect on the University's teaching programme, Torrance still found time to get involved in philosophical and theological discussions with such leading Oxford lights as Austin Farrer, Raymond Klibansky, Eric L. Mascall and especially the Scottish philosopher Donald MacKinnon.

Parish ministry: Alyth, 1940–3

Every Barth has a Safenwil, a period of pastoral ministry which forces correlation of the themes of systematic theology with the realities of human existence. For Torrance, it was imperative to gain experience of ministry, in order to bring a serious and solid dose of reality to his academic reflection. Oxford had been a good experience; it could not, however, go on for ever. Torrance wanted to minister, and be forced to correlate life and theology. In addition, some in the Church of Scotland felt that it was inappropriate that Torrance should be engaged in further study when the country was at war. Many parish ministers in the kirk were now serving as chaplains in the armed forces, resulting in a shortage of ministers at home.

Aware of this point, Torrance wrote to the Secretary of the Church and Ministry Department of the Church of Scotland to inform them that he would like to serve in a parish. Following his ministerial training at New College, Torrance had been licensed by the Presbytery of Edinburgh as a 'probationer minister', which would lead to ordination once a parish had called him. Two churches expressed interest in Torrance as their minister: the Barony Parish in Alyth in the Presbytery of Meigle, Perthshire, and Kinross, forty miles from Edinburgh across the Forth estuary. It was arranged that Torrance should meet with the elders from both parishes. Torrance preferred the elders from Alyth, who in turn liked Torrance (their judgements here no doubt being assisted by a recommendation that they had received from Professor James S. Stewart).

---

[1] For a useful memoir of the OICCU, with occasional inaccuracies, see John Reynolds, *Born Anew: Historical Outlines of the Oxford Inter-Collegiate Christian Union, 1879–1979*. Oxford: Centenary, Executive and Standing Committees of the OICCU, 1979. On the SCM, see J. Davis McCaughey, *Christian Obedience in the University: Studies in the Life of the Student Christian Movement of Great Britain and Ireland, 1930–1950*. London: SCM Press, 1958; David L. Edwards, *Movements into Tomorrow: A Sketch of the British SCM*. London: SCM Press, 1960.

Alyth Barony Parish Church.

Ordination and Induction
OF

Rev. Thomas F. Torrance, B.D.,
WEDNESDAY, 20th MARCH, 1940, at 2.30 p.m.

Officiating Ministers:
Rev. EDWARD T. HEWITT, M.A., Airlie.
Rev. R. J. WRIGHT, B.A., Rattray East.

INTRODUCTORY SERVICES,
EASTER SUNDAY, 24th MARCH, 1940.

11.15 a.m.—Rev. Professor HUGH WATT, D.D., New College, Edinburgh.
6 p.m.—Rev. THOMAS F. TORRANCE, B.D.

The Programme for Torrance's Ordination and Induction at Alyth, 1940.

During the absence of a parish minister at Alyth, the Presbytery of Meigle had appointed Revd Robert Hastie of the neighbouring parish church of St Andrews, Blairgowrie, to act as Interim-Moderator. Hastie arranged for Torrance to preach at St Andrew's Church, Blairgowrie, and ensured that members of the Alyth Vacancy Committee were present to hear him. Torrance preached on Herod and John the Baptist in the morning, and in the evening on John 3.7: 'You must be born again.' He sufficiently impressed the visitors from Alyth that they resolved to take the matter further. The next step was for him to conduct and preach at a morning and evening service at the Barony Parish, so that the Alyth congregation could determine whether they wished to call him as their Minister. Torrance was duly ordained as Minister at 7.15 p.m. on Wednesday 20 March 1940. Amongst those present was Torrance's father, who had now retired to Edinburgh from his missionary work in Sichuan. Hastie, knowing of Torrance's interest in Calvin, presented him with a full set of Calvin's commentaries, which Torrance would use extensively in his sermon preparation.[2]

Torrance fondly recalls Alyth as 'a lovely old town', which then had about 3,000 inhabitants.[3] It was situated close to the border between Perth and Angus, at the lower end of the foothills which run from the Grampians down to the plain of Strathmore. The Burgh of Alyth had been established at the base of a 300-foot high hill. The Barony Kirk was situated beside a picturesque bridge over the local burn. The manse was located in Cambridge Street, towards the west end of the town.

Torrance's first sermon as Minister of Alyth Barony Parish Church – to use its full title – took place in the evening of Easter Sunday, 24 March. His preaching over his first period at Alyth shows him to be a man who is passionately concerned to turn nominal Christians into believers, and believers into disciples. Torrance's sermons of this period were generally meticulously typed up in single spacing on 5" × 8" paper, and stored in brown manila envelopes with details of the occasions on which they had been preached, and the pages of handwritten notes on which they were based. It is impossible to avoid comparing Torrance with Hugh Ross Mackintosh, whether as preacher or theologian. Torrance's sermons of the period were clearly written to challenge as much as to reassure his congregations. For example, his first Christmas sermon culminated with a plea for personal conversion:

[2] It may be noted that Barth also made extensive use of Calvin's commentaries in his sermon preparation at Safenwil: see, for example, Karl Barth and Eduard Thurneysen, *Revolutionary Theology in the Making: Barth–Thurneysen Correspondence 1914–25*. London: Epworth Press, 1964, 12–13.

[3] Torrance, 'My Parish Ministry: Alyth, 1940–3', unpublished typescript, 3.

After Bethlehem there is only one thing in all the world that really matters, and that is *personal attachment to Jesus Christ our Lord.* . . . Christ must be born in every heart that loves him. God's reconciliation with the world in Christ goes every whit as deep as that; personal attachment to Jesus Christ cannot come short of the most intimate of personal relationships. Indeed, until Christmas means to you the birth of Christ in your heart, you will never experience Christmas at all![4]

Earlier that month, he had preached on the theme of 'Foreign Missions', stressing the critically important role of missionary work in the modern world, and the urgent need to proclaim and respond to Christ as Saviour and Lord.

We must recapture for ourselves in this generation the gospel message of the New Testament, and preach that with uncompromising vigour and faith. We must point the heathen to Christ, and say: Behold your King! Behold your God! . . . We must point them to the cross, and tell them that Christianity is a religion of suffering – and only there through that great humiliation can men be forgiven and come to know God in Jesus Christ. Christianity is God's attack upon man and all his pride.[5]

Even in his more explicitly theological sermons of the period, Torrance never failed to make pastoral and evangelistic connections for his congregations. This is seen most clearly in a sermon on the Trinity, preached in November 1940, in which Torrance explored the theological, pastoral and spiritual depths of 2 Corinthians 13.14 – a passage which his congregation knew well from its formal liturgical use, but which Torrance clearly believed needed unpacking and application. The sermon represents a remarkable piece of homiletics, in which Torrance at one and the same time explains the basic themes of the doctrine, explores its relevance, and applies it to the situations of those in his congregation. For example, here is Torrance explaining the concept of 'grace' to his congregation:

The fact that God stooped down to our earth and in love donned the garment of human flesh is what our text calls the GRACE of our Lord Jesus Christ. Grace is the love of God in princely condescension. It is the love of God to those who do not deserve his love, the indifferent and disloyal, whose only claim is their need. Love may exist between equals, or it may rise to those above us, or flow down to those in any way beneath us. But GRACE, from its very nature, has only one direction which it can take. Grace always flows down.

⁴ Torrance, sermon on 2 Corinthians 5.19, preached 25 December 1940.
⁵ Torrance, sermon on 1 John 2.2, preached December 1940. For the theme of a personal relationship with Christ in the writings of Mackintosh, see Redman, 'Participatio Christi'.

Having made this point, Torrance then proceeded to apply it in a demand for real personal faith on the part of his congregation members:

> There are too many people in the church who are only religious. Their religion consists simply in a belief in God – and in the end it doesn't matter very much what God they believe in. Theirs is simply a bare religion with not much room for Jesus Christ in it. Why is it that so many people are apt to be content with a bare religion with only a creator for their God? Why is it that so many people in modern times are apt to be unitarian, whether in explicit faith or in virtual practice? It is because in Jesus Christ, *God comes too near them* – and they only want a God that is far-off and distant. It would spoil their selfish enjoyment; it would mean a radical alteration in their way of life; it would cost too much; hurt too much, to have a God so close to them that he had come down into the world and become man.

Torrance then clinched this point with some lines which clearly reflect the influence of his much-loved mentor, Hugh Ross Mackintosh:

> Be sure that in your life Jesus Christ occupies the most central place, for it is only through him and in him that you can really have to do with God at all. When you look into the face of Jesus Christ and see there the face of God, you know that you have not seen that face elsewhere, and could not see it elsehow.[6]

In addition to his preaching, Torrance led a series of weekly 'Bible Classes', at which he would deliver a talk based on the passage they were to study, or a more general theme. The notes for those talks over the period 1940–1 (virtually all of which are based on New Testament passages and themes) show Torrance to have a strong concern to explain and apply the themes to both the understanding and the spiritual lives of his congregation. He visited his entire congregation during his time as Minister of Alyth, and regularly read the Bible and prayed with them.

Torrance found that one area of Christian doctrine which many of his congregation found unsettling was the doctrine of grace. The difficulty first came to his notice when John Welch, a local ploughman who had been converted at one of Dwight L. Moody's evangelistic campaigns, asked Torrance to preach some sermons on the letter to the Romans. Welch enjoyed reading Luther's commentary on Galatians, and felt that it would be good to hear Torrance expound Romans. Torrance obliged; in later 1942 and early 1943, he preached on a series of passages from the letter. His sermon on Romans 3.24, preached on 24 January 1943, identified the critical issue as being how someone can be right with God. Throughout

---

[6] Torrance, sermon on 2 Corinthians 13.14, preached November 1940. See also 'A Sermon on the Trinity', *Biblical Theology* 6 (1956) 40–4.

the sermon, Torrance stressed the sinfulness of humanity, and its total inability to put itself in a right relationship with God. Only God can put someone in the right, on account of the cross of Christ. 'Man stands as a guilty sinner before God – he is in the wrong – and the heart of God goes out to him in all his infinite love and mercy.' Yet a human response is needed to what God has done in Christ. Using a down to earth analogy, Torrance concluded:

> The cross of Christ means that God has paid all our debts himself – your debts and mine – all of them. He has given you a cheque covering all your debts – *but* have you gone to the bank and cashed it?

The series of sermons, which focused particularly on justification by grace, caused one elder (and, as it turned out, some others) considerable anguish. Did he mean, they asked Torrance, that their work within the church did nothing to put them in the right with God? Torrance assured them that this was indeed his meaning – and that of St Paul. Yet it conflicted with the intuitive human feeling that religious activity was in some sense meritorious. Torrance would encounter the same difficulty later in his ministry, and would later use his experiences to illustrate the radical nature of the doctrine of justification to his students at New College.

Yet Torrance was also continuing his theological reflection at a more academic level than his preaching and pastoral work might demand. This was stimulated to no small extent by John MacConnachie, Minister of St John's Church, Dundee, and noted particularly for his writings on Karl Barth. MacConnachie persuaded Torrance to become a member of the Angus Theological Club, which met regularly in Dundee. Torrance attended these meetings as often as he could, and found them a stimulus to his thinking and writing. Despite his parish duties, particularly his heavy preaching responsibility, Torrance found time to work on some journal articles and reviews, publishing eight such pieces during his time at Alyth. His review of Cornelius van Til's inept analysis of the theology of Barth and Brunner may be singled out for particular mention at this point.[7]

Yet it is arguable that one of his most significant pieces was an essay that remains unpublished, and was produced for private circulation. A discussion group of leading theologians from throughout Great Britain had been called into being by J. H. Oldham (1874–1969) as a kind of

---

[7] Torrance, Review of *The New Modernism: An Appraisal of the Theology of Barth and Brunner*, by C. van Til, *The Evangelical Quarterly* 19 (1947), 144–9.

theological think-tank.[8] The group, known simply as 'the Moot' (the Old English term for a 'gathering' or 'debate') included John Baillie, H. A. Hodges, Sir Walter Moberley and Alec Vidler. The group met for the first time over the period 1–4 April 1938 at High Leigh in Herefordshire, and set itself a broad agenda aimed to influence the thinking of a future generation. When the Second World War broke out, it seemed to some that the group might well be able to take a leading role in the period of theological reconstruction which they believed would lie ahead, once the War had ended.

However, Baillie began to gain the impression that the theological viewpoints represented within 'the Moot' were distinctly out of line with those which he knew to be gaining ground amongst students at Edinburgh – namely, the ideas associated with Karl Barth. Baillie found himself having to inject Barthian notions into the Moot, while at the same time ensuring that the group understood that he did not regard himself as a Barthian. It was not the easiest of positions to maintain. Hodges (1905– 76) was then Professor of Philosophy at Reading University, and had a particular interest in the writings of Wilhelm Dilthey. At the twelfth meeting of the Moot (August 1941), Hodges presented a paper entitled 'Christian Thinking Today', in which he argued that it was necessary 'to discover and draw out those impulses in humanity which [Christianity] is meant to satisfy, so that the relevance and excellence of it may be felt'. Baillie clearly thought that this line of approach was diametrically opposed to that which was gaining ground among a younger generation of theologians. He therefore proposed that a younger theologian with a knowledge of and sympathy for the Barthian position should be invited to contribute a paper – and named Torrance as his first choice. Torrance was duly approached, and accepted. He was able to finish the paper by the end of 1940, and sent it directly to Baillie.

Torrance's paper was written 'straight out from a few pencilled notes'; even so, it was a substantial piece of writing, taking up seventeen pages of closely-typed foolscap pages. Although Torrance was clearly being invited to write from a Barthian perspective, he chose to make virtually no explicit reference to Barth. Indeed, the approach, in Torrance's view, would have appealed far more to Karl's philosopher brother Heinrich than to Barth himself. However, since Torrance attacked the same ideas which Barth was known to have rejected, it was inevitable that his paper would be treated as 'Barthian' in tone, particularly by Baillie himself, even though

[8] For details, see Keith W. Clements, 'John Baillie and "The Moot"', in Fergusson, *Christ, Church and Society*, 199–219.

it faithfully reflected the general theological perspective which was gaining a substantial following from about 1935 among Edinburgh's many divinity students.

In a bold opening statement, Torrance declared that he was 'in total agreement with the professor's aim', but that he disagreed 'both with his analysis of the situation and therefore with the method which he proposes to solve it'.[9] For Torrance, Hodges seemed to be arguing that the issue was primarily one of communication. Hodges had declared that it was necessary to 'try to make [Christianity] intelligible, so that anyone who sees it as a vision may be able to assure himself that it is not a mirage'. For Torrance, this seemed to imply that Christian truth was in some way already available in the common stock of human ideas as a whole. For Torrance, Christian truth came through revelation, not through some common set of naturally derived ideas, common to all humanity. 'Christian truth is not something that we already have, and to be looked for along the converging lines of human thinking; it is something which must be brought TO our thinking.' Nevertheless, Torrance felt able to agree with Hodges that there was a need to ensure that Christian truth was communicated effectively, and distanced himself from certain 'Barthian' approaches to this matter:

> That means that it cannot be helped if the outsider is blind to Christian truth. Something far more than language and thought will be necessary to make him see. 'Except a man be born again, he cannot see.' There will therefore always be this tension between the communication of the Christian faith, and its reception by the world. At the same time, I feel with Professor Hodges that we cannot absolve ourselves from failure in putting the Christian convictions as clearly as we can. The 'Barthian' is so apt to preach the Gospel, and then leave it to God; but if we believe that the Incarnation establishes once and for all the fact that we can only apprehend God in human thought forms, then we must do our utmost to shape those thought forms in a way in which they will really be human, really relevant to the present human situation.[10]

Yet this could lead to the possibility of accommodating or reducing Christianity to modern thought forms, and losing sight altogether of its distinctive outlook, content and approach – above all, its origins in divine self-revelation, rather than human insight.

> It is quite false to try and force Christianity into the framework of the modern system of ideas at whatever cost to itself, and it would amount to an equal betrayal to return to the more congenial categories of another age. If

---

[9] Torrance, 'Christian Thinking Today', unpublished paper, 3.
[10] Torrance, 'Christian Thinking Today', 4–5.

Christianity is anything, it is living; if its genius is Grace, then we must be prepared to take the initiative ourselves, and not simply try to fit in our Christian message with present day thinking. New categories have certainly developed in the philosophical discussion of the centuries, and we cannot escape from these even if we would – at the same time we may do well to remember that our very language is so steeped in a pagan tradition that very often the words which we use have a whole philosophy within themselves, and we shall have to use our words carefully.[11]

Finally, Torrance addressed Hodges' third argument: it is necessary 'to discover and draw out those impulses in humanity which [Christianity] is meant to satisfy'. Torrance emphatically refuted this. 'It is from the very centre of the Christian faith that we are to work out a new orientation towards thinking today, and not from the analysis of religious awareness.'[12] It was necessary to work outwards from the central doctrines of the Christian faith, not inwards from a general philosophical or pheno-menological analysis of human experience.

There can be no doubt that Torrance's paper irritated Hodges. For example, Torrance suggested that Hodges' use of the term *Weltanschauung* was inappropriate, and muddled the rather different notions of *Weltanschauung* and *Lebensanschauung* – citing Dilthey in support of his point. Hodges, who considered himself an expert on Dilthey, was not entirely pleased with being challenged on the interpretation of this point. Torrance also spent some time analysing the finer points of recent German-language philosophy, suggesting that Hodges had perhaps become a little muddled in his thinking, or at least the terms in which he expressed it. Hodges replied virtually immediately to Torrance's piece, with a somewhat bad-tempered paper entitled 'Barthianism and Christian Thinking', which implied that Baillie had made a bad choice in approaching Torrance.[13] What was the point in continuing with the Moot if Torrance was right?[14] It is clear that other members of the Moot also found Torrance's style and approach to be difficult, for various reasons. In a diplomatic letter to Torrance, J. H. Oldham suggested that the discussion headed off in a different direction, and that Torrance's paper was not really discussed within the body of the meeting.[15] In fact, the general drift of discussion within the December meeting of the Moot seems to have

---

[11] Torrance, 'Christian Thinking Today', 12.
[12] Torrance, 'Christian Thinking Today', 17.
[13] H. A. Hodges, 'Barthianism and Christian Thinking', unpublished paper, 1.
[14] Hodges, 'Barthianism and Christian Thinking', 6–7.
[15] Oldham to Torrance, 15 January 1942. For a study of Oldham, see Keith W. Clements, *Faith on the Frontier: A Life of J. H. Oldham*. Edinburgh: T&T Clark; Geneva: WCC, 1999.

been that the Torrance paper was something of a waste of their time, in that it clearly did not relate well to their agenda.

Elsewhere, Torrance was establishing his reputation as an eloquent and able exponent of a critical approach to prevailing currents of thought within the Church of Scotland. This can be seen from a paper entitled 'The Place and Function of the Church in the World', delivered by Torrance on 21 January 1942 to a special meeting of the Presbytery of Meigle, which included the Barony Parish.[16] In this paper, Torrance reflected on the tendency of the church to become identified with human culture and civilization, and thus to lose its distinctive identity and mission. The church 'has so compromised her message with the ideas of the modern world that she is now not in a proper position to stand over against the world and deliver the pure Word of God with passion and conviction'. It is significant that Torrance saw the Second World War as provoking a crisis, in which the identity and mission of the Christian church demanded to be recovered; after all, Barth had similar feelings about the First World War while in Safenwil. Torrance thus issued a call for a recovery of Christian authenticity, and supremely for the church to make the proclamation of the gospel its foremost task. The church exists by mission, just as fire exists by burning – and that mission must be recovered at all costs.

After three years in the ministry at Alyth, Torrance felt sure that the time had come to serve in the British Army. He was reluctant, however, to sign up with the Royal Army Chaplain's Department, in that the commission that he would receive would mean that he would have to serve on after the War had ended. Torrance was convinced of the need to get back into theological ministry in Scotland as soon as possible, and was reluctant to stay on in the Army after the War was over.

War service: 1943–5

Early in 1943, Torrance travelled to Edinburgh, and presented himself at the headquarters of the Church of Scotland at 121 George Street. In addition to inquiring about how he could sign up with the Royal Army

---

[16] *The Place and Function of the Church in the World*, published privately at Alyth on 26 January 1942 by the Presbytery of Meigle. The discussion was held against the background of the General Assembly Commission for the Interpretation of God's Will in the Present Crisis (chaired by Professor John Baillie, and usually simply known as the 'Baillie Commission'). On this, see Andrew R. Morton (ed.), *God's Will in a Time of Crisis: A Colloquium Celebrating the 50th Anniversary of the Baillie Commission*. Edinburgh: Centre for Theology and Public Issues, University of Edinburgh, 1994.

Chaplain's Department, he needed to find out what arrangements could be made for the pastoral care of the people in Alyth during his absence. In the end, however, events took a slightly different – and rather more agreeable – turn than he had anticipated. A number of kirk organizations were based at 121 George Street, including the Church of Scotland Huts and Canteens. On his arrival, Torrance ran into Dr Charles Warr of St Giles' Cathedral, Edinburgh. It was to prove a providential encounter.

The 1940 General Assembly of the Church of Scotland was conscious of a need to provide both pastoral care and practical assistance to Scottish soldiers on wartime service. It therefore established a 'Committee on Hut and Canteen Work for H.M. Forces', with a brief to develop work of this kind. The organization which resulted from this was widely known simply as the 'Huts and Canteens' organization; one of its senior personnel was Charles Warr.[17] By July 1940, the organization had established itself in the Middle East, under its first director in the region, Duncan MacGillivray. For the first thirty months of its existence, the Middle East office of the Huts and Canteens was located in the vestry of St Andrews Church, Jerusalem. Work was also begun in Cairo; a hut was established at the Abbassia Barracks, on the outskirts of the city. It was not long before this hut was simply known as 'Scots Corner', on account of the large number of Scottish soldiers who made use of its facilities.[18]

At the time of his accidental meeting with Torrance in Edinburgh, Warr was trying to find a replacement for George Campbell, who had served the organization centred in Cairo, and was now in the process of returning home to his parish. Warr knew that Torrance was familiar with the Middle East, and immediately offered him a position with the organization. If he accepted, he would be guaranteed a posting to Cairo and Jerusalem within weeks.

The offer was tempting, and it did not take Torrance long to agree to Warr's request. Arrangements were soon made for pastoral care for Alyth during Torrance's absence. Kenneth Mackenzie (who was married to Torrance's younger sister Margaret) would in the meanwhile act as *locum tenens* during his absence. The formalities took several weeks, after which Torrance travelled to Edinburgh to bid farewell to his parents, and then to join a troopship. They sailed southwards, heavily laden with troops to reinforce the 51st Highland Division and other units, bound for the North

---

[17] For this neglected organization, which was to prove so important to Torrance, see Lewis L. L. Cameron, *A Badge to be Proud of: A History of the Church of Scotland Huts and Canteens, 1939–1972*. Edinburgh: Church of Scotland, 1972. The organization was wound up at the General Assembly of the Church of Scotland on 26 May 1972.

[18] For a full account of 'Scots Corner', see Cameron, *A Badge to be Proud of*, 37–67.

African port of Algiers. It was an uneventful voyage. Although German submarines and bombers were active in the area, Torrance's worst moment was merely being seasick in the Bay of Biscay. Torrance found himself doing much pastoral work throughout the voyage, and preached a sermon on 'Christ as Personal Saviour and Lord'.

On arrival at Algiers, Torrance spent a few days at the Officers' Transit Camp, awaiting travel instructions to Cairo. None came. Torrance wandered round Algiers, noting the massive build-up of British and American forces in preparation for the planned (but still highly secret) assault on Sicily. After two weeks, Torrance lost his patience, and hitched a ride on a Dakota to Tripoli. Here he met Duncan MacGillivray, who headed up the Church of Scotland Huts and Canteens in the Middle East. MacGillivray had no idea that Torrance had arrived in Algiers, and promptly made arrangements for him to be flown to Cairo, and take up where George Campbell had left off.

Torrance dreamed of such military exploits as being the man who tore down the Nazi flag from the summit of Mount Olympus. In fact, no such distinction came his way while serving in the Middle East. Some had the privilege of undertaking top secret missions behind enemy lines. Torrance's first major mission, however, was to deliver a massive consignment of Turkish Delight to the Scottish Horse Regiment, an armoured regiment based in Tobruk and Tripoli who were preparing for the invasion of Italy. Torrance's mission involved driving over 1,500 miles of desert, and took him and his driver Jock Patterson three and a half days. Rumours of impending action circulated ceaselessly, although most came to nothing. The closest that Torrance came to seeing some real action was when the major Allied assault on the Aegean islands got under way. It went disastrously wrong.

Theologically, it was not a particularly exciting time – but it could hardly have been expected to be so. The demands of his pastoral work were such that Torrance found himself with little time available for reading. His parents sent him what they could, including two major works with Edinburgh connections published in 1943 – Leonard Hodgson's *Doctrine of the Trinity* (the Croall Lectures for 1942–3), and William Manson's *Jesus the Messiah* (the Cunningham Lectures). At the 19th General Hospital, Torrance encountered H. E. W. Turner (Chaplain of Lincoln College, Oxford), whom he had come to know during his time at Oriel College in 1940, and who subsequently became Professor of Theology at Durham University. While browsing through a Cairo store, Torrance came across a copy of Emil Brunner's *Divine Imperative*, which he presented to Duncan MacGillivray when he learned that he had become engaged, and that he was to be best man at the wedding in Jerusalem in March 1944. The wedding allowed Torrance to revisit many sites he knew in Palestine from his earlier sojourn in the area.

Yet Torrance's future was unclear. The regiments to which he was attached kept moving on to fresh duties, leaving him behind to attend to their replacements. At one point, he was asked to consider being appointed as minister of St Andrew's Church and Hospice in Jerusalem, a position which would have continued after the War. However, Torrance was convinced that he was called to serve in theological ministry in Scotland, and declined the offer. There was a serious shortage of army chaplains at this point, and it gradually became clear that ways could be found to combine Torrance's responsibility in Huts and Canteens with a chaplaincy role. Despite renewed pressure to join the Royal Army Chaplains' Department, Torrance continued to resist this option. In his view, he was already doing a chaplain's job; furthermore, he had no intention of remaining in the army once the War had been won.

In the end, Torrance's break came through Major-General Denys Reid, noted for his distinguished service in a series of long-range desert patrols across North Africa. Reid was the son of a Church of Scotland minister in Inverness, and wanted a Church of Scotland chaplain for the 10th Indian Division, which was then preparing to sail for active service in Italy.[19] Torrance was duly loaded, along with his mobile canteen truck,[20] onto a small cargo ship heavily laden with tanks, which set sail for the port of Taranto, from which he made his way to Ortona, on the eastern end of the battle line. Torrance established his canteen in the ruins of a monastery, and set about arranging for a local bakery to make biscuits and cakes from the flour, eggs and sugar he was able to provide.

As the Allied advance northwards continued, Torrance found himself traversing Italy. In Rome, he met up with J. K. S. Reid, who was acting as chaplain to a parachute battalion. Together, they explored the Vatican and St Peter's. Torrance then went on to visit the Collegio di Sant' Anselmo, where he knew one of the professors though correspondence. He was allowed to borrow some works from the college library. A final shopping trip (which he referred to as his 'holy grocery') allowed Torrance to pick up two sets of Aquinas' *Summa Theologica* and *Summa contra Gentiles* for his brothers. Later, once the mountains overlooking Florence had been captured, he drove to Quaracchi, and bought some of the

---

[19] Details of its campaign can be found in *Teheran to Trieste: The Story of the Tenth Indian Division*. Bombay: Times of India Press, [n.d.].

[20] On these trucks, see Cameron, *A Badge to be Proud of*, 85–91.

Torrance on war service in Italy, 1944.

theological works published there, including the two-volume edition of Peter Lombard's *Sentences* and Duns Scotus' *Opus Oxoniense*. Karl Barth had regularly engaged with Peter Lombard in his Basel seminars, and Torrance found the volumes reminding him of those halcyon days in Switzerland before the War. In Florence, he later picked up Heinrich Barth's pamphlet on St Augustine, and a copy of Pico della Mirandola's writings.

Torrance was not directly involved in the fighting. Nevertheless, what was going on around him made a deep impression on him. One particular incident would remain indelibly imprinted in his memory. It took place on 17 October 1944, when the King's Own Royal Rifles launched an attack on the hamlet of San Martino. The San Martino–Sogliano ridge was particularly difficult to attack on account of its strong defences. For example, San Martino cemetery had high, thick walls which provided ideal cover for the defending German troops. Part of the assault had to take place at night, under the illumination of searchlights. Torrance served as a stretcher bearer, and found himself under fire at several points during the night.

When daylight filtered though, I came across a young soldier (Private Philips), scarcely twenty years old, lying mortally wounded on the ground, who clearly had not long to live. As I knelt down and bent over him, he said: 'Padre, is God really like Jesus?' I assured him that he was – the only God that there is, the God who had come to us in Jesus, shown his face to us, and poured out his love to us as our Saviour. As I prayed and commended him to the Lord Jesus, he passed away.[21]

In one sense, this was merely another casualty of war. Yet Torrance found the situation to be deeply moving, and rich with theological significance. Hugh Ross Mackintosh had constantly stressed the importance of seeing God in Jesus, despite the widespread theological tendency to isolate Jesus from God. Torrance has never forgotten that incident, nor its impact upon him.

That incident left an indelible impression on me. I kept wondering afterwards what modern theology and the Churches had done to drive some kind of wedge between God and Jesus, and reflected on the damage done by natural theology to Christology and the proclamation of the Gospel! The evangelical teaching which I had from Karl Barth was considerably reinforced on the battlefield. There is no hidden God, no *Deus Absconditus*, no God behind the back of the Lord Jesus, but only the one Lord God who became incarnate in him. Years later in my Aberdeen parish an old lady who had not very long to live said to me one day: 'Dr Torrance, is God really like Jesus?' I was startled, for those were the very same words I had heard on that battlefield in Italy. What have we been doing in our preaching and teaching in the church, to damage in the faith of our people the relation between their faith in Jesus Christ and God? How important was the teaching of Jesus in the gospel about the mutual and exclusive relation between him and God the Father, which H. R. Mackintosh used to stress in his lectures given to us in Edinburgh! . . . That was the problem, a refracted or damaged relation between Jesus and God, the hiddenness of God, which I found in Donald Baillie's book, *God was In Christ,* in which he could only think out the relation between God and Man in Christ as a paradox.[22]

Although Torrance was fully occupied with the pastoral welfare of his regiment, he gradually found that his thoughts were beginning to turn back to theology. He had been invited to give some lectures to Church of Scotland chaplains in May at Assisi. His task in preparing these lectures was made easier by Brigadier Smith, who dug out a typewriter which he had captured some time ago in Eritrea, and loaned it to Torrance. Torrance entitled the lectures 'Theology and Action'.[23] As it happened, the Second World War ended in Europe shortly before Torrance gave the lectures, and he found himself having to arrange a series of thanksgiving services for the troops. The result was that he did not feel adequately prepared to give the lectures, and was up at 7.30 every morning working away at the text in order to try and get things ready. In the one surviving lecture, Torrance stresses the centrality of the death of Christ upon the cross, and its powerful message, even to a world wrecked by war:

> Why is it then that the cross has become the dearest and the most sacred emblem of the Christian faith, the religion of love? Why does it produce saints, when, it seems, it ought to produce sceptics? This is the fact of the matter: – Put God in heaven and Jesus on the cross allowed to die, and you destroy your faith, for you cannot believe in a God who allowed that. On the other hand, it makes us utterly despair of man, for if that is what we have done, what hope is there of the world ever living in love and brotherhood after this war? *But* (and this is the gospel) *put God on the cross* and you alter the whole situation, for then the cross is not the picture of God's unconcern or careless disregard. Rather it is the picture of God's utmost concern, nay, a picture or his actual intervention in the affairs of men, for it means that God Almighty has come down into the midst of human sin and shame, not only to bear our sin, but to destroy it for ever. That is the incomprehensible cast and design of his glory, that in the cross we have the invasion of God striking in desperate anguish at the heart of evil.[24]

For Torrance, the cross had to be of central importance, not simply to our thinking about redemption (important though that is), but also to our whole way of thinking, and doing theology. The cross is both the foundation and criterion of authentically Christian theology, allowing the church to regain her own identity in the world, and avoid being swept along by the latest current of thought.

> A Christian theology which must perforce use the language of the day, a language steeped in an alien tradition and fashioned by the thinking of centuries of secular philosophy, must be prepared always to put these ideas into the crucible of the cross, so that they die and rise again new creatures in Christ. That must happen continually in the mind and soul of the Christian; the refashioning of his mind. New categories must be built into the matrix of his mind, until he have the mind of Christ and Christ be formed in him. That is the task of Christian theology in the world today . . . and unless Christian

---

[23] The text of all but one of these lectures has been lost. For the one that survived, see Torrance, 'In hoc signo vinces', published in November 1945.

[24] Torrance, 'In hoc signo vinces', 15.

theology makes use of the cross at the very centre of its sacred task, pressing to the surface all the pagan and anti-Christian ideas seeded into the human soul, reshaping the church's mind at every crisis in the road, and giving her such a firm grip upon the image and the mind of Christ that she will be able to face decisively all that confronts her, the Christian church will not survive these days of pagan and demonic onslaught, far less the insidious absorption of the Christian faith in the inherently pantheistic and monistic outlook of the natural man.[25]

With these words, Torrance may be seen to have set a personal theological agenda of some considerable depth. But how could this agenda be advanced? The question of his future could not now be ignored. He was not a member of the Royal Army Chaplains' Department, and hence would not be required to remain in uniform now that the War was over. He could now begin to turn his thoughts to the future. One possibility that was being actively canvassed was that he should return to Oxford. The Provost of Oriel, Sir W. D. Ross, was convinced that Torrance should be the next minister of St Columba's Church in Oxford, and had written to the Church of Scotland headquarters at 121 George Street to say so.

Torrance thus preached to the congregation of St Columba's after his return from Italy on 22 July 1945. It was a powerful sermon, contrasting exemplarist understandings of the cross with the full-blooded orthodox interpretation of the death of Christ. The sacrificial service of so many members of the armed forces during the War was widely interpreted as a paradigm of the cross. The death of Jesus was to be seen as an example of heroic self-giving love, the kind of behaviour which he intended to inspire in his followers. Torrance weighed in heavily against such an interpretation, which he felt was fatally compromised by its failure to deal with the seriousness of the human predicament.

> I wonder if you were ever tempted . . . to believe that Christianity is just human nature at its best? That is the most powerful and dangerous plea that is being put forward just now in challenge to our Christian faith. It is the idea that Christianity is just the spirit of self-sacrifice, which you find in human nature already, developed to its highest . . . We folk today are sickened with the thought of slaughter and the waste of human life – but we also want to face the facts. Here's a realist who says: The Cross, a picture of love! You might as well take your children to see a public execution in Germany, and say 'Behold a picture of love'. No one but a madman would do that – and yet the cross *was* a public execution. We dare not eliminate the horrors from it without evacuating it of

---

[25] Torrance, 'In hoc signo vinces', 20.

its intense significance. But horror though there be, there is a meaning behind it that transforms all its ugliness into beauty; that does bring love and life out of death. And the meaning is this: God stooped to that in order to redeem. 'He loved me, and gave himself for me.' 'He sent his son to be the propitiation for our sins'. It is that insight, by no means an easy or an obvious, but a costly one, that enables us to see love at last – not simply the love that lays down one's life for friends, not simply heroic love, but a deed of *sovereign* love, the love that is able to turn ashes into beauty.[26]

Attractive though it would have been to return to Oxford and minister at St Columba's, Torrance felt that his future lay elsewhere. Yet if a ministry in Oxford was out of the question, then where was he to go? Torrance felt that he should really return to Alyth, and had explained the reasons for this early in 1945 to Duncan MacGillivray, who was then visiting Italy to monitor the progress of Church of Scotland work among the armed forces. Torrance had by then been away from the Barony Parish Church for two years. MacGillivray attempted to dissuade him from leaving Huts and Canteens, offering him overall charge of some exciting new projects which the organization was planning in the Balkans. And if he didn't like the Balkans, what about Burma? But Torrance was set in his way of thinking.

In late May, he learned officially that he would be returning to England. On his arrival in London, he went to St Martin in the Fields, a large Anglican church in Trafalgar Square. He wanted to pray and meditate, giving thanks for being kept safely throughout the War, and entrusting the future to God.

> I wanted to pray and meditate, before I returned to Edinburgh. I was overwhelmed with the fact that I had come back alive, and even uninjured. In my prayer and meditation I asked the Lord what he wanted me to do. I believe he had spared me for some purpose – it was indeed that belief that gave me courage and again and again had sustained me in the face of death and destruction – although I often felt ashamed when I was preserved while others were not. I had committed myself to him unreservedly for what he wanted me to do. I never forget those moments in St Martin's in the Fields, and whenever I am back in London, I try to visit it again, in renewed thankfulness for God's gracious preservation and blessing to me in my work for him, and in renewal of my unreserved commitment to him in the service of the Lord Jesus Christ and the Gospel.[27]

---

[26] Unpublished sermon on 1 John 4.10, also delivered in May 1943 in the chapel of Glasgow University.

[27] Torrance, 'War Service', 66–7.

Parish ministry: from Alyth to Beechgrove, 1945–50

Torrance resumed ministry in Alyth in the late summer of 1945. His first major undertaking was the systematic visitation of his congregation members, particularly those who had suffered losses during the War. A number of issues now pressed upon him. In the first place, he wanted to finish off his Basel doctorate on the doctrine of grace in the apostolic fathers. Yet his personal life was also in the process of changing. During his time in Edinburgh before the War, Torrance had met Margaret Edith Spear. Although Margaret was English, she was at that time a student at Atholl Crescent Domestic Science College in Edinburgh. Margaret had become a friend of Torrance's sister Margaret; both were regular members of the Evangelical Union at Edinburgh University. Margaret had spent four years during the war nursing in London at St Thomas' Hospital, which had been bombed thirteen times during the Blitz. In May 1946, she returned to Edinburgh to spend some time visiting Margaret Torrance, who had just returned on her first furlough from Central Africa. During this visit, Torrance finally realized that this was the woman he wanted to marry. They became engaged on 24 May at Combe Down, near the city of Bath in England's West Country, shortly before Torrance returned to Basel to face his doctoral *Rigorosum*.[28] They would be married at Combe Down on 2 October of that same year.

First, however, there was the matter of the *Rigorosum*. Torrance returned to Basel after becoming engaged, and spent several weeks refreshing his knowledge of German, partly through attending lectures by Karl Ludwig Schmidt and Emil Brunner (who was lecturing in Basel while Barth was in Bonn). In the event, Torrance took his *Rigorosum* along with Christoph Barth, whom he had got to know well during his earlier period at Basel. In Torrance's case, the examination was conducted by Karl Ludwig Schmidt, Oscar Cullmann and Fritz Lieb. The outcome of both examinations was successful; Torrance was awarded his doctorate *magna cum laude*. Torrance's thesis was published in its original paper-bound form by Oliver & Boyd of Edinburgh in 1946; a hard-bound edition was issued by the same press in 1948. The book filled an important gap in the literature, and furthered Torrance's growing reputation as a significant figure in the field of historical theology.

---

[28] For those familiar only with North American and British doctoral examinations, it may be helpful to add that the *Rigorosum* can be thought of as a doctoral examination at which the candidate may be questioned on any aspect of theology, and not merely that on which he has chosen to specialize.

Torrance pictured during his time at Basel, 1946.

Yet Torrance had given thought, especially during his wartime service, to institutional developments which would be needed to consolidate the revival of Scottish theology, and especially Barthian perspectives, in the postwar period. It was quite clear to Torrance that there was an urgent need for academic theological societies and journals. He founded the Scottish Church Theology Society in 1945, recognizing the need to consolidate the growing interest in theology in the region. Further developments would follow in due course, most notably the launch of the *Scottish Journal of Theology* in 1948 (which Torrance had already projected and developed further in discussion with J. K. S. Reid, who had also seen military service in Italy). Finally, Torrance founded the Society for the Study of Theology in 1952. It is easy to note these three developments; yet each represented the outcome of a long process of reflection and planning, focusing on the institutional developments which would be the necessary precondition for theological consolidation.

Torrance, however, saw himself both as an heir and interpreter of the Reformed tradition, particularly in relation to Calvin. He also found time to work on an aspect of Calvin's theology which was of some importance to him – theological anthropology. The question of Calvin's understanding of human nature, and particularly the nature and epistemic capacity of human nature in consequence of it being created in the image of God, had featured prominently in the 1934 debate between Karl Barth and Emil Brunner, and had proved to be a divisive matter subsequently. Torrance believed that Barth and Brunner were 'shooting past each other' on this matter, and wanted to sort it out.[29] The work was published in 1949 by Lutterworth Press, and is now regarded as something of a landmark in British Calvin studies.

Torrance's long-term objective was to pursue an academic career in the service of the church. The possibility of such a career first arose seriously in January 1947, when Sir Hector Hetherington, Principal of Glasgow University, wrote to Torrance to invite him to apply for the Chair of Divinity which had become vacant within the University through the resignation of Professor Fulton. Since 1929, Glasgow had two chairs of systematic theology, as a result of the church union of that year. The senior chair was generally referred to as the 'old' chair of systematic theology; it was this chair which became vacant. The second chair was associated with Trinity College, and was occupied by John G. Riddell

---

[29] It is interesting to note that Barth explicitly refers to Torrance only once in the *Church Dogmatics*, on precisely this issue: see *Church Dogmatics* IV/1, 367, where Barth registers disagreement with Torrance over whether the doctrine of human corruption is to be formulated as a consequence of the doctrine of grace.

Torrance pictured with his parents and baby Thomas at the front door of the Barony Manse, Alyth, 14 July 1947.

during the period 1934–47. In the event, university politics intervened, with the result that an internal appointment was made, with Riddell being transferred from the Trinity College chair to the 'old' chair. Although Torrance was then invited to consider applying for the new vacancy which resulted, he declined to do so. Although Torrance recommended George S. Hendry for the position, in the event it was offered to Ian Henderson, who took up his position in 1948.

So Torrance remained in Alyth. Alyth was a small parish, and this had the advantage of allowing Torrance to get on with some academic work while fulfilling his pastoral duties. However, the limitations of the position became increasingly clear as Torrance's family grew. The stipend of £400 was not really enough to meet the needs of a growing family. Thomas Spear Torrance was born at Alyth on 3 July 1947. Two more children would follow: Iain Richard Torrance, born in Aberdeen on 13 January 1949; and Alison Meta Elizabeth Torrance, born in Edinburgh on 15 April 1951.[30]

---

[30] At the time of writing (1998), Thomas is an economist and philosopher of science at Heriot-Watt University, Edinburgh; Iain is a theologian and patristic scholar at the University of Aberdeen, serving both as an editor of the *Scottish Journal of Theology* and on the Académie Internationale des Sciences Religieuses; Alison graduated in medicine, and is currently a general practitioner in Edinburgh.

A few days after the birth of Thomas, a delegation of elders came to visit Torrance from Beechgrove Church in Aberdeen. They wanted to know if Torrance would be open to the possibility of moving to Aberdeen, and becoming their Minister. James S. Stewart, who had also served as Minister to the parish from 1928 to 1947, had been called to the Chair of New Testament Language, Literature and Theology at New College, Edinburgh. Stewart suggested that Torrance would be an ideal person to be their Minister.

The idea had some attractions for Torrance. The first minister of the parish had been none other than Hugh Ross Mackintosh, who served the parish from 1901 to 1903, after which he was called to lecture at New College, Edinburgh. Torrance felt that he would be following a distinguished tradition were he to proceed to Beechgrove. In addition, Professor A. M. Hunter, who held the New Testament chair at King's College, Aberdeen, and was then acting as *locum tenens* in Beechgrove Church, was also a positive influence on Torrance.

There were also two additional considerations which made Torrance take the possibility seriously. First, the position carried with it a larger stipend than Alyth – £700 instead of £400. With the needs of his family in mind, Torrance could not overlook the importance of this point. Second, a move to Aberdeen would allow him contact with the Faculty of Divinity, and stimulate his academic ministry. In addition, his friend Donald MacKinnon, a noted philosopher, was based at King's College, Aberdeen. It seemed that this would indeed be a suitable move. On 24 September, Torrance travelled to Aberdeen to take services and preach at Beechgrove. The congregational report was favourable, and the decision was taken to call Torrance. In early November, the Torrance family moved to Aberdeen, and settled in at 39 Forest Road. Torrance was inducted as the new minister of Beechgrove Church on Thursday 13 November.

Beechgrove was a larger and busier parish than Alyth, and Torrance found himself with more to do than he would have liked. Although articles and reviews flowed from his pen, it became clear that there would not be much opportunity for researching and writing the major academic studies which he believed were needed, and which he believed he could undertake. He found that he could make use of some of the sermons which he had already delivered at Alyth; some of these would eventually find their way into later published collections, including the 1957 volume *When Christ Comes, and Comes Again.*[31] His Basel doctoral thesis would

---

[31] *When Christ Comes, and Comes Again*. London: Hodder & Stoughton, 1957.

Beechgrove Parish Church, Aberdeen.

appear in a different format in 1948. Torrance now had two substantial books and a significant number of articles and reviews, as well as initiatives relating to societies and journals, to his credit. But he could not remain at Beechgrove for ever. Where would he go next?

It must be stressed that, at a personal level, Torrance was very happy at Beechgrove, and made a positive and lasting appeal to his congregation. It is no accident that Torrance was invited to preach as part of the centenary celebrations at Beechgrove Church on 2 November 1997.[32] His difficulty related to his academic work: he was so engaged in the business of parish ministry that he felt that he would not be able to achieve what he believed to be his calling – to be a theologian who could support the missionary and evangelistic work of the church. In an interview published in 1990, Torrance stressed that he had no doubts that his long period in various forms of ministry was invaluable to his theological development.

---

[32] This was not, of course, the first time he had been invited back. See his sermon preached at Beechgrove on 10 December 1967, which was printed in full, at the request of church members, in the January 1968 edition of the parish magazine.

My ten years in parish ministry … enabled me to think *theologically* and not pseudo-psychologically. Again and again I found that the fundamental theological questions were the very stuff of the deepest anxieties of the human heart, questions such as 'Is God really like Jesus?' I discovered repeatedly that to minister effectively required a firm grasp of the gospel and of the theology of the incarnation.[33]

The call to New College, 1950

It was clear that Torrance believed that his future lay as a professor at New College, Edinburgh, the institution at which he had been a student back in the 1930s. Hugh Ross Mackintosh – who had once served at Beechgrove – was clearly something of a role model for Torrance at this stage. Colleagues on the faculty at New College had indicated to Torrance that they fully expected him to join them there at some point in the future. But when? And in what capacity?

To understand what happened next, we need to consider developments within the Department of Ecclesiastical History at New College, Edinburgh. After the merger of the University Faculty of Divinity and New College in the mid-1930s, two chairs of church history existed side by side, and were usually referred to as the 'university chair' and the 'church chair'. The former was held by John Henderson Seaforth Burleigh (appointed 1931) and the latter by Hugh Watt (appointed 1919).[34] In 1950, Watt retired, only to find himself called to the Moderatorship of the General Assembly of the Church of Scotland. But who would succeed Watt in the 'church chair'?

Torrance did not see himself as a church historian, although he fully recognized the importance of historical theology. When, in the early part of 1950, he was sounded out about the possibility of succeeding Watts, he dismissed the possibility, for two reasons. First, he had only served for two and a half years at Beechgrove. It would have been unseemly and inconsiderate to leave after such a short period. Second, he was not really a church historian.[35] However, none of those whose advice he sought regarded these as serious difficulties. On Sunday 26 March 1950, the news of Torrance's call to the 'church' chair of ecclesiastical history at Edinburgh was announced to the congregation at

---

[33] 'Thomas Torrance', in Bauman, *Roundtable*, 113.
[34] See Wright and Badcock, *Disruption to Diversity*, 102–4.
[35] Torrance explained his reservations in 'Minister's Letter on Call to the Chair of Church History, New College, Edinburgh (John 21.18–19)', *Beechgrove Church* (April 1950), 1–3. For the congregational tribute to Torrance, see p. 3.

Beechgrove, and later confirmed at the General Assembly of the Church of Scotland.

It was not (at least, from Torrance's perspective) an ideal appointment. But it brought Torrance to a chair at New College. A door had finally opened, apparently allowing Torrance to enter into the sphere of ministry to which he believed that he had been called.

CHAPTER 5

Professor at Edinburgh, 1950–79

TORRANCE returned to his *alma mater* in the late spring of 1950. The Torrance family soon settled down at 21 South Oswald Road, a large house which suited the family well as the children grew up. Torrance's initial teaching responsibilities were in the general area of church history, focusing particularly on the Reformation in Germany and Switzerland. His lectures dealt mainly with the theology of John Calvin, John Knox and the Scots reformers, although he also held a seminar on the life and thought of the early church, using Henry Melvill Gwatkins' textbook. Torrance's engagement with the leading Scottish religious writers of the past strengthened his sense of belonging to, and working within, a distinctly Scottish theological tradition.

It is probably fair to say that Torrance's lectures during his brief period as Professor of Church History tended to deal with 'historical theology', rather than 'ecclesiastical history' in the stricter sense of that term. This observation is of some importance; as we have seen, Torrance saw himself primarily as a theologian, rather than as a historian. The Chair of Church History was thus not the position which Torrance really wanted, although it might serve as a point from which some other more suitable position might arise. But what? And when?

From Church History to Dogmatics

Torrance's opportunity arose in 1952, when G. T. Thomson (who had not been in good health) announced his retirement from the Chair of

New College, Edinburgh.

Christian Dogmatics. Thomson had succeeded H. R. Mackintosh in this Chair, and it was clear to Torrance that the pending vacancy would suit his own interests and concerns ideally. He had already followed in Mackintosh's steps once, by being called to Beechgrove Church; why not follow him a second time, into the Chair of Christian Dogmatics at New College? Torrance asked to be considered for the vacant chair. He was quite clear that dogmatics was both his strength and his passion. The move thus seemed to him both natural and appropriate.

Yet there was something of a problem here, in the person of John Baillie, who can be argued to have dominated and determined Edinburgh divinity since his arrival at New College in 1934. As one perceptive study of the development of New College, Edinburgh, comments: 'New College theology in the 1940s was to be almost synonymous with the name of John Baillie.'[1] In effect, Baillie now had such a reputation within the

[1] George Newlands, 'Divinity and Dogmatics', in Wright and Badcock, *Disruption to Diversity*, 117–34, 125.

scholarly world at large, and within New College in particular, that it could be said that he defined the theological position for which New College, and Edinburgh divinity in general, stood. Torrance happened to represent a rather different theological stance, for which neither John Baillie nor his brother Donald had much sympathy. Torrance would be 39 in 1952, with more than a quarter of a century lying ahead before he would reach the compulsory age of retirement. A radical reorientation of Edinburgh divinity was a serious possibility if Torrance were to be allowed to have the Chair of Christian Dogmatics.

Baillie himself was due to retire in 1956, and would thus not be in any position to resist such change if Torrance were to be called to the Chair. The department of church history was clearly seen by Baillie as a safe repository for potential theological agitators, where their opportunities to influence the theological development of students was minimal. Resistance by Baillie to this move was thus inevitable. A further consideration was that Baillie believed that Torrance was particularly good, both as a teacher and researcher, on the history of doctrine, and thus wished him to remain in a position which seemed to suit him and the faculty well. In Baillie's view, Torrance was perfectly suited to his present position, and should stay there if he were to remain at Edinburgh.

It would not be the first time that Baillie had successfully headed off a Barthian challenge. One such challenge had arisen earlier, in the person of George S. Hendry. We may consider this point further, as it casts some light on Baillie's attempt to block Torrance's sideways move from church history to dogmatics. In a perceptive essay on the reaction to Barth in Scotland, Alec C. Cheyne suggests that Scottish theologians could be divided into four broad camps in terms of their reaction to Barth:

> The first, those who were only superficially influenced, and in consequence continued the liberal tradition without much change; the second, whose entire outlook was affected, but in the end withheld their whole-hearted approval; the third, those who may be described as real if cautious admirers; the fourth, those in whom we can discern the unqualified zeal of out-and-out converts.[2]

Cheyne (rightly, in my view) assigned David Cairns of Aberdeen to the first group; both John and Donald Baillie to the second; H. R. Mackintosh to the third; and George S. Hendry to the fourth. It was fairly clear to all that John Baillie disliked Hendry, not least on account of what he regarded as his uncritical Barthianism. This can be seen in his review of Hendry's

[2] Alec C. Cheyne, 'The Baillie Brothers', in Fergusson, *Christ, Church and Society*, 3–37, 33.

1935 Hastie Lectures at Glasgow, published in 1937 as *God the Creator*.[3] This book was regarded as 'rather Barthian' in its approach. Hendry was a theologian-minister at the Bridge of Allan, and it seemed to many that he should be called to a chair in systematic theology.

Such a possibility opened up in 1947, when the Free Church Chair of Systematic Theology at Glasgow University became vacant. Baillie was able to use his influence to ensure that such an appointment was effectively blocked. In an interesting turn of events, President John Mackay of Princeton Theological Seminary (an old school friend of John and Donald Baillie in Inverness) invited Hendry to take up the Charles Hodge Chair of Theology a few years later. There can be no doubt that there was a perception that a theologian who was unfortunate enough to be stereotyped as 'Barthian' by the Baillies would have some difficulty in finding academic employment. Torrance himself recalls one private discussion with a Scottish theologian, who had studied at Basel, who had come to the conclusion that his prospects for employment were seriously limited – unless he were to alter publicly his theological commitments in a more liberal direction.

At the time at which Torrance requested transfer from church history to dogmatics, Baillie was both Principal of New College and Dean of the Faculty of Divinity. He was therefore in a powerful position to determine the choice of Thomson's successor. The transfer, however, went through, despite Baillie's opposition.[4] Baillie appears to have been a little rankled by this development, and declined to allow Torrance an inaugural lecture to mark the occasion. Torrance has always suspected this reflected Baillie's dislike of his inaugural lecture in the Chair of Church History, which pointedly adopted an approach to the notion of 'progress' which contrasted sharply with that set out in Baillie's *The Belief in Progress* (1950).[5] The outcome of this transfer would prove decisive in terms of Edinburgh's theological profile worldwide. If Baillie determined that profile in the 1940s, Torrance would determine it throughout the 1960s and 1970s.

From 1952 to 1956, Torrance and Baillie taught alongside each other. Baillie lectured on what might be termed 'divinity' in the general sense of

---

[3] Baillie's review may be seen in *British Weekly* (25 March 1937), 287.

[4] An administrative loose end which required tidying up concerned the future of the 'church' chair in ecclesiastical history; in effect, this position was 'frozen', and the gap thus created filled by a succession of lecturers, beginning with James S. McEwan (Torrance's travelling companion in the Holy Land: see p. 41).

[5] John Baillie, *The Belief in Progress*. London: Oxford University Press, 1950. It is instructive to compare the ideas in this volume with Torrance, 'History and Reformation', *Scottish Journal of Theology* 4 (1951), 279–91.

the term, which would be referred to as 'philosophical theology' in other contexts. Torrance lectured on 'Christian dogmatics', which could be taken to cover the general field of systematic theology. Torrance taught students for the final two years of the three-year Bachelor of Divinity degree.[6] He delivered a major lecture course on 'Christology and Soteriology' to second year students; in the third year, he lectured on 'Church, Ministry and Sacraments'.[7]

Inevitably, there was some tension between Torrance and Baillie over the teaching programme. For example, lectures on the doctrine of God – including the doctrine of the Trinity – were deemed to fall within the more general topic of 'divinity', and thus assigned to Baillie in the first year. Being denied the possibility of lecturing at Edinburgh on the doctrine of God, and especially the doctrine of the Trinity, was a severe disappointment to Torrance. It is important to note that Torrance wrote little on the doctrine of God (especially the doctrine of the Trinity) during his time as Professor of Christian Dogmatics; his major works in this field tend to date from after his retirement. Torrance's generally evangelical course of lectures on Christology and soteriology were countered by Baillie, who taught on his brother Donald's book *God Was in Christ*. For those who chose to specialize in Christian dogmatics, Torrance also offered a final year seminar on seminal patristic texts, such as Athanasius' *Letters to Serapion*, Books 2 and 3 of his *contra Arianos*, and Hilary of Poitiers' *de Trinitate*. At this stage, the texts in question were all studied in the original languages.

Baillie and Torrance also lectured to postgraduate students who were undertaking theological research. Here, Torrance was more or less completely at liberty to teach what he liked; this allowed him to offer lecture courses on themes close to his own heart – for example, 'the theology of Karl Barth' and 'theology and science'.

Torrance had already delivered a major course of lectures on virtually every aspect of Christian theology at Auburn Theological Seminary during the academic year 1938–9. These lectures had been painstakingly typed out in full, and represent a remarkably comprehensive and well thought through approach to their subject. Torrance's teaching at Auburn included

---

[6] Until the 1960s, the Edinburgh Bachelor of Divinity degree was a three-year degree open only to graduates. The creation of what came to be known as the 'first B.D.' (meaning an undergraduate degree which could be entered directly from school), taken over four years, would change the structure of the teaching programme significantly.

[7] In our analysis, we shall use the typescript of the final rescension of both courses of lectures, dating from the 1970s. It seems that Torrance intended to publish the 'Christology and Soteriology' lectures at some point.

a substantial course of lectures on Christology and Soteriology, extending to more than 350 pages of typescript. His later Edinburgh lectures are clearly based upon the Auburn Lectures, in terms of the structure of the lecture course, the material which is deployed, and the general approach taken. To illustrate this, we may compare the structure of the lecture courses, and some representative passages in the Auburn and Edinburgh lectures.

The structure of the Auburn Lecture course entitled 'The Doctrine of Christ' can be set out as follows. Seventeen individual lectures were delivered, roughly one-third of which deal with soteriology in the strict sense of the term.

1. Introduction
2. The Encounter with Christ
3. The Gospel Testimony to Christ
4. The Apostolic Testimony to Christ
5. The Significance of Christ for Faith
6. The Incarnation
7. The Pre-Existence of Christ
8. The Humiliation of Christ
9. The Significance of the Humanity of Christ
10. The Significance of the Divinity of Christ
11. The Person and Work of Christ
12. The Background of the Cross
13. The Mediation of Christ
14. The Atonement on the Cross
15. Forgiveness and Reconciliation
16. The Resurrection of Christ
17. The Ascension and Second Advent of Christ

The Edinburgh lectures consisted of twenty-four lectures, with the material being arranged in substantially the same manner. Although there are some minor alterations (for example, the final Edinburgh lecture is simply entitled 'Eschatology'), there can be no doubt of the fundamental continuity between the two series of lectures.

This continuity can also been seen in terms of the contents of the lectures. To illustrate this point, we may consider Torrance's discussion of the biblical witness to Jesus Christ in the two lecture series.

Auburn[8]

If we are to approach Christ in the right light we have to approach Him in His own light and in the categories that His person creates for Himself. His person is His own self-authentication; He never appealed to external authority, and refused to be brought under the judgment of men, though of course He was ever willing to be confessed by men. He even went so far as to assert that judgment concerning His person was a supernatural act; for nobody knew the Son except the Father, and only those who shared the Holy Spirit might partake of the same knowledge or revelation. Thus to return to the words of Melanchthon: 'Hoc est Christum cognoscere, beneficia ejus cognoscere.' We must assert that they cannot be construed in any rational way as the theologians of Ritschlian Luthertum tried. The theologians of later Lutheranism reversed the dictum of the Reformer. Whereas they made central the judgment of man on Christ, for Melanchthon what was central and important was the fact that Christ spoke to us, not what we thought of Him. In the theology of the Reformation the whole emphasis was on the glory of God. It is not because Christ brings us beneficia that He is the Son but because He reveals God to us do we know ourselves as sheltered and healed in him.

Edinburgh[9]

If we are to approach Christ truly, we must approach Him in His own light and in the understanding which His own person creates for Himself. His person is His own self-authentication. He never appeals to external authority, and refuses to be brought under the judgment of men. Judgment concerning Him, said Jesus, was a supernatural act. Nobody but the Father knows the Son, and those to whom it is revealed by the Father. Only those who share the Holy Spirit with which the Father has anointed the Son can share in knowledge of Christ. But to return to the words of Melanchthon: 'This is to know Christ, to know His benefits' – he meant the words not as Ritschl and others interpreted them, for whereas what they made central was the fact that Christ acts upon us, and so reveals Himself to us. The primary emphasis is on the glory of God. It is not because Christ brings us benefits that He is the Son of God, but because He reveals God to us in Himself we know ourselves to be sheltered and healed in Him.

It will be clear that there is an organic relation of continuity with development between these lectures, with the fundamental themes of the Auburn Lectures being taken up and redeveloped in the Edinburgh lectures. The nature of the development can be summarized in the following terms:

[8] Torrance, 'The Doctrine of Christ', unpublished Auburn Lectures, 27–8.
[9] Torrance, 'The Doctrine of Christ', unpublished Edinburgh lectures, Lecture 3, 'The Biblical Witness to Jesus Christ', 2.

1. A general tightening up of style, in which points are made more crisply and precisely than previously.

2. A general updating of material to include the many developments subsequent to Auburn, including the appearance of later works of Karl Barth, and new theological luminaries, including Wolfhart Pannenberg and Jürgen Moltmann.

These developments are all typical of a classic major lecture series, delivered and refined over the years. On the one hand, Torrance's fundamental approach remains more or less the same; on the other, the material which he feels obliged to deal with shifts in line with wider developments. For example, Ritschl plays a much more significant role in the Auburn Lectures than in those subsequently delivered at Edinburgh, partly on account of the diminishing relevance of Ritschl and Ritschlianism after the Second World War.

In the case of the lectures on 'Church, Ministry and Sacraments', we encounter a completely new set of material. Torrance had not dealt with these subjects at length at Auburn, although there were points at which he touched upon them – for example, in a very general eight-page discussion of the nature and purpose of the sacraments.[10] Torrance's eighteen lectures[11] on this theme reflect many of the denominational distinctives of the Church of Scotland, in that this lecture course was of particular relevance to those preparing for ministry in that church. For example, the twelfth lecture in the series was entitled 'Lawful Ministry and Ordination in the Church of Scotland'. It is important to note that Torrance's lecturing in this field coincided with his activity in ecumenical discussions, in which the nature and proper place of the church, ministry and sacraments were at the top of the agenda. We may consider this further in what follows.

Ecumenical engagement: a Reformed perspective

The 1950s and 1960s represented the high-water mark of the ecumenical movement. This movement, which aimed to bring about the recovery of unity between the Christian churches, is usually considered to have begun in Edinburgh, in that it emerged from the Edinburgh Missionary

---

[10] Torrance, 'The Doctrine of the Holy Spirit: The Sacraments', unpublished typescript.

[11] Torrance later added a nineteenth lecture, dealing with the Christian doctrine of marriage, which is basically the expanded version of a sermon preached at the Kirk of the Greyfriars on 26 May 1963, and which was revised and enlarged on 11 November 1963.

Conference, held at New College in 1910.[12] This conference was attended by some 1,200 delegates, representing 160 mission agencies, and led to the formation of the International Missionary Council. This conference had already played a significant role in the Torrance family history (see p. 10): Torrance's father had attended the conference (although not as an official representative) after serious difficulties had arisen over his position in Chengdu with the China Inland Mission, and as a result of discussions at the conference, he returned to the city as a representative of the American Bible Society. It was subsequent to his return to Chengdu that he met and married Annie Elizabeth Sharpe. At the human level, Torrance could be said to owe his existence to this conference.

The ecumenical movement really gained momentum after the Second World War, with the formation of the World Council of Churches on 23 August 1948.[13] The new enthusiasm for unity between the churches led to a remarkable number of 'bilateral dialogues' between churches, including conversations between representatives of the Church of Scotland and the Church of England, held over the period 1949–51. The results of these conversations were held to be sufficiently encouraging to warrant more extended discussions between the churches. Torrance was appointed as a representative of the Church of Scotland.[14] The group met three times in Edinburgh, once at Durham, and twice at Lambeth Palace.

Yet it is arguable that Torrance's main contribution to ecumenical dialogue lay not so much in his personal participation in the bilateral conversations of the time, but in his rigorous exploration of the fundamental theological principles which he considered to be the necessary basis of such dialogue. For example, Torrance responded extensively to the two volumes of preparatory studies for the World Council of Churches meeting at Amsterdam in 1948.[15] The Third World Conference on Faith and Order, which met at Lund in August 1952, raised important issues concerning the theology of the church, which Torrance addressed in a

[12] For the history of the movement, see Ruth Rouse and Stephen Neill (eds), *A History of the Ecumenical Movement 1517–1948*. London: SPCK, 1954.

[13] For the standard account of its origins and influence, see G. K. A. Bell, *The Kingship of Christ: The Story of the World Council of Churches*. Harmondsworth: Penguin, 1954; M. E. Brinkman, *Progress in Unity? Fifty Years of Theology within the World Council of Churches*. Grand Rapids, MI: Eerdmans, 1995. For a somewhat more scurrilous view of the events, see Stephen Neill, *God's Apprentice*. London: Hodder & Stoughton, 1991, 205–39.

[14] For the final outcome, see *Relations between Anglican and Presbyterian Churches: A Joint Report*. London: SPCK, 1957. See also J. K. S. Reid, *Presbyterians and Unity*. London: Mowbrays, 1962, 69–85.

[15] 'Concerning Amsterdam. I. The Nature and Mission of the Church: A discussion of volumes I and II of the Preparatory Studies', *Scottish Journal of Theology* 2 (1949), 241–70.

Torrance pictured with members of the Conference on Anglican–Presbyterian Relations in 1956. From left to right: Rt Revd Eric Graham, Bishop of Brechin; Professor William Tindal, New College, Edinburgh; Principal John H. S. Burleigh, New College, Edinburgh; Revd F. J. Taylor, Principal, Wycliffe Hall, Oxford; Principal R. D. Whitehorn, Westminster College, Cambridge; Professor John Baillie, New College, Edinburgh; Rt Revd W. D. L. Greer, Bishop of Manchester; Rt Revd R. R. Williams, Bishop of Leicester; Professor William Manson, New College, Edinburgh; Professor S. L. Greenslade, University of Durham; Rt Revd A. E. J. Rawlinson, Bishop of Derby; Professor Thomas F. Torrance, New College, Edinburgh.

series of works around this time.[16] In particular, his 1955 study *Royal Priesthood* addressed many of the issues which surfaced as of significance at this period, and developed the key idea of 'bishop in Presbytery' as a

[16] Most notably, 'Where Do We Go from Lund?', *Scottish Journal of Theology* 6 (1953), 53–64; 'The Atonement and the Oneness of the Church', *Scottish Journal of Theology* 7 (1954), 245–69. Torrance's major writings on ecumenical issues in the 1950s were gathered together in *Conflict and Agreement in the Church*. I: *Order and Disorder*. London: Lutterworth Press, 1959; *Conflict and Agreement in the Church*. II: *The Ministry and the Sacraments of the Gospel*. London: Lutterworth Press, 1960. Torrance (along with Georges Florovsky, Anders Nygren and Edmund Schlink) was instrumental in persuading Lund to establish a commission on Christ and the Church.

means of resolving certain difficulties in the dialogue between Reformed and episcopal churches (particularly the Church of England).[17]

One of the most important issues raised by Torrance at this point was the need to recover the eschatological orientation of the doctrine of the church.[18] It was clear to Torrance that the Reformation witnessed both a recovery of the relevance of eschatology, as well as a degree of divergence over how that eschatology was to be understood.

> Broadly speaking, their divergence may be characterised by saying that while Lutheran eschatology was mainly an eschatology of judgement, going back to early Latin Fathers like Cyprian with their emphasis on the decay and collapse of the world, Reformed eschatology was mainly an eschatology of resurrection, going back to the early Greek Fathers with their emphasis upon the renewal of the world through the incarnation of Christ.[19]

For Torrance, this eschatological element of faith is a significant element of Calvin's understanding of the nature of the church, and gives the reformer's views on this theme their distinctive colouring:

> For Calvin, predestination is the *prius*, eschatology the *posterius*, of the Christian faith, and between the two the whole life of the church on earth is to be understood ... This means, however, that the whole life of faith and union with Christ is exercised in eschatological tension (*suspensio*) between the *prius* manifested in the calling of God, and the *posterius* of final revelation and redemption, and in a wondrous anticipation or foretaste of the glorious consummation. In other words, the eschatological relation involved in Christian faith is at once the relation between the heavenly and the earthly here and now, and the relation between the present and future.[20]

Torrance believed that this eschatological element of the Reformation doctrine of the church required to be injected into contemporary ecumenical discussions. This is probably best seen from the major 1949 article, engaging with the preparatory volumes published for the Amsterdam meeting of the World Council of Churches in 1948.[21] For

---

[17] For the background, see *Conflict and Agreement in the Church*, I, 82–5.

[18] Of the many works of relevance to this point, see particularly his *Kingdom and Church: A Study in the Theology of the Reformation*. Edinburgh: Oliver & Boyd, 1956.

[19] *Kingdom and Church*, 5. Note particularly the link that Torrance perceives between Reformed theology and the general Greek patristic testimony; this theme would be developed more thoroughly later, particularly in his tracing a direct line of development and continuity from Athanasius through Calvin to Barth.

[20] *Kingdom and Church*, 108–9.

[21] 'Concerning Amsterdam. I'. All references are from this article. The four volumes were published under the general title *Man's Disorder and God's Design* by SCM Press in 1948. The individual titles were: 1: *The Universal Church in God's Design*; 2: *The Church's Witness to God's*

Torrance, the unity of the church was to be understood as 'an eschatological reality that both interpenetrates history and transcends it, as a given unity even in the midst of disorder and as a promised unity beyond it'.

This insight established a perspective which allowed the debate over what constituted the *esse* and *bene esse* of the church to be seen in its proper perspective. These debates tended to centre on the question of what historic forms of ministry were essential to the identity of the church; Torrance insisted that the validity of the church's ministry could not be determined with reference to specific historical forms which have emerged within the church's history.

> If the given unity of the church is essentially eschatological, then the validity of all that she does is conditioned by the Parousia and cannot be made to repose upon any primitive structure of unity already complete in the naturally historical realm.

Torrance thus points out that it is 'understandable that when the early church was faced with the dangers of Gnosticism it should appeal to an actual succession of bishops to attest the historicity of its claims'. Yet this does not mean that this chronological precedent can be transmuted into a theological principle. Furthermore, the same objective might today be more effectively achieved in another manner – for example, by historical criticism.[22]

Furthermore, the eschatological perspective on matters, urged so strongly by Torrance, renders questionable any attempt to identify a specific *historical* feature of the church as being essential to the identity of the church:

> Whenever we speak of any structure or form as belonging to the *esse* of the church, must we not go on to add that this very structure and this very form will therefore be preserved when heaven and earth pass away and the new heaven and the new earth will be revealed? If we have no authority for holding that such a structure or form belongs to the church as the final eschatological reality, have we any right to say it belongs to the *esse* of the church? . . . Certainly the book of Revelation mentions a heavenly presbytery ('four and twenty

---

Design; 3: *The Church and the Disorder of Society*; 4: *The Church and the International Disorder*. Torrance's analysis focused on the first two volumes only. Note here also Torrance's important 1952 essay 'Eschatology and Eucharist', in D. M. Baillie and J. Marsh (eds), *Intercommunion*. London: SCM Press, 1952, 303–50.
    [22] 'Concerning Amsterdam. I', 243–4.

elders') whereas it mentions no heavenly episcopate! . . . Of course it is difficult
indeed to draw dogmatic concepts out of the Apocalypse, and perhaps not
justifiable, but it seems clear nevertheless that the more we think the biblical
eschatology into the doctrine of the church, the more our differences will tend
to disappear, though doubtless not without great heart-searching in our several
traditions.[23]

Developing this point further, Torrance argued that any understanding of
the church which failed to recognize the eschatological element in its
identity was vulnerable to corruption and distortion through an improper
immersion in the world – an immersion which could compromise its
God-given mission:

> The church will be unable to carry out this divine mission and function in the
> world unless she recovers more and more the eschatological character of her
> true being. The great shame and disorder of the church is that she has
> collaborated with the disorder of the world and clothed herself with so many
> of its forms and fashions that so often she is too committed to the world and
> too compromised with it to be able to deliver the revolutionary Word of the
> Gospel with conviction and power . . . The church must be prepared as part of
> her dying and rising with Christ to mortify the deeds of the body, to lay her
> worldly form upon the altar of the Cross and in the shedding of old ways and
> habits, in the refashioning of her order, to release the Gospel effectively to the
> world of today.[24]

It will thus be clear that Torrance was mounting a critique of those who
argued that the *esse* of the church was to be defined with reference to
traditional forms of ministry. What to some (especially, in Torrance's view,
Anglo-Catholics within the Church of England) were divinely ordained
practices and traditions might need to be seen as 'old ways and habits'
which needed to be set aside – partly because they would have no place in
the New Jerusalem, and partly because they served no discernible function,
in that what they once achieved could now be achieved more effectively
in other manners.

While Torrance addressed a number of major issues in his writings
around this time, it is clear that most of his attention focused on the areas
of the church, ministry and sacraments. For example, Torrance was
Convener of the Church of Scotland Commission on Baptism (1954–62),
and was responsible for the publication of five interim reports (1955–9)

---

[23] 'Concerning Amsterdam. I', 251. Torrance clearly finds this idea in Calvin, who regarded 'all
orders of the church in terms of eschatological suspension'. See the important discussion in *Kingdom
and Church*, 134–9.
[24] 'Concerning Amsterdam. I', 268–9.

and the Final Report (1960).[25] Although Torrance subsequently gained a reputation in relation to the concept of revelation, the doctrine of God, and the relation of Christian theology and the natural sciences, his initial work at Edinburgh centred on what might be termed 'church-related issues'. In part, this can be seen as reflecting the particular Chair which he held at Edinburgh: the Chair of Church History seemed a particularly appropriate platform from which to engage with the major issues confronting the ecumenical movement. Were not many of the issues which divided the churches to be traced back to the Reformation? And was not Torrance to be seen as a specialist in the theology of that movement? There is no doubt that Torrance was initially seen as a reliable and informed representative of the Reformed tradition, steeped in a knowledge of its history and theology, with a deep personal sense of commitment to Reformed church life. While Torrance's later works, especially in the field of science and theology, would broaden his reputation, Torrance never ceased to be seen as a major representative of the Reformed tradition, concerned for both academy and church. It was perhaps inevitable that he would be invited to become the Moderator of the General Assembly of the Church of Scotland for the year 1976–7, towards the end of his tenure of the Chair of Christian Dogmatics.

The Moderator of the General Assembly of the Church of Scotland holds office for a period of one year, which places considerable restrictions upon the long-term influence which may be exerted through the position. For many, this consideration was of the utmost importance: the last thing that the Kirk needed was someone possessed of strong views, stridently held and proclaimed, who would be in office long enough to put some of them into effect. The one-year period of office is often viewed as an attempt to limit the ability of any one individual over the Kirk in general, and its General Assembly in particular.

Aware of the limits which attended his position, Torrance nevertheless made it clear that he intended to attempt to use his influence on the Kirk in several areas in which he believed it to need redirection. In the first place, he believed that a note of serious theological reflection needed to be injected into the life and thought of the church. Good pastoral care and preaching were not, in Torrance's view, opposed to each other; rightly understood, theology was a means for the enabling and informing of pastoral ministry. Linked with this, Torrance believed that there was a

---

[25] The Secretary of the Baptism Commission was John Heron, who was also one of the founding directors of *Scottish Journal of Theology*. His son Alasdair later became a lecturer at New College under Torrance, before becoming Professor of Reformed Theology at the University of Erlangen, and for many years was a co-editor of *Scottish Journal of Theology*.

The General Assembly of the Church of Scotland in session in the presence of Queen Elizabeth II and the Duke of Edinburgh, 1977. Torrance is seated on the elevated chair, directly below the royal party.

need to ensure that firm links were forged between theology and aspects of modern life and thought, including economics and the natural sciences.

A second particular area of concern related to the situation in South Africa. The Reformed Church in South Africa had come to be associated with the development and maintenance of apartheid, a radical programme of racial separation which had evoked outrage. Torrance was vigorously opposed to apartheid, which he regarded as having Nazi roots. It was therefore a matter of some considerable importance to him to do what he could to interact with the situation.

During the 1950s, Torrance's ecumenical activities were focused on conversations between the Church of Scotland and the Church of England (1950–8), and various aspects of the work of the World Council of Churches. Torrance was present at the Faith and Order Conference at Lund in August 1952, and served on the Faith and Order Commission from 1952 to 1962. He was also present at the World Council of Churches meeting at Evanston, Illinois, in 1954. In 1974, he served on the Reformed–Roman Catholic Study Commission on the Eucharist, which met at Woudshoten, in the Netherlands. Yet it is arguable that the most important ecumenical activity in which Torrance engaged began after his retirement from the chair of Christian Dogmatics at Edinburgh in 1979.

In 1977, Torrance visited the Ecumenical Patriarch and other leaders of the Greek Orthodox Church on behalf of the World Alliance of Reformed Churches, with the proposal that their churches should enter into serious dialogue with a view to achieving some degree of theological consensus on the doctrine of the Trinity.[26] This led to a series of meetings at Istanbul and Geneva between 1979 and 1983, which achieved sufficient progress to warrant the involvement of all fourteen Orthodox churches. An expanded discussion group met at Geneva, Leuenberg and Minsk over the period 1986–90, and was eventually able to issue an 'Agreed Statement on the Holy Trinity' at Geneva on 13 March 1991. This document is of considerable interest and importance, and can be seen as resonating with Torrance's growing engagement with issues of Trinitarian theology subsequent to his retirement. His writings in this field are of such importance that they will be considered in detail later (see pp. 159–74).

Barth's successor at Basel?

Karl Barth had indicated on several occasions that he would have liked Torrance to be his successor in the chair of dogmatics at Basel. For Barth, Torrance was 'an extraordinarily gifted young theologian', with a great future ahead of him.[27] Nevertheless, this was merely Barth's personal preference, and was not necessarily binding on the Faculty of Theology. Yet as the date of Barth's retirement loomed larger, the need to find a worthy successor to him became increasingly pressing. On 30 January 1961, Oscar Cullmann, who would become Rektor of the University of Basel, wrote to Torrance, asking him to allow his name to go forward for the chair which would become vacant through Barth's retirement at the end of the summer term.[28] The tone of the letter was warm and inviting,

---

[26] For an early recognition, from the Orthodox side, of the potential ecumenical importance of Torrance's Moderatorship, see George D. Dragas, 'The Significance for the Church of Prof. T. F. Torrance's Election as Moderator of the General Assembly of the Church of Scotland', *Ekklesiastikos Pharos* 58 (1976), 214–26. In 1973 Torrance was consecrated as a Protopresbyter within the Patriarchate of Alexandria by the Archbishop of Axum, on the occasion of his being invited to Addis Ababa to commemorate the death of Athanasius the Great in 373, and to celebrate the conclusion of an agreement between Chalcedonian and non-Chalcedonian Christians, which Torrance had initiated in 1954.

[27] See the commendatory letter of Barth, dated 11 April 1947.

[28] Cullmann to Torrance, 30 January 1961. The letter set out the teaching obligations and financial package which were associated with the chair, and noted that Torrance's familiarity with Basel would greatly assist him in settling in.

stressing the positive advantages of the move to Torrance. Cullmann, however, needed a swift reply.

Initially, the offer seemed very attractive. It would, in Torrance's view, have been a wonderful privilege to succeed Barth. Both he and his wife knew and liked Switzerland. In addition, Torrance's wife had some Swiss-German Moravian relatives in the region, and was generally enthusiastic about the possibility. Yet the job would have been demanding, in that it involved giving four hours of lectures a week in German. Although Torrance had lectured and preached in German before, the thought of having to sustain such a heavy teaching load in a foreign language was not particularly attractive. Torrance's initial reaction was to suggest to Cullmann that, at the very least, he would require the services of a full-time secretary to cope with the writing of these lectures.

On further reflection, it became clear to Torrance that the move would not be appropriate. His children were, at that stage, going through school, and none of them spoke German. As they would have been obliged to enrol at German-language schools in Basel, Torrance felt that their education would have been seriously impaired by their move. The cumulative weight of the difficulties seemed to point inescapably towards a negative response to the proposal from Basel. With some sadness, he declined. Basel subsequently went on to appoint Heinrich Ott as Barth's successor, in a move rumoured to have been influenced perhaps more by pressure from the Cantonal Government than by Ott's theological capacities.

It is difficult, and arguably not of great importance, to ascertain how Torrance's career might have developed had he accepted the invitation. New avenues of research and teaching might well have opened up to him. However, it can be said with some confidence that two aspects of his theological work which he himself regarded as of considerable significance would have been adversely affected. First, Torrance's work has always been linked with his activities as a leading representative of the Church of Scotland. Although the move to Basel would have allowed Torrance to maintain his links with Reformed theology and church life in general, he would not have had the close involvement with the Church of Scotland, culminating in his work as its Moderator. More significantly, there are excellent reasons for suggesting that Torrance's interest in the natural sciences, which began to develop properly in the late 1960s, might not have developed at all, let alone to the same extent, had he moved to Basel.

Torrance regarded his decision not to accept the Basel offer as one of the two most difficult decisions he had ever had to make.[29] He believed

---

[29] The other difficult decision was to reject the 1939 offer from Princeton University: see p. 58.

that his decision to remain at Edinburgh, though difficult, was correct. He did not give serious consideration to any other possibilities during his time as Professor of Christian Dogmatics. Nevertheless, a moment came when he was asked to consider a significant modification of his role at New College. In 1968, the position of Principal and Dean of New College became vacant, and Torrance was requested to consider filling this position. Under new regulations which were introduced in that year, the office of Principal was only to be held for four years. Nevertheless, Torrance felt that he was quite unsuited for this position. He was a scholar and teacher, not an administrator. Torrance recalled John Baillie, a former Principal, once being asked how many committees he served on. '87!' was his immediate reply. Torrance, who cordially disliked committee work, felt that this was an honour he could well do without. Despite being asked to reconsider his decision, Torrance remained firm. New College would have to find another Principal.

A new Principal was duly found. John McIntyre, who had been appointed to the Chair of Divinity in October 1956 in succession to John Baillie,[30] became Principal and Dean of New College in 1968, and served in those capacities until 1974. Under McIntyre, New College moved decisively towards a commitment to Religious Studies and away from the more traditional concentration of Christian dogmatics. It was decided not to incorporate 'religious studies' elements into the Bachelor of Divinity programme, and to avoid the option of adding a 'Religious Studies' department alongside those already represented within New College – such as New Testament, Old Testament and Christian Dogmatics.[31] The Bachelor of Divinity would continue to be a degree primarily aimed at those intending to be ordained in the Church of Scotland (although being open to those who did not); a new degree in religious studies would be offered alongside this. McIntyre appointed Elizabeth Maclaren to coordinate the new teaching programme, which was first offered in the academic year 1971–2. Although this development lay more than a decade in the future, it was perhaps inevitable that the department of Christian dogmatics would end up becoming a department of theology and religious studies.

Torrance was troubled by these developments, and felt that the specific appointments being made and general direction being taken under McIntyre were to the impoverishment of New College and its wider reputation. By 1970, Torrance had established Edinburgh as one of the

---

[30] The two other candidates considered for the position were David Cairns and J. K. S. Reid.

[31] For a full analysis, see Frank Whaling, 'Religious Studies', in Wright and Badcock, *Disruption to Diversity*, 151–65.

Torrance accepting the Templeton Prize at the Guild Hall, London, 1978. Also included in the photograph are James I. McCord (President, Princeton Theological Seminary) and Sir John M. Templeton.

most significant centres in the world for the study of Christian theology; that reputation could not help but be called into question by the shifts into religious studies promoted by McIntyre.

There were those who wondered whether there was some form of personal agenda involved. Such suspicions deepened in 1979, the year of Torrance's retirement. McIntyre had been appointed Acting Principal of Edinburgh University at this point, and was thus in a position of considerable influence when it came to making senior appointments within the University. James Mackey, a radical Roman Catholic with fairly tenuous links to that church, was appointed as Torrance's successor in the newly designated Thomas Chalmers Chair of Theology.[32] The contrast between the styles of theology associated with Torrance and Mackey could not have been greater.

Yet this account of Torrance's career cannot be allowed to be seen to end on such an ambivalent, perhaps even negative note. In the first place,

---

[32] The appointment caused consternation and an angry debate at the General Assembly of the Church of Scotland that year. For an account of the debate, see *The Scotsman*, 26 May 1979, 1.

Torrance speaking at the Palais des Académies, Brussels, in 1981 at the joint meeting of the Académie Internationale de Philosophie des Sciences and the Académie Internationale des Sciences Religieuses in honour of Stanislas Dockx, OP.

we must note that in 1978, he had been awarded the immensely prestigious Templeton Prize for Progress in Religion, in recognition of his seminal writing in the field of science and Christian theology. This can be seen as a remarkable and highly public recognition of the significance of his academic career. It also allowed Torrance to retire slightly earlier than was strictly necessary, thus allowing him to devote much more time to research and writing than was possible while he held the Chair of Christian Dogmatics at Edinburgh.

A further possibility opened up at this stage. James I. McCord, who served as President of Princeton Theological Seminary over the period 1959–83, suggested to Torrance that he might consider leaving Edinburgh for a position at Princeton. Aware of the pressures under which Torrance had struggled at Edinburgh, McCord promised that there would be few administrative responsibilities associated with the position which he had in mind. However, Torrance felt that it would not have been appropriate to move his family to New Jersey at this stage, and resolved to spend his 'retirement' in Edinburgh.

Torrance's career thus cannot be said to have 'ended' in 1979. In his memoir marking the occasion of Torrance's retirement in 1979, John McIntyre prophetically remarked that 'retirement' would hardly be an appropriate term to designate the 'new found busyness' which enveloped Torrance on the formal ending of his New College responsibilities.[33] As events would prove, Torrance's 'retirement' can only be thought of in terms of a cessation of administrative and teaching duties. The writing, speaking and research continued at a remarkable rate. Torrance's list of published works contains roughly 320 works which originated during his twenty-nine-year period as a professor at Edinburgh. Since retiring from that position in 1979, he has added a further 260 items, including two of his most significant works – *The Trinitarian Faith* (1988) and *The Christian Doctrine of God* (1996).[34]

It will be clear that the time has come to explore the ideas for which Torrance established his reputation as one of the most productive, creative and important theologians of the twentieth century. Having set the scene for those ideas, we must now turn to a detailed and sustained engagement with the leading themes of the theology of Thomas F. Torrance.

---

[33] John McIntyre, 'Thomas Forsyth Torrance', *New College Bulletin* 10 (August 1979), 2.
[34] It may be noted that Torrance counts these two works among the three most important of his writings. The third is, as might be expected, *Theological Science* (1969).

PART TWO

The Contours of a Scientific Theology

Introduction

TO engage with Torrance's theological *oeuvre* is to become aware
of both its internal intellectual coherence and the breadth of its
vision. Torrance, for example, is one of the few major academic
theologians to have engaged with the natural sciences in a distinguished
and sustained manner. Yet that engagement is not undertaken on the
basis of a series of *ad hoc* assumptions, but on the basis of a rigorous and
comprehensive vision of the nature of theology, and its proper place within
the constellation of intellectual disciplines in general. Torrance's understanding of theology allows him to see the person and work of Christ, the
concept of revelation, the doctrine of the Trinity and the scientific
approach to the investigation of the world as facets of one comprehensive
and coherent theological method, rather than as isolated episodes within
an essentially fragmented discipline.

Part of the intrinsic importance of Torrance's theological programme is
that it represents the development and application of what is clearly a
Barthian approach to theology.[1] Torrance spent the academic year 1937–8
studying theology at the University of Basel under the direction of Karl
Barth himself, and expressed an interest in writing a doctoral thesis on
the scientific structure of theology. Barth dissuaded him, believing that
he was too young to undertake such an ambitious project. Yet it may be

---

[1] It is interesting to note that the single sentence to mention Torrance in John Macquarrie's
Twentieth-Century Religious Thought treats him purely as an advocate of Barthianism: John
Macquarrie, *Twentieth-Century Religious Thought*. Revised edition. London: SCM Press, 1971, 390.

argued that Torrance's theological programme represents precisely such an exploration and application of the scientific nature of theology, including the exploration of boundaries and borderlands which Barth himself had tended to disregard.[1] Torrance must therefore be regarded as a figure of considerable importance in relation to the reception and development of the Barthian legacy, particularly in the English-language world. For example, Torrance's careful yet positive attitude to natural theology, rightly understood, represents a major development of Barth's thinking, and is clearly laden with significance for the engagement between theology and the natural sciences.

The second part of this work thus aims to deal with Torrance's theological programme. In the light of the considerable substance of this programme – considered both in terms of its intellectual range and the number of publications in which it is conveyed – it will not be possible to offer more than a survey and preliminary engagement with Torrance's theology. It is intended to offer more substantial and detailed engagement with aspects of that theology in future monographs. Given Torrance's major contribution to the shaping of the Barthian heritage, it is entirely appropriate that we begin by considering the impact of Torrance upon English-language Barth-reception.

---

[1] The most important of those is the relation between Christian theology and the natural sciences: see Harold P. Nebelsick, 'Karl Barth's Understanding of Science', in J. Thompson (ed.), *Theology beyond Christendom: Essays on the Centenary of the Birth of Karl Barth*. Allison Park, PA: Pickwick Publications, 1986, 165–214. Yet it must, of course, be pointed out that Barth addressed some issues on which Torrance has not chosen to focus in depth, such as the foundations and structure of Christian ethics: see, for example, John Webster, *Barth's Ethics of Reconciliation*. Cambridge: Cambridge University Press, 1995; *idem, Barth's Moral Theology: Human Action in Barth's Thought*. Edinburgh: T&T Clark, 1998.

CHAPTER 6

Torrance and British Barth-Reception

KARL BARTH is widely acknowledged to be one of the greatest theological luminaries of all time, establishing a theological landmark which requires to be addressed by both those sympathetic and those inimical to his position. The question of how his ideas came to be appropriated and adapted in the English-speaking world is therefore of considerable importance. 'Reception' is a term used to refer to the manner in which intellectual developments are actively assessed and appropriated by a community of discourse, whether religious or secular.[1] Although the normal associations of the term might suggest that it denotes a passive acceptance, the term properly and technically denotes an active process of evaluation, assimilation and propagation of any intellectual or cultural development, including the theories of the natural sciences. One can thus speak of the 'reception of the Copernican theory' or 'the reception of Darwinism'.[2] Indeed, as I point out elsewhere, there

---

[1] The term can thus be used to refer to the manner in which literary themes, images or writers are appropriated: see, for example, Anthony J. Harding, *The Reception of Myth in English Romanticism*. Columbia, MO: University of Missouri Press, 1995; Alain Montandon, *La réception de Laurence Sterne en Allemagne*. Clermont-Ferrand: Association des publications de la Faculté des Lettres et Sciences Humaines, 1985; James R. Perkin, *A Reception-History of George Eliot's Fiction*. Rochester, NY: University of Rochester Press, 1995.

[2] V. N. Brotóns, 'The Reception of Copernicus in Sixteenth-Century Spain: The Case of Diego de Zúñiga', *Isis* 86 (1985), 52–78; A. Ellegerd, *Darwin and the General Reader: The Reception of Darwin's Theory of Evolution in the British Periodical Press, 1859–1872*. Gothenburg: Acta Universitatis Gothenburgensis, 1958; T. F. Glick, *The Comparative Reception of Darwinism*. Austin, TX: University of Texas Press, 1972. For aspects of the distinction between 'response' and 'reception', see Roger Greenacre, 'Two Aspects of Reception', in G. R. Evans (ed.), *Christian Authority*. Oxford: Oxford University Press, 1988, 40–58.

are significant parallels between the manners in which the scientific and theological communities assess and appropriate ideas.[3]

The manner in which major European theologians are received within the English-speaking world is in itself a matter of considerable interest. Martin Luther and John Calvin are excellent examples of theologians whose ideas were appropriated in manners specific to the English-speaking world – a process which involved not a little adaptation and modification during its course.[4] 'Reception', it must be stressed, may take place on the basis of what some might argue to be an inaccurate or skewed inter- pretation of the theologian in question. It concerns the perceived relevance of a writer for a context. Occasionally, that perception may rest upon an accidental misreading of a text, often due to translation difficulties; on other occasions, it may rest upon a deliberate decision to interpret the theologian in a specific manner.

As Ola Sigurdson points out in his excellent recent study of Swedish Barth-reception since 1947, the debate between Stanley Fish and Wolfgang Iser on the hermeneutics of reception makes it clear that there are many possible and legitimate manners of interpreting texts; it is therefore intensely problematic to suggest that one specific interpretation of Barth is 'right', and others 'wrong'.[5] This point must be appreciated from the outset, as it enables us to avoid the largely sterile debate over whether Torrance 'got Barth right'. Barth interpretation is a developing and contested discipline, in which a 'settled' or 'received' view (for example, von Balthasar's assertion that Barth shifted from being a 'dialectical' to an 'analogical' theologian after his book on Anselm of Canterbury) is subject to challenge and modification.[6] Reception is an ongoing process involving debate within a community, not a once-and-for-all event. The important point which demands to be addressed is the specific nature of Torrance's interpretation of Barth, both in terms of what he said and its potential significance for Christian life and thought, and the manner in which this perception is related to English-language Barth-reception.

It must, however, be pointed out in this connection that Barth himself clearly regarded Torrance as a faithful expositor of his ideas. In 1959, Barth

[3] McGrath, *Foundations of Dialogue in Science and Religion*, 160–4.

[4] For example, see Charles D. Cremeans, *The Reception of Calvinistic Thought in England.* Urbana, IL: University of Illinois Press, 1949.

[5] Ola Sigurdson, *Karl Barth som den andre: En studie i den svenska teologins Barth-reception.* Stockholm: Brutus Östlings Bokförlag Symposion, 1996, 333–4.

[6] See the important revisionist study of Bruce L. McCormack, *Karl Barth's Critically Realistic Dialectical Theology: Its Genesis and Development 1909–1936.* Oxford: Clarendon Press, 1995. For an early response, see the article review of Colin Gunton, in *Scottish Journal of Theology* 49 (1996), 483–98.

presented Torrance with a copy of *Der Gefangenen Befreiung!*, in which he had inscribed the words 'Mit herzlichen Dank für viel Treue!'.[7] The use of the specific term *Treue* ('faithfulness', or perhaps 'trustworthiness') is significant, in that it indicates that Barth felt both that Torrance had properly understood him and was sympathetic towards his general position. The same point is evident in Barth's suggestion that Torrance should be a member of the committee which would complete the *Church Dogmatics* in the event of his premature death, and also in Barth's desire that Torrance should succeed him at Basel on his retirement (see p. 102). While there are those who suggest that Torrance radically misunderstood Barth, it must be pointed out that Barth does not appear to have shared that viewpoint, and that Barth's views on Torrance's portrayal of his ideas must be given their due weight in this matter. But this is to rush ahead of our narrative; we must return to the issue of how Barth came to be received in the English-language world.

We begin by noting that Barth was something of an unknown quantity in the English-language world of the 1920s.[8] Although two general surveys of 'the theology of crisis' appeared in 1925,[9] the first major studies devoted specifically to Barth to be published in English were both due to Scots writers. In 1927, John McConnachie (1875–1948) published an exposition and evaluation of Barth's theology, focusing particularly on Barth's restoration of the category of revelation. McConnachie's account of Barth was generally appreciative, although he was critical of aspects of Barth's theology (such as its apparent failure to work out the proper relation of the historical Jesus and the risen Christ).[10]

A year later, Hugh Ross Mackintosh argued that, despite Barth's predilection for iconoclasm, a positive theological programme could be discerned as emerging from his more recent writings. It is only at the end

---

[7] 'With warm thanks for much faithfulness.' Torrance subsequently returned the compliment, without indicating its source: see T. F. Torrance, *Karl Barth: Biblical and Evangelical Theologian*. Edinburgh: T&T Clark, 1990, xii.

[8] For a general assessment of English-language Barth-reception, see Richard H. Roberts, 'The Reception of the Theology of Karl Barth in the Anglo-Saxon World: History, Typology and Prospect', in S. W. Sykes (ed.), *Karl Barth: Centenary Essays*. Cambridge: Cambridge University Press, 1989, 115–71. This richly documented essay may be regarded as essential reading for our theme.

[9] Adolf Keller, 'The Theology of Crisis', *The Expositor* 3 (March 1925), 164–75; (April 1925), 245–60. It should be pointed out that Keller (1872–1963) was not British; the first major indigenous assessment of Barth's theology is due to McConnachie (see the following note).

[10] J. McConnachie, 'The Teaching of Karl Barth: A New Positive Movement in German Theology', *Hibbert Journal* 25 (1926–7), 385–400. For an assessment, see J. McPake, 'John McConnachie as the Original Advocate of Karl Barth in Scotland: The Primacy of Revelation', *Scottish Bulletin of Evangelical Theology* 14 (1996), 101–14.

of Barth's Romans commentary, Mackintosh commented, that we find any real engagement with the positive Christological dimensions of revelation. Yet, Mackintosh concluded, 'this distribution of accent might yet change, and if it changes, Barth will prove an even greater and more revolutionary Christian force than at this hour'.[11] Mackintosh here put his finger on the central issue which also troubled Barth himself: how to move from a negative programme of criticism of human religious constructions to a positive programme based on God's self-revelation.

That programme is set out in the *Church Dogmatics*, and it can be argued that it was not until the publication of the first half-volume of this major work that it became clear that Barth was indeed to set out the positive programme requested by Mackintosh. McConnachie had read and digested this work by February 1933, and offered a substantial account of its significance in his major work *The Barthian Theology and the Man of Today*.[12] By 1936, Barth's name had become better known, and the theological programme with which he was associated had begun to gain a higher profile.[13] A number of major individual works were translated and published in that year, including *Credo* and *God in Action: Theological Addresses*. Yet the most important event in relation to British Barth-reception was the appearance of the first half-volume of the *Church Dogmatics*, translated by G. T. Thomson. As events would prove, this was not to presage the immediate translation of the entire *Church Dogmatics*. Nevertheless, it was a harbinger of what was to come, and stimulated many to learn theological German in order to drink deeply from this new wellspring of theological stimulation.

The contribution to the Barth Festschrift of that year, edited by Ernst Wolf, included contributions by four British writers: J. McConnachie, Norman W. Porteous, G. L. B. Sloan and Sir E. C. Hoskyns. Of these, the first three mentioned were Scottish, the last English. All the

[11] H. R. Mackintosh, 'Leaders of Theological Thought: Karl Barth', *Expository Times* 39 (1928), 536–40.

[12] J. McConnachie, *The Barthian Theology and the Man of Today*. London: Hodder & Stoughton, 1933. See also his earlier work, *The Significance of Karl Barth*. London: Hodder & Stoughton, 1931.

[13] Works which had appeared by this stage included: J. H. Morrison, 'The Barthian School I: An Appreciation', *Expository Times* 43 (1931), 314–17; N. W. Porteous, 'The Barthian School II: The Theology of Karl Barth', *Expository Times* 43 (1931), 341–6; A. J. MacDonald, 'The Message and Theology of Barth and Brunner', *Theology* 24 (1932), 197–207, 252–8, 324–32; M. Chaning-Pearce, 'The Theology of Crisis', *Hibbert Journal* 32 (1933–4), 101–74, 437–49; R. W. Stewart, 'The Theology of Crisis: A Criticism', *Hibbert Journal* 32 (1933–4), 450–4; H. Jochums, 'Dialectical Theology in the English-Speaking World', *Union Seminary Review* 46 (1935), 313–20 (which, while focusing on North America, also deals with Great Britain); J. McConnachie, 'The Barthian Theology in Great Britain', *Union Seminary Review* 46 (1935), 302–7.

evidence indicates that early interest in and enthusiasm for Barth's theology was particularly associated with Scotland. Among Barth's few English supporters at this time, particular attention should be directed to F. W. Camfield, then a Congregationalist theologian, who subsequently published a major study of Barth in 1933 entitled *Revelation and the Holy Spirit: An Essay in Barthian Theology*.[14] McConnachie's contribution to that volume took the form of a survey of the influence of Barth in Scotland and England.[15] In this essay, McConnachie pointed out one of the factors inhibiting a positive appropriation of Barth in Great Britain was the obstinate fact that few British pastors were in a position to read Barth in the original German.[16] Barth's influence, in McConnachie's view, was most marked in the case of professors of theology, theological students and younger pastors.

As we have seen, Torrance began his studies at New College in 1934, and soon formed the impression that Barth was indeed a theological lodestar for the future. Nevertheless, Torrance viewed Barth as standing in the great tradition of orthodox Christianity, developing and sustaining some of the central themes of Athanasius and Calvin. Barth was never regarded by Torrance as a writer who could be detached from the great tradition of Christian theology, but was rather viewed as a representative of that tradition who both embodied its values and virtues and encouraged renewed and sustained engagement with its themes. Torrance's time at Basel (1936–7) allowed him close access to both the person and ideas of Barth, and generated a positive estimation of both. Yet it is quite improper to suggest that this estimation was uncritical.

Torrance would subsequently become a major figure in relation to English-language Barth-reception. To understand his role in this important process, we need to consider regional factors affecting the reception of Barth's theology, and some of the more fundamental elements of the process of reception itself. We shall begin by considering some of the regional issues which relate to Barth-reception.

---

[14] F. W. Camfield, *Revelation and the Holy Spirit: An Essay in Barthian Theology*. London: Elliot Stock, 1933. This book was originally a doctoral dissertation at the University of London. It may be added that Camfield was moved to learn German to deepen his knowledge of Barth as a result of reading McConnachie's 1927 article 'The Teaching of Karl Barth'.

[15] J. McConnachie, 'Der Einfluss Karl Barths in Schottland und England', in E. Wolf (ed.), *Theologische Aufsätze*. Munich: Kaiser Verlag, 1936, 529–70. Although the article is intended to cover both Scotland and England, McConnachie warns his readers that his knowledge of the English situation is somewhat attenuated (566). His comments on the Church of England at the time are probably best disregarded.

[16] McConnachie, 'Der Einfluss Karl Barths', 560.

Barth-reception: regional perspectives

Any attempt to understand the complexities of English-language Barth-reception must attempt to identify some of the local factors which were involved in the process. There can be no doubt that one of the major factors which is of critical importance in relation to the manner in which Barth is viewed is the dominant theological mode of discourse in the region in question. Writers such as Edward E. Said and Wesley A. Kort have shown how the 'ruling discourse' determines the rules of admission to public discussion, and eliminate their rivals through a process of trivialization.[17] To illustrate this point, we may compare the reaction to Barth in three very different theological environments: Scandinavia, in which the dominant theological mindset is that of Lutheranism; England, in which Anglicanism has had a considerable influence; and Scotland, in which the dominant theological perspective is Reformed.

Scandinavia

Scandinavian church life and theological reflection has been deeply shaped by the Lutheran Reformation.[18] It is widely agreed that there are potential tensions between Barth's mature theology and that of both Luther and confessional Lutheranism,[19] particularly (though by no means exclusively) concerning the relation of the law and gospel.[20] Although Scandinavian theology has become markedly less Lutheran since about 1980, there can be no doubt that the 'ruling discourse' of Scandinavian theology from 1920 to 1960 was that of confessional Lutheranism. The manner in which Barth was received within Scandinavian theology has been carefully

[17] See Wesley A. Kort, *Bound to Differ: The Dynamics of Theological Discourse*. University Park, PA: Pennsylvania State University Press, 1992.

[18] See Risto Saarinen, 'Protestant Theology: Scandinavia', in A. E. McGrath (ed.), *The Blackwell Encyclopaedia of Modern Christian Thought*. Oxford: Blackwell, 1993, 515–20.

[19] A. Siemens, 'Karl Barth der Vollender der lutherischer Reformation?', *Theologische Beiträge* 8 (1977), 31–5; A. Peters, 'Karl Barth gegen Martin Luther?', in R. Slenckza and R. Teller (eds), *Rechenschaft des Glaubens: Aufsätze*. Göttingen: Vandehoeck & Ruprecht, 1984, 92–129; G. Ebeling, 'Karl Barths Ringen mit Luther', in G. Ebeling, *Luther Studien* III. Tübingen: J. C. B. Mohr, 1985, 428–573; G. Ebeling, 'Aber die Reformation hinaus? Zur Luther-Kritik Karl Barths', *Zeitschrift für Theologie und Kirche* 83 (1986), 33–75; A. E. McGrath, 'Karl Barth and the *Articulus iustificationis*: The Significance of His Critique of Ernst Wolf within the Context of His Theological Method', *Theologische Zeitschrift* 39 (1983), 349–61; J. Webster, 'The Grammar of Doing: Luther and Barth on Human Agency', in J. Webster, *Barth's Moral Theology: Human Action in Barth's Thought*. Edinburgh: T&T Clark, 1998, 151–78.

[20] See, for example, B. Klappert, 'Erwägungen zum Thema: Gesetz und Evangelium bei Luther und K. Barth', *Theologische Beiträge* 7 (1976), 140–57; W. Joest, 'Karl Barth und das lutherische Verständnis von Gesetz und Evangelium', *Kerygma und Dogma* 24 (1978), 86–103.

studied,[21] and allows us to gain some insights into the general principles involved. There is no doubt that the predominantly Lutheran theological ethos of Scandinavian academic theology predisposed it against Barth's more Reformed perspective, particularly in relation to the critical function of the *articulus iustificationis* and the complex issue of the interaction of *lex* and *evangelium*,[22] and the Christological question of the *communicatio idiomatum*, on which Lutheran and Reformed theology had long-standing differences of interpretation.

The most significant schools of thought within Scandinavian academic theology are those associated with Sweden. A tradition of Barth interpretation was established within Swedish Lutheran theology as early as 1926, which later theologians within this confessional tradition repeated, with little more than superficial amendments.[23] Sweden had been noted for its hostility towards Reformed theology in both the sixteenth and seventeenth centuries; this hostility towards Reformed modes of thought (which are often depicted as 'outsiders' to Swedish religious culture) continued into the early twentieth century. In his careful study of Barth-reception, Sigurdson paints a remarkable picture of theological provincialism in the region, characterized by a refusal to take seriously anything which threatens the settled assumptions of the region.

The writer who may be argued to have set the prevailing Swedish tradition of Barth interpretation in place is Torsten Bohlin (1889–1950), Professor of Theological Ethics at Uppsala, noted as an interpreter of Kierkegaard. It is of the utmost significance to note that Bohlin analyses Barth within the context of Kierkegaard-intrepretation.[24] In his study *Tro och uppenbarelse: En studie till teologins kris och 'krisens teologi'* (Faith and revelation: A study in the crisis of theology and the 'theology of crisis'), Bohlin argued that the main characteristic of Barth's theology was the metaphysical dualism and discontinuity between God and humanity. The term 'metaphysical' had generally negative overtones within the Swedish

---

[21] See Aleksander Radler, 'Der Einfluss des theologischen Werkes von Karl Barths auf die skandinavische Theologie', *Neue Zeitschrift für systematische Theologie und Religionsphilosophie* 29 (1987), 267–93.

[22] For the best analysis of Barth's relation to Luther, see Gerhard Ebeling, 'Karl Barths Ringen mit Luther'.

[23] For a general analysis, see Sigurdson, *Karl Barth som den andre*. Sigurdson concentrates on Barth-reception after 1947, although he offers valuable perspectives on the formation of the tradition of Barth interpretation which emerged in the prewar period. I have to confess that Sigurdson seems to me to continue to view Barth through Lutheran eyes, not least in terms of his understanding of both the *Deus absconditus* and the *extra Calvinisticum* (for example, see his comments at pp. 121–2).

[24] A point noted by Radler, 'Der Einfluss des theologischen Werkes von Karl Barths auf die skandinavische Theologie', 268–70.

theological community of the period. Bohlin suggested that two distinct strands could be discerned within Kierkegaard's thought: a personal and existential strand, related to personal experience; and an intellectualist and metaphysical strand. Barth, according to Bohlin, was foolish enough to fasten on to this latter strand, whereas the true genius of Kierkegaard lay in relation to the former. The rival school of theology at Lund – represented by writers such as Gustaf Aulén, Ragnar Bring and Anders Nygren – has often been portrayed as more positive towards Barth. Nevertheless, Bohlin's general line of interpretation continued to be affirmed at Lund, even as late as the 1960s.[25]

Whereas Swedish Barth-reception was significantly influenced by the creation of a linkage between Barth and Kierkegaard, the situation in Norway and Denmark developed along different lines.[26] A Lutheran agenda is especially evident in the case of the Danish theologian Regin Prenter, who mounted a vigorous critique of Barth's discussion of the 'two natures' doctrine from a Lutheran perspective.[27] In his *Den dialektiske teologi* (The dialectical theology), the prominent Norwegian pietist writer Ole Hallesby (1879–1961) offered a cautious welcome to Barth's critique of experientially based theologies, while clearly having reservations elsewhere.[28]

It may be noted that German was the second language of most Scandinavian academics, so that gaining access to Barth's ideas was not a particular problem. The most fundamental issue appears to have been the perceived degree of incommensurability between Barthianism and traditional Lutheran dogmatics. This may have been heightened by additional factors (such as the unfortunate decision to view Barth as a misguided follower of Kierkegaard); nevertheless, the intrusion of a clearly confessional agenda appears to have been the most decisive consideration to lead to the emergence of a generally hostile and critical reaction to Barth in this region.

[25] Radler, 'Der Einfluss des theologischen Werkes von Karl Barths auf die skandinavische Theologie', 273–7; more detailed analysis in Sigurdson, *Karl Barth som den andre*. Gustaf Wingren is a particularly good example of a later Swedish writer to maintain this line of criticism against Barth: see Gustaf Wingren, *Theology in Conflict*. London: Oliver & Boyd, 1958, 23–128.

[26] Radler, 'Der Einfluss des theologischen Werkes von Karl Barths auf die skandinavische Theologie', 277–86; Kjetil Hafstad, *Das Geschichtsverständnis Karl Barths*. Munich: Kaiser Verlag, 1985.

[27] Regin Prenter, 'Karl Barths Umbildung der traditionallen Zweinaturlehre in lutherischer Beleuchtung', *Studia Theologica* 11 (1957), 1–88.

[28] Hafstad, *Das Geschichtsverständnis Karl Barths*, 23–4.

England

The dominant form of Christianity in England is that associated with the Church of England, and generally known as 'Anglicanism'.[29] As the national church, the Church of England tended to reflect the values of English society as a whole. The foreign languages regarded worthy of serious study were primarily French and Italian, rather than German. In 1882, Matthew Arnold wrote of the 'provincial unconsciousness of the English',[30] apparently intending this to be understood as a reference to the tendency of the English to disregard events and ideas originating beyond Calais as devoid of real significance. It must be stressed that this is a dangerous generalization, and it is a relatively simple matter to identify English theologians and philosophers who were well aware of the importance of intellectual developments in Germany and elsewhere. Nevertheless, such thinkers found themselves swimming against the prevailing current. In 1936, one perceptive critic noted that Barth had yet to disturb 'the placid provincialism of English theological thought'.[31]

The perceptions of German-language theology in Anglican circles during the 1930s were generally negative in tone. A widespread hostility towards German theology developed during the nineteenth century, and persisted into the twentieth. German theology was widely portrayed as rationalist, devoted to the godless and new-fangled discipline of biblical criticism.[32] Throughout the Victorian period, the English national church retained a principled commitment to traditional Christian doctrines which its senior members tended to fear was not echoed by their German counterparts.[33] The accuracy of these perceptions is, of course, open to serious challenge; nevertheless, they existed, and were unquestionably reinforced through the rise of anti-German sentiment after the outbreak of War in 1914. After the Great War of 1914–18, it became politically

---

[29] For an overview, see P. D. L. Avis, *Anglicanism and the Christian Church*. Edinburgh: T&T Clark, 1989; Alister E. McGrath (ed.), *Handbook of Anglican Theologians*. London: SPCK, 1998.

[30] G. W. E. Russell (ed.), *Letters of Matthew Arnold 1848–88*. 2 vols. London: Macmillan, 1895, vol. 2, 201.

[31] M. Chaning-Pearce, 'Karl Barth as a Post-War Prophet', *Hibbert Journal* 35 (1936–7), 365–79 (365).

[32] An excellent survey may be found in Robert Morgan, 'Non Angli sed Angeli: Some Anglican Reactions to German Gospel Criticisms', in S. Sykes and D. Holmes (eds), *New Studies in Theology* I. London: Duckworth, 1980, 1–30.

[33] See the comments of the translators of August Neander's *Life of Jesus Christ*. London, 1848, ix–x, particularly their reference to 'the *dread* with which German theology is regarded by many English and some American divines'.

incorrect to devote much attention to German theology.[34] Barth was, of course, Swiss. Yet the fact that he wrote in German led many to draw the conclusion that he was a German,[35] and thus to be marginalized.

In my analysis of Barth-reception in Scandinavia, I drew attention to the importance of some of the theological distinctives of confessional Lutheranism in relation to the perception of Barth. The Church of England has long been regarded as theologically minimalist,[36] with no real interest in systematic theology. This might therefore be taken to mean that there were no fundamental theological considerations which might predispose Anglicans towards or against Barth's ideas. In fact, the situation is somewhat more complex, and requires a little explanation.

During the final quarter of the nineteenth century, many theologians within the Church of England began to regard the doctrine of the incarnation as the lynchpin of Christian orthodoxy. The defence of the divinity of Jesus Christ was specifically linked with the concept of 'incarnation'. Earlier apologetic works – such as Henry Parry Liddon's *Divinity of our Lord and Saviour Jesus Christ* (1867) – did not make this concept of central importance, even if it could be argued to be implicit within their general approach. This general trend reached its zenith in the final decade of the century. In 1899, with the publication of *Lux Mundi*, with the highly significant subtitle *A Series of Studies in the Religion of the Incarnation*,[37] the sixth contribution to the collection had the highly suggestive title 'The Incarnation as the Basis of Dogma'.[38]

It is perhaps cruel – and not a little unjust – to suggest that the Church of England was an organization in search of a theological rationale, which serendipitously happened upon precisely such a *raison d'être* in the notion of the incarnation. Nevertheless, it can be shown that the theme of the incarnation came to assume a major, possibly dominant, theological role for Anglicanism until the Second World War, as can be seen from a study

---

[34] J. K. Mozley, *Some Tendencies in British Theology from the Publication of* Lux Mundi *to the Present Day*. London: SPCK, 1951, 47; Roberts, 'Reception of the Theology of Karl Barth', 118–25.

[35] Sadly, the trend continues: see, for example, the reference to 'the German theologian Karl Barth' in Kenneth Leech, *True God: An Exploration in Spiritual Theology*. London: SPCK, 1985, 302.

[36] For a classic analysis of this perception, see Stephen Sykes, *The Integrity of Anglicanism*. London: Mowbrays, 1978.

[37] Charles Gore, the editor of the collection, had indicated his preference for the title *The Religion of the Incarnation*. For further study, see Peter Hinchliff, 'The Church', in R. Morgan (ed.), *The Religion of the Incarnation*. Bristol: Bristol Classical Press, 1989, 136–57.

[38] R. C. Moberly, 'The Incarnation as the Basis of Dogma', in C. Gore (ed.), *Lux Mundi*, 10th edn, London: John Murray, 1890, 215–72. Moberly avoids offering any definition of what he understands by the term 'incarnation', apparently assuming that its meaning is as self-evident as is its function as a guarantor of orthodoxy.

of the writings of two of the more theologically competent Archbishops of Canterbury, William Temple (1881–1944) or Arthur Michael Ramsey (1904–88).

A tradition of Barth-interpretation arose within Anglicanism which held that Barth was hostile to the incarnation. It is virtually impossible to know quite how this perception arose, nor who created it. Yet the fact of its existence and potency is an integral aspect of Anglican history. The Anglican writer Geoffrey Bromiley, whose contribution to the translation of the *Church Dogmatics* must be fully acknowledged, relates the following anecdote, which illustrates this point perfectly:

> By and large the Anglican world has not given itself to the study of Barth that his work deserves. Though it is many years ago now, I remember talking with a learned bishop who on no less authority than that of William Temple suggested that Barth's view of revelation undercut the incarnation. I could not resist replying with one of Barth's shorter statements: 'To say "revelation" is to say "the Word became flesh"'.[39]

With occasional exceptions, then, Anglicanism was predisposed to dismiss Barth.[40] This, of course, is no longer the case; since about 1970, it has become clear that many younger Anglican writers have found Barth a congenial dialogue partner, even if that dialogue might be both critical and appreciative.

Scotland

As John McConnachie pointed out in his 1935 assessment of Barth's influence in Scotland, there were excellent prima-facie reasons for supposing that Barth's British influence might be at its greatest in Scotland.[41] Our brief analysis of theological factors implicated in Barth-reception would certainly point in this direction. The established Church of

[39] Geoffrey Bromiley, 'The Influence of Barth after World War II', in N. Biggar (ed.), *Reckoning with Barth*. London: Mowbray, 1988, 9–23(21). For reflections on the difficulty of securing a fair hearing for Barth in England at this time, see Daniel Jenkins, 'Mr Demant and Karl Barth', *Theology* 39 (1939), 412–20.

[40] One of Barth's few advocates within Anglicanism was Edwyn Clements Hoskyns, Dean of Corpus Christi College, Cambridge. Hoskyns had studied under Adolf von Harnack at Berlin in 1907, and taught in the field of New Testament. He was widely mocked, both by his colleagues in the Cambridge Faculty of Divinity and those students who attended his lectures. See Owen Chadwick, *Michael Ramsey: A Life*. Oxford: Oxford University Press, 1990, 27–9; Roberts, 'Reception of the Theology of Karl Barth', 127–8. The comments of Charles Raven, *The Gospel and the Church: A Study of Distortion and Its Remedy*. London: Hodder & Stoughton, 1939, 140–7, can be taken as an indication of the hostility felt towards Barth at Cambridge at this time.

[41] McConnachie, 'Der Einfluss Karl Barths', 561–2.

Scotland was strongly Calvinist in terms of its theological heritage, in contrast to the Lutheranism of Scandinavia. One obvious consequence of this would be the absence of the Lutheran confessional distinctives (such as the emphasis on the *articulus iustificationis*, the tension between *lex* and *evangelium*, and a specific approach to the question of the *communicatio idiomatum*) which had proved so effective an obstacle to Barth's reception in Scandinavia. A further point which might be made here is that Barth makes frequent reference to the *Confessio Scotica*,[42] the Scots Confession of Faith of 1560.

For McConnachie, a significant obstacle to Barth-reception lay in the lingering influence of Ritschlianism within the Scottish theological faculties. Nevertheless, this was in irreversible decline in the early 1930s. We have already had cause to note the gradual shift of Hugh Ross Mackintosh during the 1930s from a Ritschlian to a Barthian perspective (although one can never really say that Mackintosh was 'Ritschlian' or Barthian, in that he maintained something of a critical distance from both viewpoints). By the middle of the 1930s, there was a much more sympathetic reception for Barth, especially at Edinburgh. Barth's appreciative foreword to Heinrich Heppe's *Reformed Dogmatics* clearly indicated Barth's interest in the historic Reformed tradition, and thus commended him to many within the dogmatics departments of the five Scottish Universities – all of which, it must be stressed, were at that stage the more or less exclusive preserves of the Church of Scotland.

Yet perhaps the most significant factor in establishing Barth as a significant theological presence in Scotland was the long-established Scottish tradition of seeing 'Christian dogmatics' as an integral element of Christian theology. The contrast is perhaps best seen by contrasting the approaches adopted to the teaching of theology at the University of Oxford and the University of Edinburgh in the 1930s. Oxford theology was primarily historical in tone; the issue was to establish what had been believed, without the supposition of any necessary connection between what had been believed in the past and what was to be believed in the present. It can be argued that the model adopted in the Scottish faculties of theology paralleled that which was established at major Reformed schools of theology throughout Europe (such as the Reformed academies at Geneva, Leiden and Heidelberg) in the seventeenth centuries,[43] in which

---

[42] See, for example, *Church Dogmatics* I/2, 658; II/1, 185, 445, 457; II/2, 62, 84, 154, 308; IV/1, 704, 709.

[43] See Richard Stauffer, 'Calvinism et les universités', *Bulletin de la société d'histoire du protestantisme français* 126 (1980), 27–51; H. Meylan, 'Collèges et académies protestantes en France au XVIᵉ siècle', in *Actes du 95ᵉcongrès national des sociétés savantes*. 2 vols. Paris: Imprimerie nationale, 1971, vol. I, 301–8.

an emphasis upon dogmatics was seen as *de rigueur*. At Edinburgh, the emphasis was on assisting students to answer major theological questions – such as 'What is the meaning of Jesus Christ for me?'[44] Barth could therefore be seen as a recent contributor (although a particularly radical and exciting one) to a long-standing theological tradition, stretching back through Herrmann to Ritschl and Schleiermacher.[45]

This is not to say that Oxford in particular, or England in general, lacked an interest in systematic theology, or failed to produce systematic theologians. It is to point out that there was no English *institutional commitment to and investment in Christian dogmatics*. In contrast, the five Scottish faculties of divinity, especially Edinburgh, had a strong commitment to the positive teaching of Christian dogmatics as a core element of theological education. The high profile of Christian dogmatics, along with the clear assumption of the importance of the discipline, meant that dogmatic issues were taken seriously. It can therefore be argued that it was inevitable that, as Barth's star rose in the German-language firmament, this would be reflected in the teaching and research of the Scottish universities.

Yet the process is not quite as simple as this brief analysis might suggest. Having noted some regional factors which were clearly of some importance in relation to Barth-reception, we must now focus on some specific issues to allow us to understand the major role played by Torrance in the English-language reception of Barth.

The mechanics of Barth-reception

There are four elements which are known to be of significance in relation to the successful English-language reception of any major foreign-language intellectual, whether theological, political or philosophical.

1. Translation of the most important works of the individual into English. The linguistic competence of British theologians in particular is notoriously limited. It is a well-known fact that the only German-language theologians to receive substantial scholarly attention in English-language theology are those whose works have been translated into English.

---

[44] An example offered by McConnachie, 'Der Einfluss Karl Barths', 562.
[45] For an interesting exploration of this linkage, see H. L. Stewart, 'Schleiermacher, Ritschl, Barth: A Sequence', *Hibbert Journal* 50 (1951–2), 10–17.

2. A journal dedicated or sympathetic to the viewpoint of the theologian in question. The views of the Vienna Circle, for example, were diffused and developed through the journal *Erkenntnis*, founded in 1930 and edited by Otto Carnap and Hans Reichenbach.

3. A publishing house which is prepared to handle primary and secondary material relating to the individual. In the case of Barth himself, this critical function was performed by Christian Kaiser Verlag (Munich).

4. A platform from which a rising generation of students may be influenced. The most common form of such a platform is a leading university faculty. In the case of the Vienna Circle, the University of Vienna provided the platform in question.[46]

We may consider these elements individually in greater detail as they bear specifically on English-language Barth-reception, and consider the manner in which Torrance was involved in each.

The translation: the Church Dogmatics

By 1937, a substantial number of the early works of Barth had been translated into English, most notably, the second edition of the Romans commentary (translated by E. C. Hoskyns) and the first half-volume of the *Church Dogmatics*. It was, however, clear that the sheer immensity of Barth's theological output, supremely in relation to the *Church Dogmatics*, meant that any informed assessment and appropriation of Barth in the English-speaking world would depend on the production of a reliable English translation of this major work.

There were, however, some problems. George T. Thomson, who had produced the English translation of I/1 in 1936, showed no inclination to extend his endeavours to the remainder of the series. In addition, it became clear that there were some serious weaknesses with the translation he had produced, in that certain philosophical notions absent from the original German were, in effect, imported through the translation process, and thus attributed to Barth by those readers who were unable or unwilling to compare the translation with the original German. These difficulties are hinted at by Torrance, in his discussion of criticisms directed against Barth by English-language logico-analytical writers:

---

[46] For details, see K. Menger, 'Memories of Moritz Schlick', in E. Gadol (ed.), *Rationality and Science: A Memorial Volume for Moritz Schlick*. Berlin: Springer Verlag, 1982, 83–103.

When I examined the German text, I realized that they had been misled by the use of logical terms such as 'deduce' or 'infer' in G. T. Thomson's translation which did not accurately reproduce the original text. In it Barth had studiously avoided that kind of language, for his theological conceptions were *not logically* but *ontologically* derived, in much the same way in which our basic concepts in empirico-theoretical science are derived . . . Thus it became clear to me that a new translation of *CD* I.1 was needed.[47]

But how was the massive undertaking of a complete translation of the *Church Dogmatics* to be undertaken?

Even while in parish ministry, Torrance had begun to plan for the preparation of a complete English translation of the *Church Dogmatics*. It was not until 1952 that Torrance was able to begin the project in earnest. Once he was settled into the Chair of Christian Dogmatics at Edinburgh, he was able to give careful thought to how to undertake the task. The difficulties were immense. How could consistency be assured within the translation, in that it was clear that a number of translators would be required for the undertaking? And how could the complexities of Barth's theological German – not to mention his stylistic peculiarities, such as his 'long and carefully balanced sentences' – be handled?

A model already existed. The English translation of Schleiermacher's *Christian Faith* had taken place at two levels: editorial and translation. The editors (H. R. Mackintosh and J. S. Stewart) exercised general supervision of the project, and supervised (and contributed to) the work of translation, which was undertaken by a team of eight translators, including Donald Baillie. A comparable model suggested itself for the larger project of the *Church Dogmatics*: an editorial team of two persons would be able to supervise and contribute to the translation process, while at the same time discharging much of the work to a larger team. One of those two editors would be Torrance himself; but who would the other be? It was clear to Torrance that it was essential to have the project co-directed by someone whose mastery of the German language was matched by a corresponding theological competence. He found precisely such a person in Geoffrey W. Bromiley.

Although Bromiley was a specialist in historical theology, and published some excellent studies in his own right,[48] it is fair to suggest that he will be remembered primarily as a superb translator of German theology into English. He would go on to translate several other major works of

---

[47] See Torrance, 'My Interaction with Karl Barth', in *How Karl Barth Changed My Mind*, edited by Donald K. McKim. Grand Rapids, MI: Eerdmans, 1986, 52–64.

[48] For example, *Thomas Cranmer: Theologian*. London: Lutterworth Press, 1956.

systematic theology from German, including Helmut Thielicke's *Evangelical Faith* and Wolfhart Pannenberg's *Systematic Theology*.[49] It is, however, for his translation of the *Church Dogmatics* that he will be chiefly remembered.

The greatest difficulties were presented by I/2. Thomson had managed to get some work done on this before his health had declined, with the result that §§13–20 were complete, leaving §§21–4 untranslated. These were duly completed by Dr Harold Knight. However, Thomson's translation was not entirely consistent within itself, nor faithful to Barth's distinctive forms of thought. As a result, the translation had to be reworked several times before Torrance and Bromiley were satisfied with the result. The general intention was to produce two part-volumes per year. In the event, the entire project was not completed until 1977. The reason for this delay was the need to retranslate I/1 (completed in 1975); only then could the final index volume be published (1977).

It will therefore be clear that Torrance played a decisive role in this critical aspect of Barth-reception. It might be argued that others could have done this; perhaps there is some truth in that. Yet the simple fact of history is that Torrance saw the need for the translation, and set in place the editorial and linguistic logistics necessary to undertake the massive task.

The journal: the Scottish Journal of Theology

Torrance founded the *Scottish Journal of Theology*, with J. K. S. Reid, in 1948. The initial publisher was Oliver & Boyd, an eminent religious publisher based in Edinburgh, which had earlier published Torrance's Basel D.Theol. thesis in both its forms. In part, the journal was intended to reflect and stimulate the high level of academic theological discussion within Scotland. Torrance had already founded the Scottish Church Theology Society on his return from war service in 1945, and the journal could be seen as an extension of his vision for the renewal of theology within Scotland as a servant of the church and its mission. It was not the easiest of matters to establish a journal in the immediate postwar period. Paper, for example, was in short supply. Torrance approached Oliver & Boyd to see if they might be interested in publishing the new journal. Their expression, initially of interest and subsequently of commitment, was probably helped along to no small extent when Torrance secured a promise of supplies of paper from Dr Patrick Russell, who owned a local paperworks.

---

[49] For an account of Bromiley's work, see the introduction to James E. Bradley and Richard A. Muller (eds), *Church, Word, and Spirit: Historical and Theological Essays in Honor of Geoffrey W. Bromiley*. Grand Rapids, MI: Eerdmans, 1987.

The journal rapidly acquired an international reputation,[50] and can be regarded as contributing significantly to Torrance's international profile.[51] In due course, the journal would be supplemented by a series of 'occasional papers', which actively furthered theological and scholarly debate in areas of importance.

The journal would, however, also act as a vehicle for sympathetic discussion and promotion of Barthian ideas within the English-language world. The reaction to Barth in other British theological journals tended to be cool and unreceptive. By the late 1930s, many had dismissed Barth as a fading presence, a star whose brief luminosity was now in terminal decline.[52] The *Scottish Journal of Theology* took a rather different line. The first volume included a significant article by John McConnachie on the 'Uniqueness of the Word of God',[53] in which Barthian ideas were treated sympathetically.

It would be quite ludicrous to suggest that the journal took an uncritically pro-Barth stance, or that it chose to devote its pages more or less entirely, or even predominantly, to matters relating to Barth. The journal reflected accurately many of the academic concerns of the era. It simply allowed Barth's perspective to be heard. In this respect, *Scottish Journal of Theology* cannot be directly compared to *Erkenntnis*, which was founded with the specific agenda of promoting the ideas of the Vienna Circle. Nevertheless, Torrance's personal theological commitment, as editor, ensured that the new journal would act as a forum for the discussion and dissemination of Barthianism within the English-speaking world. As events proved, the journal proved to be one of the few international English-language journals to assume such a role, and it is therefore entirely proper to credit Torrance with establishing and setting in place this second element in the process of Barth-reception.[54]

The publisher: T&T Clark

The publication of Barth's *Church Dogmatics* in English, and the possible publication of a substantial number of secondary studies on Barth's

[50] See the comments of John Howard, 'New College Library', in Wright and Badcock, *Disruption to Diversity*, 187–202, 192.

[51] Readers might like to consult the bibliography provided at the end of this volume, and note the substantial number of articles and reviews which Torrance contributed to the journal.

[52] See, for example, H. C. Rouse, 'The Barthian Challenge to Christian Thought', *Baptist Quarterly* 7 (1934–5), 256–63.

[53] John McConnachie, 'The Uniqueness of the Word of God', *Scottish Journal of Theology* 1 (1948), 113–35.

[54] *Scottish Journal of Theology*, now edited by Iain Torrance and Bryan Spinks, continues to be a significant theological forum under its present publishers, T&T Clark. A cumulative index of its first fifty years of articles and reviews was published in 1998.

theology, required an academic publisher willing to take the considerable commercial risks involved in such a massive enterprise. The sheer size of the complete *Church Dogmatics* pointed to a potentially major investment of time and resources. If the work failed to sell adequately, it could have spelt financial ruin to the publisher. In a number of languages, it proved necessary to publish the work by subscription – that is, by raising the funds necessary for publication in advance, on the basis of individuals subscribing to the series as a whole. Torrance was able to persuade Sir Thomas Clark, director of the leading Edinburgh legal and religious publisher T&T Clark,[55] to publish the work on a commercial foundation, trusting that the sales of the work would cover their production costs.

By 1950, T&T Clark was firmly established as the leading Scottish theological publisher, a position which it retains to the present day.[56] The company had published many translations of works of theology, including: series such as the Ante-Nicene Christian Library; the works of St Augustine; the Calvin Translation Society series of Calvin's letters, commentaries and treatises; and the 180 volumes of the Foreign Theological Library (1846–91). More significantly, perhaps, they had also published the translation of the *Hauptwerken* of two leading German liberal Protestant theologians – F. D. E. Schleiermacher's *Christian Faith* (published in 1927), and A. B. Ritschl's *Christian Doctrine of Justification and Reconciliation* (published in 1900). Barth was now widely seen as a successor to these two luminaries of continental Protestant theology. It was therefore entirely natural for G. T. Thomson (then at Aberdeen) to approach T&T Clark in 1933 and suggest a translation of what was then available of Barth's *Church Dogmatics*. In the event, Thomson only proved able to translate the first half-volume. In one sense, therefore, Torrance may simply be said to have built on a foundation laid by Thomson, in securing T&T Clark. Nevertheless, the important role played by Torrance in securing a publisher for this series cannot be overlooked. The third element in English-language Barth-reception owed much to Torrance.

The platform: Edinburgh University Faculty of Divinity

The final element we must consider is the 'platform' – that is, the base from which Barthian ideas would be studied, developed and disseminated. The classic platform for the dissemination of an academic school of thought is a university faculty, through which a rising generation of

---

[55] On the origins and early history of this publishing house, with particular reference to its theological commitments and concerns, see John A. H. Dempster, *The T. & T. Clark Story: A Victorian Publisher and the New Theology*. Edinburgh: Pentland, 1992.

[56] See the comments of Wright and Badcock, *Disruption to Diversity*, xxii–xxiii.

students can be exposed to the ideas in question. An excellent example of such a theological 'platform' in the recent past is provided by the University of Marburg during the final decade of the nineteenth and first decade of the twentieth centuries, when it was noted for its commitment to the ideas of Wilhelm Herrmann, and thus attracted theologians as diverse as Hugh Ross Mackintosh, Rudolf Bultmann and Karl Barth.[57] More recently, we might note the case of Yale Divinity School in relation to 'postliberalism'.[58]

Herrmann's period at Marburg is instructive for a number of reasons, not least of which is the sheer length of his academic tenure. Herrmann arrived at Marburg in 1879, and remained there until his retirement in 1917. The reputation of the faculty increased steadily, particularly in 1886, after the arrival of Adolf von Harnack. Student numbers soared, with large numbers of international students being attracted to Marburg on account of its distinctive position. The distinctive ethos of the faculty was closely linked with Herrmann's personal theological commitments.

As we noted earlier (p. 89), the significance of a long academic tenure for the shaping of the ethos and reputation of a theological faculty had not gone unnoticed by John and Donald Baillie. When Torrance asked to be allowed to transfer from the Chair of Church History at New College to the Chair of Christian Dogmatics in 1952, the Baillies were well aware that a move was being mooted which could lead to a theologian of decidedly pronounced views occupying a leading position in both Edinburgh and Scottish theology, which he would continue to hold for more than a quarter of a century. His potential influence on a generation of students could be profound, and might establish Edinburgh as a centre of Barthianism. What the Baillies feared was, of course, what Torrance rather hoped for.

Yet it must be pointed out that it is quite incorrect to suggest that Barth was first introduced or commended at Edinburgh in the 1950s. As we have stressed, Barth first began to be studied seriously at New College during the 1930s, primarily as a consequence of the influence of Hugh Ross Mackintosh. The Faculty of Divinity at New College, Edinburgh, were, of course, far from uniformly persuaded of the merits of Barth. One of the most significant voices raised against Barth was that of John Baillie.

---

[57] Marburg was also home to one of the two most influential German neo-Kantian schools of philosophy, under Paul Natorp (1854–1924) and Ernst Cassirer (1874–1945). For details, see H. Hermelink and S. A. Kähler, *Die Philipps-Universität zu Marburg 1527–1927*. Marburg: N. G. Elwertsche Verlagsbuchhandlung, 1927.

[58] See B. J. Kellenberg, 'Unstuck from Yale: Theological Method after Lindbeck', *Scottish Journal of Theology* 50 (1997), 191–218.

Writing in 1930, John Baillie commented on the difficulties which he experienced in digesting – let alone assimilating! – the writings of Karl Barth. 'Barth's own writings were at first found very indigestable by British and American theologians, and not least by the present writer.'[59] Baillie was hostile to Barthianism for a number of reasons, not least its apparent refusal to take seriously the agenda of the Renaissance and Enlightenment, and especially its premature rejection of much that was of permanent value in the pre-Barthian tradition:

> I believe any effective and significant post-Barthian movement must go *through* Barthianism, not repudiating the remarkable contribution which it has made to all our thinking but entering fully into its heritage, while at the same time correcting its deficiencies and also recovering for us much that was of value in those early ways of thought which were too brashly jettisoned.[60]

Baillie joined the Faculty of Divinity at Edinburgh in 1934, and must be regarded as a significant modulating factor in Barth-reception from that point onwards, and particularly during the 1940s. The intellectual ascendancy of Baillie's theological style at Edinburgh during this period has often been noted.[61] Although there are clearly points at which Baillie welcomed Barthian insights (for example, its critique of the optimism of post-Enlightenment theology), the dominant tenor of his evaluation is studiedly negative.[62] Baillie had little sympathy with what he regarded as extreme forms of liberalism, against which he understood Barth to have reacted. Barthianism was thus to be viewed essentially as 'an over-reaction to an over-reaction'.[63]

Torrance's appointment as Professor of Christian Dogmatics at Edinburgh was thus the portent of a major shift in Edinburgh's perceived theological commitments, attracting large numbers of students (especially from North America) sympathetic to (or at least interested in) Barth. While Torrance's opponents referred to his period as Professor of Christian Dogmatics as 'the Barthian captivity',[64] it is a simple fact of history that Edinburgh's reputation as a centre of excellence in systematic theology

[59] John Baillie, 'Looking before and after', *Christian Century* 75 (2 April 1958), 400–1.

[60] John Baillie, 'Some Reflections on the Changing Theological Scene', *Union Seminary Quarterly Review* 12 (January 1957), 7.

[61] See, for example, the comments of George Newlands, 'Divinity and Dogmatics', in Wright and Badcock, *Disruption to Diversity*, 117–34, 125.

[62] For a useful evaluation of Baillie's theology, see Fergusson, 'John Baillie: Orthodox Liberal'.

[63] George Newlands, 'John and Donald Baillie', *Modern Believing* 39 (1998), 22–8, 23. Baillie himself seems to have read surprisingly little Barth, and probably never got beyond I/2 of the *Church Dogmatics*: see Fergusson, 'John Baillie: Orthodox Liberal', 151 n. 70.

[64] See Newlands, 'Divinity and Dogmatics', in Wright and Badcock, *Disruption to Diversity*, 127.

reached its climax during this period, and thus afforded a significant platform for the development and dissemination of Barthian ideas and approaches.

In considering this fourth element of Barth-reception, we can again see the critical importance of Torrance. The radical reorientation of Edinburgh from the gentle and subtle liberalism of John Baillie to the (to its critics) rather more strident orthodoxy of Karl Barth was due to the personal influence of Torrance, who occupied precisely the position of influence required to effect the transformation.

In this section, we have explored in a little detail the mechanics of Barth-reception. Ideas do not just get 'received'; resources must be put in place to enable this process to happen. We have identified four such resources which were instrumental in relation to English-language Barth-reception. In one case, Torrance may be regarded as building upon a foundation laid by another, in that G. T. Thomson had already secured the agreement of T&T Clark to publish part of the *Church Dogmatics*. In this case, Torrance built upon and extended Thomson's work in a very significant manner. In the case of the remaining three elements, however, Torrance must be regarded as having had a decisive impact on English-language Barth-reception, in that he set these elements in place *de novo*. It could be argued that others might have done the same at a later stage, in a different manner, and at a different location; the fact remains, however, that Torrance had the vision to set them in place before anyone else, and must therefore take a substantial degree of whatever credit is due for the subsequent major expansion in Barth's influence.

But how did Torrance himself view Barth? What was so important about Barth that moved Torrance to devote so much of his academic career to exploring and commending his ideas? In what follows, we shall attempt to gain an understanding of how Torrance viewed Barth.

Torrance on the significance of Barth

The stature of Barth as one of Christianity's most significant theologians is no longer disputed. Yet the nature of that significance remains a matter of some debate. In his careful and thoroughly researched study of the reception of Barth in the Anglo-Saxon world, Richard H. Roberts offers a typology of the responses to Barth, noting that these responses are often to be understood as developments within Anglo-Saxon theology which are stimulated by the intervention of Barth's theology,[65] rather than a direct appropriation of Barth's theology, in part or in whole.

---

[65] Roberts, 'Reception of the Theology of Karl Barth', 142–59.

In view of the importance of Torrance's understanding of Barth to the development of English-language theology in the twentieth century, we may explore the way in which Torrance used Barth in the lectures he delivered at a very early stage in his career.

Torrance's use of Barth in the Auburn Lectures, 1938–9

In the academic year 1938–9, Torrance delivered a series of lectures at Auburn Theological Seminary in New York State (see pp. 51–5). These lectures were never intended to be published. By this stage in his career, Torrance had read the first two half-volumes of the *Church Dogmatics* in German, and had found them immensely stimulating to his thinking. In that these volumes deal particularly with the concept of revelation and the doctrine of the Trinity, it is to be expected that they might well exercise a significant impact on Torrance's Auburn Lectures on 'revelation' and 'the doctrine of God'.

To illustrate the tone and approach of the lectures, and especially to consider Torrance's early use of Barth, we may consider the major lecture entitled 'The Christian Doctrine of Revelation'.[66] The fifty-nine pages of this lecture develop an approach to the concept of revelation which clearly corresponds to some aspects of Barth's approach, yet which can be seen to stand firmly within the grand tradition of Scottish theology, particularly that which Torrance found in the writings and lectures of H. R. Mackintosh.

Revelation is to be understood as 'an objective unveiling' of God, coupled with 'a making of that unveiling real to our vision by a taking away of the scales of our eyes which were hitherto too dimmed and diseased to behold the light'.[67] We can surely discern here an echo of the characteristic Barthian notion of *Offenbarkeit* – the idea that revelation is not revelation until it is recognized and received as revelation; and that this process of recognition is not something which we can commence or complete by virtue of our human resources, but which is a work of God from its beginning to its end. Revelation is to be considered as an *event* – 'a positive Word of God addressed to men'.[68] It is something which subverts 'the whole natural approach of man',[69] in that it challenges the autonomy of the human mind. Revelation is thus not 'an extension of

---

[66] Torrance, 'Christian Doctrine of Revelation'. The structure of the typescript suggests that the material was broken down into four major sections (pp. 1–14, 15–27, 28–39, 40–59), which probably were delivered as individual lectures.

[67] 'Christian Doctrine of Revelation', 5.

[68] 'Christian Doctrine of Revelation', 6.

[69] 'Christian Doctrine of Revelation', 7.

our natural knowledge',[70] in that it does not invite us to advance further down the road on which natural unaided human reason has taken us thus far. It stands in contradiction to this:

> Revelation must be thought of as the approach of reality to man, not as the approach of man to reality. The latter is discovery; the former a divine communication ... Christianity does not set out from anything positive within man; it sets out from something positive that comes to man, and comes from beyond. Man is sought and found; he does not seek and find. We are concerned with a movement of God to man; not a movement of man to God.[71]

Torrance affirms that human nature is incapable of bridging the revelational abyss between the divine and the human from its side. It is dependent for its knowledge of God upon that gap being bridged in an act of revelation by God, and God alone. For Torrance – and here the Barthian echoes are unmistakeable – theology is a response to revelation, not an independent human activity based upon human reason or experience:

> We have nothing to teach except what we hear from God. We have nothing to minister to the hungry souls of our people except what we ourselves have been given in the way of bread from him who claimed to be the 'bread of life'. Our theology, too, which is but an attempt, by means of human thought and speech, to scrutinize what we have been given in this revelation and to say it over again for our generation; what we do here is say after God what antecedently he had said in revelation about that revelation and all that it contains.[72]

A point of critical importance concerns the manner in which revelation is conveyed through Christ and through the Bible. Torrance affirms that revelation 'is God speaking in person – *Deus loquentis persona*'.[73] The Bible is to be thought of as a witness to divine revelation – that is, a witness to Christ. The relation of the Bible to Christianity cannot be regarded as being parallel to that of the Qur'an to Islam. In his discussion of this point, Torrance follows the general Barthian approach of regarding the Bible as a witness to revelation, which may become the Word of God:

> For the Christian, the Bible is not primarily an oracle-book, or a manual of instruction, though it may be regarded as that; it is the testimony to the living Christ who is himself the revelation of God, and to that Christ the Book is related in a relation of subordination. As Luther said: 'the Scriptures are the

---

[70] 'Christian Doctrine of Revelation', 8.
[71] 'Christian Doctrine of Revelation', 9.
[72] 'Christian Doctrine of Revelation', 4.
[73] 'Christian Doctrine of Revelation', 52.

crib wherein Christ is laid'. The crib must not be mistaken for the Christ. The Bible is not as such the immediate Word of God, though it is the only book that may become the Word of God.[74]

At several points in his discussion of revelation, Torrance cites from Barth (or uses phrases which are strongly reminiscent of Barth) to reinforce the points which he was making; these citations are generally taken from either a collection of texts edited by John Baillie and Hugh Martin, published shortly before Torrance set sail for New York, or from the original German language edition of the first half-volume of the *Church Dogmatics*.[75] Yet it is clear that Torrance is in no way basing himself uncritically or exclusively upon Barth. At point after point, we find references to his teachers at Edinburgh, most notably Mackintosh and Lamont. For example, Torrance cites with appreciation Mackintosh's memorable aphorism: 'A religious knowledge of God, wherever existing, comes by revelation; otherwise we should be committed to the incredible position that a man can know God without his willing to be known.'[76] As has often been pointed out, the early 1930s saw a dramatic increase in interest within Scottish theology in the Barthian emphasis on the priority of revelation, and it is entirely possible that Torrance here speaks as a representative of the 'revivification of the Word of God' within Scottish theology at this time, linked with writers such as John McConnachie.

For Barth, there was the most intimate of connections between the actuality of revelation and the doctrine of the Trinity. It is therefore of considerable interest to examine the section of Torrance's major lecture course on 'The Christian Doctrine of God' to deal with the doctrine of the Trinity.[77] Although Torrance's presentation of the doctrine is fresh and invigorating, it is clear that he is deeply influenced by Barth at this point:

> [The doctrine of the Trinity] is the basis and presupposition of the Revelation of God: and when we ask Who God is Who reveals Himself, we must answer, the Triune God, the God who reveals Himself as Father, Son and Holy Ghost.[78]

Torrance develops this point by stressing the correspondence between God's person and God's acts, noting that God is antecedently what God's revelation demonstrates to be the case:

---

[74] 'Christian Doctrine of Revelation', 54.
[75] See John Baillie and Hugh Martin (eds), *Revelation*. London: Faber, 1937, which is cited by Torrance, 'Christian Doctrine of Revelation', 10–11.
[76] 'Christian Doctrine of Revelation', 18.
[77] Torrance, 'Christian Doctrine of God', 90–111.
[78] Torrance, 'Christian Doctrine of God', 90.

We are dealing with the acts of God, the acts of God in redemption, those acts in which His Person and His acts are identical, those acts which go back to His essence and while distinct from His essence are His nature in manifestation towards men. But what he is in His acts He is antecendently in Himself if those acts are real and valid manifestations of God, if that is to say, they are real in which we have not merely an empty manifestation of God but God Himself there: manifestations of God which are full of content, a content which is God Himself.[79]

Torrance explores the foundations of the Trinity with particular reference to Jesus Christ, again noting the revelational presuppositions and implications of this point. Once more, Barthian ideas and language saturate his analysis:

We begin with the fact of God's revelation in Jesus Christ, that is with the self-revelation of God in an act which is Himself in action. Here we have three things to say of which Scripture tells in revelation.

  (a) Here we have GOD revealing Himself. We have an act in which GOD is the Subject, and as persistent Subject. That is so in all His acts and attributes, as we have seen.

  (b) We have here God REVEALING Himself THROUGH HIMSELF. That is to say we have an act in which God is the operator, the actor. God can only be known through Himself, because His Being is the I am that I am, the Being grounded in and through Himself . . .

  (c) But in this act of self-revelation, we have God revealing HIMSELF – here we have the object of the Subject to the Predicate – the Object of the Revelation of God which is Through God. This Object of the revelation is Jesus Christ our Lord.[80]

The verbal and conceptual dependence upon Barth at this point can be seen by noting the extent to which Torrance cites from or alludes to the first half-volume of Barth's *Church Dogmatics* in these lectures.[81]

Torrance's lectures on the Trinity and the doctrine of revelation were never published. While he was able to make use of much of the Auburn material relating to Christology and soteriology in his subsequent teaching career at Edinburgh, he was never permitted to lecture on the doctrine of God.

---

[79] Torrance, 'Christian Doctrine of God', 91.

[80] Torrance, 'Christian Doctrine of God', 92.

[81] Torrance, 'Christian Doctrine of God', 94, 96, 97, 101, 102, 106. Barth is the only theologian to be cited to any significant extent in this section of the lectures; Brunner is cited twice at 95. All the Barthian citations are from the German edition of the first half-volume of the *Church Dogmatics*, with one citation from *Credo* (106).

Torrance's interpretation of the significance of Barth

As we have seen, Torrance is to be seen as one who sought to introduce and interpret Barth's theology to the English-speaking world, as one who had himself found it deeply satisfying. Yet it was not until 1955 that Torrance directly addressed the topic of the significance of Karl Barth.[82] Up to that point, Torrance's works had tended to concentrate on issues relating to the history and theology of the Reformation, and a series of issues of relevance to the ecumenical movement. It is, of course, possible to argue that Barthian concerns lay behind some of these writings: for example, *Calvin's Doctrine of Man* can be seen as an attempt to clarify some of the issues attending the Barth–Brunner debate of 1934, in which the issue of Calvin-interpretation was of some importance.

Although Torrance's sympathy for Barth was well known, his published writings up to about 1955 do not reflect this with quite the clarity which one might expect. For example, we have noted how Torrance's 1941 Moot paper was widely interpreted as 'Barthian', although there is little within the paper that is explicitly or distinctively Barthian in character or tone. A label had been applied to Torrance, and it would remain with him for the remainder of his career. In practice, it is entirely proper to refer to Torrance in this manner, provided that the term is not understood to mean 'an uncritical disciple of Barth'. As we shall see, Torrance had the highest regard for Barth, while at the same time reserving the right to criticize where he felt that this was appropriate.

In his 1955 assessment of Barth, Torrance affirms that Barth 'is incontestably the greatest figure in modern theology since Schleiermacher, occupying an honoured position among the great élite of the church – Augustine, Anselm, Aquinas, Luther and Calvin'.[83] In view of later

[82] 'Karl Barth', *Expository Times* 66 (1955), 205–9. This is not to say that Barth is absent from the previous eighty-five published works; it is simply to point out that this was the first occasion on which Torrance chose to mention Barth's name explicitly in this manner. The occasion of this 1955 article was the publication of the first part-volume of the English translation of the *Church Dogmatics*, under the editorial direction of Torrance and G. W. Bromiley in 1956. Torrance entered into a brief published debate with Professor Brand Blanshard in 1952 over the latter's attack on 'The Theology of Crisis', as reported in *The Scotsman*, (9 April 1952). See Torrance, 'The Theology of Karl Barth' (14 April), 4; Blanshard's reply (16 April), 6; Torrance again (19 April), 6; Blanshard (22 April), 6; Torrance again (23 April), 6; Blanshard (30 April), 6. These brief pieces were polemic in tone and intent, and cannot be seen as sources for a definitive statement of Torrance's early views on Barth, despite the manner in which they are used by Bruce L. McCormack, *Karl Barth's Critically Realistic Dialectical Theology*, 4–5 n. 10.

[83] 'Karl Barth', 205. Later in the article, he narrows this group down to Anselm, Calvin and Schleiermacher: 208. Later still (209), he stresses that Barth stands in the tradition of Calvin.

developments, it is pertinent to note that Athanasius is not mentioned. In effect, Torrance identifies those whom he regards as the leading theological lights of the Christian church, and indicates that Barth is to be allowed a place of honour among them.

Torrance argues that Barth's 'comprehensive grasp and wrestling with the whole history of Christian thought makes him essentially a catholic theologian'.[84] Barth is to be seen as belonging to the tradition of Christian theology as a whole, rather than simply functioning as a leader of a new movement of thought. This point is important in relation to Torrance's agenda, in that it indicates the necessity and propriety of engaging with Barth as part of the great tradition of Christian theology. For Torrance, one of Barth's more significant achievements was to rescue the theological heritage of John Calvin from the scholasticism of his later followers, and give it a new lease of life.[85]

It is not accurate to see Torrance as someone who attempted to transplant a fundamentally German-language theology to Great Britain, particularly Scotland. Had not Scottish theology benefitted from its interaction with Calvin, through Knox? Torrance clearly has a strong sense of the existence of a distinctive Scottish Reformed theological tradition, nourished from a number of continental sources (such as Calvin and, later, Barth) yet retaining its distinctive Scottish identity.[86] Torrance's constant reference, virtually universally positive, to the personal influence and positive teachings of Scottish writers such as Hugh Ross Mackintosh, must serve as a reminder that Torrance saw himself as continuing and representing a distinctively 'Scottish voice' in modern theology. That voice may well have developed its resonance through interaction with other traditions and approaches; nevertheless, Torrance clearly saw Scotland as being heir to a distinct theological tradition, which merited continuing development. Torrance himself does not use this analogy, yet it is impossible to overlook the possibility that Torrance is to Barth what Knox is to Calvin.

At this early stage, Torrance identifies four broad areas in which Barth has made a signal contribution to modern theology:

[84] 'Karl Barth', 205.

[85] This did not endear Torrance to those who felt that Reformed scholasticism was in itself an admirable thing, and an entirely legitimate expression of Calvin's thought. See, for example, the hostile and dismissive critique of Torrance's assessment of Barth by Richard A. Muller, 'The Barth Legacy: New Athanasius or Origen Redivivus? A Response to T. F. Torrance', *Thomist* 54 (1990), 673–704.

[86] See his 'From John Knox to John McLeod Campbell: A Reading of Scottish Theology', in Wright and Badcock, *Disruption to Diversity*, 1–28; *Scottish Theology, from John Knox to John McLeod Campbell*. Edinburgh: T&T Clark, 1996.

1. In relation to the 'whole nature of theology' as a discipline, particularly in relation to setting out the scientific nature of theology and grounding it securely in Scripture.

2. In providing a 'far more adequate account of the person and work of Christ than we have known for centuries'.

3. In allowing the ecumenical dimension of theology to be rediscovered. (During the 1950s, Torrance was heavily engaged in ecumenical discussions (see pp. 94–8), and this aspect of Barth's theology appears to have been particularly important to him at this time.)

4. In his emphasis on 'the new humanity in Jesus Christ Incarnate, Crucified and Risen'. Torrance here stresses the importance of the concept of 'physical resurrection' as part of the Christian hope.[87]

No uncritical admirer of Barth, Torrance notes his apparent failure to deal adequately with 'the doctrine of a living union with Jesus Christ'.[88] In response to Torrance's suggestion, Barth included an account of the theme of 'union with Christ' within §71, dealing with 'the vocation of man'.[89] We may here sense a strong echo of the concern of Hugh Ross Mackintosh for this theological theme, which he regarded as essential to a full-blooded Christology.[90]

Our concern in this study is particularly with the manner in which Torrance addresses the relation of the natural sciences and theology. It may therefore be helpful to focus on the manner in which Torrance found Barth to be a particularly significant positive theological stimulus to this dialogue. Two aspects of Barth's theology may be regarded as being of especial importance:

1. His emphasis on theology as a discipline with its own distinct methodology, imposed upon it by virtue of the specific nature of its subject matter.

2. His rejection of epistemological dualism.

Each of these points merits further discussion, which we shall provide in what follows.

---

[87] 'Karl Barth', 208–9.

[88] 'Karl Barth', 209. For a later formulation of these and other criticisms, see *Karl Barth: Biblical and Evangelical Theologian*, 131–3.

[89] See *Church Dogmatics* IV/3.2, 481–680. The theme is discussed at 539–40.

[90] Redman, 'Participatio Christi'.

Theology as a science

We may open our discussion of this point by considering the debate between Barth and Heinrich Scholz over whether, and in what manner, theology could be considered to be a science.[91] (At this point we should note that the German term *Wissenschaft*, widely translated as 'science', is perhaps better translated as 'discipline', due to the tendency on the part of English-speaking readers to equate 'science' with '*natural* science'.) For Scholz, the 'scientific' (*wissenschaftlich*) status of a subject was essentially determined logically in terms of the methods which it applied, which required to take the form of an axiomatic and deductive approach, based upon clearly formulated propositions. For Barth, the scientific status of a subject was determined by the peculiar nature of its subject, with the result that theology cannot be judged on the basis of criteria which might be appropriate in other disciplines, precisely because their subject-matter differed radically from that of theology.[92]

For Torrance, Barth thus views theology as a science which 'elaborates a method only in the actualization of knowledge'. In other words, it does not set out with a predetermined or preconceived understanding of 'method', but allows its subject-matter to determine that method. As Torrance states this principle:

> The fundamental principle that I have been concerned with is a very simple one, but its implications are deep and far-reaching when worked out consistently over the whole range of human knowledge. We know things in accordance with their natures, or what they are in themselves; and so we let the nature of what we know determine for us the content and form of our knowledge.[93]

This insight – which Torrance develops with particular rigour in his *Theological Science* – must be regarded as of fundamental importance to our study, and will be explored in considerably greater detail later in this work (see pp. 209–11).

At this stage, however, it is important to note that Torrance argues that this approach is due to Barth. In a careful study of Barth's concept of 'dogmatic science', and particularly his view on the distinctive nature of theological inquiry, Torrance sets out his view that each science must

[91] See Heinrich Scholz, 'Wie ist eine evangelische Theologie als Wissenschaft möglich?', *Zwischen den Zeiten* 9 (1931), 8–53.

[92] See the discussion in *Church Dogmatics* I/1, 7–9.

[93] *The Ground and Grammar of Theology*. Charlottesville, VA: University of Virginia Press; Belfast: Christian Journals, 1980, 8.

proceed *kata physin* (that is, according to the nature of its subject), before tracing this approach to Barth:

> All scientific activity is one in which the reason acts strictly and precisely in accordance with the nature of its object, and so lets the object prescribe for it both the limits within which it may be known and the mode of rationality that is to be adopted toward it ... This is precisely the procedure which Barth adopted in scientific dogmatics – as we can see very clearly in his brilliant interpretation of Anselm's theological method, and in the way in which he has worked out his own epistemology in strict obedience to the nature of the concrete object of theological knowledge, God come to us in Jesus Christ ... The procedure common to theological science and all other genuine science is one in which the mind of the knower acts in strict conformity to the nature of what is given, and refuses to take up a standing in regard to it prior to actual knowledge or in abstraction from actual knowledge.[94]

The rejection of dualism

As we have seen, Torrance initially located Barth in a theological tradition which stretched back to Augustine. In 1962, however, we can discern shifts beginning to take place which reflect a growing concern over the issue of dualism, and increasing suspicion over the nature of Augustine's approach to theology. In an extended introduction to a collection of Barth's early writings,[95] Torrance adds Athanasius to the list of theological giants, whose numbers must now include Barth.[96] This may seem a trivial point to note; nevertheless, it is actually of some importance, in that it relates to Torrance's perception that an unresolved epistemological dualism, whose roots could be discerned in Augustine, lay behind much western theology. Such a dualism was both improper in itself, and inhibited the dialogue with the post-Einsteinian natural sciences – which, for Torrance, deliberately eschewed such a dualist approach.

Initially, Barth's appeal to many British theologians (such as John McConnachie) concerned his emphasis on the primacy of revelation. However, it is clear that, while Torrance concurred with that emphasis, he came to regard Barth's views on the nature and substance of that revelation as being of considerable importance, not least in relation to the overcoming of an epistemological dualism which he discerned within western theology. Torrance's growing interest in the interaction of

---

[94] *Karl Barth: Biblical and Evangelical Theologian*, 67–8.
[95] 'Introduction' to Karl Barth, *Theology and Church, Shorter Writings 1920–1928*. London: SCM Press, 1962, 7–54.
[96] 'Introduction', 7.

Christian theology and the natural sciences, particularly linked with his understanding of the development of Christian theology, led him to the view that much western Christian theology was grounded upon dualist foundations. Torrance argued that the traditional form of natural theology was an excellent example of a theological discipline which both rested upon and reflected this dualism (see pp. 188–92).

Increasingly, Torrance came to identify a group of theologians who developed a unitary approach to the Christian faith, and especially the question of the relation between God and the world. For Torrance, a telltale sign of such forms of dualism was the positing of a distinction between 'God' and 'revelation'. Torrance found in Athanasius, Calvin and Barth a group of writers who espoused such a unitary approach. It is important to notice that Augustine, who features prominently in Torrance's earlier lists of theological luminaries, begins to slip away from favour, precisely because of Torrance's growing conviction that his theology rested on unacceptable dualist assumptions.

Thus Torrance argues that Irenaeus, Athanasius, Cyril of Alexandria and others maintained a unitary approach to theology at a time when Alexandrian theological culture, under Arian influence, was inclined to dualism. This point is made particularly clearly in the conclusion of *Theological Science* (1969), in which Torrance notes the unitary nature of God's being and acts:

> Dogmatic thinking arises from the fact that God has acted in human history in a final and saving way, and that what He has given us in His revelation is Himself, His own divine being: His Being in His Act; His Act in His Being.[97]

For Torrance, this fundamental insight is safeguarded Christologically, and expressed in the concept of the *homoousion*, a point made with particular clarity in the essay 'The Logic and Analogic of Biblical and Theological Statements in the Greek Fathers'.[98] Nicene theology, which Torrance believes to be essential to a right understanding of the relation of Christian theology and the natural sciences, is seen as something which was articulated by Athanasius and safeguarded by Calvin and Barth.

In contrast, Torrance argued that Augustine developed a dualist approach, which led to serious imbalances in his own theology, and the medieval theological heritage which was grounded upon it. It is therefore important to note that, in his assessment of Calvin, Torrance tends to

[97] Torrance, *Theological Science*, London: Oxford University Press, 1969, 343.
[98] Torrance, 'The Logic and Analogic of Biblical and Theological Statements in the Greek Fathers', in *Theology in Reconstruction*. London: SCM Press, 1965, 30–45, especially 34–7.

stress his indebtedness to Greek patristic theology, rather than the more customary tendency to stress his Augustinian roots. In his essay 'Karl Barth and the Latin Heresy',[99] Torrance identifies a trend in western theology, which he traces back to Tertullian and Augustine, which 'abstracted knowledge of God from its objective ground in his self-revelation'. This inevitably leads to theology being understood as 'a set of doctrinal propositions abstracted from the substance of the faith and systematically connected together'.

Torrance argues that this dualist tendency can be seen clearly both in the Catholic scholasticism of the Middle Ages and the Protestant scholasticism of the post-Reformation era. Calvin, in Torrance's view, was able to break free from it; his followers, however, lapsed into dualist scholastic modes of thought shortly afterwards.[100] Barth's genius was to recover the integrity of divine revelation as the *self-revelation of God*, avoiding the dualist tendency to speak and think of that revelation in abstractive formal relations. Barthian slogans such as 'God reveals himself as Lord' and 'God himself is the content of his revelation' are seen by Torrance as representing a strategic recovery of the unitary foundation of theology. From about 1965 onwards, it is clear that Torrance comes to regard Barth's permanent significance as lying in his recovery of the epistemological significance of the *homoousion*. There is thus a direct link, in Torrance's view, between Athanasius, Calvin and Barth in this matter.

Torrance illustrates this in a number of manners, especially in his 1986 essay 'Karl Barth and Patristic Theology'.[101] Here, Torrance notes how both Calvin and Barth draw heavily on an Athanasian heritage. One example will illustrate the general tenor of Torrance's analysis. One of Barth's most striking and oft-repeated phrases is that revelation is *Deus loquentis persona*, 'God speaking as a person'.[102] Torrance points out (correctly) that this phrase is due to Calvin, who deploys it in his analysis of the nature of God's revelation in Scripture.[103] Torrance then argues that

---

[99] Torrance, 'Karl Barth and the Latin Heresy', *Scottish Journal of Theology* 39 (1986), 461–82.

[100] See further Torrance, 'The Deposit of Faith', *Scottish Journal of Theology* 36 (1983), 1–28. This aspect of Torrance's evaluation of Barth has been vigorously resisted by those who hold that Reformed Orthodoxy does not require correction at this point. For example, see Richard A. Muller's rather intemperate and muddled criticism of Torrance in 'Barth Legacy'. For Muller's own views on the matter, see his 'Scholasticism Protestant and Catholic: Francis Turretin on the Object and Principles of Theology', *Church History* 55 (1986), 193–205.

[101] Torrance, 'Karl Barth and Patristic Theology', in *Theology beyond Christendom: Essays on the Centenary of the Birth of Karl Barth*, edited by John Thomson. Allison Park, PA: Pickwick Publications, 1986, 215–39.

[102] For example, see *Church Dogmatics* I/1, 304.

[103] See Calvin, *Institutes* I.vii.4.

Calvin's use of the phrase is a recognizable allusion to a section of Athanasius' *de incarnatione*.[104] This suggestion might not meet with universal assent, although it must be stressed that it is known that Calvin had a high regard for Athanasius' treatise on this subject. The point that Torrance is making is clear: there is a direct continuity (both verbal and substantial) between Athanasius, Calvin and Barth, which is of central importance to the interaction of theology and the natural sciences.

It will therefore be clear that the question of the nature of revelation, especially in relation to its Christological foundations, is of critical importance to Torrance, and plays a major role in relation to his understanding of, for example, the significance of Karl Barth, the value of the Athanasian tradition, the place of natural theology, and particularly the relation of Christian theology and the natural sciences. It is therefore imperative that we turn directly to consider Torrance's understanding of the nature of revelation, which forms the substance of the following chapter.

[104] Athanasius, *de incarnatione* 3.

CHAPTER 7

Revelation and Salvation: The Place of Jesus Christ in Christian Theology

IN the previous chapter, we noted Torrance's pivotal role in relation to
English-language Barth-reception. Yet it is quite improper to regard
Torrance as some slavish imitator of Barth. It is widely agreed that
Torrance's significance lies in the creative interpretation and application,
not simply of Barth's approach to theology, but of the broader 'great
tradition' of which Barth is a recent representative. Perhaps this is at its
clearest in relation to the issue of the nature of revelation, which forms
the substance of the present chapter.

Yet while Torrance is rightly to be seen as standing within a firmly
Barthian tradition, he has developed that tradition in a manner of
considerable importance for the issue of a 'scientific theology'. Torrance
may be regarded as having restored natural theology to its traditional
place within Reformed theology, while at the same time taken seriously
the objections which Barth raised against it.

Early views: the Auburn Lectures

Torrance spent the academic year 1938–9 teaching at Auburn Theological
Seminary in New York State (see pp. 47–56). His lectures for this period
indicate a strong interest in the issue of revelation, and map out a coherent
approach to the issue in which can be discerned many of the themes
which feature prominently in his later works.

147

Torrance opens his lecture series 'The Christian Doctrine of Revelation' with a vigorous defence of its necessity. Unless God tells us who he is and what he is like, we cannot hope to have access to this knowledge. We are dependent upon God to speak to us, to break the silence and draw aside the veil so that we may behold what lies beyond it.

> Our knowledge of God is one given to us by God himself in an act of self-communication. He speaks, and breaks the silence; He draws away the clouds of heaven and reveals to us His heart, or rather he comes down through the veil out of His eternal sanctuary and manifests himself to us in our world and in our word.[1]

The opening sections of the lecture course clarify the meaning of the concept of 'revelation', and indicate its necessity for a Christian dogmatics. Revelation forces us to think a posteriori rather than a priori, in that we are obligated to respond to God's prior self-revelation. Revelation is about God graciously willing to be known, so that authentic human knowledge of God is not to be compared to a Prometheus, snatching the secrets of the gods. Torrance thus approvingly cites Hugh Ross Mackintosh's dictum: 'A religious knowledge of God, wherever existing, comes by revelation; otherwise we should be committed to the incredible position that a man can know God without His willing to be known'.[2]

Torrance then moves on to deal with the question of the 'possibility of revelation'.[3] If God is to reveal himself to us, then this 'must be through a presentation of God Himself to us'. Appealing to the fundamental Athanasian principle that only God can reveal God, Torrance insists that 'nothing else will suffice for a revelation of God than God Himself'. There is a fundamental gulf between God and humanity, which can only be bridged from God's side by God. If the living God is to be known, then it must be through an *act of God*. 'We cannot know God except *through* His acts, except *by* His acts, except *in* His acts.' Yet creation can be regarded as an act of God. Does this therefore legitimate a natural theology? Developing this point further, Torrance argues that revelation consists of an act 'in which God reveals *Himself* to us'.

> We must, therefore, hold these two points together in a single thought: namely, that we must know God through His acts, and yet we must know the Personal Being of God, for nothing else will convey Him. No! not even an act of creation,

for creation is as such an act in which something distinct from God is brought into existence. That means therefore that we can only know God in an ACT in which HIS ACT AND PERSON are IDENTICAL, in which God's presence, personal presence, is present in His act, in which the act is the Person and the Person is the Act.

It therefore follows that 'nothing but God Himself in Person will suffice to bridge the gulf between man and God'. Creation and providence alike are to be seen as acts of God in which 'God does not actually convey Himself'.

The question now becomes: what act are we talking about? Torrance opens his discussion of this question by stressing that, if we are to be confronted with an act of God, this must take place in human history and in terms of human culture and language. God must enter into our situation if he is to impart and communicate himself.

> If revelation is really to be revelation to man, fallen and historical man, then it must actually come to him in his ruined situation and come in terms of his ideas and language ... In other words, the Word of God to come across to men must come down to their level and become human, for it would be by becoming human that it could take upon itself all the ideas and language of men in which they converse and think. This is the great Christian doctrine of the Incarnation – of the Word becoming flesh, of the Word who was in the beginning with God and who was God and through whom all things were created that were created becoming flesh and tabernacling among men – in Jesus Christ our Lord.[4]

It is this 'inhomination of God' which makes possible human speech and thought concerning God, and which leads to the formulation of the doctrine of the Trinity.

Torrance's analysis of the doctrine of the Trinity in the Auburn Lectures opens by stressing the interconnectedness of the doctrine of revelation with the doctrine of the Trinity, in a manner which faithfully echoes Barth's concerns in *Church Dogmatics* I/1:

> Here we come to that section of the doctrine of God which may be said to be the distinctively Christian doctrine – for it is private to Christianity alone, and has only appeared in philosophical accounts so far as they have been borrowed from Christian theology, for example, as we have it in Plotinus, Proclus or Hegel. But while formally this is the distinctive element in the Christian doctrine as compared with the other so-called doctrines of God, it is *the* Christian doctrine itself, and upon which all the Christian teaching of God is

---

[4] Torrance, 'Christian Doctrine of Revelation', 33–4.

founded. It is the basis and presupposition of the Revelation of God: and when we ask who God is who reveals himself, we must answer, the Triune God, the God who reveals himself as Father, Son and Holy Ghost.[5]

In the doctrine of the Trinity, we speak of a God who reveals and redeems; a God who acts, and whose being may be known in and through those acts. God reveals himself through himself – that is, God [the Father] reveals himself [the Son] through himself [the Holy Spirit].[6] The identity of the revealer with the revelation inevitably leads to the discernment of a trinitarian structure to that revelation; yet the discernment of that structure within the *ordo cognoscendi* is posterior to its prior existence within the *ordo essendi*. As the process of distinguishing between 'the one who reveals' and 'the one who is revealed' proceeds, the trinitarian structure of both the revealer and revelation can be discerned. Although Torrance moves on to address certain specific aspects of the doctrine (such as the relation between *persona* and *hypostasis*),[7] it is clear that his primary interest is the exploration of the nexus of the doctrines of revelation and the Trinity. It is the grounds of the doctrine, rather than its specific conceptualities, which occupy his attention at this stage. Yet Torrance's thinking on the foundations of the doctrine of the Trinity would continue to develop throughout his career. The nature and extent of this development is perhaps best seen by considering his later analysis of the foundations of the doctrine of the Trinity, in which a Barthian emphasis on the theological linkage between the Trinity and revelation is subtly transformed into something much more comprehensive. We shall consider this at the appropriate point in our analysis of his trinitarian theology (p. 167).

The Auburn Lectures date from an early stage in Torrance's career. Nevertheless, they set out a remarkably coherent approach to the theme of revelation which established the framework within which Torrance would work for the remainder of his career. The strong criticism of human attempts to find and represent God unaided are set alongside a positive understanding of revelation in Christ. Torrance makes reference to Barth in the course of this presentation; it is, however, the Barth of the first two half-volumes of the *Church Dogmatics*, rather than the more iconoclastic critic of the Romans commentary, that we encounter. Revelation is affirmed in strongly positive terms, and firmly anchored to Jesus Christ, and the biblical witness to him.

---

[5] Torrance, 'Christian Doctrine of God', 90.
[6] Torrance, 'Christian Doctrine of God', 92–3.
[7] Torrance, 'Christian Doctrine of God', 107–11.

The Christological foundations of revelation

It will be clear from the analysis of the Auburn Lectures on revelation that Torrance regards revelation as being Christologically grounded. In Christ, we find God entering into the world of human life and language in a form which is adapted to human intelligibility (the theme of 'accommodation', so important for Calvin, can clearly be discerned here).[8] For Torrance, this 'accommodation' is not some human invention, but is grounded in God's gracious decision to reveal himself in this manner.

> Clearly, for the eternal Word of God to become understandable and communicable in the mode and character of word to man, he had to share to the full in the space–time distinctions and connexions of human existence in this world, and operate within the finite conditions of created rationality. This is not to say, of course, that he ceased to be the Word he is in the Creator, but rather that he appropriated human form within the frame of earthly life and action and speech in such a way as to take up the frail and finite conditions of the creature into himself ... In Jesus Christ the Word has become a physical event in space–time, meets us in the indissoluble connection of physical and spiritual existence, and is to be understood within the co-ordinate levels of created rationality.[9]

God has thus condescended to be known as he is in himself. No disjunction can be accepted between God as he is in himself and as he is in his self-revelation.

The importance of the *homoousion* for Torrance's understanding of theological history can be seen from his 1964 essay 'A New Reformation'.[10] In this essay, Torrance set out the importance of the *homoousion* for two great epochs in church history – the patristic period and the Reformation. Torrance argues that a number of unbiblical assumptions crept into Christian thinking during the first few centuries. The two assumptions which Torrance identifies as being of particular importance are:

1. God does not intervene in the world of space and time, in that God is immutable and changeless.

2. The Word of God revealed in Christ is not grounded in the eternal being of God, but is detached and separated from him. For this reason, it is changeable.

---

[8] For the theme in Calvin, see Ford Lewis Battles, 'God Was Accommodating Himself to Human Capacity', *Interpretation* 31 (1977), 19–38.

[9] Torrance, *God and Rationality*. London: Oxford University Press, 1971, 142.

[10] Torrance, 'A New Reformation?', *The London Holborn and Quarterly Review* 189 (1964), 275–94.

Both these assumptions, for example, could be argued to lie behind Arianism. One of the tasks of Christian theology was therefore to eliminate these dualist assumptions.

For Torrance, the doctrine of the *homoousion* – 'the doctrine that Jesus Christ as the Word and Son of God belongs to the divine side of reality, and is himself very God come into our world to redeem and recreate us' – offered a critically important corrective to these trends. Without the *homoousion*, Torrance argues, it would have to be concluded that 'all Christian imagery and conceptuality of God are essentially correlative to creaturely existence, and have no objective truth in God corresponding to them'.

There is, then, no difficulty in the assertion that Christology was of central importance to the patristic theological debates. At this point, a difficulty might seem to arise. The Reformation, as is well known, focused on a series of major issues, soteriological and ecclesiological – yet not Christological. Christology was not a subject of major debate, either between the Protestant Reformers and their Catholic opponents, or between individual Reformers. This would, at least at first sight, raise some serious difficulties for Torrance's view of the importance of the *homoousion*.

Torrance is aware of this line of criticism, and meets it in a number of ways. First, he notes that the Reformation revived the 'central relation of Christ to the Holy Scriptures'. There can be no doubt that this theme was of major importance to Luther and Calvin. As Luther put it, Christ is 'the mathematical point of Holy Scripture',[11] just as Scripture 'is the swaddling clothes and manger in which Christ is laid'.[12] John Calvin made a similar point: 'This is what we should seek ... throughout the whole of Scripture: to know Jesus Christ truly, and the infinite riches which are included in him and are offered to us by God the Father.'[13]

Torrance further argues that the patristic and Reformation periods may be seen as applying the *homoousion* in different respects; the patristic

[11] *D. M. Martin Luthers Werke. Kritische Gesamtausgabe: Tischreden.* Vol. 2. Weimar: Böhlau, 1883– , 439.

[12] *D. M. Martin Luthers Werke. Kritische Gesamtausgabe: Deutsche Bibel.* Vol. 8. Weimar: Böhlau, 1883– , 12.

[13] *Ioannis Calvini opera quae supersunt omnia.* 59 vols. Brunschweig and Berlin: Schwetschke, 1863–1900, vol. 9, 815. There are some thoughtful explorations of related themes to be found in John D. Morrison, 'John Calvin's Christological Assertion of Word Authority in the Context of Sixteenth Century Ecclesiological Polemics', *Scottish Journal of Theology* 45 (1993), 465–86. For the Christocentric orientation of the Reformation doctrine of Scripture in general, see J. K. S. Reid, *The Authority of Scripture.* New York: Harper & Row, 1957, 29–72; Brian A. Gerrish, 'The Word of God and the Words of Scripture: Luther and Calvin on Biblical Authority', in *The Old Protestantism and the New.* Chicago: University of Chicago Press, 1982, 51–68.

period saw it being applied in the area of Christology, whereas the Reformation saw it being applied in the area of soteriology. The 'Act of God in his Being' is thus to be set alongside the 'Being of God in his Act'.

> The fathers of the early church were concerned in the *homoousion* to assert the belief that when God communicates himself to us in Christ it is none other than God himself in his own divine Being that is revealed. The fathers of the Reformation were concerned to apply the *homoousion* to salvation in Christ, insisting that when God gives himself to us it is none other than God himself who is at work. God himself is active in his saving gifts and benefits – that is to say, they applied the *homoousion* to the doctrine of *grace* ... Grace is none other than Christ, God communicating himself to us, the unconditional and sovereignly free self-giving of God the Lord and Saviour of men.

Torrance thus argues that the two Reformation doctrines of justification by grace and predestination (or election) may be regarded as representing a recognition that 'in all our relations with God, in thinking and acting we have to reckon with the absolute priority of God'.

In this discussion of the Reformation, it is important to note that Torrance studiously avoids representing the Reformation as a recovery of 'Augustinianism'. For many theologians in the Reformed tradition, this would have been a perfectly acceptable way of viewing the Reformation.[14] Torrance, however, regards 'Augustinianism' as being tainted with the spectre of a dualism between God and the world (see p. 143), especially in relation to God and revelation. Where others, for example, stressed the continuity between Calvin and Augustine,[15] Torrance chooses to place the emphasis upon Calvin's positive relationship with Greek patristic Christianity[16] – for example, noting that the 'predominating patristic influence' on Calvin must be understood to be Chrysostom's biblical expositions and commentaries.[17] Similarly, Torrance argues that whereas Luther's doctrine of union with Christ was heavily influenced by Augustine, Calvin's owes its distinctive shape to Cyril of Alexandria. We shall return to this matter in our discussion of Torrance's natural theology, at which point the issue of dualism becomes particularly pressing (see p. 192).

---

[14] See, for example, the analysis of Benjamin B. Warfield, *Calvin and Augustine*. Philadelphia: Presbyterian and Reformed Publishing Co., 1956, especially the *dictum* 'The Reformation, inwardly considered, was just the ultimate triumph of Augustine's doctrine of grace over Augustine's doctrine of the church' (322).

[15] See the careful study of Luchesius Smits, *Saint Augustin dans l'oeuvre de Jean Calvin*. Assen: Van Gorcum, 1957.

[16] See, for example, his argument that Calvin's theology of the Trinity draws heavily on that of Gregory of Nazianzus: *Trinitarian Perspectives: Toward Doctrinal Agreement*. Edinburgh: T&T Clark, 1994, 21–40.

[17] See Torrance, 'Karl Barth and Patristic Theology'.

Torrance's analysis of the application of the *homoousion* in Christology and soteriology naturally brings us to consider his approach to these areas of theology in more detail.

The relation of Christology and soteriology

One of the most distinctive features of Christian theology since the nineteenth century has been the recognition that it is not possible to separate Christology and soteriology into two neat watertight compartments, which may be considered in isolation from each other. Thus in his *Christian Faith*, Schleiermacher had pointed out the close connection between the 'natural heresies' of Christianity, two of which were soteriological, and two Christological.[18] In the 1870s, Albrecht Benjamin Ritschl had argued for the inseparability of the two disciplines on essentially Kantian grounds, in that something can be known only in terms of its impact upon us. In the 1880s, Charles Gore pointed out the close connection between deficient Christologies and soteriologies, concluding that 'the Nestorian Christ is the fitting Saviour of the Pelagian man'.[19] Paul Tillich had famously declared that 'Christology is a function of soteriology'.[20] Wolfhart Pannenberg had also noted the close connection, while wishing to retain an emphasis on the need to ground Christology in history, rather than in soteriology: 'A separation between Christology and soteriology is not possible, because in general the soteriological interest, the interest in salvation, in the *beneficia Christi*, is what causes us to ask about the figure of Jesus.'[21]

Torrance's reflections on the relation of the person and work of Christ are thus to be set against a background of theological reflection which encouraged the recognition and affirmation of a close link between the two areas of theology. Nevertheless, Torrance's approach to the subject rests upon quite distinct grounds, which reflect his fundamental theological convictions. For Torrance, Christology and soteriology are held together in an inseparable unity by the fact that each is grounded in and articulates the *homoousion*. We can illustrate this by the way in which

---

[18] Friedrich Schleiermacher, *The Christian Faith*. Edinburgh: T&T Clark, 1928, 98–9.

[19] Charles Gore, 'Our Lord's Human Example', *Church Quarterly Review* 16 (1883), 282–313 (298).

[20] Paul Tillich, *Systematic Theology*. 3 vols. London: SCM Press, 1978, vol. 2, 150. See also the discussion at 168–70.

[21] Wolfhart Pannenberg, *Jesus – God and Man*. London: SCM Press; Philadelphia: Westminster Press, 1968, 38–9. Pannenberg's concern here is to refute the anti-historical tendencies he discerned within Tillich's approach.

Torrance argues that Barth used Greek patristic ideas to 'redress the theology of the Reformation by bringing to light the essential inner connection between revelation and reconciliation'.[22] Torrance's argument involves the positing of a fundamental connection between revelation and grace in terms of the self-imparting of the divine reality. Torrance finds Barth making this point in an essay of 1934 on the theme of revelation, in which Barth draws a parallel between the theological debates of the fourth and sixteenth centuries:

> Revelation is God himself! Twice the Christian church was compelled to contend for the victory of this knowledge. The first time it was in the fourth century when the doctrine of the Trinity was at stake, i.e., the acknowledgement of the essential deity of Jesus Christ and the Holy Spirit. In consummating this acknowledgement in a dogma, the church gave expression to this: exactly in believing revelation, the church believes God himself... The second battle for this same truth was fought in the sixteenth century, when the Reformation doctrine of free grace was at stake. The reformers were concerned about a right understanding of the justification of the sinner. They contended that it was an act in which the gift which is bestowed on the sinner is identical with the giver of the gift.[23]

Barth here clearly sees a direct parallel between the Christological and soteriological conflicts of the fourth and sixteenth centuries, with the common theme being the self-impartation of God in revelation and reconciliation.[24]

Torrance thus argues that Barth is able to establish the essential inner connection between revelation and reconciliation by grounding each in the *homoousion*.

> The application of the *homoousion* to the Word made flesh means that the Word of God embodied in Jesus Christ is identical with the Word in the eternal being of God: God the eternal Word is the actual content of his revealed Word to us in Jesus Christ and his gospel ... The application of the *homoousion* to the grace of God means that grace is to be understood as the impartation to us not of an impersonal something (an *aliquid*) from God, but of God himself. In Jesus Christ and in the Holy Spirit God freely gives himself to us in such a living personal way that the gift and the giver are one and the same and cannot be detached from each another.[25]

---

[22] See Torrance, 'Karl Barth and Patristic Theology'.

[23] Karl Barth, 'Revelation', in *God in Action*. Edinburgh: T&T Clark, 1936, 3–19 (13–14).

[24] This theme would be developed still further in Torrance's elaboration of the significance of the doctrine of the Trinity. See in particular *Christian Doctrine of God*, 144–7.

[25] 'Karl Barth and Patristic Theology.'

The role of the humanity of Christ in Torrance's doctrine of revelation and redemption should be noted. Torrance notes that, for Barth, the humanity of Christ reveals not only the saving act of God but also true knowledge of God within that saving act. Torrance thus points out that Dietrich Bonhoeffer must be thought of as an 'epistemological Apollinarian', in that he fails to establish a proper place for the humanity of Christ in his understanding of revelation.[26] A seminal element of Torrance's understanding of soteriology is that of the vicarious humanity of Christ.[27] Although Torrance's understanding of the nature and grounds of salvation shows clear affinities with that of Calvin (particularly in relation to the theme of the sacrifice of Christ),[28] the dominant theological influence at this juncture is that of Athanasius.[29] Torrance expresses a concern that the forms of dualism which he discerns within strands of western theology has led to the doctrine of redemption being 'expounded in terms of external relations between Christ and sinful people'.[30] The radical distinction between the person and the works of Christ, so typical of Protestant theology, is to be critiqued as a consequence of a dualism which should have no place in Christian theology.

Torrance finds in Athanasius an exemplary statement of an understanding of redemption which is grounded in a unitary understanding of the inner relations of Christ as mediator on the one hand, and Christ's external relationship with humanity on the other. Atonement does not involve an adjustment in the external relationships between Christ and humanity; it consists of a correlation and correspondence between Christ's flesh and ours, in that believers are incorporated into Christ through union with him.[31] In redemption, the Son of God 'appropriated from us our body and soul and made them his own', in order that we might be fully redeemed.

> [Athanasius] understood the humanity of Jesus Christ as the humanity of
> him who is not only Apostle from God but High Priest taken among men,
> and the saving work of Christ in terms of his *human* as well as his divine

[26] *Theological Science*, 292 n. 1.

[27] Christian D. Kettler, *The Vicarious Humanity of Christ and the Reality of Salvation*. Lanham, MD: University Press of America, 1991, 121–54.

[28] Torrance's emphasis on the high priestly role of Christ has important echoes in Calvin, particularly his commentary on Hebrews: see his comments on the 'reformation of the Roman mass' in *Conflict and Agreement in the Church*, II, 137–40.

[29] It must, of course, be noted that Calvin's soteriology has been influenced by Athanasius at points, so that an indirect Athanasian influence may derive from this route.

[30] *Theology in Reconciliation: Essays towards Evangelical and Catholic Unity in East and West*. London: Geoffrey Chapman, 1975, 230.

[31] For Torrance's discussion of this theme in Athanasius, see *Theology in Reconciliation*, 226–31.

agency – it is the human priesthood and the saving mediatorship of Jesus Christ in and through his human kinship with us that Athanasius found so significant.[32]

Torrance thus insists that there is an inseparable link between substitution and incorporation. Christ does not merely take our place as our representative in redemption; he incorporates us into himself. Christ's substitutionary bearing of human sin is not an external matter, but rests on the assumption of human nature.

> That is not something which takes place externally, as if he carried our infirmities and sins in some exterior way, for it took place in and with the Incarnation of the Son into our actual humanity where we suffer from corruption, slavery to sin, curse and death and divine judgement. That is to say, Athanasius sought to take with full seriousness the fact that Christ was 'made sin' and 'made a curse', the just for the unjust, and so bore upon himself and in himself for our sakes 'the whole inheritance of judgement that lay against us'.[33]

Torrance's insistence on the unitary structure of the doctrines of incarnation and atonement is perhaps best studied from the fifth chapter of *The Trinitarian Faith,* a lecture entitled 'The Incarnate Saviour' which was originally delivered at Princeton Theological Seminary in 1981, and a subsequent lecture (also delivered at Princeton Theological Seminary) in 1992.[34] Torrance stresses the manner in which Athanasius links the doctrines of incarnation and atonement. The incarnation, understood as 'an act of God *himself* in which he really became man, and took the whole nature of man upon himself',[35] thus undergirds the atoning work of Christ, in that 'the redemptive work of Christ was fully representative and truly universal in its range'.[36] By taking our human nature upon himself in the incarnation, God acts in Christ *instead of* and *in the place of* all humanity.

> Through his incarnation the Son of God has made himself one with us as we are, and indeed made himself what we are, thereby not only making our nature his own but taking on himself our lost condition subject to condemnation and death, all in order that he might substitute himself in our place, discharge our debt, and offer himself in atoning sacrifice to God on our behalf. Since sin and its judgement have affected the actual nature of death as we experience it,

---

[32] *Theology in Reconciliation*, 228.

[33] *Theology in Reconciliation*, 153.

[34] *Trinitarian Faith*, 146–90; 'Incarnation and Atonement in the Light of Modern Scientific Rejection of Dualism', in Torrance, *Preaching Christ Today*, 41–71.

[35] *Trinitarian Faith*, 150.

[36] *Trinitarian Faith*, 155.

Christ has made our death and fate his own, thereby taking on himself the penalty due to all in death, destroying the power of sin and its stronghold in death, and thus redeeming or rescuing us from its dominion.[37]

Torrance argues that the 'Nicene theology', characterized by its profound interlocking of creation and redemption, incarnation and atonement, thus offers a means of maintaining the central themes of the Christian faith, against distortions which were bound to emerge within the Hellenistic culture of the period.

It should also be noted that these lectures set Torrance's thinking on the identity and significance of Christ within the framework of a unitary mode of thought which refuses to acknowledge the dualism typical, in Torrance's view, of much western theology. Marcion's radical antithesis between the creator God and the redeemer God illustrates this dualism, as does Arius' conception of the manner in which the divine and the human 'relate to one another merely tangentially without in any way intersecting one another'. For Torrance, Einstein's unitary way of approaching nature was characterised by its integration of empirical and theoretical factors, so that ontology and epistemology are 'wedded together'. As noted above, precisely this same point is made at the theological level by the *homoousion*, which Torrance declares to have 'destroyed the epistemological and cosmological dualisms endemic in Hellenic culture'.[38]

It will thus be clear that Torrance regards the *homoousion* as providing the ontological foundation for Christian theology. As Torrance consistently affirms, epistemology is grounded ontologically; the entire Christian theological enterprise is thus securely anchored in the ontological reality of the incarnation. Yet this raises the whole question of the extent to which God can be known *remoto Christo*, to use the phrase deployed by Anselm of Canterbury in his *Cur Deus homo*. Torrance's insistence upon the ontological grounding of revelation naturally leads us to consider his understanding of the doctrine of the Trinity. We shall begin by considering some of the writers who influenced Torrance's thinking on this significant issue.

---

[37] *Trinitarian Faith*, 157.

[38] Torrance returns to this point in his discussion of the Trinity. Of particular importance is his concern to avoid any distinction between the 'economic' and 'essential' approaches to the Trinity: *Christian Doctrine of God*, 7 n. 16. He also suggests that the view that God can be known in his 'energies' but not in his 'being' (found, for example, in Gregory Palamas, but capable of being traced back to Maximus) reflects a similar dualism: *Trinitarian Perspectives*, 38 n. 69.

Influences on Torrance's approach to the Trinity

Every writer is influenced by others, whether they choose to concede this point or not. Torrance is quite clear that his thinking on the Trinity is heavily influenced by three individuals: Athanasius, Hugh Ross Mackintosh and Karl Barth.[39] In what follows, we shall consider the nature of those influences, and the light which they shed both on Torrance's trinitarian theology and his theological method in general.

However, it is important to note that Torrance's approach to the history of theology – especially the Alexandrian theology of the fourth century – is important in relation to a proper understanding of his theological method. Torrance does not approach the theology of either the patristic period or the Reformation from the perspective of one who regards such theology as ideas fashioned by the prevailing ideologies and intellectual fashions of the day. Rather, Torrance regards both periods – and supremely the theologies of Athanasius and Calvin – as a paradigmatically obedient response to the inner structure and logic of the Christian faith, which remains both a challenge and stimulus to contemporary theologizing. Such theologians of the past regarded theology as a response to reality, both in terms of its objective ontological constitution and its formal revelation in the Christian proclamation – to which theology is a proper and necessary response.

To study the theology of an Athanasius, for example, is thus to 'bring to light the inner theological connections which gave coherent structure to the classical theology of the ancient Catholic Church'.[40] Athanasius, Calvin and Barth, in different manners, were aiming to explicate and unfold the intellectual vision of the Christian faith, on the basis of the fundamental assumption that this faith was grounded in the bedrock of a reality which ultimately transcended human attempts to describe it, yet which was capable of being reflected faithfully in the terms and conceptualities of Christian theology. For Torrance, to study Athanasius or other representatives of the great tradition is thus to take upon oneself the task of engaging with the reality to which the Christian faith bears witness. It is to engage with a tradition which submitted itself to 'biblical patterns of thought governed by the Word of God and the obedient hearing of faith'.[41]

[39] *Christian Doctrine of God*, ix.
[40] *Trinitarian Faith*, 2.
[41] *Trinitarian Faith*, 69.

Athanasius

The high regard in which Torrance held Athanasius is evident at point after point in his theological analysis. For example, Torrance's careful exploration of the vicarious humanity of Christ clearly reflects Athanasian concerns and conceptualities. The central place which Torrance ascribes to the *homoousion* can also be argued to rest on Athanasian foundations, as can Torrance's vigorous rejection of any form of theological dualism, particularly in relation to the doctrines of revelation and redemption. It is therefore to be expected that Athanasius would prove a fertile source of theological stimulation to Torrance's discussion of the Trinity.[42]

Torrance regards Athanasius as adopting a scientific theological approach to the doctrine of the Trinity, in that his approach 'took its start and controlling norm from the revealing and saving acts of God'.[43] The doctrine of the Trinity is therefore a legitimate response to God's self-revelation in Christ, and is not to be regarded as an improper consequence of an inappropriate form of philosophical speculation. 'Athanasius set about trying to order theological understanding of the ways and acts of God in accordance with their proper principle (*arche*), as it becomes revealed to us in the Incarnation.'[44] It is particularly important to observe how Torrance stresses the role of the 'Nicene concept "of one being with the Father" (*homoousious to Patri*)', which is seen both as the foundation and criterion of trinitarian theology. The roots of the doctrine of the Trinity may thus be said to be Christological, in that its origins can be discerned as lying within the struggle to make sense of the significance of Christ in relation to God.

> It was to *theologia* of this kind that Athanasius assimilated the scientific method that had been developed in Alexandria, namely, rigorous knowledge according to the inherent structure or nature (*kata physin*) of the realities investigated, together with the development of the appropriate questions and the apposite vocabulary demanded by the nature of the realities as they become disclosed to us. It is in this way that theology adapts its method to its proper subject-matter, and allows its proper subject-matter to determine the appropriate forms of

[42] The major essay of 1974 on the theology of Athanasius should be noted in this context: 'Athanasius: A Reassessment of His Theology', *Abba Salama* 5 (1974), 171–87. Torrance deals with Athanasius' doctrine of God primarily in terms of the doctrine of creation, and engages with trinitarian vocabulary primarily in relation to the issue of the legitimacy of the use of non-biblical terms in theological discourse. While trinitarian issues are implicit throughout the essay, a full discussion of Athanasius' approach to the Trinity would not appear for a further decade: 'The Doctrine of the Holy Trinity according to St Athanasius', *Anglican Theological Review* (1987), 395–405.

[43] Torrance, *Trinitarian Perspectives*, 9.

[44] *Theology in Reconciliation*, 250.

thought and speech about God. So far as scientific theology is concerned, this means that we are forced to adapt our common language to the nature and reality of God who is disclosed in Jesus Christ, and even where necessary to coin new terms, to express what we thus apprehend.[45]

Torrance's understanding of Athanasius' role in formulating a scientific theological approach to the Trinity includes a number of elements which demand further discussion.

1. The doctrine of the Trinity is held to represent the proper outcome of an intellectual engagement with God *kata physin*. We can see here the foundational principle of Torrance's scientific theology being brought into play. For Athanasius, the nature of God was disclosed to be such that trinitarian thinking was the only appropriate response to the reality thus encountered. Torrance notes a similar type of scientific thinking in the eighth book of Clement of Alexandria's *Stromateis*. We shall explore this 'kataphysic' approach to theological science in more detail later (p. 209).

2. The realist assumptions of theological science allow direct correlations to be established between the self-revelation of God and God himself. 'What God is in the economy of his saving operations towards us in Jesus Christ he is antecedently and inherently and eternally in himself.'[46] Although Torrance uses Barthian revelational language at this point, he clearly regards precisely the same considerations to underlie Athanasius' wrestling with the revelational and soteriological implications of the *homoousion*.

3. Torrance notes how Athanasius is obliged to forge or justify the use of new theological terms, as a consequence of this intellectual engagement with the self-revelation of God.[47] Existing words have to be invested with additional or new meanings; at points, the conceptualities which result from an analysis of God's self-revelation demand new categories of ideas and words. Torrance notes that precisely the same processes can be discerned within the natural sciences.

The fundamental principle which underlies Athanasius' trinitarian theology at this point is, according to Torrance, to be seen at work both in later responsible Christian theology (such as that of Barth), and in the natural sciences themselves. Athanasius may predate the modern rise of

---

[45] *Theology in Reconciliation*, 241.
[46] *Theology in Reconciliation*, 253.
[47] *Theology in Reconciliation*, 242–51.

the natural sciences; yet his fundamental approach can be discerned as underlying them. The doctrine of the Trinity is thus not to be seen as a retreat into mysticism, or the outcome of intellectual speculation going far beyond the cautious language and conceptualities of Scripture. It is to be seen as the proper outcome of scientific engagement with the reality of God, as God is disclosed in Christ. In one sense, the doctrine of the Trinity is to be seen as the culmination of a scientific theology – not its contradiction.

It might be argued at this point that Torrance is retrospectively projecting the methods and concerns of scientific theology onto an Athanasius who was innocent of such notions. This concern must be taken seriously; for example, there is some risk of anachronism in suggesting that Athanasius was a 'scientific theologian', when a concern for theology *qua* science can be argued to be a later development. Yet it can be pointed out, in response to this objection, that precisely such notions had indeed been developed within the Alexandrian tradition by both *physikoi* and *theologikoi* from as early as the second century; furthermore, it can be argued that the writings of the sixth century thinker John Philoponos reflect such developed notions of 'science'.[48] Yet Torrance's point is, in any case, independent of the precise historical circumstances: Athanasius, he argues, insisted that God, like any other reality, had to be investigated and conceptualized in a manner and terms appropriate to his own nature.

It is important to note that Torrance suggests that some of the difficulties within the Orthodox view on the Trinity are to be traced, not to Athanasius, but to Basil of Caesarea.[49] The particular difficulty that Torrance identifies concerns the Cappadocian response to the charge of an implicit tritheism within their understanding of the Trinity. The Cappadocians met this charge partly by affirming the unity of God in terms of the Father as the one 'principle' or 'origin' and 'cause' of both Son and Spirit. This, according to Torrance, inevitably led to the conclusion that both the *existence* and the specific *mode of existence* of Son and Spirit were due to the Father. Torrance argues that this could not but lead to serious difficulties in relation to the question of the procession of the Spirit.[50]

---

[48] See Torrance, 'John Philoponos of Alexandria, Sixth Century Christian Physicist', *Texts and Studies.* vol. 2. London: Thyateira House, 1983, 261–5.

[49] See the careful analysis in *Trinitarian Faith*, 313–26.

[50] For the argument, see *Trinitarian Faith*, 313–20. Note particularly the suggestion that dualist assumptions (absent from Athanasius) were thus incorporated into the Cappadocian understanding of the relation of the Trinity to the world.

It will thus be clear that Torrance adopts a critical perspective on the Orthodox approach to the Trinity. The focus on Athanasius reflects Torrance's conviction that this writer develops a unitary conception of the Trinity, formulated in response primarily to soteriological and ontological considerations. It is not the eastern tradition in general which is to be commended, but a particular formulation of that tradition. Torrance is critical of the later development of that tradition (initially in Basil, but subsequently in Maximus the Confessor and Gregory Palamas).[51]

Hugh Ross Mackintosh

At first sight, it might seem strange for Torrance to include Hugh Ross Mackintosh among those who shaped his thinking on the Trinity. To put the matter in a somewhat pointed manner, Mackintosh never gave this particular doctrine his focused attention. Torrance attended Mackintosh's lectures on Christian dogmatics at New College during the academic year 1935–6. A careful study of Torrance's notes taken during those lectures indicates that the course focused on Christology and soteriology, with additional lectures devoted to such matters as the nature of revelation, the attributes of God, the doctrine of providence, and the nature of religion. The doctrine of the Trinity was not, in general, treated in this manner.[52]

In once sense, therefore, Torrance's specific views on the Trinity cannot be traced to Mackintosh. However, this is to fail to notice Mackintosh's persistent emphasis on the Christological basis of the Christian knowledge of God.[53] Although Mackintosh tended to present his incarnational theology primarily from a soteriological perspective, his Christology was rigorously ontological.[54] Where others chose to operate with psychological or ethical categories in their exploration of Christology, Mackintosh remained committed to ontological categories. As Torrance frequently pointed out, the *homoousion* can be discerned as playing a foundational

---

[51] Note his criticisms of the view (fully developed in Palamas) that God can be known in his 'energies' but not in his 'being': *Trinitarian Perspectives*, 38 n. 69.

[52] For an important exception, however, see the careful discussion of 'Christ and the Divine Trinity', in Mackintosh, *Doctrine of the Person of Jesus Christ*, 508–26.

[53] See Torrance, 'Hugh Ross Mackintosh'; Redman, 'H. R. Mackintosh's Contribution to Christology and Soteriology in the Twentieth Century'; Redman, 'Participatio Christi'.

[54] Mackintosh must be regarded as avoiding the dangers which Pannenberg rightly discerned as lurking within predominantly soteriological approaches to Christology: Wolfhart Pannenberg, *Jesus – God and Man*, 47–9. See further Torrance, 'Hugh Ross Mackintosh', 162–3; Alister E. McGrath, 'Christology and Soteriology: A Response to Wolfhart Pannenberg's Critique of the Soteriological Approach to Christology', *Theologische Zeitschrift* 42 (1986), 222–36.

role in Mackintosh's entire thinking on the identity of Christ and the nature of God.[55]

Furthermore, Torrance found in Mackintosh a clear statement of the interconnectedness of the being and action of God – an aspect of Torrance's thought which some have tended to attribute to Barth's influence, yet which has its roots in a work of Scottish theology published in 1912. For Torrance, Mackintosh

> used to insist that we hold inseparably together Christian conceptions of God *for us* and of God *in himself*, that is, conceptions of God that arise out of the evangelical pattern or economy of God's saving revelation in history and conceptions of God which are expressions in time of eternal personal distinctions in God. And so he steered a course in his lectures through any divergence between what are called notions of 'the economic Trinity' and notions of 'the immanent or ontological Trinity'.[56]

To note Mackintosh's influence at this point is not in any way to detract from the importance of Barth; it is rather to note that there already existed a theological tradition, indigenous to Scotland, which would prove a fertile ground for Barthian ideas when these began to take root in the 1930s.

Karl Barth

Barth is a major influence upon Torrance's trinitarianism, as he is for Torrance's theological reflection in general. Not only can Barth be given substantial credit for the rehabilitation of the doctrine of the Trinity in the twentieth century, he also contributed significantly to the substance of that doctrine. However, it would be quite wrong to suggest that Torrance is an uncritical or 'slavish' admirer of Barth; as we have seen, one of Torrance's most significant achievements has been the active development of the Barthian heritage to allow its active engagement with the natural sciences. Torrance singles out Barth's doctrine of the Trinity as one of the leading features of his theology, and it is appropriate to note what Torrance considers to be Barth's distinctive emphases.[57] We shall here note two themes which are clearly of importance to Torrance's positive exposition of this doctrine.

---

[55] Torrance, 'Hugh Ross Mackintosh', 163.

[56] *Christian Doctrine of God*, 7. The allusions are taken from Mackintosh, *Doctrine of the Person of Jesus Christ*, 512–15. This work should not be confused with a shorter study, published in the same year with a similar title: *The Person of Jesus Christ*. London: SCM Press, 1912.

[57] *Karl Barth: Biblical and Evangelical Theologian*, 118–20, 193–7. See also *Karl Barth: An Introduction to His Early Theology, 1910–1931*. London: SCM Press; New York: Harper & Row, 1962, 113–18.

The first point is that the foundations of the doctrine of the Trinity are not to be sought so much in explicit biblical statements on the matter, but primarily in the structure of the revelation to which Scripture bears witness. For Torrance, Barth locates the grounds of the doctrine of the Trinity in 'our actual knowledge of God mediated through Holy Scripture'. God himself is the content of his revelation – an insight (and verbal formula) which Torrance regularly repeats throughout his analysis of the doctrine of the Trinity. 'The one divine act of revelation is internally threefold: God is himself at once the Subject, Object and Predicate of revelation.'[58] Barth thus developed his doctrine of the Trinity through an analysis of the basic structure of divine revelation. This approach can be seen in Torrance's Auburn Lectures; it can also be discerned, although in a significantly modified form, in his later writings on the Trinity, in which soteriological considerations are also taken into account.

The second point of significance is Barth's distinctive emphasis on the relation of 'God's being in his act' and 'God's act in his being'. This theme is developed at a number of points in the Auburn Lectures, and is clearly seen by Torrance as of critical importance to the doctrine of the Trinity, not least on account of its implications for a unitary conception of theology.[59] Torrance discerns an identical theme in the writings of Athanasius, and regards this general principle as essential to responsible trinitarian reflection.

John Calvin

Torrance, as we have seen, singles out the three theologians noted above as being of particular importance in relation to his trinitarian theology. Yet it is fair to argue that Calvin may be regarded as playing a highly significant role for Torrance's thinking, not least on account of the way in which the Genevan writer can be seen as modelling an approach to the Trinity which is grounded in the insights and methods of the Reformation on the one hand, and yet which is sensitive to and appreciative of the insights of the Greek patristic tradition on the other.[60]

Torrance regards Calvin as being of particular importance in relation to the formulation of the doctrine of the Trinity in the context of the new concern for theological and doxological conformity to Scripture, which was so characteristic of the sixteenth-century Reformation. How could

---

[58] *Karl Barth: Biblical and Evangelical Theologian*, 118.

[59] *Karl Barth: Biblical and Evangelical Theologian*, 194–7.

[60] See the important comparison of Calvin with Gregory Nazianzen in *Trinitarian Perspectives*, 21–40.

the complex trinitarian vocabulary, which went far beyond the biblical idiom, be justified within the Reformed tradition? For Torrance, Calvin offered a judicious and positive response:

> Calvin will have nothing to do with a narrow biblicism that condemns the use of non-biblical words in the interpretation and explanation of what is attested by the Scriptures. Granted that we must allow the Scriptures to govern our thinking and speaking of God, that should not prevent us from explaining intricate and difficult biblical matters in clearer words, provided that they serve the truth of the Scripture devoutly and faithfully, and are used but sparingly and modestly.[61]

Christianity as a trinitarian faith

One of Torrance's greatest regrets is that he was unable to lecture on 'the doctrine of God' while Professor of Christian Dogmatics at Edinburgh. This area was deemed to be more philosophical in orientation, and had hence been treated as the territory of philosophical rather than dogmatic theologians. It was, however, an area in which Torrance took a keen interest from his student days onwards. A careful survey of Torrance's massive theological output shows that the doctrine of the Trinity is *explicitly* addressed only on a few occasions throughout his professional career until his retirement in 1979.[62] While it can be argued that Torrance's emphases on the priority of revelation and the importance of the incarnation can be understood to make implicit trinitarian claims, these are not explored explicitly or in detail until after Torrance's retirement from the Chair of Christian Dogmatics at Edinburgh.[63] Thereafter, what can only be described as a torrent of substantial studies appeared, culminating in the major studies *The Trinitarian Faith* (1988) and *The Christian Doctrine of God* (1996).[64]

The Trinitarian Faith can be regarded as a one-volumed dogmatics, setting out the leading themes of the Christian faith within a rigorously trinitarian framework. The dominant theological presence is that of Athanasius. While some might suggest that Athanasius has been read from a Barthian perspective, this must be viewed as a somewhat superficial

---

[61] *Trinitarian Perspectives*, 45.

[62] An important exception should be noted: one of the texts which Torrance dealt with in his graduate seminars at Edinburgh was Hilary of Poitiers's *de Trinitate*.

[63] Among the very few works to engage explicitly with the doctrine of the Trinity, we may note in particular: 'Sermon on the Trinity'; 'Toward an Ecumenical Consensus on the Trinity', *Theologische Zeitschrift* 31 (1975), 337–50.

[64] Torrance counts these two works, along with *Theological Science* (1969), as the three most important of his writings.

judgement. In reality, Barth is being critiqued – subtly, obliquely and graciously – from an Athanasian perspective.[65]

The foundations of the doctrine of the Trinity

Torrance stands within the Reformed tradition, which regards Scripture as of fundamental importance for Christian theology. Torrance thus stresses the propriety of establishing the scriptural foundations of the doctrine of the Trinity. These are not, however, to be sought in isolated proof-texts, but in the totality of the biblical witness to the acts and being of God:

> The Holy Scriptures are to be interpreted not in an analytical or discursive way but in terms of the integrated witness which they bear together to the fulfilment of God's eternal purpose for the salvation of the world as it has been brought to its focus and has been actualized in Jesus Christ, in whom God in all his fullness has chosen to dwell ... [We must ensure that] the conceptual connections that arise compulsorily in our mind are objectively and ontologically controlled by the intrinsic connections in God's self-revelation and self-interpretation as Father, Son and Holy Spirit. Hence in our approach to the Holy Scripture we must be quite ruthless with ourselves in discarding all concepts of an *a priori* or extraneous derivation so that the truth of the Word of God may be allowed to shine through the biblical text and generate in our minds appropriate conceptual forms with which to articulate it and bring it to doctrinal expression.[66]

For Torrance, the distinctive pattern of divine being and activity which is disclosed within Scripture focuses on the person of Jesus Christ – a pattern which is formalized in the concept of the *homoousion*.

We have already noted the immense importance which Torrance attaches to the concept of the *homoousion* (pp. 151–8). In view of the critical role which this concept comes to play in his theology, it would be entirely legitimate to suggest that it is the cornerstone on which much of his distinctive theological reflection rests. Whereas in the Auburn Lectures, Torrance primarily locates the rationale for the Trinity within an analysis of the factuality of divine self-revelation, his later expositions of the doctrine make extensive use of an analysis of the complex interaction of revelation and redemption, and their common focus on the person of Jesus Christ. This, for Torrance, is the stimulus which inevitably leads to the shaping of the contours of the Christian doctrine of God, in the

---

[65] The chapter dealing with the procession of the Spirit and its relevance to the *filioque* clause may be studied with profit in this respect: *Trinitarian Faith*, 231–47.

[66] *Christian Doctrine of God*, 44.

specific form of the Trinity. The *homoousion* defines 'the Christological pattern that will appear throughout the whole body of Christian dogmatics'.

> The Christian doctrine of God is to be understood from within the unique, definitive and final self-revelation of God in Jesus Christ his only begotten Son, that is, from within the self-revelation of God as God become man for us and our salvation.[67]

The Christological foundations of the doctrine of the Trinity are to be sought in 'God's gracious condescension to be one with us, and his saving assumption of us to be one with himself'. Torrance explicitly links revelation and salvation, refusing to introduce any bifurcation between these aspects of the divine economy. The Nicene emphasis upon the 'Being of God in his Act' and the Reformation emphasis upon the 'Act of God in his Being' are thus mutually affirmed and correlated. 'Divine revelation and atoning reconciliation take place inseparably together in the life and work of the incarnate Son of God'.[68]

The Trinity and the stratification of truth

Torrance's increasing interest in the natural sciences led him to pay particular attention to the notion of 'levels of truth', and the implications of this for theological science. Einstein, Torrance notes, had argued that true science involved the development of a system of stratification, in which research disclosed different 'levels' or 'layers' of concepts. The clearest statement of this idea can be found in his analysis of 'the stratification of truth' in the 1985 work *Reality and Scientific Theology*.[69] The complexity of the world is such that we can only penetrate it to some limited extent, and gain at best a partial and incomplete understanding of its structures and relations. A purely phenomenalist approach to knowledge must be rejected as failing to recognize the manner in which scientific knowledge is actually gained.

> This means that knowledge is gained not in the flat, as it were, by reading it off the surface of things, but in a multi-dimensional way in which we grapple with

---

[67] *Christian Doctrine of God*, 1.

[68] *Christian Doctrine of God*, 144.

[69] *Reality and Scientific Theology*, The Margaret Harris Lectures, Dundee, 1970. (Theology and Science at the Frontiers of Knowledge, No. 1) Edinburgh: Scottish Academic Press, 1985, 131–59. Although Torrance tends to identify Einstein as the main source of this multi-level and multi-layer approach to truth, the ideas of Michael Polanyi must also be regarded as having provided a major stimulus to Torrance's reflections on the manner in which truth is discerned and uncovered (pp. 228–32).

a range of intelligible structures that spread out far before us. In our theoretic constructions we rise through level after level of organized concepts and statements to their ultimate ontological ground.[70]

The methodology which this understanding of truth determines can be seen as advancement to deeper levels of understanding, in which each level rests upon what has already been uncovered, yet casts additional light upon it.

> We start with our ordinary experience in which we operate already with some sort of order in our thought which is essential for our understanding of the world around us and for rational behaviour within it. We assume that the world is intelligible and accessible to rational knowledge ... we operate on the assumption that by means of thought we can understand in some real measure the relations between events and grasp their orderly sequence and consistent structure.[71]

That initial perception of orderedness and structure, however, turns out to be a starting point for a more penetrating and discerning investigation, in which successive layers of truth are identified and uncovered, and their inner relationships established.

> What we are concerned with in science, however, is to deepen our grasp of that orderly structure. We select a few basic concepts in our experience and apprehension of the world, try to work out their interconnections, and organize them into a coherent system through which like a lens we can gain a more accurate picture of the hidden patterns and coherences embedded in the world. We carry out this activity in other fields of investigation and try to connect together the various structures we discover latent in them, thus widening and at the same time unifying the progress of our science.

The basic process which Torrance declares to be essential to the natural sciences can also be applied to theological science. It is at this point that we can return to Torrance's analysis of the foundations of the Trinity, in that he argues that an understanding of the Trinity is arrived at through progression through a series of layers or levels of investigation.

The primary object of reflection is Jesus Christ. As we have stressed, Torrance regards the person of Jesus Christ, as he is 'clothed in the gospel' (to use a phrase originally deployed by Calvin and endorsed by Torrance)

---

[70] *Reality and Scientific Theology*, 136. Torrance's critique of phenomenalism in relation to both natural and theological science is best seen in *Divine and Contingent Order*, 1–25;

[71] *Reality and Scientific Theology*, 147. There are interesting parallels at this point with George Lindbeck's understanding of the relation between first-order and second-order theological statements: see George Lindbeck, *The Nature of Doctrine*. Philadelphia: Westminster, 1984.

as the cornerstone of all authentically Christian theological reflection. But that process of reflection, Torrance argues, is multi-levelled. The first level (which could be defined as 'incipient theology') is the *evangelical and doxological* level.[72] This could be thought of as the basic level of Christian experience and living, 'the level of our day-to-day worship and meeting with God in response to the proclamation of the Gospel'. At this level, God is apprehended intuitively, 'without engaging in analytical or logical process of thought'.[73] Torrance here cites approvingly the dictum of Hugh Ross Mackintosh, to the effect that the inner life of God 'is apprehended by us for the sake of its redemptive expression, not for the internal analysis of its content'.[74]

At this level, the Christian believer has an experience of the reality of God as a 'basic undefined cognition which informally shapes our faith'. The Christian experience of worship, reading of Scripture, and an intuitive awareness of the reality of God constitute the point of departure for further theological reflection.

> Our minds become inwardly and intuitively adapted to know the living God. We become spiritually and intellectually implicated in patterns of divine order that are beyond our powers fully to articulate in explicit terms, but we are aware of being apprehended by divine Truth as it is in Jesus which steadily presses for increasing realization in our understanding, articulation and confession of faith.[75]

Through participation in the worship of the Christian community and engaging with the Scriptures (Torrance occasionally speaks of 'indwelling' Scripture, thereby stressing the personal engagement he envisages), the 'trinitarian pattern of God's self-revelation implicit in them becomes stamped on our minds'. At this stage, this pattern is more appreciated or intuited than subjected to rigorous analysis – yet the intuitive apprehension of the ordering of the Christian *kerygma* and *didache* must be

[72] *Christian Doctrine of God*, 88–90.

[73] Torrance uses the terms 'intuitive' and 'intuition' to refer to the means by which believers directly apprehend the reality of God. His use of the terms must be seen in the light of their earlier use in Einstein and Polanyi. The importance of this point is best seen from the serious misreading of Torrance by Ronald Thiemann, which seems to rest on the assumption that Torrance equates 'revelation' and 'intuition': Ronald F. Thiemann, *Revelation and Theology: The Gospel as Narrated Promise*. Notre Dame, IN: University of Notre Dame, 1985, 32–3. It seems that Thiemann glosses the term 'intuition' with Kierkegaardian connotations, apparently unaware of Torrance's different reading of the term's intellectual pedigree and associations.

[74] *Christian Doctrine of God*, 91, citing from Mackintosh, *Doctrine of the Person of Jesus Christ*, 526.

[75] *Christian Doctrine of God*, 89. See also the discussion of 'the trinitarian structure of theology' in *Reality and Scientific Theology*, 160–200, especially 161–2.

regarded as the essential foundation for the process of theological reflection which will follow.

It will be evident that this first stage of theological engagement corresponds to the natural scientist discerning some patterns of order and regularity within nature, prior to a detailed engagement with them. As noted above (p. 170), Torrance argues that Einstein's understanding of scientific method begins with the intuitive perception of 'some sort of order' within nature; on the basis of this perception, the scientist will then proceed to a more rigorous investigation of the structure and grounds of that ordering.[76] For Torrance, theological science begins by immersion within the Christian community of worship and prayer, in which the believer absorbs the language of the Christian faith, shares its 'evangelical and doxological' experience, and begins to appreciate the 'evangelical pattern or economy of the redeeming acts of God in Jesus Christ'. It is from this point that theological reflection begins.

Torrance thus argues that the second stage in this process of engagement is the *theological level*. This secondary level of engagement involves moving on from the primary level of 'experiential apprehension' of God, and discerning the structures which lie within it.

> By forming appropriate intellectual instruments with which to lay bare the underlying epistemological patterns of thought, and by tracing the claims of connection throughout the coherent body of theological truths, [theologians] feel their way forward to a deeper and more precise knowledge of what God has revealed of himself, even to the extent of reaching a reverent and humble insight into the inner personal relations of his Being. Our concern at this secondary level, however, while distinctly theological, is not primarily with the organic body of theological knowledge, but with penetrating through it to apprehend more fully the economic and ontological and trinitarian structure of God's revealing and saving acts in Jesus Christ as they are presented to us in the Gospel.[77]

The decisive transition which Torrance envisages in moving from the primary to the secondary level of reflection can be summarized thus: the theologian progresses from the Christian experience of God to an apprehension of the general theological structures which underlie this experience. It will be clear that this can be understood to apply to a series of Christian doctrines; in the specific case of the Trinity, Torrance argues that the transition in question is from 'the intuitive incipient form of an understanding of the Trinity' to 'the economic Trinity'.[78]

---

[76] *Reality and Scientific Theology*, 137–48.
[77] *Christian Doctrine of God*, 91.
[78] *Christian Doctrine of God*, 91–8.

Attention now focuses on 'God's redemptive revelation of himself through himself', a concept which is particularly associated with the term *oikonomia*. At this level, theological inquiry is directed towards an analysis of the self-revelation of God in history, including reflection on the relation of Jesus Christ to God in the light of the evangelical proclamation of revelation and redemption in and through him. For Torrance, the concept of the *homoousion* is of decisive importance at this juncture, in that it is to be recognized as 'the central organizing truth' of this level of theological engagement.[79]

The third level (the 'higher theological level') involves 'moving from a level of economic trinitarian relations' to 'what [God] is ontically in himself'.[80] Once more, there is a distinct parallel, according to Torrance, with the natural sciences, in which the final stage of scientific analysis is to be understood as an attempt to discern 'the objective structures of reality'.[81] The concept of the 'economic Trinity' may be said to belong to the second level of discourse; the concept of the 'essential Trinity' belongs to the third.

> In advancing from the second to the third epistemological level, we move from an ordered account of the economic activity of God toward us as Father, Son and Holy Spirit, to an ultimate set of fundamental concepts and relations whereby we seek to formulate in forms of thought and speech the hypostatic, homoousial and perichoretic relations in the eternal dynamic Communion.

Torrance argues that the transition which he envisages at this juncture corresponds to the patristic movement from *oikonomia* to *theologia*, when the organizing truth, complementing *homoousion*, is *perichoresis*, the mutual or coinherent indwelling of the three divine persons in the eternal communion of their one Being. In the course of this third and final phase, some significant developments in theological vocabulary take place, with implications which need to be noted.

1. New words require to be invented, in order to give expression to the new insights resulting from such theological speculation.

2. Words already in usage develop new associations, or have existing associations refined or redefined within the controlling paradigm of trinitarian thought. For example, the terms 'spirit' and 'being' underwent a radical shift in meaning away from a hitherto impersonal association towards 'an intensely personal meaning'.[82]

---

[79] *Christian Doctrine of God*, 96–8.
[80] *Christian Doctrine of God*, 93, 98–107.
[81] *Reality and Scientific Theology*, 144–7.
[82] *Christian Doctrine of God*, 103.

3. The fragility of theological terms must not be construed as an indication of their inappropriateness in this regard, nor as implying that their referent shares their ambiguity. 'All true theological concepts and statements invariably fall short of the God to whom they refer so that . . . their fragility and inadequacy as concepts and as human statements about God must be regarded as part of the correctness and truthfulness of their reference to God.'[83]

4. Despite the fragility of human language as a means to refer to God, there is no case to be made for employing purely negative modes of discourse concerning God. The nature of God is such that 'committed rational worship and praise through godly ways of thought and speech that are *worthy* of God' are essential elements of a responsible Christian theology.[84]

Torrance regards this terminological evolution as an essential aspect of this theological engagement, and warns against the danger of using such *redefined* terms in their original pre-Christian senses.[85] A further concern which Torrance notes in relation to this third level of theologizing is that it runs the risk of becoming detached from its moorings in God's self-revelation in history, and becoming little more than speculation and possible invention.

> We must keep a constant check on these refined theological concepts and relations to make sure that they are in definite touch with the ground level of God's actual self-revelation to us and our evangelical experience of his saving activity in history, and that they remain empirically correlated with the saving truths and events of the Gospel, otherwise they tend to pass over into mythological projections of our own rationalizations into Deity.[86]

The trajectory of trinitarian theological reflection and formulation set out by Torrance can thus be represented broadly as follows:

Experience of God $\rightarrow$ *Economic Trinity* $\rightarrow$ *Essential Trinity*

These three levels are mutually correlated; while, for example, the ontological Trinity is revealed in Christian experience, that experience is

---

[83] *Christian Doctrine of God*, 110–11.

[84] *Christian Doctrine of God*, 111.

[85] Torrance explores this with particular reference to the debate over the masculinity of trinitarian language: see especially 'The Christian Apprehension of God the Father', in *Speaking the Christian God: The Holy Trinity and the Challenge of Feminism*, edited by Alvin F. Kimel, Jr. Grand Rapids, MI: Eerdmans, 1992, 120–43.

[86] *Christian Doctrine of God*, 109.

ultimately grounded in the ontological Trinity. As we shall note when dealing with Torrance's appropriation of the ideas of Michael Polanyi (see pp. 228–32), the essential point here is that the distinguishing of different levels of reality must not be considered as an affirmation of their independence so that one or other may be dispensed with or treated as redundant or superseded. The ontological Trinity cannot be regarded as independent of the economic Trinity, nor of Christian trinitarian experience. Nor is Torrance for one moment suggesting that lower levels within the stratification of truth are to be regarded as false or redundant; they are all to be regarded as interconnected responses to their object. A failure to recognize the mutual interconnectedness of these levels of discourse can lead to theological reflection becoming divorced from Christian experience on the one hand, or from its proper ontological foundations on the other.

On the basis of this analysis of the foundations of the doctrine of the Trinity, it will be clear that Torrance's thinking on this matter has progressed considerably since the 1930s. An initial engagement with the actuality of revelation has given way to a stratified engagement with the entire Christian experience of revelation and redemption. The same Barthian concerns may be discerned within this later approach; nevertheless, they have been incorporated into a coherent approach which brings together strands of the thought of writers as apparently diverse as Athanasius, Einstein, Polanyi and Mackintosh.

This chapter has focused particularly on the concept of revelation, and the manner in which Torrance explores its implications for a scientific theology. Yet this emphasis on revelation raises a question of major importance. In what manner and sense can God be 'known' through nature? What are the dangers of this viewpoint? What opportunities does it offer to Christian theology? In view of the considerable importance of this question in relation to Torrance's views on the relation of Christian theology and the natural sciences, we shall move on to consider his understanding of the purpose and place of natural theology.

CHAPTER 8

The Place and Purpose of
Natural Theology

THE desire to encourage a dialogue between Christian theology and the natural sciences is widely regarded as eminently desirable. Yet there is at least an apparent paradox within this affirmation. The natural sciences have achieved their considerable epistemological successes through the direct engagement with the natural world, uncovering its ordering, and offering both explanations of that ordering and means by which these can be evaluated. To any theologian who places an emphasis upon the priority of divine revelation, this engagement raises a serious problem. Is not the scientific engagement with nature diametrically opposed to the theological need to engage with God's self-revelation? Furthermore, is not the theological equivalent of an engagement with nature little more than an invitation to reduce revelation to nature, and theology to anthropology?

From a Barthian perspective, these are very serious matters. Torrance, as the leading British interpreter of Barth, was acutely aware of the force of these considerations. Barth held that the claim to a natural knowledge of God was one element in the sinful human tendency towards self-affirmation in the face of God. If God could be known through nature, his self-revelation could be disregarded. 'Natural theology, as such, arises out of man's natural existence and is part of the whole movement in which he develops his own autonomy and seeks a naturalistic explanation for himself within the universe'.[1] To concede the legitimacy of natural

---

[1] *Karl Barth: Biblical and Evangelical Theologian*, 141–3.

theology would thus be to compromise the entire principle of the priority and necessity of God's self-revelation. Yet some account of the manner in which Christian theology engages with the natural order is clearly essential if the dialogue with the natural sciences is to progress. How can these apparently incompatible considerations be held together?

One of Torrance's most significant theological achievements concerns his careful relocation of the place of natural theology within the Reformed tradition in general, and the Barthian heritage in particular. His understanding of the purpose and place of natural theology has not merely been of major importance in encouraging and fostering the dialogue between Christian theology and the natural sciences; it has encouraged a new engagement with the doctrine of creation, and its implications for this dialogue. We may begin our analysis of his achievement by considering the debate over the place and purpose of natural theology within the Reformed tradition.

Natural theology and the Reformed tradition

The concept of 'natural theology' is contested, and a number of interpretations of the notion can be found in philosophical theology. In general terms, however, the term is widely taken to reflect the notion that at least something of God can be known from the natural order. This theme was developed during the Middle Ages, and can be shown to be an integral element of the theology of Thomas Aquinas, particularly in those of his writings which were directed towards a non-Christian audience.[2] In the sixteenth century, the emerging Reformed tradition developed a highly sophisticated theory of natural theology, which on the one hand stressed its subordinate role to divine revelation, while on the other noting its not insignificant apologetic implications and possibilities.

For Calvin, God reveals his glory, wisdom and power through the natural order, so that none might be without knowledge of his reality and significance for their lives.

> There is within the human mind, and that by natural instinct, a sense of divinity. This we take to be beyond controversy. So that no-one might take refuge in the pretext of ignorance, God frequently renews and sometimes increases this awareness, so that all people, recognizing that there is a God and

---

[2] An excellent example being the *Summa contra Gentiles*. See Norman Kreitzmann, *The Metaphysics of Theism: Aquinas's Natural Theology in Summa contra Gentiles*. I. Oxford: Clarendon Press, 1997. On the related issue of natural law, see Anthony J. Lisska, *Aquinas's Theory of Natural Law*. Oxford: Clarendon Press, 1996.

that he is their creator, are condemned by their own testimony because they have failed to worship him and to give their lives to his service ... There are innumerable witnesses in heaven and on earth that declare the wonders of his wisdom. Not only those more arcane matters for the closer observation of which astronomy, medicine, and all of natural science (*tota physica scientia*) are intended, but also those which force themselves upon the sight of even the most unlearned and ignorant peoples, so that they cannot even open their eyes without being forced to see them.[3]

Nevertheless, Calvin insists that this knowledge of God is neither complete nor saving; this full knowledge of God is only to be had through Scripture.[4] Calvin does not attempt to develop a natural theology in the sense of a source of knowledge of God which is autonomous, and can be arrived at independently of God's revelation in Scripture. Nevertheless, Calvin lays the foundation for the notion that something of God may be known from the natural order, and that the full revelation of God in Scripture confirms and completes this limited natural knowledge of God. Further development of the theme took place subsequently within the Reformation tradition, both at the Genevan Academy and in the Reformed schools of theology elsewhere, particularly in the Netherlands.[5]

This concept of natural theology received a particularly significant development within the confessional element of the Reformed tradition. The Gallic Confession of Faith (1559) argues that God reveals himself to humanity in two manners:

First, in his works, both in their creation and their preservation and control. Second, and more clearly, in his Word, which was revealed through oracles in the beginning, and which was subsequently committed to writing in the books which we call the Holy Scriptures.[6]

---

[3] *Institutes* I.iii.1, 2. The use made of Cicero in this connection is important: see Emil Grislis, 'Calvin's Use of Cicero in the *Institutes* I:1–5: A Case Study in Theological Method', *Archiv für Reformationsgeschichte* 63 (1971), 5–37. Torrance notes Calvin's relation to the fifteenth-century humanist writer Lorenzo Valla in this matter: *The Hermeneutics of John Calvin*. Monograph Supplements to *Scottish Journal of Theology*, edited by A. I. C. Heron and I. R. Torrance. Edinburgh: Scottish Academic Press, 1988, 97–8, 100–2.

[4] *Institutes* I.vi.1. For a full discussion, see Edward A. Dowey, *The Knowledge of God in Calvin's Theology*. New York: Columbia University Press, 1953; T. H. L. Parker, *Calvin's Doctrine of the Knowledge of God* 2nd edn. Edinburgh: Oliver & Boyd, 1969.

[5] See Michael Heyd, 'Un rôle nouveau pour la science: Jean Alphonse Turrettini et les débuts de la théologie naturelle à Genève', *Revue de théologie et philosophie* 112 (1983), 25–42; John Platt, *Reformed Thought and Scholasticism: The Arguments for the Existence of God in Dutch Theology*. Leiden: Brill, 1982; Martin Klauber, 'Jean-Alphonse Turrettini (1671–1737) on Natural Theology: The Triumph of Reason over Revelation at the Academy of Geneva', *Scottish Journal of Theology* 47 (1994), 301–25.

[6] *Confessio Gallicana*, 1559, article 2, in E. F. K. Müller (ed.), *Die Bekenntnisschriften der reformierten Kirche*. Leipzig: Böhme, 1903, 221–2.

A related idea was set out in the Belgic Confession (1561), which expanded the brief statement on natural theology found in the Gallic Confession. Once more, knowledge of God is affirmed to come about by two means:

> First, by the creation, preservation and government of the universe, which is before our eyes as a most beautiful book, in which all creatures, great and small, are like so many characters leading us to contemplate the invisible things of God, namely, his eternal power and Godhead, as the Apostle Paul declares (Romans 1:20). All of these things are sufficient to convince humanity, and leave them without excuse. Second, he makes himself known more clearly and fully to us by his holy and divine Word; that is to say, as far as is necessary for us to know in this life, to his glory and our salvation.[7]

The two themes which emerge clearly from these confessional statements can be summarized as follows:

1. There are two modes of knowing God, one through the natural order, and the second through Scripture.
2. The second mode is clearer and fuller than the first.

This basic framework is of considerable importance in relation to the development of the 'two books' tradition within Reformed theology, especially in England, which regarded nature and Scripture as two complementary sources of our knowledge of God. Thus Francis Bacon commended the study of 'the book of God's word' and the 'book of God's works' in his *Advancement of Learning* (1605). This last work had considerable impact on English thinking on the relation of science and religion. For example, in his 1674 tract *The Excellency of Theology compared with Natural Theology*, Robert Boyle noted that 'as the two great books, of nature and of scripture, have the same author, so the study of the latter does not at all hinder an inquisitive man's delight in the study of the former'.[8] At times Boyle referred to the world as 'God's epistle written to mankind'. Similar thoughts can be found expressed in Sir Thomas Browne's 1643 classic *Religio Medici*:

> There are two books from whence I collect my divinity. Besides that written one of God, another of his servant, nature, that universal and publick manuscript, that lies expansed unto the eyes of all. Those that never saw him in the one have discovered him in the other.[9]

---

[7] *Confessio Belgica*, 1561, article 2, in Müller, *Die Bekenntnisschriften der reformierten Kirche*, 233.
[8] Robert Boyle, *Works* ed. R. Birch. 6 vols. London: Rivingtons, 1882, vol. 4, 1–66.
[9] Cited in Harold Fisch, 'The Scientist as Priest: A Note on Robert Boyle's Natural Theology', *Isis* 44 (1953), 252–65 (258).

This metaphor of the 'two books' with the one divine author was of considerable importance in holding together Christian theology and piety and the emerging interest and knowledge of the natural world in the seventeenth and early eighteenth centuries.[10] It may be regarded as an integral element of the Reformed tradition prior to Barth. It illustrates a theme of major importance for Torrance: the potential role of a properly constituted and contextualized natural theology in relation to the right understanding of the relation of Christian theology and the natural sciences.

Yet at this point a major difficulty must be noted. As we have pointed out, Torrance was a noted defender of the general theological approach adopted by Karl Barth – an approach which was characterized by its conspicuously hostile attitude to natural theology. One of Torrance's most significant achievements is the development of the Barthian critique of natural theology in such a manner that its fundamental principle was retained, while broadening its applicability. To understand the point at issue, we may begin by considering Barth's critical approach to natural theology.

Barth's critique of natural theology

Barth's hostility towards natural theology rests on his fundamental belief that it undermines the necessity and uniqueness of God's self-revelation. If knowledge of God can be achieved independently of God's decision to reveal himself, or independent of the specific form of that self-disclosure in Christ, then it follows that humanity can dictate the place, time and means of its knowledge of God.[11] Natural theology, for Barth, represents an attempt on the part of humanity to understand itself apart from and in isolation from revelation, representing a deliberate refusal to accept the necessity and consequences of revelation. One of Barth's central concerns is to expose the myth of human autonomy, and identify its consequences for theology and ethics.[12] The human desire to assert itself and take control over things is seen by Barth as one of the most fundamental sources of

[10] See, for example, Frank E. Manuel, *The Religion of Isaac Newton*. Oxford: Clarendon Press, 1974, 31; Arthur R. Peacocke, *Creation and the World of Science*. Oxford: Oxford University Press, 1979, 1–7.

[11] On this general point, see Regin Prenter, 'Das Problem der natürlichen Theologie bei Karl Barth', *Theologische Literaturzeitung* 77 (1952), 607–11.

[12] On the theme of autonomy in Barth's writings, see John Macken, *The Autonomy Theme in the Church Dogmatics: Karl Barth and His Critics*. Cambridge: Cambridge University Press, 1990; Thies Gundlach, *Selbstbegrenzung Gottes und die Autonomie des Menschen: Karl Barths Kirchliche Dogmatik als Modernisierungschrift evangelischer Theologie*. Frankfurt/Bern: Peter Lang, 1992.

error in theology, leading to the erection of theological towers of Babel –
purely human constructions, erected in the face of God. The quest for
autonomy lies at the heart of original sin:

> It is quite clear throughout Barth's analysis of sin that the target he had in view
> was the 'modern' idealistic conception of consciousness as structured by the
> autonomous generation (and realization) of tasks. Where for the theologians
> of the Ritschlian school (as well as for neo-Kantian philosophy) the develop-
> ment of the 'free' (which is to say, autonomous) personality is synonymous
> with the creation of an ethical agent, for Barth, the desire for autonomy is the
> original sin. The quest for autonomy is the source of individualism, dis-
> organization, and chaos in society.[13]

For Barth, there is a close link between natural theology and the theme
of human autonomy. As Barth understands the concept, natural theology
concerns the human desire to find God on humanity's own terms. Natural
theology thus appears to posit a second source of revelation alongside
Jesus Christ, as he is attested in Scripture. The affirmation of a natural
theology appears to contradict the fundamental principle that God reveals
himself in Christ, implying that God reveals himself in nature independent of his self-revelation in Christ. For Barth, revelation is only to be
had through the revelation of God, as a consequence of God's gracious
decision that he is to be known. There is no manner in which God can be
known outside and apart from God's self-revelation.[14]

Barth's view here would appear to represent an intensification of the
consensus of the Reformed tradition. Calvin, as we have noted, argues
that human nature has the capacity to know something of God from
nature. Nevertheless, Calvin points out that the natural innate tendency
of human nature is to use this capacity in an improper or misguided
manner, and thus to fall into idolatry, worshipping the creation rather
than its creator. For Calvin, it is necessary for this natural knowledge of
God to be seen and interpreted in the light of revelation. There is thus a
subtle and nuanced correlation between natural and revealed theology.

Barth, however, saw any form of affirmation of natural theology as
tantamount to an assertion of human autonomy in theology. Thus Barth
expressed serious anxieties concerning the statements set out by both the
Gallic and Belgic Confessions:

---

[13] Bruce L. McCormack, *Karl Barth's Critically Realistic Dialectical Theology*, 167.

[14] This point is stressed at point after point: see, for example, *Church Dogmatics* II/1, 3–4, 69;
206–7. The general point at issue can be studied in Ingrid Spieckermann, *Gotteserkenntnis: Ein
Beitrag zur Grundfrage der neuen Theologie Karl Barths*. Munich: Kaiser, 1985; McCormack, *Barth's
Critically Realistic Dialectical Theology*, 241–88.

Natural theology was able to attain new forms and find new points of entry which were soon revealed in the teaching of the 16th century enthusiasts both inside and outside the Church. It could again recommend itself to a martyr Church – this time the French – in such a way that, in contradiction to Calvin's proposal, the mischief could be done which may now be read in article 2 of the *Confessio Gallicana*, from which it quickly spread to the *Confession Belgica* (art. 2–3). And once the Reformers were dead ... it could impress itself on their disciples as the indispensable prolegomena of theology, a part of the same development by which the Evangelical Churches allowed themselves, almost without thinking, to be steered into a new position as State Churches.[15]

As can be seen from this citation, Barth saw a fatal connection between natural theology and allegiance to the state. Barth detected in the writings of Emil Brunner a particularly insidious approach to natural theology, given the political situation of the 1930s, as Nazism became a significant political and ideological force in Germany. For Barth, Brunner's concept of a 'point of contact' (*Anknüpfungspunkt*) seemed tantamount to a reversion to the classic pagan notion that the human soul represents a 'spark of the divine'. In addition, Brunner's essay on natural theology appeared at a highly contentious time (1934); Brunner's approach seemed to Barth to play into the hands of the pro-Hitler 'German Christians'.[16] Barth's radical insistence that revelation came only through Christ and Scripture – embodied in the Barmen Declaration – can be seen as emphasizing his rejection of natural theology.

1. Jesus Christ, as he is attested for us in Holy Scripture, is the one Word of God which we have to hear and which we have to trust and obey in life and in death. We reject the false teaching, that the church could and should acknowledge any other events and powers, figures and truths, as God's revelation, or as a source of its proclamation, apart from and besides this one Word of God ...

3. The Christian church is the congregation of brothers and sisters in which Jesus Christ acts presently as the Lord in Word and sacrament, through the Holy Spirit. As the church of forgiven sinners, it has to bear witness in the midst of a sinful world, with both its faith and its obedience, with its proclamation as well as its order, that it is the possession of him alone, and that it lives and wills to live only from his comfort and his guidance in the expectation of his

---

[15] *Church Dogmatics* II/1, 127.

[16] For the reasons, see Joan O'Donovan, 'Man in the Image of God: The Disagreement between Barth and Brunner Reconsidered', *Scottish Journal of Theology* 39 (1986), 433–59.

appearance. We reject the false teaching, that the church is free to abandon the form of its proclamation and order in favour of anything it pleases, or in response to prevailing ideological or political beliefs.[17]

It will therefore be clear that Barth's attitude to natural theology rests partly on his concern that the assertion of the human autonomy to find God in whom or where it pleases inevitably leads to the enslavement of theology to prevailing cultural and ideological currents. Only by firmly anchoring theology to 'Jesus Christ, as he is attested for us in Holy Scripture' can theology maintain its true character as a response to God's revelation.

Yet it is important to note that in later sections of the *Church Dogmatics*, Barth appears to take a stance to the issue of the relation of knowledge of God in creation and knowledge of God through revelation which seems much closer to that associated with Calvin. For example, consider the following statement:

> It is given quite irrespective of whether the man whom it addresses in its self-witness knows or does not know, confesses or denies, that it owes this speech no less than its persistence to the faithfulness of the Creator ... However corrupt man may be, they illumine him, and even in the depths of his corruption he does not cease to see and understand them ... they are not extinguished by this light, nor are their force and significance destroyed ... As the divine work of reconciliation does not negate the divine work of creation, nor deprive it of meaning, so it does not take from its lights and language, nor tear asunder the original connection between creaturely *esse* and creaturely *nosse*.[18]

Similarly, in the lecture fragments of the *Church Dogmatics*, published posthumously, Barth sets out reasons for supposing that something of God can be known from creation, so that God 'is objectively a very well known and not an unknown God'. Nevertheless, he stresses that these impressions should not be 'systematised in the form of a natural theology'.[19] These later statements seem to differ in tone from those found earlier in the *Church Dogmatics*; it is, however, probably improper to suggest that this softening in the tone of Barth's expression should be seen as representing a theological shift on the issue.

[17] 'Theological Clarification of the Present State of the German Evangelical Churches (1934)', sections 1, 3, in W. Niesel (ed.), *Bekenntnisschriften und Kirchenordnungen der nach Gottes Wort reformierten Kirche*. Zürich: Evangelischer Verlag, 1938, 335–6.

[18] *Church Dogmatics* IV/3, 139.

[19] *The Christian Life*. Edinburgh: T&T Clark, 1981, 120–2.

As we noted earlier, there are reasons for suggesting that there is a connection between natural theology and a positive interaction with the natural sciences – an area in which Torrance would make an especially significant contribution. Torrance's development of the Barthian position is therefore of considerable importance, and merits careful study. It is also of importance in the light of a number of significant criticisms which have been directed against Barth's views on natural theology, most notably James Barr's vigorous defence of natural theology on biblical grounds.[20]

In his 1991 Gifford Lectures, Barr argues that the interpretation of the Bible has been subjected to a 'Barthian captivity' on this matter. Responding to Barth's Gifford Lectures of 1938, Barr argues that much of Barth's critique of natural theology rests on inadequate foundations. Although Barr's primary concern is to set out the biblical foundations for natural theology (a concept, incidentally, which he does not rigorously define),[21] he argues that Barth's rejection of the concept rests upon inadequate grounds. For example, Barth's assertion of a link between natural theology and National Socialism is argued to rest on a 'vast misdiagnosis'.[22]

For such reasons, it is important to explore the manner in which Torrance develops Barth's approach. Before considering Torrance's own views on natural theology, we shall deal with the manner in which he defends and restates the views of Barth.

Torrance's interpretation of Barth on natural theology

It is clear from recent studies that there is considerable interest in Torrance's reworking of Barth's attitude to natural theology, but as a development within a clearly 'Barthian' approach to theology, yet also as a significant contribution in its own right to the dialogue between theology and the natural sciences.[23] Torrance's most sustained engagement with Barth's views on natural theology are to be found in the 1970 study 'The Problem of Natural Theology in the Thought of Karl Barth'.[24] We shall

[20] James Barr, *Biblical Faith and Natural Theology*. Oxford: Clarendon Press, 1993.

[21] For what seem to be hints of definition(s), see Barr, *Biblical Faith and Natural Theology*, 95, 142–9, 187–91.

[22] Barr, *Biblical Faith and Natural Theology*, 113.

[23] See Ray S. Anderson, 'Barth and a New Direction for Natural Theology', in Thompson, *Theology beyond Christendom*, 241–66; Wolfgang Achtner, *Physik, Mystik und Christentum: Eine Darstellung and Diskussion der natürlichen Theologie bei T. F. Torrance*. Frankfurt/Bern: Peter Lang, 1991, 158–87.

[24] 'The Problem of Natural Theology in the Thought of Karl Barth', *Religious Studies* 6 (1970), 121–35.

therefore explore the main lines of Torrance's interpretation of Barth on
the basis of this work.

Torrance stresses that Barth does not reject natural theology on the
grounds of rational scepticism or some form of *via negationis* which denies
a positive knowledge of God. The issue concerns the human desire to
conduct theology on anthropocentric foundations. Torrance affirms that
one of Barth's most fundamental objections to natural theology concerns
the innate human tendency to develop and assert its own autonomy.

> The claim to a natural knowledge of God, as Barth understands it, cannot be
> separated out from a whole movement of man in which he seeks to justify
> himself over against the grace of God, and which can only develop into a natural
> theology that is antithetical to knowledge of God as he really is in his acts of
> revelation and grace. From this point of view, the danger of natural theology
> lies in the fact that once its ground has been conceded it becomes the ground
> on which everything else is absorbed and naturalized, so that even the
> knowledge of God mediated through his self-revelation in Christ is
> domesticated and adapted to it until it becomes a form of natural theology.[25]

Torrance argues that Barth came to this conclusion as a result of his study
of the development of German Protestant theology since the Enlightenment, and notes the particular importance of the rise of Nazism as a
catalyst for Barth's misgivings in this matter.

If all theology proceeds from God's self-revelation in Christ, then it
would seem that there is no place for natural theology. Yet Torrance makes
the point that, even at this point, Barth is not denying the possibility or
even the actuality of natural theology. His point is that natural theology
'is undermined, relativized and set aside by the actual knowledge of God
mediated through Christ'. Torrance here draws a parallel between salvation
and revelation.

> Just as when we are justified by the grace of God in Jesus Christ all our natural
> goodness is set aside, for we are saved by grace and not by our own works of
> righteousness, without there being any denial of the existence of natural
> goodness, so here, in the epistemological relevance of justification by grace,
> our natural knowledge is set aside, for we know God through his own grace
> and not by our own efforts of reason, without there being any denial of the
> existence of natural knowledge.

Barth neither denies the existence of a natural knowledge of God, nor
does he mount a metaphysical critique of its foundations. Rather, he
argues that such a knowledge stands in opposition to the Word of God. It

[25] 'Problem of Natural Theology', 125.

is, as Barth himself put it, a relation to the truth in the form of opposition to the truth.[26]

It is thus the implication that natural theology is a self-sufficient and autonomous discipline, which leads to a knowledge of God apart from and in opposition to revealed theology, which Torrance believes to be the fundamental difficulty that Barth identifies in relation to the subject.

> What Barth objects to in natural theology is not its rational structure as such, but its *independent* character, i.e. the autonomous rational structure which it develops on the ground of 'nature alone' in abstraction from the active self-disclosure of the living God.

As such, natural theology has a proper and significant place *within the ambit of revealed theology.* That is to say, Barth's objection to natural theology lies in a conceived danger – that such a natural theology will be seen as an independent and equally valid route to knowledge of God, which may be had under conditions of our choosing. Yet this danger is averted if natural theology is itself seen as a subordinate aspect of revealed theology, legitimated by that revealed theology rather than by natural presuppositions or insights. To put it another way, the authorization for natural theology lies not in its own intrinsic structures, but in divine revelation itself, which both legitimates it and defines its scope.

> Barth can say that *theologia naturalis* is included and brought to light within *theologia revelata*, for in the reality of divine grace there is included the truth of the divine creation. In this sense Barth can interpret, and claim as true, the dictum of St Thomas that grace does not destroy nature but perfects and fulfils it, and can go on to argue that the meaning of God's revelation becomes manifest to us as it brings into full light the buried and forgotten truth of the creation. In other words, while knowledge of God is grounded in his own intelligible revelation to us, it requires for its actualization an appropriate rational structure in our cognising of it, but that rational structure does not arise unless we allow our minds to fall under the compulsion of God's being who he really is in the act of his self-revelation and grace, and as such cannot be derived from an analysis of our autonomous subjectivity.[27]

A further factor which Torrance implicates in relation to Barth's early attacks on natural theology is a form of dualism (see pp. 141–5), which he argues has its origins in Augustine and Luther, and was conditioned by a Kantian dichotomy between the noumenal and phenomenal world:

---

[26] See *Church Dogmatics* I/2, 305, which offers an analysis of Romans 1 and Acts 17: 22–31, widely regarded as the two most important New Testament *loci* for a natural theology.

[27] 'Problem of Natural Theology', 128–9.

There is certainly a deep and persistent problem in Barth's thought here which cannot be glossed over, one that has its roots in an *Augustinian and Lutheran dualism*. He owed it not simply to a residual influence upon him of Wilhelm Herrmann of Marburg, but to his fascination with the young Luther whose thought was then being brought to light in the new *Lutherforschung* ... It was the Augustinian dualism lying behind all this that helped him to develop the brand of existentialism that is found in several editions of his *Commentary on Romans*, and it was into a form of this that he tended to be flung back as he sought to combat the kind of synthesis (Augustinian–Thomist) between the divine and the human advocated by the Jesuit theologian Eric Pryzwara.[28]

Torrance developed this idea of a pervasive dualism within post-Reformation Protestant theology in his later essay 'Karl Barth and the Latin Heresy' (1986). He argued that Barth broke free from such a dualism, and recovered an essentially Athanasian position which refused to accept any fundamental distinction between God and God's revelation.[29]

Torrance therefore argues that Barth's fundamental concern can be identified and honoured. There is indeed a danger that natural theology might become an independent route to knowledge of God, bypassing and thereby marginalizing Jesus Christ and Scripture. Yet if *theologia naturalis* is seen within the ambit of *theologia revelata*, this difficulty is eliminated. Torrance believes that the situation is illuminated by exploring the relation of geometry and physics, in the light of Einstein's theory of relativity.

Since the rise of four-dimensional geometries which have brought to light a profound correlation between abstract conceptual systems and physical processes, geometry can no longer be pursued simply as a detached independent science, antecedent to physics, but must be pursued in indissoluble unity with physics as the sub-science of its inner rational structure and as an essential part of empirical and theoretical interpretation of nature. As such, however, its character changes, for instead of being an axiomatic deductive science detached from actual knowledge of physical reality it becomes, as Einstein said, a form of natural science.[30]

Yet there is a potential difficulty here. Is there not a danger that Torrance will compromise – indeed, that he may even have compromised – his own approach, which insists upon the priority of theology? In a careful study of the manner in which religious theorists have deployed

[28] 'Problem of Natural Theology', 122. Emphasis in original.

[29] This argument is also developed further in his essays 'Deposit of Faith' (1983) and 'Substance of the Faith' (1983), which should be consulted at this point. They are unquestionably among the most important of Torrance's shorter writings.

[30] 'Problem of Natural Theology', 129.

mathematical and physical analogies, Frederick Norris raises the possibility that Torrance may have allowed an analogy drawn from outside the realm of theology to determine the relation between natural theology and dogmatics.[31] In practice, it seems more likely that Torrance simply found the Einsteinian analogy as a convenient way of illustrating something which he already knew to be true on other grounds. In other words, the analogy is to be understood as illustrative, not determinative or constitutive.

The point Torrance is making is that geometry can be seen as an independent discipline, having no essential relation to physics; or, following Einstein's approach, it can be seen as properly belonging within the discipline of physics, in which it can be seen in its proper light, and be allowed to achieve its full potential. The same point can then be made concerning natural theology in relation to revealed theology.

> Natural theology can no longer be pursued in its old abstractive form, as a prior conceptual system on its own, but must be brought within the body of positive theology and be pursued in indissoluble unity with it. But then its whole character changes, for pursued within actual knowledge of the living God where we must think rigorously in accordance with the nature of the divine object, it will be made *natural* to the fundamental subject-matter of theology and will fall under the determination of its inherent intelligibility.[32]

Barth does not deploy this comparison at any point within his writings; indeed, there is little evidence that Barth had engaged with the relativistic issues involved. Torrance indicates that he discussed this with Barth prior to his death, and secured Barth's approval for the comparison as a means of setting out his views on the matter.[33]

Torrance thus argues that, providing natural theology is not seen as an independent, autonomous or detached discipline in its own right, it is to be viewed as an integral aspect of the overall project of theology. The significance of this point is such that it merits much more detailed analysis, as it is clearly of fundamental importance to Torrance's understanding of the relation of theology and the natural sciences, which we shall consider in the following chapter.

[31] Frederick W. Norris, 'Mathematics, Physics and Religion: A Need for Candor and Rigor', *Scottish Journal of Theology* 37 (1984), 457–70 (466–7).

[32] 'Problem of Natural Theology', 129.

[33] See *Space, Time and Resurrection*. Edinburgh: Handsel Press, 1976, ix–xi. The conversation referred to dated from the late summer of 1968, a few weeks before Barth's death. The essay in which Einstein explored this point should be consulted: Albert Einstein, 'Geometry and Experience', in *Ideas and Opinions*. London: Souvenir Press, 1973, 232–46.

Torrance's attitude to natural theology

Torrance's earlier statements on natural theology tend to suggest that nothing of any significance can be known of God, apart from divine revelation. Torrance's Auburn Lectures of 1938–9 can be cited in this respect, as they illustrate well the criticisms which Torrance directed against the notion of natural theology at this early stage in his thinking. Torrance here argues that the term 'revelation' is to be understood as an affirmation that 'God does not keep Himself hidden to Himself, wrapped up in His eternal and awful Majesty, but turns towards us in grace and imparts Himself to us in saving revelation'. This being the case, it follows that:

> Revelation means immediately the refutation of all else that purports to be knowledge about God. Revelation means that all other knowledge is not knowledge at all. If revelation means the revelation of what is otherwise not known and is hidden, then it puts out of court our ordinary knowledge about God – yes, even our religious knowledge gained through the examination of our moral or mystical experience. All indirect revelation – as it is called – or all general revelation is confuted by the fact of revelation.[34]

It is clear that the point at issue is that of the impossibility of an independent source of revelation within the natural order, which Torrance regards as quite unacceptable.

Yet Torrance is careful to argue that, *seen from the standpoint of faith*, creation can be seen and recognized for what it is – something that God has created.

> Once we have known God, known him as Redeemer and so as Creator, we do come to see that the heavens declare the glory of God and the firmament showeth His handiwork. Granted that, but that is possible because we know God already. That is, the world is then a kind of symbol which helps us realize the God we already know by an act in which He has conveyed to us His presence and person.[35]

As we noted earlier (pp. 148–9), Torrance insists that creation, while being an act of God, is not to be thought of as an act of God in which God imparts himself as a Person. For Torrance, the notion of revelation is specifically linked to an act 'in which God confronts us with His person', in which he 'imparts Himself'.

---

[34] Torrance, 'Christian Doctrine of Revelation', 11.
[35] Torrance, 'Christian Doctrine of Revelation', 32. The biblical allusion is Psalm 19.1.

Torrance and the classic Reformed tradition

As we noted earlier, two major sources for the Reformed understanding of natural theology are to be found in the writings of John Calvin, and the confessional material of the Reformed churches. Torrance engaged in dialogue with both these significant resources in relation to this question. In his 1947 essay 'The Word of God and the Nature of Man', Torrance notes approvingly Barth's argument that the actuality of God's self-revelation cuts the ground from under any natural theology, which is thus shown up as the 'shadow-side' of divine revelation.[36] Both in this article, and in his later study *Calvin's Doctrine of Man*, Torrance hints that there might be reasons for suggesting that Barth and Calvin are not totally in agreement with each other on natural theology, although he notes that Barth could be argued to have identified and preserved the essential thrust of Calvin's argument. Torrance is clear that the Reformed position on natural theology is a corollary of its teaching on grace. Using words which strongly echo the teachings of Hugh Ross Mackintosh, Torrance affirms that:

> Reformed theology takes its stand only within the inference from grace. When we come to know God in the Face of Jesus Christ, we know that we have not seen that Face elsewhere, and could not see it elsehow. Christ is the Way, the Truth and the Life, and there is no door, nor way, leading to the Father but by him. And so that natural wisdom of the world about God is made foolishness at the cross, and our natural knowledge is completely set aside by the new creation.[37]

A similar attitude is adopted towards the confessional material in *The School of Faith* (1959), in which Torrance insists that creation can only be understood to have revelatory significance from within the standpoint of the covenant. It cannot be regarded as having an *independent* or *autonomous* revelatory significance, in that it requires to be interpreted within the framework of a revealed theology of creation, incarnation and redemption.

> The whole world of signs which God in his covenant mercy has appointed to correspond to him only has revealing significance, and therefore can be interpreted only, in relation to his covenant will for communion with man and in the actualization of that covenant in the course of his redemptive acts in history. Thus while the whole of creation is formed to serve as the sphere of divine self-revelation, it cannot be interpreted or understood out of itself, as if

[36] Torrance, 'The Word of God and the Nature of Man', in F. W. Camfield, *Reformation Old and New: Festschrift for Karl Barth*. London: Lutterworth Press, 1947, 121–41.
[37] 'Word of God and the Nature of Man', 134.

it had an inherent likeness or being to the Truth, but only in the light of the history of the covenant of grace and its appointed signs and orders and events in the life of the covenant people ... In this way, Reformed theology certainly holds that God reveals himself in creation, but not by some so-called 'light of nature', and it certainly holds that God's revelation makes use of and is mediated through a creaturely objectivity, but it does not hold that an examination of this creaturely objectivity of itself can yield knowledge of God.[38]

In this analysis, Torrance explicitly critiques the notion of *analogia entis* – the idea, especially associated with Thomas Aquinas, that there exists some intrinsic likeness between creator and creation arising from the creative action of God.[39] The fact that there exists some form of correspondence between the creator and creation is not due to an inherent relation of likeness, but to the free and gracious decision of God that some such correspondence shall exist. We are thus dealing with an *analogia gratiae* rather than an *analogia entis*. There is no intrinsic capacity on the part of nature to convey God, nor is the created element as such part of the content of revelation. For Torrance, revelation must be understood to be *self-revelation of God*.

It will thus be clear that Torrance considers a 'natural theology' which regards itself as independent of God's self-revelation as a serious challenge to Christian theology. Natural theology has its place under the aegis of revelation, not outside it. In its improper mode, a 'natural theology' is an approach to theology which leads to the introduction of 'natural' or 'commonsense' concepts into theology without first establishing the warrant for doing so on the basis of revelation. In this sense of the term, Barth was entirely justified in critiquing natural theology, which could only lead to the 'assimilation of God to history and of revelation to history, and thus the reduction of theology to anthropology'.[40]

In this sense, 'natural theology' must be regarded as a serious threat to responsible Christian theology. In one of his earliest published writings, Torrance argued against the intrusion of natural theology into the doctrine of predestination.[41] Torrance's point is that it is fatally easy to introduce metaphysical ideas – for example, 'omnipotence' or 'eternity' – into the Christian understanding of predestination:

---

[38] Torrance, *The School of Faith: The Catechisms of the Reformed Church*, translated and edited with an introduction. London: James Clarke, 1959, liii.
[39] Torrance stresses this point from the outset – as for, example, in his 1938–9 Auburn Lectures: see Torrance, 'Christian Doctrine of Revelation', 22.
[40] *Karl Barth: Biblical and Evangelical Theologian*, 136.
[41] Torrance, 'Predestination in Christ', *Evangelical Quarterly* 13 (1941), 108–41.

Omnipotence, as the late Professor H. R. Mackintosh urged so often, is what God does, and it is from His 'does' rather than from a hypothetical 'can' that we are to understand the meaning of the term. What God does, we see in Christ. He is in His Person and action the Almightiness of God – the Almightiness of love and holiness. It is in fact a natural theology which, by introducing into the Christian apprehension of God a foreign body, causes all the mischief – and there is no doctrine where natural theology causes more damage than in the doctrine of predestination.[42]

Yet alongside this uncritical appropriation of 'natural' ideas and concepts, there is an approach to natural theology which is grounded in God's self-revelation, and views itself as located within and subordinate to that revelation. It is this view of natural theology which Torrance seeks to defend, both in terms of its theological legitimacy and its relevance for the dialogue between Christian theoloogy and the natural sciences.

Natural theology and the contingency of creation

It is important to note the role which the doctrine of creation plays in Torrance's reflections on the place of a reconstructed natural theology. The doctrine of creation *ex nihilo* is, for Torrance, the foundation of the idea that the world is contingent, and dependent upon God for its being and order. This allows for the notional separation of natural science and theology, while at the same time insisting that, rightly understood and conceived, the two enterprises can be seen as thoroughly compatible.

It was with the Reformation that there was revived the biblical idea of God who creates the world out of nothing as something entirely distinct from himself while yet dependent upon him for its being and order. This at once emancipated the study of nature from philosophical preconceptions and led to the disenchantment of nature of its secret divinity. Men realized that they could understand nature only by looking at nature, and not by looking at God. God means us to examine nature in itself, to learn about it out of itself, and not from the study of the Holy Scriptures or theology. But it was the clear and unambiguous doctrine of God as the creator of nature out of nothing that emancipated nature in this way for the investigations of empirical science. We know God by looking at God, by attending to the steps he has taken in manifesting himself to us and thinking of him in accordance with his divine nature. But we know the world by looking at the world, by attending to the ways in which it becomes disclosed to us out of itself, and thinking of it in accordance with its creaturely nature. Thus scientific method began to take shape both in the field of natural science and in the field of divine science.[43]

---

[42] Torrance, 'Predestination in Christ', 114.
[43] Torrance, *God and Rationality*, 39.

It will be clear that Torrance's careful discussion of the manner in which the creation can be said to have revelatory potential opens the way to some very significant developments. Torrance insists that creation can only be held to 'reveal' God from the standpoint of faith. Nevertheless, to one who has responded to revelation (and thus who recognizes nature as God's creation, rather than an autonomous and self-created entity), the creation now has potential to point to its creator. The theologian who is thus a natural scientist (or vice versa) is thus in a position to make some critically important correlations. While the neutral observer of the natural world cannot, according to Torrance, gain meaningful knowledge of God, another observer, aided by divine revelation, will come to very different conclusions.

Dualism and natural theology

Perhaps the most important exploration of the role of natural theology is to be found in the discussion of 'The Transformation of Natural Theology', which formed part of the 1978 Richards Lectures, given at the University of Virginia at Charlottesville.[44] In this lecture, Torrance pointed out the Athanasian insight that knowledge of God and knowledge of the world share the same ultimate foundations in the rationality of God the creator. There is no need to invoke a distinction between 'natural' and 'supernatural' knowledge, in that these are both integrated within Athanasius' understanding of God and the world.[45]

Nevertheless, this model became distorted, due to the rise of various forms of dualism, found in the writings of Thomas Aquinas and others. Inevitably, this led to the acceptance of 'an explicit division between natural and supernatural knowledge' and a 'deistic disjunction between God and the world'.

This disjunction was not due to any specifically theological consideration, but rather to the adoption of cosmological and epistemological dualisms from outside the Christian faith.[46] Torrance argues that, prior to the Reformation, the dominant form of dualism could be described as 'Augustinian–Aristotelian'; after the Reformation, this was displaced by another, which Torrance designates 'Augustinian–Newtonian'. While Torrance notes a number of factors which led to the collapse of natural theology in its traditional form (including Humean scepticism concerning the notion of causation, the Kantian critique of natural theology

---

[44] Published as Torrance, *The Ground and Grammar of Theology.*
[45] *Ground and Grammar of Theology,* 77–8.
[46] *Ground and Grammar of Theology,* 78–9.

within the limits of pure reason, and the impact of the views of the Vienna Circle), he insists that the primary problem lies in the persistence of the dualist foundations of natural theology. This being the case, the reconstruction of natural theology depends upon its transformation – and specifically, upon its liberation from dualist modes of thinking.

> If natural theology is to have a viable reconstruction, it can only be on the basis of a restored ontology in which our thought operates with a fundamental unity of concept and experience, or of form and being, within a contingent but inherently intelligible and open-structured universe.[47]

So where are such approaches to be found within the Christian tradition? For Torrance, one of the great strengths of both Athanasius and Barth was their sustained exposition and defence of non-dualist modes of thought. Barth's critique of natural theology thus simultanously identifies its vulnerability and points the way towards its reconstruction.

> If the God whom we have actually come to know through Jesus Christ really *is* Father, Son and Holy Spirit in his own eternal and undivided Being, then what are we to make of an independent natural theology that terminates, not upon the Being of the Triune God – i.e., upon God as he really is in himself – but upon some Being of God in general? Natural theology by its very operation abstracts the existence of God from his act, so that if it does not begin with deism, it imposes deism upon theology. If really to know God through his saving activity in our world is to know him as Triune, then the doctrine of the Trinity belongs to the very groundwork of knowledge of God from the very start, which calls into question any doctrine of God as the One God gained apart from his trinitarian activity – but that is the kind of knowledge of God that is yielded in natural theology of the traditional kind.[48]

It will be clear that Torrance has made two moves which are of critical importance here. First, he deploys the term 'natural theology of the traditional kind' to designate an approach to natural theology which was critiqued by Barth and rested upon dualist foundations. The use of the phrase immediately suggests that there are *other* approaches to natural theology which have validity – such as that which Torrance will himself develop. Secondly, Torrance explicitly sets a proper natural theology within a trinitarian context, linked with both revelation and salvation through

[47] *Ground and Grammar of Theology*, 86–7. Torrance notes that precisely this kind of natural theology is to be found in Eric L. Mascall, *The Openness of Being: Natural Theology Today*. London: Darton, Longman & Todd, 1971.
[48] *Ground and Grammar of Theology*, 89.

Christ.[49] We shall return to explore the implications of this emphasis upon a Trinitarian approach to theology at a later stage in this work.

Having noted Barth's critique of the traditional approach to natural theology, Torrance indicates the manner in which this reconstruction is to take place:

> Barth's opposition to the traditional type of natural theology, which is pursued as an independent system on its own, antecedent to positive or revealed theology, rests upon a radical rejection of its dualist basis and constitutes a return to the kind of unitary thinking we find in classical Christian theology as exemplified by Athanasius, in which theology is committed to one coherent framework of thought that arises within the unitary interaction of God with our world in creation and incarnation, and in which we are unable to make any separation between a natural and supernatural knowledge of God.[50]

Torrance therefore argues that there is an urgent need for theology to set to one side the disruption of the unity of form and being which underlies dualistic modes of thought, and restore this unity along the lines mapped out by classical Christian theology. Torrance is adamant that this is *not* 'a call to theology to submit itself to some alien way of thinking'; rather, it is to be seen as an invitation to rediscover and return to its own proper epistemic basis, which has become corroded and distorted through the intrusion of cosmological and epistemological influences.[51] Theology and the natural sciences thus stand together in their mutual affirmation of the rationality and intelligibility of the world.

It will therefore be clear that Torrance's reformulation of the problem of natural theology is of major importance to the development of a positive relation between theology and the natural sciences. We are now in a position to begin a detailed study of the aspect of Torrance's theology which has attracted the most attention, and which may be regarded as his most important contribution to modern theology – the development of a scientific theology.[52]

---

[49] For further discussion of this point, see Torrance, *Transformation and Convergence in the Frame of Knowledge: Explorations in the Interrelations of Scientific and Theological Enterprise.* Grand Rapids, MI: Eerdmans, 1984, 293.

[50] *Ground and Grammar of Theology*, 93.

[51] *Ground and Grammar of Theology*, 96.

[52] See, for example, A. I. C. Heron, *A Century of Protestant Theology.* Philadelphia: Westminster Press, 1980, 209–14; Daniel W. Hardy. 'Thomas F. Torrance', in D. F. Ford (ed.), *The Modern Theologians*. 2 vols. Oxford: Blackwell, 1989, vol. 1, 71–91. This important essay was omitted from the second edition, although some material relating to Torrance was included in the new essay by Ted Peters, 'Theology and the Natural Sciences': David F. Ford (ed.), *The Modern Theologians*. 2nd edn. Oxford: Blackwell, 1997, 649–68, with special discussion of Torrance at 657–9.

CHAPTER 9

Theology and the Natural Sciences

IN 1978, Torrance was awarded the Templeton Foundation Prize for Progress in Religion on the basis of his extensive contributions to the discussion of the interaction of Christian theology and the natural sciences. There can be no doubt that this is the area of study for which Torrance is especially highly regarded. This chapter will deal with some of the major themes to emerge from Torrance's mature analysis of these issues, which is to be found in a series of publications from 1969, including perhaps his best-known work in this field – *Theological Science* (1969). Torrance's substantial commitment to the 'Faith and Order' agenda, which had its origins at Lund in 1952 and continued until 1962, placed severe limits on the amount of time he was able to devote to this area of theology; once he was relieved of this ecumenical responsibility, he was able to devote the time to the field which he believed it merited.

We have already noted the important role which Torrance ascribes to natural theology, and the significance of this in relation to Torrance's interpretation and application of the theological legacy of Karl Barth. Yet Torrance's understanding of the purpose and place of natural theology can be argued to reflect his growing appreciation of the importance of forging rigorous links between theology and the natural sciences. The present chapter will explore certain key aspects of Torrance's exposition of this relationship in writings dating from about 1963.

Theology and science: Torrance in relation to Barth

It will be clear that one of the most interesting aspects of Torrance's under-standing of the relation between theology and the natural sciences is the light which it casts upon Torrance's appropriation of the Barthian theo-logical legacy. As we have noted, Torrance is no uncritical disciple of Barth, and has expressed reservations concerning aspects of Barth's theology. It is perhaps in relation to the question of the connection between theology and natural science that the divergence between the two thinkers becomes clearest. It is therefore of considerable importance to explore this divergence in some detail.

The first point which needs to be stressed is that Barth appears to have had little genuine knowledge of the working methods and assumptions of the natural sciences.[1] Barth's relatively few pronouncements on the natural sciences suggest that he regarded them as having little relevance for theology. Barth's discussion of Darwinism is slight and unsatisfactory, although it could be argued that the point which Barth wishes to make in relation to Darwin's theory of evolution does not require a detailed engagement.[2] There is no attempt to engage with the theory of relativity in particular, or the intellectual achievement of Albert Einstein in general, at any point in the *Church Dogmatics*. In effect, Barth treats Christian theology and the natural sciences as non-interactive disciplines, each with their respective fields of competence.[3]

Barth's generally wary attitude towards the natural sciences is perhaps best illustrated from his decision not to become involved in the 'Göttingen Conversations' of 1948–59.[4] These conversations can be seen as arising from a lecture delivered in May 1937 by Max Planck, entitled 'Religion and Natural Science'. In his lecture, Planck argued for the interdependence of religion and the natural sciences, and affirmed his belief that they had much to say to each other. His words had a considerable impact on a number of religiously inclined scientists of the time, who developed the idea of pursuing the agenda set out in Planck's lecture. The intervention of the Second World War made this problematic, and it was not until after the War that the project could be taken further.

[1] For a detailed analysis, see Nebelsick, 'Karl Barth's Understanding of Science'.

[2] *Church Dogmatics* III/2, 88.

[3] This approach is more fully developed in the writings of Langdon Gilkey. See Langdon Gilkey, *Nature, Reality and the Sacred: The Nexus of Science and Religion*. Minneapolis: Fortress, 1993. Gilkey's comments on Barth in an earlier work should be noted: Langdon Gilkey, *Religion and the Scientific Future: Reflections on Myth, Science and Theology*. New York: Harper & Row, 1970, 26–9.

[4] A full account of this may be found in Harold Nebelsick, *Theology and Science in Mutual Modification*. Belfast: Christian Journals, 1981, 159–66.

Günter Howe, a mathematical physicist who became involved in the conversations, had heard Barth lecture on the role of theology at Hamburg in 1931, and had – in his own words – been 'converted to theology' in consequence. It seemed obvious to Howe that Barth would be able to provide precisely the kind of theological input and reflection which the 'Göttingen Conversations' required.[5] Howe had absorbed Barth's views on the nature of theology as a science; while there are indications that he was uneasy concerning Barth's radical separation of theology and the natural sciences, he clearly regarded Barth as an important potential contributor to a dialogue in this field. Howe hoped that Barth would be joined by Karl Heim, representing the theological dimension of the dialogue; physicists of the calibre of Carl Friedrich von Weizsäcker, Werner Heisenberg and Pascual Jordan had all indicated their availability and interest.

Barth declined to attend the initial meeting, or subsequent meetings. It is difficult to avoid the conclusion that important opportunities were missed, not least in relation to forcing Barth to confront some major questions which he appeared to have treated somewhat lightly in the past. Torrance, who discussed this matter with Barth, drew the conclusion that Barth's decision not to become involved did not rest on any antipathy towards the natural sciences as such. Rather, Barth's misgivings concerned the Kantian presuppositions which lay behind the approach to quantum theory adopted by Howe and Heim.

Torrance's position is significantly different, and must be regarded as the most significant point of difference from Barth – especially when taken together with the issue of natural theology, to which it is closely linked conceptually.[6] As we noted in our study of Torrance's intellectual development, his Edinburgh years exposed him to the influence of writers – such as Daniel Lamont – who held that the interaction of the natural sciences and Christian theology could be both significant and positive.

---

[5] For details, see Günter Howe, *Die Christenheit im Atomzeitalter: Vorträge und Studien*. Stuttgart: Klett, 1970.

[6] Other areas in which Torrance indicates a divergence from Barth may be noted, although they are not as significant as the point under consideration. First, Torrance argues that Barth, at points, lapses into a form of 'sacramental dualism', which is inconsistent with his more integrative approach elsewhere. Second, he argues that Barth has not paid sufficient attention to the doctrine of the Holy Spirit, which remains an underdeveloped aspect of Barth's theology. Third, he suggests that Barth has misread Calvin's doctrine of election. Fourth, he chides Barth for failing to emphasize the notion of 'a living union with Jesus Christ'. For example, see *Ground and Grammar of Theology*, 93; *Transformation and Convergence in the Frame of Knowledge*, 285–7; *School of Faith*, lxxvii; 'Karl Barth', 208–9; *Theology in Reconciliation*, 99–100; *Karl Barth: Biblical and Evangelical Theologian*, 138–9. It is interesting to speculate that one may discern the influence of Hugh Ross Mackintosh behind some of these criticisms, particularly the fourth. See p. 140.

Lamont had also introduced Torrance to the writings of Karl Heim; although Torrance remained critical of what seemed to him to be an excessive reliance upon Kantian categories, he nevertheless found Heim's general attitude to the sciences attractive. Heim was quite clear that Christian theology was under an obligation to interact with both the natural order and the natural sciences. To ignore the issues thrown up by the natural sciences is, according to Heim, 'a rebellion against God, who has placed us in a reality which inevitably confronts us with questions of this kind, and who has given us an intelligence which cannot rest until we have sought for some sort of answer to these questions'.[7]

There is no doubt that Torrance felt that Barth's failure to engage with the natural sciences constituted perhaps his most serious weakness.[8] As will become clear in what follows, Torrance regards the natural sciences – rightly understood – as an immensely significant ally in the struggle for theological integrity. It should be noted that Torrance's use of the natural sciences is selective, and focuses virtually exclusively on 'a certain kind of physical science'.[9] Torrance's immensely learned and sustained engagement in this field is not merely of considerable importance in itself; it offers a significant criterion of dissimilarity between Torrance and Barth, which has considerable implications for the issue of the reception, interpretation and development of the Barthian heritage.

We may begin our exploration of this matter by considering the origins of Torrance's interest in the relation of the natural sciences and Christian theology. Torrance published relatively little on this matter before the 1959 Hewitt Lectures were finally published, in a significantly extended and developed form, in 1969.[10] In the light of Torrance's subsequent development, his early views on the interaction of natural science and theology are of considerable interest. These have been over-looked by those who have explored Torrance's understanding of the relation of science and religion and who have, in consequence, allowed it to be understood that Torrance's interest in this area was a relatively late development. We may therefore take some time to explore those early views, as they are set out in the unpublished typescript of a major lecture series on this theme, delivered at Auburn Theological Seminary during the academic year 1938–9.[11]

---

[7] Karl Heim, *Christian Faith and Natural Science*. London: SCM Press, 1953, 30.

[8] See the comment in *Transformation and Convergence in the Frame of Knowledge*, x.

[9] Hardy, 'Thomas F. Torrance', 86.

[10] Some questions of relevance to the issue are touched on in 'Reason in Christian Theology', *Evangelical Theology* 14 (1942), 22–41.

[11] All citations are from the 61-page unpublished typescript, entitled 'Science and Theology'.

The Auburn Lectures on science and theology

As noted earlier in this narrative (pp. 47–56), Torrance spent an academic year lecturing on various aspects of Christian theology at Auburn Theological Seminary. It is important to note that Auburn Theological Seminary is located in New York State, which is also home to Cornell University. The significance of this point is easily overlooked. New York State was the backdrop against which a ferocious intellectual battle over the relation of science and Christian theology was waged in the second half of the nineteenth century. The origins of Andrew Dickson White's *History of the Warfare of Science with Theology in Christendom* (1896) – widely regarded as one of the icons of the 'warfare' model of the relation of science and religion – lie in the circumstances surrounding the foundation of Cornell University. Many denominational schools (including Auburn Theological Seminary) felt threatened by the establishment of the new university, and encouraged attacks on the fledgling school and White, its first president, accusing both of atheism.

Angered by this unfair treatment, White decided to launch an offensive against his critics in a lecture delivered in New York on 18 December 1869, entitled 'The Battle-Fields of Science'. Once more, science was portrayed as a liberator in the quest for academic freedom. The lecture was gradually expanded until it was published in 1876 as *The Warfare of Science*. The material gathered in this book was supplemented by a further series of 'New Chapters in the Warfare of Science', published as articles in the *Popular Science Monthly* over the period 1885–92. The two-volumed book of 1896 basically consists of the material found in the 1876 book, to which this additional material was appended.[12] In lecturing on the theme of 'science and theology', Torrance was entering into a highly polarized debate, with specific local associations, in which the majority of his audience would be disposed to consider that there was a serious, and possibly insuperable, tension between the natural sciences and Christian theology. A survey published in the United States in 1916 showed that only 40 per cent of active natural scientists had any form of religious commitments. This was seen as confirming the popular conception of a serious tension between traditional Christian faith and the natural sciences, and was widely held to suggest that the future could only lead to

---

[12] For further discussion, see David C. Lindberg and Ronald L. Numbers, 'Beyond War and Peace: A Reappraisal of the Encounter between Christianity and Science', *Church History* 55 (1984), 338–54; Colin. A. Russell, 'The Conflict Metaphor and Its Social Origins', *Science and Christian Faith* 1 (1989), 3–26.

the erosion of religious belief in the face of a scientifically undergirded secularism.[13]

Torrance thought otherwise. As we noted earlier, Daniel Lamont had proved an invaluable stimulus to Torrance's thinking on the relation of the natural sciences and theology during his studies at Edinburgh. The course of lectures we are about to examine are of considerable importance, as the germs of his mature approach to this critically important theme can be discerned in these early lectures. As is so often the case with lectures delivered early in an academic's career, Torrance's Auburn Lectures on science and theology can be seen as serving the dual purpose of informing an audience and clarifying the lecturer's thinking at the same time.

One of the most important tasks which Torrance faced was the neutralizing of the notion that science and theology were in conflict. From the outset, Torrance set out to clarify the various senses in which the term 'science' was used, aiming to demonstrate that the term does not necessarily carry anti-religious associations. Two significantly different (though arguably related) senses of the term can be discerned:

1. The term is used to connote 'exactness', both in relation to the attempt to liberate our thought from prejudice and inaccuracy and particularly to 'carry out the work in hand as clearly and systematically as possible'. Science could thus denote the general concept of 'careful and impartial investigation proceeding by carefully defined method'.

2. The term can be used to refer to 'that activity of the mind which investigates by certain well-defined methods the world of empiric [*sic.*] actuality, the world of phenomena in abstraction from its relation to individual and personal situations and values'.[14]

Torrance noted that the first sense of the term 'science' could easily be applied to theology. Nevertheless, he stressed the importance of ensuring that the 'exactness and freedom from preconceived notions' must not be allowed to violate the object of study in question – a theme to which he would return in greater detail later.

For Torrance, science and theology are not to be understood as two non-interacting disciplines, as if each could exist in hermetically sealed

---

[13] James H. Leuba, *The Belief in God and Immortality: A Psychological, Anthropological and Statistical Study*. Boston: Sherman, French & Co., 1916. For the impact of this study, see George M. Marsden, *The Soul of the American University: From Protestant Establishment to Established Nonbelief*. New York: Oxford University Press, 1994.

[14] 'Science and Theology', 1.

compartments of the mind, with interaction excluded as a matter of principle:

> It is the same mind which carries on the two different tasks, and at the back of the mind in each case there is a belief in the ultimate consistency of things as they are in themselves, though how far the results which accrue from work in these two separate fields can therefore be coordinated is a question yet to be faced ... In science the scientist concerns himself with natural causality, with things as they manifest themselves in the actual processes of nature. In religion, we have to remember that the will of God has entered into events ... Indeed, it may be said to be the prerogative of religion to see and live by the fact that everything is viewed within the operations of providence.[15]

Torrance sees the indisputable fact 'that there is a principle of order in the universe' as an excellent illustration of this point. Science can uncover and illustrate such order. But can it account for it? Theology, on the other hand, is able to offer an account of that ordering, in that it reflects the nature of God.

Although these lectures date from a very early stage in Torrance's career, we can see his characteristic emphasis upon the complementarity of the disciplines of science and theology (if both are properly understood, and their respective limitations acknowledged) emerging. Torrance argues that the natural sciences aim at accurate description and generalization – but cannot strictly be said to offer explanations. 'Science cannot tell us anything about the ultimate origin or ends of things. If these questions are to be answered, they must be answered within the sphere of religion.'[16] At this point, Torrance's emphasis upon the significance of revelation becomes clear. In attempting to clarify the proper relation between science and religion, he develops the following significant line of argument:

> Science only informs us what light is thrown upon reality by the empirical observation of the facts of external nature. When science claims that this is all that can be said, it is no longer science but the species of philosophical theory called naturalism ... When applied to man, science interprets his nature in terms of chemical constitution, physics and biology. This is certainly one side of the truth, but it is not the whole truth. It is in so far as it is right a Christian truth. The Bible says that man is as grass, of dust and will return to dust. But religion will not allow us to rest on this side of the truth as if it were all the truth. It would indeed be convenient to think of ourselves as mere animals or as chemical episodes. But revelation comes in, and we are disturbed. We are not allowed to adopt the naturalistic view of ourselves. We are challenged by a

[15] 'Science and Theology', 1–2.
[16] 'Science and Theology', 11.

transcendental claim from God upon us ... Naturalism cannot be answered but by revelation ... <u>Unless God speaks to man, he is nothing more than a chemical episode.</u>[17]

Revelation is thus understood to disclose the true identity and goal of humanity and the created order, thus allowing insights which the natural sciences cannot, by their very nature, acquire:

> It can be said that science simply describes the behaviour of things as pheno-mena but cannot offer an explanation in the sense of being able to relate this behaviour to the final underlying reality. It is simply impossible for science, *qua* science, ever to grasp the ultimate nature of reality with which we are dealing, for it transcends the abstract mathematical patterns into which our minds stamp it and the laws which govern the relations of these patterns to one another.[18]

The final section of the lectures is devoted to discussion of personal involvement in scientific and theological knowledge. This is an issue to which Torrance would return in later works, making extensive use of the writings of Michael Polanyi (1891–1976), particularly his *Personal Knowledge: Towards a Post-Critical Philosophy* (1958). In the lectures of 1938–9, we can see Torrance beginning to explore issues directly related to those which are associated with Polanyi – on the basis of resources available at that time. Torrance here relies upon ideas developed in the writings of Martin Buber (1878–1965), especially the influential work *I and Thou* (1922, English Translation 1958). In this work, Buber argued that two fundamentally different manners of understanding the relation between a thinker and the world could be identified, as follows:

1. An *I–It relationship*, in which the active subject (the 'I') acquires an abstract knowledge of a passive object (the 'It').
2. An *I–Thou relationship*, in which the active subject (the 'I') encounters and engages with an active reality (the 'Thou'), and is transformed by the nature of the encounter.

Using this framework as a basis for his analysis, Torrance sets out two different ways of understanding the involvement of the individual in the knowledge which that individual acquires.

> The characteristic attitude of science and all kindred ways of knowing is characterised by the subject–object attitude, of the I–It attitude, as it has been called ... Here the subject, a knowing mind, sets his object over and against him with a view to investigating it as thoroughly and dispassionately as possible.

---

[17] 'Science and Theology', 14–15.
[18] 'Science and Theology', 42.

Here the subject's attention is directed towards the object, and now toward himself. Here the 'I' has no real place – for, it is urged, self-consciousness interferes with concentration upon objects.[19]

Alongside this detached 'observer attitude',[20] Torrance sets a 'person attitude' or 'I–Thou attitude', which he regards as essential to a proper knowledge of ourselves and the world. In particular, Torrance argues, there is a need to recognize that God cannot be treated as an 'It', but necessarily is to be recognized as a 'Thou'. 'To objectify God is not to speak of God at all, not of the Absolute "Thou", but merely of an *idea* about what we think to be God.'[21]

For Torrance, this distinction between two different attitudes is of fundamental importance to understanding the relation of science and theology. Torrance does not derive this distinction from any philosophical school, but sees it as the corollary of an authentically Reformed theology. As can be seen from the above, Torrance is able to deploy a number of philosophical writers to develop the notion; this does not, however, imply that he derived those ideas from them. The simple fact of the matter is that Torrance derived these ideas on other grounds, and then used writers such as Buber to lend added rigour to his analysis and discussion. The writings of Michael Polanyi would later offer Torrance a framework to develop and extend these insights; those fundamental insights, however, were already in place.

For Torrance, the two disciplines of science and theology offer qualitatively different types of knowledge:

Science proceeds always on the assumption that it deals with objects. It approaches things from the outside, from a distant, detached point of view, with a view to manipulating them. It is disinterested and dispassionate ... It works by a manipulation of forces, blind forces – where the personal coefficient is quite eliminated – at least for all purposes of science. We do not approach God in this way – in a detached, cool manner, characterised by disinterestedness and dispassionate observation. We do not approach Him at all; He approaches us and is the Reality that confronts us and calls us to a halt; calls us to a decision, to personal relations with Himself. Thus we cannot objectify God; we cannot deduce Him from nature, or derive Him by means of argument ... Any attempt to approach him any other way, as in natural theology for example, is an attempt to evade God, to evade the reality that confronts us ... All that we can do in religion is to reply to God who confronts and addresses us.[22]

[19] 'Science and Theology', 47–8.
[20] 'Science and Theology', 50.
[21] 'Science and Theology', 55.
[22] 'Science and Theology', 57–8.

There are unquestionably Barthian themes in this passage, not least the emphasis on God addressing humanity, and the rejection of natural theology. Yet it is significant to observe the dialogue partners which Torrance explicitly cites or to which he implicitly alludes in these lectures. The lectures are generously spiced with quotations from leading British philosophers of religion or science, including Arthur Eddington, C. E. M. Joad, F. R. Tennant and A. E. Taylor. It is of particular importance to note that the basic approach of Daniel Lamont's *Christ and the World of Thought* (1934) can be discerned at many points in the lectures.[23] Significantly, Torrance attributes the general framework which he deploys to continental writers such as Martin Buber (especially his highly influential study *I and Thou*), Søren Kierkegaard, Martin Heidegger, Karl Heim and Friedrich Gogarten, and also to Daniel Lamont.[24] *Karl Barth is never cited explicitly throughout the course of lectures.* The entire lecture series can thus be argued to rest upon the theological ideas which Torrance encountered while a student at New College, Edinburgh (1934–7).

Finally, we need to note the evangelistic emphasis and thrust which is found here, as it is throughout Torrance's early writings. It might seem that a lecture course on the relation of science and theology offered little scope for an evangelistic appeal. Yet Torrance concluded his lectures with what seems remarkably like an altar call:

> How glibly and dispassionately we can talk about God and discuss whether or not he is the creator and ground of the universe! But it is quite another thing to hear God challenging us all in Christ to the Great Decision. Our equanimity is disturbed and all the natural man in us bristles. Challenge comes forth to us all the same, and it is like the sound of many waters. 'Behold I stand at the door and knock. If any man will hear my voice and open the door, I will come in and sup with him and he with me.' Jesus stands today as always in Pilate's judgment Hall, waiting for the verdict of the world: 'What think ye of Christ?' 'What shall I do then with Jesus who is called the Christ?'[25]

During the 1940s and 1950s, Torrance busied himself with the detailed study of historical theology. His appointment to a chair at New College and his editorship of *Scottish Journal of Theology* led to a growing involvement in ecumenical matters. Yet throughout this period, the issue of the relationship of the natural sciences and theology was never absent from his mind. The issues which he had begun to explore in 1938–9

---

[23] For example, see 'Science and Theology', 40, 43, 48–9, 50–1, 59–60.
[24] 'Science and Theology', 47.
[25] 'Science and Theology', 61.

remained with him. The Second World War prevented him from doing much in the way of thinking in this area. Torrance himself suggests that his attitude towards the natural sciences began to develop further after 1946, during which time he became acquainted with a cousin of his wife, Dr (later Sir) Bernard Lovell. Yet it was as a result of Torrance's first invitation to deliver a major endowed lecture series that he was able to set out his developing ideas on the theme of the interaction of science and theology. Torrance was invited to deliver the 1959 Hewett Lectures at three institutions: Union Theological Seminary, New York; Andover Newton Theological School, Newton Center, Massachusetts; and the Episcopal Theological School, Cambridge, Massachusetts. He chose as his theme that of 'theological science'. Writing up the lectures took nearly ten years. With their publication, Torrance became firmly established as one of the leading thinkers in this area, a reputation which was consolidated by a series of substantial publications which followed in due course.

Rather than survey each of these publications, the present chapter will analyse a number of leading themes which can be discerned within Torrance's analysis of the interaction of science and theology. We shall begin by considering whether theology can be considered as a science.

Theology as a science

In what sense, if any, may theology be considered to be a science? The question has been debated since the Middle Ages. Augustine tended to contrast *scientia* and *sapientia*, arguing that Christian teaching was to be understood as 'wisdom' (that is, orientated towards God as the highest good), rather than 'science' (that is, knowledge relating to temporal matters).[26] The rise of theology faculties within medieval universities led to a new interest in the relation between theology and other intellectual disciplines, and hence the question of whether theology could be understood as a 'science' in the sense of a discipline with agreed methodological criteria. The debate can be studied with profit from twelfth-century sources, but is widely agreed to have reached a defining point in the thirteenth.[27] Thomas Aquinas' magisterial discussion of the scientific

---

[26] Rudolf Lorenz, 'Die Wissenschaftslehre Augustins', *Zeitschrift für Kirchengeschichte* 67 (1955), 29–60, 213–51. See also Torrance's comments at the 1990 session of the Académie Internationale de Philosophie des Sciences, published as 'The Transcendental Role of Wisdom in Science', *Science et sagesse: Entretiens de l'Académie Internationale de Philosophie des Sciences, 1990*, edited by Evandro Agazzi. Fribourg: Éditions Universitaires Fribourg Suisse – Universitätsverlag Freiburg Schweiz, Fribourg, 1991, 63–80.

[27] See the excellent survey in M.-D. Chenu, *La théologie comme science au XIIIe siècle*. 3rd edn. Paris: Librairie J. Vrin, 1989.

character of theology[28] demonstrates a keen sense of the new intellectual climate resulting from the rediscovery of Aristotle, particularly the new interest in syllogistic logic.

It must be stressed that Aquinas' understanding of the nature of a science does not necessarily include the associations which come naturally to an English-speaking person today, for whom the word 'science' tends to mean 'natural science'.[29] For Aquinas, as for his age, the term related primarily to rigorous demonstration of conclusions grounded on secure premises. For Aristotle, 'science' meant 'demonstrated knowledge' – that is, affirmations which rested on evidence.

The debate took on a new life in the twentieth century, largely on account of Barth's landmark discussion of the 'scientific' character of theology.[30] Barth's fundamental principle is that the 'scientific' status of a subject is determined primarily by its subject matter, and secondarily by its method. In this, Barth can be seen as following insights explored by Martin Kähler, who stressed that 'every particular subject requires its own form of scientific (*wissenschaftlich*) analysis'.[31]

In 1931, Heinrich Scholz laid down an essentially methodological definition of 'scientific' thinking as a direct challenge to Barth's approach.[32] Scholz laid down three 'minimum conditions' which should be met if 'scientific (*wissenschaftlich*)' status was to be accorded to a subject.

1. The subject should be capable of stating its contents in terms of propositions, the truth of which is affirmed. Scholz makes it clear that this assertion necessarily includes the principle of non-contradiction.

2. All of the propositions in question must relate to one and the same discipline (*Wissenschaft*), and must be capable of formulation as statements concerning this aspect of reality. Scholz may have Schleiermacher's understanding of theology in his sights at this point,

---

[28] *Summa Theologiae* Ia q. 1 a. 2.

[29] An excellent example of the confusion which this caused can be seen from the misleading title for Wolfhart Pannenberg's major work *Wissenschaftstheorie und Theologie* (1976), which was translated as *Theology and the Philosophy of Science*. For a careful study of the tensions between *Geisteswissenschaften* and *Naturwissenschaften*, see Wilhelm Dilthey, *Einleitung in die Geisteswissenschaften*. Göttingen: Vandenhoeck & Ruprecht, 1982.

[30] Gerhard Sauter, 'Die Begründung theologischer Aussagen – wissenschaftstheoretisch gesehen', *Zeitschrift für Evangelische Ethik* 15 (1971), 299–308.

[31] Martin Kähler, *Wissenschaft der christlichen Lehre*. 2nd edn. Leipzig: A. Deicher, 1893, 14.

[32] Heinrich Scholz, 'Wie ist eine evangelische Theologie als Wissenschaft möglich?', *Zwischen den Zeiten* 9 (1931), 8–53.

in that Schleiermacher did not regard the discipline of theology as relating to one single subject, and further argues that the various theological disciplines are linked only by pragmatic considerations.

3. The truth-claims which are implicit in the propositions in question must be capable of being tested. Scholz, interestingly, avoids stipulating the precise manner of such 'testing', arguing that theological statements cannot be verified. It is clear that Scholz's concern here is to avoid the suggestion that theology is some kind of 'personal confession of faith' which lies beyond criticism or questioning.

Barth vigorously contested Scholz' conditions, declaring that they were 'unacceptable' and compromised the essence of Christian theology.[33] Theology was to be seen as having the responsibility to 'criticize and revise language about God by the standard of the principle peculiar to the church'.[34] Barth's concern here is that the possibility of doing theology may be determined in advance by epistemological considerations, rather than be determined by its unique object, if Scholz' stipulations are conceded. Nevertheless, Scholz was not the only critic who accused Barth of denying the scientific status of theology. In January 1923, Adolf von Harnack, the doyen of German liberal Protestant theology, penned an open letter to the journal *Die christliche Welt*, in which he addressed fifteen questions to those who he described as the 'Despisers of Scientific Theology (*Verächter der wissenschaftlichen Theologie*)'.[35] For Harnack, a 'science' had only one method and only one task – 'the pure cognition of its object'. In one sense, Barth may be said to agree with this; their divergence lay on whether precisely the same method was appropriate for each and every object. Barth's insistence that theology was concerned with *die eine Offenbarung Gottes* distanced him from Harnack.

Barth's is not, of course, a view universally held within the theological community; Wolfhart Pannenberg might be noted as an excellent representative of a theologian who considers that Scholz's conditions should be met by a 'scientific' theology.[36] Nevertheless, it must be pointed out that Pannenberg's works of this period tend to operate with the notion of revelation as a publicly accessible event. Revelation is conveyed in history (*Geschichtsoffenbarung*), which is accessible to any who care to observe

---

[33] Barth, *Church Dogmatics* I/1, 8.
[34] Barth, *Church Dogmatics* I/1, 5.
[35] See H. M. Rumscheidt, *Revelation and Theology: An Analysis of the Barth-Harnack Correspondence*. Cambridge: Cambridge University Press, 1972.
[36] Wolfhart Pannenberg, *Theology and the Philosophy of Science*. London: Darton, Longman & Todd, 1976, 269.

it.[37] Pannenberg's views on the scientific character of theology may thus be argued to rest upon a prior understanding of the nature of revelation and its mode of apprehension – an understanding which is not shared by either Barth or Torrance.

Torrance sides with Barth, at least in intention, in this debate. Yet it is clear that Torrance's awareness of the importance of the natural sciences leads him to posit connections and interactions which Barth could not have conceived, a matter to which we shall return later (p. 211). At this stage, we shall stress their commonalities. Both affirm that the distinctive nature of theology is determined by its object, which is defined as God revealed in Jesus Christ. As we have seen, Torrance invokes the theological principle of the *homoousion* in making the point that this epistemological insight is ontologically determined. God already is in himself what he is in his historical self-revelation in Christ. Epistemology is thus correlated with ontology. Torrance had stressed this point from 1938 onwards. As he put it in his Auburn Lectures, the *ordo cognoscendi* is only possible on account of the *ordo essendi*.[38]

Perhaps the general concerns of Barth and Torrance can best be set out in terms of two statements, which they require to be held alongside one another.

1. Theology is a human discipline which aims to use human reason to produce, to the extent that this is possible, an ordered account of what can be known of its object. It shares this desire to yield an ordered account of things with other sciences.

2. Theology alone recognizes the self-revelation of God in Christ as its object, and hence as the sole foundation and criterion of its affirmations.

Both Torrance and Barth are concerned to maintain the second of these two statements, believing that any modification or reduction to it will inevitably lead to a loss of theological identity. Yet both concede the basic human need, observed in any science (*Wissenschaft*) to offer an ordered account of its object.

---

[37] See the seminally important essay in Wolfhart Pannenberg (ed.), *Offenbarung als Geschichte*. Göttingen: Vandenhoek & Ruprecht, 1961, 98–102. For comment, see Paul Althaus, 'Offenbarung als Geschichte und Glaube: Bemerkungen zu W. Pannenbergs Begriff der Offenbarung', *Theologische Literaturzeitung* 97 (1962), 321–30; Ignace Berten, *Histoire, révélation et foi: dialogue avec Wolfhart Pannenberg*. Paris/Brussels: Éditions du Centre d'études pastorales, 1969; Mauro Pedrazzoli, *Intellectus quaerens fidem: fede–ragione in W. Pannenberg*. Rome: Studia Anselmiana, 1981, 55–98.

[38] Torrance, 'Christian Doctrine of God', 93.

[Handwritten annotation at top of page: "Its a question of whether "science" should be determined/identified by its METHOD or by its PURPOSE. The object of study should determine the methodology. Thus method cannot be universalized."]

Torrance clearly believes that both these principles can be maintained if it is affirmed that all intellectual disciplines or sciences are under an intrinsic obligation to give an account of reality according to its distinct nature (*kata physin*).[39] 'Theology and every scientific inquiry operate with the correlation of the intelligible and the intelligent.'[40] Yet that correlation involves an obligation to 'think only in accordance with the nature of the given'.[41] If the distinctive characteristic of a science is to give an accurate and objective account of things, in a manner appropriate to the reality being investigated, it follows that the 'scientific' nature of an undertaking does not depend primarily upon the method to be employed, but upon the identification of the object to be studied. Both theology and the natural sciences are to be seen as a posteriori activities, which are a response to 'the given'. In the case of the natural sciences, 'the given' is the world of nature; in the case of theology, 'the given' is God's self-revelation in Christ.

Torrance thus maintains the scientific character of theology, while insisting that there is no generalized methodology which can be applied woodenly and uncritically to all sciences. In that each science deals with a different object, it is under an obligation to respond to that object according to its distinctive nature. The methods which are appropriate to the study of one object cannot be abstracted and applied uncritically and universally. Each science develops procedures which are appropriate to the nature of its own particular object in which it 'has solved its own inductive problem of how to arrive at a general conclusion from a limited set of particular observations'.[42]

Although Torrance shows himself aware of the twentieth-century debate over the scientific status of theology, he grounds the debate over the scientific character of theology at a much earlier period in Christian theology – the Alexandrian tradition, reflected in the writings of such major theologians as Clement of Alexandria and Athanasius, and also in the works of John Philoponos (c. 490–c. 570).[43] After years of neglect, Philoponus is finally emerging as an important figure in relation to both the development of the natural sciences, and also the interaction of

---

[39] *Theological Science*, 10.
[40] *Reality and Scientific Theology*, xii.
[41] *Theology in Reconstruction*, 9.
[42] *Theological Science*, 106.
[43] On Philoponos and the Alexandrian tradition, see H.-D. Saffrey, 'Le chrétien Jean Philopon et la survivance de l'école d'Alexandrie au Vie siècle', *Revue des études grecques* 67 (1954), 396–410. For his critique of Aristotelian science, see R. K. Sorabji (ed.), *Philoponus and the Rejection of Aristotelian Science*. Ithaca, NY: Cornell University Press, 1987, 1–40.

Christian theology with that development.[44] One of the most fundamental themes that can be discerned within his writings is that of the ontological homogeneity of creation – that is to say, that the totality of the creation is to be regarded as continuous in regard to its being, distinguished by differences within that continuity, rather than various degrees of being. Although this theme can be seen clearly developed in the writings of Gregory of Nyssa, the scientific implications of the theme were only developed fully by Philoponus. Thus Philoponus insisted (against Aristotle and most of his contemporaries) that both celestial and terrestrial events were governed by the same fundamental physical principles.[45]

The theological implications of this are considerable, and are picked up and developed by Torrance. Torrance's recognition of Philoponus' theological importance was stimulated in part by his reading of Shmuel Sambursky's *Physical World of Late Antiquity*, which singled out Philoponus for special discussion.[46] Torrance was able to visit Sambursky (who was head of the Department of the History and Philosophy of Science at the Hebrew University) during 1976, when he visited Israel in his capacity as Moderator of the General Assembly of the Church of Scotland.

Torrance argues that Alexandria became the centre of an approach to scientific method which was of considerable importance both to the development of the natural sciences and to Christian theology.[47] Given the fundamental principle of the ontological homogeneity of creation, it follows that its constituent elements are not distinguished ontologically, and may thus be studied by the same fundamental method. Nevertheless,

---

[44] For example, note the appreciation of the importance of Philoponus' critique of Aristotle's views on the eternity of heavenly bodies found in Harold Nebelsick, *The Renaissance. The Reformation and the Rise of Science*. Edinburgh: T&T Clark, 1992, 13.

[45] See the discussion in Alan Scott, *Origen and the Life of the Stars: A History of an Idea*. Oxford: Clarendon Press, 1991, 166.

[46] S. Sambursky, *The Physical World of Late Antiquity*. London: Routledge & Kegan Paul, 1962. Torrance's personal copy of this work is annotated extensively, especially at pp. 154–75, dealing with Philoponus' views on physics. Richard Sorabji, who did so much to renew interest in Philoponus, had relatives near Edinburgh, which allowed Torrance to discuss Philoponus with his most distinguished British exponent. Torrance also recalls being stimulated in this respect by some of the writings of Stanley L. Jaki, although his impression was that Jaki tended to mention, rather than engage in any great depth with Philoponus' ideas. It may also be noted that in 1974 Iain Torrance went to Oxford for his doctoral research, aiming to specialize in Greek patristic material preserved in Syriac. Torrance encouraged his son to undertake research on Philoponus; however, the lack of reliable texts led him to specialize in Severus of Antioch instead.

[47] See especially 'The Implications of Oikonomia for Knowledge and Speech of God in Early Christian Theology', in Felix Christ (ed.), *Oikonomia: Heilsgeschichte als Thema der Theologie. Oscar Cullmann zum 65 Geburtstag gewidmet*. Hamburg: Herbert Reich, 1967, 223–38; *Theology in Reconciliation*, 215–66; 'John Philoponos of Alexandria'.

the affirmation of 'different sorts of being, distinguished not by degree but simply by difference'[48] leads to the notion that each of these constituent elements must be studied in a manner appropriate to its distinctive nature.

For Torrance, this 'kataphysic' approach to theology rested on the rigorous application of the principle that scientific inquiry is to be conducted strictly *kata physin*, according to the nature or reality of things. Torrance regards Philoponus – the author both of theological works and an early treatise on the correct use of the astrolabe – as embodying this 'kataphysic' approach to science, whether theological or physical. The parallels between theological and physical sciences lie in the 'kataphysic' approach underlying them both; their divergence relates to the very different natures of the realities to which they relate, and of which they seek to offer accounts.

Theology thus has a right to take its place among the sciences. On the one hand, it shares the common human desire to wish to explore, correlate and extend knowledge; on the other, it responds to a unique object, which determines the entire nature of the intellectual engagement in question. Although the term 'science' can here be taken to refer to any human intellectual discipline, it is clear that Torrance envisages a particularly significant affinity between theology and the *natural* sciences, in that both are a posteriori responses to 'the given', in which human ideas are correlated with a reality which is independent of the knower. As Torrance understands theology, both theology and the natural sciences therefore adopt a realist epistemology. This point requires further discussion, as it is integral to Torrance's intellectual vision.

Realism in science and theology

Torrance is widely credited with having formulated 'the most highly developed version of realism' available in modern theology.[49] For Torrance, true knowledge must be understood to represent a genuine disclosure to the mind of that which is objectively real. Both Christian theology and the natural sciences operate with an understanding of knowledge which has its 'ontological foundations in objective reality'. Any intellectual

---

[48] I borrow this phrase from Robert Jenson, *God after God: The God of the Past and the God of the Future*. Indianapolis: Bobbs Merrill, 1969, 120. Jenson bases the phrase on his discussion of Gregory of Nyssa's insistence that the fundamental distinction is between the creator and the creation, not between various levels within that creation.

[49] See, for example, Hardy, 'Thomas F. Torrance', 87.

discipline is thus under an intrinsic obligation to give an account of that reality:

> The concept of truth enshrines at once the real being of things and the revelation of things as they are in reality. The truth of being comes to bear in its own light and in its own authority, constraining us by the power of what it is to assent to it and acknowledge it for what it is in itself. St Anselm, who developed that further in a more realist way, held truth to be the reality of things as they actually are independent of us before God, and therefore as they ought to be known and signified by us.[50]

Torrance's affirmations on the theme of 'responding to reality' convey an almost moral imperative: it is necessary and proper to be attentive and responsive to things as they actually are, and to ensure that we do all that we can to give an accurate and objective account of things, in a manner appropriate to the reality being investigated.[51]

Torrance argues that theology and the sciences share a common commitment to a realist epistemology, to which they respond in manners which are appropriate to the nature of that reality. The precise nature of this approach cannot be set out in advance (and here Torrance's implicit critique of the universalizing tendencies of the Enlightenment will be clear), but is determined by the engagement itself.

> [Theology and the sciences recognize] the impossibility of separating out the way in which knowledge arises from the actual knowledge that it attains. Thus in theology the canons of inquiry that are discerned in the process of knowing are not separable from the body of actual knowledge out of which they arise. In the nature of the case a true and adequate account of theological epistemology cannot be gained apart from substantial exposition of the content of the knowledge of God, and of the knowledge of man and the world as creatures of God ... This means that all through theological inquiry we must operate with an *open* epistemology in which we allow the way of our knowing to be clarified and modified *pari passu* with advance in deeper and fuller knowledge of the object, and that we will be unable to set forth an account of that way of knowing in advance but only by looking back from what has been established as knowledge.[52]

---

[50] *Reality and Scientific Theology*, 141.

[51] A full discussion of this point would require reference to the tradition of Scottish realism, which was well represented in Edinburgh's philosophical faculty during Torrance's student days. See S. A. Grave, *The Scottish Philosophy of Common Sense*. Oxford: Clarendon Press, 1960; Richard Olson, *Scottish Philosophy and British Physics, 1750–1880*. Princeton, NJ: Princeton University Press, 1975; M. Jamie Ferriera, *Scepticism and Reasonable Doubt: The British Naturalist Tradition in Wilkins, Hume, Reid and Newman*. Oxford: Clarendon Press, 1986.

[52] *Theological Science*, 10.

Torrance refers often and appreciatively to the realist approaches of two leading scientists, James Clerk Maxwell and Albert Einstein. To understand his particular interest in Einstein, it is necessary to consider his general understanding of the evolution of western thought, and particularly the impact of the scientific enterprise in achieving transformations within existing modalities of thought.[53] It must be stressed that these three cosmological transitions are to be set alongside theological transitions, such as the rise of Augustinianism or changes ushered in by the Reformation of the sixteenth century. For Torrance, three fundamental transitions may be discerned within western scientific and cosmological thinking, as follows.

1. The transition from primitive Hellenistic cosmology, characterized by a thorough and pervasive dualism, to a Ptolemaic cosmology. Torrance suggests that this transition is to be seen as taking place between the second and fourth centuries. As Christianity expanded from an originally Judaic intellectual context, dominated by non-dualistic ways of thinking, to one dominated by Hellenistic modes of thought, it was inevitable that Christian theology would find itself absorbing, perhaps uncritically, at least some aspects of the Ptolemaic cosmological synthesis. In that this synthesis was at least as dualist as that which preceded it, Torrance argues that Christian theology found itself encountering a number of serious difficulties concerning the manner in which God interacts with the world which reflect the intrusion of essentially dualist modes of thought into theology.[54]

2. The transition from a Ptolemaic to a Copernican and Newtonian cosmology, which took place during the sixteenth and seventeenth centuries. The rise of the Newtonian worldview led to the formulation of an essentially mechanistic understanding of the universe, which allowed no place for divine involvement or interaction with the world. For Torrance, this must therefore be seen as a modified form of dualism, so that the transition in question is from an Augustinian–Aristotelian to an Augustinian–Newtonian dualism. *How about Descartes?*

[53] Torrance discusses this general theme at a number of points, most notably *Reality and Scientific Theology*, 1–31; *Theology in Reconstruction*, 62–78; *God and Rationality*, 29–31. What follows is a general summary of these more detailed analyses. For an early (1956) anticipation of these themes, see *Kingdom and Church*, 1–6.

[54] See *Theology in Reconciliation*, 27–8, 267–8.

3. The Maxwellian–Einsteinian revolution, which abandoned the dualist assumptions of earlier understandings of the world in favour of a unitary approach based on the notion of continuous fields. In this revolution, positivist and instrumentalist approaches to science have been discarded and 'dualist cosmologies and anthropologies and epistemologies are transcended'.[55] In practice, Torrance recognizes that unresolved dualisms remain, despite Einstein's programme.[56] Nevertheless, he clearly believes that, at least in principle, the way has been opened to their elimination. Torrance thus sees Einstein and Barth as engaged on a related enterprise – the demonstration and construction of a unitary approach to reality.

This analysis of western intellectual history can, of course, be challenged. Nevertheless, it is important to note that, in essence, Torrance can be seen as developing a theological programme which, in at least two respects, parallels that associated with the *Dogmengeschichte* school, particularly the writings of Adolf von Harnack.

1. Christian theology is understood to have been compromised or distorted in consequence of its expansion from its original Palestinian context to the great intellectual centres of the Hellenistic world. Harnack and Torrance happen to disagree, at least in emphasis, on the precise nature of those distortions, and the manner in which they were introduced. Nevertheless, the fundamental assumption is that Hellenization led to distortion and a loss of the distinctiveness of the early Christian intellectual and spiritual vision.[57]

2. The distortions thus introduced can be identified through historical analysis prior to theological reconstruction. This principle of the correction of dogma through history was deployed by von Harnack to purge Christian theology of what he regarded as questionable Hellenistic intrusions, such as the concept of incarnation. Torrance's views on the identity of alien elements is somewhat different; the means by which he identifies and aims to eliminate them is, nevertheless, remarkably similar.

It is clear that Einstein plays a particularly important role in Torrance's thinking. For Torrance, Einstein is a realist thinker who grasped the

---

[55] *Theology in Reconciliation*, 77.
[56] *Divine and Contingent Order*, passim.
[57] See E. P. Meijering, *Theologische Urteile über die Dogmengeschichte: Ritschls Einfluss auf von Harnack*. Leiden: Brill, 1978; Alister E. McGrath, *The Genesis of Doctrine: A Study in the Foundations of Doctrinal Criticism*. Oxford: Blackwell, 1990.

inherent intelligibility of the world in a manner amenable to mathematical representation,[58] and who recognized the limits of the Newtonian and Kantian concepts of time and space, thus opening the way to a unitary conception of the world.[59] Einstein, for Torrance, thus restored to science a proper understanding of objectivity and the intelligible reality of the world, understood in a unitary manner, which was firmly grounded in an epistemological realism.

> The decisive point of Einstein's critique of the phenomenalist and Kantian approach to knowledge [was] when he broke through it and grounded scientific knowledge in the objective intelligibility of the universe: that is, upon an inherent relatedness that characterizes the universe independently of our perceiving and conceiving of it. This all-important point, theologically speaking, may be called the *homoousion* of physics, the basic insight that our knowledge of the universe is not cut short at appearances or what we can deduce from them, but is a grasping of reality in its ontological depth, and that we are unable to pierce through appearances and apprehend the structures of reality unless we operate with the ontological integration of form and being.[60]

Torrance regards Einstein in particular, and the natural sciences in general, as committed to a generally realist position in matters of epistemology. In this he must be regarded as justified. A long list of technological developments, widely regarded as essential to modern western existence, can be argued to rest upon the ability of the natural sciences to develop theories which may initially explain the world, but subsequently allow us to transform it. And what more effective explanation may be offered for this success than the simple assertion that what scientific theories describe is really present? As John Polkinghorne comments:

> The naturally convincing explanation of the success of science is that it is gaining a tightening grasp of an actual reality. The true goal of scientific endeavour is understanding the structure of the physical world, an understanding which is never complete but ever capable of further improvement. The terms of that understanding are dictated by the way things are.[61]

The simplest explanation of what makes theories work is that they relate to the way things really are. If the theoretical claims of the natural sciences were not correct, their massive empirical success would appear to be totally coincidental. 'If scientific realism, and the theories it draws on, were not

---

[58] *Theology in Reconstruction*, 73, 92.
[59] *Ground and Grammar of Theology*, 31.
[60] *Ground and Grammar of Theology*, 162.
[61] John Polkinghorne, *One World: The Interaction of Science and Theology*. Princeton: Princeton University Press, 1986, 22.

correct, there would be no explanation of why the observed world is as if they were correct; that fact would be brute, if not miraculous.'[62]

Richard Boyd sets out the central theses of what he terms 'scientific realism' as follows:[63]

1. 'Theoretical terms' (or 'non-observational terms') in scientific theories are to be thought of as putatively referring expressions. Scientific theories should thus be interpreted 'realistically'.

2. Scientific theories, interpreted in this realistic manner, are confirmable and are in fact often confirmed as approximately true by ordinary scientific evidence interpreted in accordance with ordinary methodological norms.

3. The historical development of the mature sciences is largely a matter of successively more accurate approximations to the truth concerning both observable and unobserved phenomena. Later theories tend to build on the observational and theoretical knowledge embodied in earlier theories.

4. The reality which scientific theories describe is largely independent of thoughts or theoretical commitments.

There can be little doubt that most natural scientists espouse a range of opinions which are recognizably 'realist' in their core affirmations, reflecting a common commitment to the ontological finality of the natural order.[64]

Nevertheless, two cautionary warnings need to be noted at this point. First, there is a considerable debate over precisely what form of realism is appropriate. Indeed, such is the extent of this variation that it once led Jarrett Leplin to remark that 'scientific realism is a majority position whose advocates are so seriously divided as to appear a minority'.[65] Secondly, the nature of Einstein's realism is the subject of debate within the scientific literature, with some writers suggesting that Einstein relates realism purely to empirical adequacy, whereas others suggest that he is more strongly realist in terms of his metaphysical commitments.[66] Torrance clearly

[62] Michael Devitt, *Realism and Truth*. Oxford: Blackwell, 1984, 108.

[63] Richard Boyd, 'The Current Status of Scientific Realism', in J. Leplin (ed.), *Scientific Realism*. Berkeley: University of California Press, 1984, 41–82.

[64] Nicholas Rescher, *Scientific Realism: A Critical Appraisal*. Dordrecht: D. Reidel, 1987.

[65] Leplin, *Scientific Realism*, 1.

[66] See Arthur Fine, *The Shaky Game: Einstein, Realism and the Quantum Theory*. Chicago: University of Chicago Press, 1986; Azaria Polikarov, 'On the Nature of Einstein's Realism', *Epistemologia* 12 (1989), 277–304; Frederico Laudisa, 'Einstein, Bell and Nonseparable Realism', *British Journal for the Philosophy of Science* 46 (1995), 309–29.

understands Einstein to be committed to a metaphysical concept of realism, rather than to the more instrumentalist notion of 'empirical adequacy'. However, even if Torrance could be argued to misread Einstein at this point, it must be noted that varieties of metaphysical realism dominate within the natural sciences, even if social historians of the natural sciences have tended to operate with rather different approaches.

Torrance's firm commitment to realism must not be understood to lead to any form of 'scientific positivism' which argues for a direct correspondence between concepts and experience.

> The fundamental difficulty with abstractive and positivist science ... is that it operates with a logical bridge between concepts and experience, both at the start and the finish, that is, in the derivation of concepts from the universe as we experience it and in the verificatory procedures relating concepts back to experience ... This is not only a difficulty, but an impossibility, for this is not and cannot be any logical bridge between ideas and existence. There is indeed a deep and wonderful correlation between concepts and experience, and science operates with that correlation everywhere, but since there is no logical bridge the scientist does not work with rules for inductive procedures, and cannot finally verify his claims to have discovered the structures of reality by logical means.[67]

Torrance operates with a complex understanding of correspondence between reality and knowledge which avoids the conceded difficulties of 'naïve realism' (which posits a direct correspondence between knowledge and reality). The general position adopted by Torrance is perhaps best described as 'critical realism',[68] a position which has gained increasing support within theological circles in recent decades. The New Testament scholar N. T. Wright offers an excellent approach to this position, which he describes as:

> a way of describing the process of 'knowing' that acknowledges the *reality of the thing known, as something other than the knower* (hence 'realism'), while also fully acknowledging that the only access we have to this reality lies along the spiralling path of *appropriate dialogue or conversation between the knower and the thing known* (hence 'critical'). This path leads to critical reflection on the products of our enquiry into 'reality', so that our assertions about 'reality'

---

[67] *Reality and Scientific Theology*, 76.
[68] See the careful study of P. Mark Achtemeier, 'The Truth of Tradition: Critical Realism in the Thought of Alasdair MacIntyre and T. F. Torrance', *Scottish Journal of Theology* 47 (1994), 355–74; John D. Morrison, 'Heidegger, Correspondence Truth and the Realist Theology of Thomas Forsyth Torrance', *Evangelical Quarterly* 69 (1997), 139–55.

acknowledge their own provisionality. Knowledge, in other words, although in principle concerning realities independent of the knower, is never itself independent of the knower.[69]

This interconnection of the knower and the known is of fundamental importance to Torrance. The interconnection, already clearly identified in the Auburn Lectures, is developed further with reference to the philosophy of Michael Polanyi, to which we shall return presently.

Nevertheless, at this point our concern is to note Torrance's vigorous defence of the principle that theology is under an obligation to offer an account of something which exists independently of the knower, and to which the knower is responsible for an attempt to convey what may be known of that external reality, in terms appropriate to its nature. Theological science may thus be conceived as 'rational recognition of and willing submission to the claims of objective reality upon us and of obligation towards the truth laid upon us by the truth itself'. Epistemology thus follows ontology, in which it is rooted and upon which it is dependent. Theological science is thus to be understood as based upon an 'ontological anchoring of belief in reality transcendent to ourselves', which thus necessitates the recognition of and response to that which is 'independently and universally true'.[70]

This point is developed in some detail in the 1978 Richards Lectures, delivered at the University of Virginia at Charlottesville. Torrance commented that the substance of these lectures would best be conveyed in the title 'The Ground and Grammar of a Realist Theology in the Perspective of a Unitary Understanding of the Creation'.[71] Torrance here argues that the essential unity of the created order (in that there is only one *logos* or principle of intelligibility within the world) allows both the natural and theological sciences to be seen as uncovering the inner coherence and rationality of the universe, in manners which are appropriate to the subject, and which are generated on its basis:

> If we seek to know things in accordance with their own interior principles and powers of signification, instead of clamping extraneous and distorting thought-forms down upon them, we develop objective forms of thought correlated with the ultimate openness of being and its semantic reference beyond itself.

[69] N. T. Wright, *The New Testament and the People of God*. London: SPCK, 1992, 35.

[70] *Christian Theology and Scientific Culture*. Belfast: Christian Journals; New York: Oxford University Press, 1980, 68.

[71] *Ground and Grammar of Theology*, ix. Similar material may be found in his *Christian Theology and Scientific Culture*, published at the same time.

Now when we allow objective being to reveal itself to us like that out of its own inner *logos* or intelligibility, our thought is thrust up against its reality, its truth of being, in such a way that it is sustained by an objective signification beyond itself and does not fall back into the emptiness of its own inventive, objectifying operations. Not only do we grasp the truth of intelligible being out of its own depth, but we let it interpret itself as we develop appropriate structures of thought under its impact upon us.[72]

Torrance's realism clearly raises the question of the nature and form of the 'reality' to which it relates. Perhaps at this point, we may see an affinity between Barth and Torrance, in that Torrance is clear that the epistemological centre and focus of responsible Christian theology is Jesus Christ.

We direct our minds to the self-giving of God in Jesus Christ and allow our minds to fall under the power of the divine rationality that becomes revealed in him. It is a rationality inherent in the reality of the incarnate Word before it takes shape in our apprehension of it (*a posteriori*), but as we allow it to become disclosed to us under our questions and find that it is opened out before us in an objective depth that far transcends what we can specify of it in our formulations (disclosure models).[73]

As we have seen (pp. 188–92), Torrance adopts a positive attitude to natural theology, viewed within the structures of systematic theology as a whole, rather than seen as an independent and autonomous entity. This is not to be seen as contradicting his Christological focus (although there are clearly differences of significance between Barth and Torrance at this point); rather, it is to be seen as an affirmation that the 'divine rationality' which is definitively revealed in Christ is to be discerned a posteriori within the creation.

Christ is thus like a lens, allowing us to see the created order in its proper light and from its proper perspective. Theology develops from 'movements of thought in which we seek to know God strictly in accordance with his own nature, and in terms of his own internal relations as they become disclosed to us through the incarnation'.[74] Torrance develops this concept in Athanasian terms, arguing that if the divine *logos* is indeed incarnate in Christ, then access to the inner divine rationality – and hence the rationality of all that God has created – comes through Christ:

---

[72] *Ground and Grammar of Theology*, 95–100 (97).
[73] *God and Rationality*, 45.
[74] *Ground and Grammar of Theology*, 151.

If God's *logos* inheres in his own Being eternally, and that *logos* has become incarnate in Jesus Christ, then it is in and through Christ that we have cognitive access into the Being of God, into his inner divine intelligibility or *logos*. There is a parallel to this, as we have had cause to see, in the way we now seek to understand nature, or the universe, in accordance with its internal rational order or intrinsic intelligibility. Hence we speak of apprehending natural realities in terms of their intrinsic structures, or, if you like, in terms of their intrinsic reason.[75]

The fundamental trajectory of Torrance's argument at this point can be summarized in terms of a set of interlocking affirmations.

1. God is in possession of an intrinsic rationality, traditionally articulated in terms of the divine *logos*.

2. That *logos* has become incarnate in Jesus Christ, so that Christology becomes the key to accessing the inner rationality of God.

3. The divine rationality is also to be seen in the created order, in which the divine *logos* can be discerned at work in the contingent yet ordered nature of the world.

4. From the standpoint of the doctrine of creation, there is therefore a place for natural theology.

5. The natural sciences are obliged to assume some such ordering of the world as an essential element of their investigation of the world.

6. Theology is therefore able to offer an account of the origins and nature of the ordering which the natural sciences uncover, yet cannot fully account for.

One aspect of the reality to which the theological and natural sciences related is the ordering of the world, which we may explore in considerably more depth.

The concept of order in theology and science

We can see something of Torrance's growing awareness of the theme of 'order', and its close connection with the theme of natural theology, from the three-page text of an informal Bible Study on 'The Language of Creation', which Torrance led during his period as minister of Beechgrove Church (1947–50).[76] Taking as his text Psalms 19 and 139, Torrance argues

---

[75] *Ground and Grammar of Theology*, 151.
[76] Torrance, 'Informal Bible Study (1): The Language of Creation', unpublished typescript. Citations drawn from throughout this short text.

that creation can be seen as expressing in some way the nature and will of God. In particular, he argued that Psalm 19 offers 'a thoroughly, startlingly modern scientific outlook on the universe ... cast in the medium of meditation, praise and worship of God'. The Psalm could be seen as a 'meditation upon the created universe, its orderly structure, echoing the law of God'. We can see here the fundamental notion that both natural law and the 'law of God' are fundamentally related to one another.

> The Hebrew Psalmists saw that the forms and patterns of created being were grounded in a structure beyond themselves that derived from the creative Word of God – their structure is a sort of created language echoing the Voice of God.

Human reflection on the ordering of the creation is thus a means of increasing our awareness of the wonder, majesty and creativity of God, and moves us to prayer and adoration.

> Man himself is in the heart of that creation, made by God to reflect His own transcendent judgments and wisdom in an orderly, faithful way of life – hence meditation upon the law of God is so important: for it orders man's life in obedience to God, and reveals the inner connections between the creature and Creator.

In his later writings, Torrance would come to place considerable emphasis upon the notion of 'contingent order'.[77] Torrance himself, however, points to others who discerned the importance of this point before him. A case in point is provided by Eric L. Mascall's much-neglected 1956 Bampton Lectures at Oxford University, which considered the theme of 'cosmology and contingency' in some detail. Mascall devoted particular attention to the question of what kind of world the Christian God might be expected to have created, on the basis of what could be known of that God. For Mascall, the answer was clear:

> It will be both contingent and orderly, since it is the work of a God who is both free and rational. It will embody regularities and patterns, since its Creator is rational, but the particular regularities and patterns which it embodies cannot be predicted *a priori*, since he is free; they can only be discovered by examination. The world of Christian theism will thus be one whose investigation requires the empirical method, that is to say, the method of modern natural science, with its twin techniques of observation and experiment.[78]

---

[77] For comment, see Colin E. Gunton, *The Triune Creator: A Historical and Systematic Study.* Edinburgh: Edinburgh University Press, 1998, 112–13.

[78] Eric L. Mascall, *Christian Theology and Natural Science: Some Questions in Their Relations.* London: Longmans, Green & Co., 1956, 94. See the comments of Torrance at *Theological Science*, 61.

We may see here important affinities with Torrance's stress upon the a posteriori nature of both scientific and theological knowledge, and also anticipations of the manner in which Torrance would develop and exploit the concept of contingent order.

For Torrance, the order which is evident within the natural world is to be understood as *contingent*. On the basis of the Christian understanding of the nature of God and the creation, there is no tension between the concepts of 'contingency' and 'orderliness'. There exists what Barth termed a 'created correspondence' between the world and God.[79] Torrance sets this point out in some detail in his essay 'Divine and Contingent Order':

> [The notion of contingent order] is the direct product of the Christian understanding of the constitutive relation between God and the universe, which he freely created out of nothing, yet not without reason, conferring upon what he has made and continues to sustain a created rationality of its own dependent on his uncreated transcendent reality ... [This doctrine of creation] liberated nature conceived as the timeless embodiment of eternal forms from a necessary relation to God, which made it impossible to distinguish nature from God; and it destroyed the bifurcation of form and matter, affirming each as equally created out of nothing and equally real in their indissoluble unity with one another in the pervasive rational order of the contingent universe under God.[80]

The order that is discerned within the world – and, indeed, upon which so much scientific reasoning is dependent – is thus to be understood as a consequence of the creative action of God. One of the fundamental dilemmas of natural science, Torrance notes, is that it cannot be proved that there is order in the world, in that such proof would imply the prior assumption of precisely such an order.[81] Torrance, of course, does not regard this as a proof for the existence of God; it is, nevertheless, an important and significant indication of the fundamental convergence between Christian theology and the natural sciences, and a clear illustration of the advantages of undertaking scientific investigation from the perspective of a Christian worldview. The fact that such order exists, and that the human mind is such that it can discern and appreciate it, has

[79] *The Christian Frame of Mind* 1st edn. Edinburgh: Handsel Press, 1985, 28.
[80] 'Divine and Contingent Order', in A. R. Peacocke, *The Sciences and Theology in the Twentieth Century*, Notre Dame, IN: University of Notre Dame Press, 1981, 81–97, 302–3 (84–5).
[81] *Ground and Grammar of Theology*, 131–2; 'Transcendental Role of Wisdom in Science', 67–8. See also *The Christian Frame of Mind: Reason, Order and Openness in Theology and Natural Science.* 2nd edn. Colorado Springs, CO: Helmers & Howard, 1989, 17–64.

'to be introduced from outside into the stock of fundamental ideas with which science operates, through the Judaeo-Christian doctrine of God and creation'.[82]

Torrance illustrates this point with particular reference to the work of James Clerk Maxwell (1831–79), which he regards as being fundamental to the advance of modern science, particularly in relation to the setting aside of dualist in favour of unitary modes of thinking about nature. On 4 November 1979, Torrance preached the sermon at the James Clerk Maxwell memorial service, held at Corsock Parish Church in Kirkcudbrightshire, marking the centenary of Maxwell's death. The sermon offered him the opportunity to set out an expansive reflection on the significance of Maxwell for the development of the natural sciences and theology. Noting Maxwell's strong Christian faith in the 'divine power and wisdom by which the worlds were created', Torrance pointed out how this led Maxwell to insist that 'nature abhors *partition*, for in nature everything is inwardly connected together'.[83] Torrance then takes this point a stage further, arguing that the form of relational thinking which Maxwell developed was grounded in Christian assumptions. Maxwell rejected 'merely mechanical ways of thinking' on the grounds that they offered only a limited perspective on nature (which, incidentally, prompted his colleague Sir William Thomson – later Lord Kelvin – to suggest that Maxwell had lapsed into mysticism).

For Maxwell, Torrance argues, the Christian doctrine of creation offers a lens through which the rationality and intelligibility of the created order can be understood and pursued further.[84] Maxwell's pursuit of the 'unsearchable riches of creation' was grounded in a 'deep intuitive grasp of God in relation to the world he had created and ceaselessly sustains'. This deep grasp of the contingent rationality of the world as a consequence of its created character gave Maxwell, according to Torrance, his characteristic trust in the ultimate intelligibility of the world, and the ability of the human mind to discern it.

Torrance links the discernment of ordering within the world with the classic concept of 'wisdom'. In a lecture published in 1991, Torrance noted the significance of the distinction between *sapientia* and *scientia* in the thought of Augustine.[85] The concept of 'wisdom', as developed by Augustine, is to be understood as referring to

---

[82] *Christian Frame of Mind* (1st edn), 41.
[83] Torrance, 'James Clerk Maxwell Memorial Sermon', unpublished 1, 4–5.
[84] See especially *Transformation and Convergence in the Frame of Knowledge*, 216–20.
[85] See 'Transcendental Role of Wisdom in Science'.

the unique insight that arises when the eye of the human mind discerns an invisible transcendent realm of immutable eternal truth upon which all *scientia* of the truths of the visible corporeal realm, gained through the rational operations of the human reason, are ultimately contingent.

What the natural sciences are forced to assume – in that it cannot be formally demonstrated without falling into some form of circularity of argument or demonstration – the Christian understanding of 'wisdom' allows to be affirmed, and correlates with the existence of a transcendent creator God, responsible both for the ordering of the world and the human ability to grasp and discern it.

> [The concept of order] arises compulsorily in our minds through direct intuitive contact with the intelligible nature of reality which we acknowledge to be the ultimate judge in all questions of truth and falsity, order and disorder. That is to say, our concept of order presupposes an ultimate ground of order transcending what we can comprehend but of which we are implicitly aware in the back of our mind, and under the constraint of which we generate order in all intellectual activity. Belief in order, the conviction that, whatever may appear to the contrary in so-called random events, reality is finally and intrinsically orderly, thus constitutes an ultimate regulating factor in all rational and scientific activity.[86]

Torrance's analysis of the relation of divine and contingent order leads him to draw three conclusions concerning the proper relationship between Christian theology and the natural sciences.[87]

1. Torrance argues that the framework renders void any model of the interaction of theology and the sciences which ascribes 'why' questions to the former and 'how' questions to the latter. They simply cannot be separated in this simplistic manner.

2. Both the natural and theological sciences operate under the 'constraint of an ultimate ground of order'. This order is found embedded in 'the structures of created being', which lies beyond our control, so that we are under an obligation to respond to it and offer an account of its 'intrinsic ontological grounds'. 'The effort of knowing is thus guided by a sense of obligation towards the truth; by an effort to submit to reality.'[88]

---

[86] 'Transcendental Role of Wisdom in Science', 67.
[87] See *Christian Frame of Mind* (1ˢᵗ edn), 24–6.
[88] Michael Polanyi, *Personal Knowledge: Towards a Post-Critical Philosophy.* 2ⁿᵈ edn. London: Routledge & Kegan Paul, 1958, 63.

3. On the basis of the doctrine of creation, there is a 'fundamental harmony between the "laws of the mind" and the "laws of nature"'. This point becomes especially clear in the remarkable convergence of mathematics and physics, a point neatly captured in Eugene Wigner's affirmation of the 'unreasonable effectiveness of mathematics in the natural sciences'.

Torrance develops this point further in an essay of 1982, entitled *Juridical Law and Physical Law*. On the basis of the concept of the contingent ordering of the universe, Torrance argues that there is an ontological foundation for the postulation of orderedness in the invariant ordering of the creation itself. While showing himself alert to the debate within the philosophy of law over the propriety and limitations of legal positivism, Torrance argues for a recognition of a unitary basis of both juridical and physical laws in the ordering of creation. 'All authentic knowledge, including legal knowledge, depends upon belief in and recognition of orderly patterns inherent in the universe.'[89] If legal science were to follow the general method of the natural science, 'it would seek to ground juridical law in the objective intelligibilities of created reality'.[90]

Torrance explores this issue with particular reference to the issue of natural law. Noting that modern western conceptions of 'natural law' are conditioned by fundamentally anthropocentric assumptions, inherited from the classic period, Torrance argues for a recovery of a notion of natural law grounded in the concept of contingent order of the universe:

> The classical Greek and Roman conception of natural law, as mediated through the eclectic tradition of the schools, was governed by an immanentist understanding of the relation of God to the cosmos in which *physis, nomos* and *logos* were run together with *theos*. This represents an equation of natural law with the immanent necessity of the divine Reason or *Logos*, and gave natural law its timeless immutable character. In later Stoic and Roman conceptions, this immanent divine law of nature was regarded as coming to full expression in the human reason, and so tended to be associated with the dignity and rights of man as belonging to him by nature.[91]

We can see here an appeal to one of Torrance's more fundamental concerns: the intrinsic dualism of the Greek worldview, which led to a distinction and division between the divine and human realms. This

---

[89] Torrance, *Juridical Law and Physical Law: Toward a Realist Foundation for Human Law* Edinburgh: Scottish Academic Press, 1982, 27.
[90] Torrance, *Juridical Law and Physical Law*, 33.
[91] Torrance, *Juridical Law and Physical Law*, 34 n. 22.

contrasts with the Judaeo-Christian conception of natural law, which, according to Torrance:

> was governed by a transcendentalist understanding of the relation of God to the creation, who does not embody his eternal *Logos* or *Reason* or *Law* in nature as his universal law, but who through the unifying and rationalizing power of his *Logos*, conceived as the Word of God, creatively imparts to the world a pervasive rational order subordinate to himself on his transcendent level as its determinant ground. Natural law thus understood refers to the God-given patterns of the universe and has to do with the intrinsic truth or objective intelligibility or order of contingent being.

It will therefore be clear that Torrance offers a synthesis of the natural, theological and legal sciences, based on their mutual grounding in the contingent order of nature.

A further aspect of the relationship between theology and the natural sciences which relates to the issue of 'order' is found in Torrance's suggestion that the doctrine of the atonement is to be set in this context.[92] Torrance argues that the significance of the doctrine of the atonement can be seen in relation to the 're-ordering of creation'. At first sight, this might seem to be little more than a restatement of the cosmic notions of redemption which are particularly associated with the Greek patristic tradition.[93] On closer inspection, a more nuanced approach emerges, based on an analysis of the notion of the ordering discerned within the world by scientific investigation. Torrance notes how the universe requires 'redemption from disorder':

> In Christian theology that redemption of the universe is precisely the bearing of the cross upon the way things actually are in our universe of space and time. It represents the refusal of God to remain aloof from the disintegration of order in what he has made, or merely to act upon it 'at a distance'. It is his decisive personal intervention in the world through the incarnation of his Word and love in Jesus Christ. In his life and passion he who is the ultimate source and power of all order has penetrated into the untouchable core of our contingent existence in such a way as to deal with the twisted force of evil entrenched in it, and thereby to bring about an atoning reordering of creation.[94]

This 'atoning reordering of creation' is to be understood as an engagement with the 'source of disorder'. The resurrection of Christ is understood as

---

[92] See *Christian Frame of Mind*, 102–5. A fuller discussion of the theme of 'disorder', which includes a discussion of the relation of disorder and entropy, can be found in *Divine and Contingent Order*, 113–28.

[93] See H. E. W. Turner, *The Patristic Doctrine of Redemption*. London: Mowbrays, 1952.

[94] *Christian Frame of Mind* 2nd edn, 103.

the means by which God 'triumphs over all the forces of disintegration and disorder in the cosmos'.[95] Redemption can thus be understood as re-ordering – that is, restoring the God-given order in which the cosmos came into being. Torrance notes that the disorder which has crept into the universe affects human nature in particular; nevertheless, redemption must be understood to embrace the whole created order, which has now fallen into disorder, and not simply humanity.

The theme of 'cosmic redemption' is thus developed in a significant manner by Torrance: redemption is to be seen as involving the re-ordering of the cosmos, including human nature but extending far beyond this. For Torrance, humanity has a special – indeed, unique – place within creation. Not only has humanity been created in the image of God; redeemed humanity has also been entrusted with the task of exercising a 'priestly and redemptive role in the world'.[96] Once healed of its internal disorder and disunity, humanity may undertake this role.

> The fact that God has taken the way of becoming man in allying himself with contingent existence and thereby effecting the redemption of the creation from within its ontological foundations, immensely reinforces the unique place of man in the universe. And in that it is redeemed man who is established at the head of the whole system of inter-level interaction throughout the created order, man's priestly function in the universe now takes on the pattern of a redemptive mission to nature. It is in this light that Christian theology must regard man's God-given role in natural scientific inquiry, that is, not only to be the constituent element in the universe whereby it unfolds and expresses its inherent rational order, but to be the instrument under God whereby physical evil and disorder are rectified and are made, contrary to what they may actually be, to serve the whole created order. However, it is only as man himself is healed of his own inward split that he may exercise a truly integrative and re-ordering role in the world around him.[97]

Redemption is thus understood as a restoration of humanity, in order that humanity may play its defined role (which, though limited, is of significance) in the restoration of the universe as a whole.

Perhaps Torrance does not develop these ideas to the extent that one might like; one is left wishing for more discussion of this potentially important line of thought. Nevertheless, even this brief discussion is sufficient to indicate the theological importance of the theme of 'order',

---

[95] *Divine and Contingent Order*, 138.
[96] *Divine and Contingent Order*, 128–42.
[97] *Divine and Contingent Order*, 138. For the idea of the scientist as the 'priest of creation' as it first occurs in the works of Robert Boyle, see Fisch, 'Scientist as Priest'.

which can be seen to link together creation and redemption, incarnation and atonement.

Michael Polanyi: philosopher of science

One of the most intriguing writers in the field of the philosophy of science is the Hungarian chemist Michael Polanyi (1891–1976).[98] Polanyi's work has been extensively cited by religious writers, including Torrance, and it is arguable that he has had far greater impact on religious writers than on his fellow scientists. Polanyi was born into a Jewish family in Budapest. In his early years, Polanyi belonged to 'the Galileo Circle', a small group of students who held that science held the key to the solution of the world's problems. This somewhat ambitious and optimistic attitude towards what Mary Midgely has termed 'science as salvation' gradually gave way to a growing interest in the spiritual side of life, inspired and nourished by Russian writers of the nineteenth century, such as Tolstoy and Dostoyevski. At the age of twenty-eight, he was received into the Roman Catholic church.

In the following year, Polanyi secured an academic teaching position at the Kaiser Wilhelm Institute for Physical Chemistry. This position became insecure through the rise of Nazism in the 1930s. The Nazis disliked having people of Jewish descent in significant academic positions, and Polanyi recognized that he would be wise to leave Germany. He obtained a position in 1933 as Professor of Physical Chemistry at the University of Manchester, in the north-west of England. As his research interests shifted, so did his teaching responsibilities: in 1948, he was appointed to a chair in social science.

Polanyi's most significant work to deal with the philosophy of science is widely agreed to be *Personal Knowledge: Towards a Post-Critical Philosophy* (1958). This work has had considerable influence on many religious thinkers, particularly within the Christian tradition, including Torrance. This wide interest in Polanyi on the part of religious writers must not be seen as a distortion of Polanyi's intentions or interests. Polanyi himself was a religious man (although it is widely agreed that the precise nature of his own religious views will probably remain unclear) and frequently addresses religious issues in his works. In a brilliant study of Polanyi's theological significance, Avery Dulles suggests that this is to be found less in his explicitly religious statements than in the theological

---

[98] See the biographical memoir by Eugene Paul Wigner and Robin A. Hodgkin, 'Michael Polanyi, 1891–1976', *Biographical Memoirs of Fellows of the Royal Society* 23 (1977), 413–48.

'transfer value' possessed by his reflections on the nature of scientific method.[99]

The way in which Torrance makes use of Polanyi is of considerable interest,[100] and there are excellent reasons for thinking that Torrance's pioneering use of Polanyi has had a significant impact on the shaping of English-language theology since about 1970. It will be clear that it is not germane to the objectives of this work to offer a comprehensive overview of Polanyi's philosophy, in much the same way as Torrance's role as an advocate of Barth did not necessitate a total engagement with the Barthian theology. Nevertheless, it is important to begin to appreciate the leading themes of Polanyi's thought which Torrance found congenial to his theological enterprise, and to his defence of theological realism in particular.

It needs to be made clear from the outset that Torrance himself regards his use of Polanyi as a means of developing and strengthening his own fundamental theological ideas, and is emphatic that those ideas are not *grounded* in Polanyi's writings. Torrance certainly uses Polanyian notions – selectively and critically, it must be noted – in exploring the implications of some of those fundamental ideas, and enjoys pointing out convergence at points of significance. Yet he does not see this as entailing any form of total commitment to Polanyi's general methods or assumptions.[101] Appreciative of Barth's strictures concerning the danger of making theology dependent upon anthropology, Torrance distinguishes between what we might term 'foundational' and 'illuminative' roles for philosophies such as Polanyi's.

---

[99] Avery Dulles, 'Faith, Church and God: Insights from Michael Polanyi', *Theological Studies* 45 (1984), 537–50. Dulles offers a list of thirteen theologians who he reckons to have been influenced by Polanyi (n. 1): Torrance is not among them.

[100] An interesting study of this relationship is to be found in Colin Weightman, *Theology in a Polanyian Universe: The Theology of Thomas Torrance*. New York: Peter Lang, 1994. This work misunderstands Torrance at a number of serious points, and appears to assume that Torrance's use of Polanyi implies a dependence upon him *tout simple*. This is certainly not what Torrance intended, nor does the evidence support such a conclusion. Torrance's views on many of the issues on which he would later deploy Polanyi as his *ancilla theologiae* appear to have been settled by 1939, as the Auburn Lectures on science and religion clearly indicate. Weightman suggests (203) that Torrance's 1959 references to the 'personal and communal dimensions of knowledge' are 'typically Polanyian'. This is a serious misreading of the situation. Torrance regards these as typically *Reformed* themes, developed and explored in the classic writings of the Reformed tradition, and which he later finds developed in (partly) congenial ways by Polanyi. See Torrance's essay 'The Place of Michael Polanyi in the Modern Philosophy of Science', *Ethics in Science and Medicine* 7 (1980), 57–95.

[101] The confusion evident in Weightman's analysis reinforces the importance of this point: see, for example, Weightman, *Theology in a Polanyian Universe*, 249–54. For a more reflective evaluation of Polanyi's role for theology, see John V. Apczynski, *Doers of the Word: Toward a Foundational Theology Based on the Thought of Michael Polanyi*. Missoula, MT: Scholars Press, 1977.

It is not clear when Torrance first encountered the ideas of Polanyi. It is certainly possible to conjecture that he was introduced to either the name or some of the ideas of Polanyi during his 1946 conversations with Sir Bernard Lovell. Lovell's term of service on the Faculty of Physics at Manchester overlapped with Polanyi, who served on the Faculty of Chemistry until 1948. The two also played tennis together regularly. Some have suggested that Lovell might have mentioned the general interests of Polanyi to Torrance, thus kindling his interest in the writer.[102] However, this possibility is rendered problematical by a number of considerations. At that stage, Polanyi was not well known, and his works were not being widely discussed. A careful reading of Torrance's published and un-published works up to 1962 shows no explicit engagement with Polanyi.

It is widely agreed that the work in which Torrance first makes extensive and explicit engagement with Polanyi is *Theological Science* (1969). This work was, as noted, based on lectures given in the United States in 1959; this has moved some to suggest that the references to Polanyi date from this earlier period.[103] Torrance is clear that this is not the case; the material relating to Polanyi was worked in during the revision of the work for publication during the 1960s.[104] It should also be noted that it was at this stage (1968–9) that Torrance joined Polanyi as a member of the Brussels-based Académie Internationale de Philosophie des Sciences.[105]

The first explicit published reference to Polanyi in Torrance's writings is found in a paper on 'The Problem of Theological Statement Today', delivered at the University of Tübingen in May 1963.[106] The citation of Polanyi relates to his observation that scientific theories have implications which extend far beyond the experience in relation to which they were originally formulated. From this point onwards, Polanyi is cited regularly and approvingly. For example, the 1964 paper 'Theological Education

[102] For example, see Weightman, *Theology in a Polanyian Universe*, 203. Weightman also implies that Torrance may have become acquainted with Polanyi's *Science, Faith and Society* on or around its publication; Torrance has no recollection of reading this, or any other work by Polanyi, before 1958.

[103] Weightman, *Theology in a Polanyian Universe*, 203.

[104] It should be noted in this respect that in 1966 Torrance sent his son Iain (who was then a student at Monkton Combe School) a copy of Polanyi's *Tacit Dimension*, which had just been published, and urged him to read it.

[105] The growing friendship between Torrance and Polanyi is evident from their correspondence over the period 1970–4, particularly Polanyi's formal request that Torrance address him using his Christian name (26 December 1972). In a letter of 16 November 1972, Polanyi spoke warmly of Torrance's 'high enterprise in linking religion to science, and finding them thus mutually revealed', indicating his agreement with this position.

[106] 'Das Problem der theologischen Aussage Heute', *Theologische Zeitschrift* 19 (1963), 318–37. English translation in *Theology in Reconstruction*, 46–61.

Today' notes the importance of Polanyi in relation to faith and commitment in theological education, drawing on insights from Polanyi's work *Personal Knowledge*.

At this point, we may pause and consider this matter in a little more detail. It is widely agreed that one of the most important themes developed by Polanyi is that of the fiduciary component of human knowledge. Polanyi asserts that all acts of human knowledge either rest upon or constitute in themselves acts of faith.

> We must now recognize belief once more as the source of all knowledge. Tacit assent and intellectual passions, the sharing of an idiom and a cultural heritage, affiliation to a like-minded community: such are the impulses that shape our vision of the nature of things on which we rely for our mastery of things. No intelligence, however critical or original, can operate outside a fiduciary framework ... Our acceptance of this framework is the condition for having any knowledge.[107]

If this is the case, it follows that theological statements are developed and tested in manners which are at the very least analogous to those associated with the natural sciences. Even doubt itself is to be seen as a fiduciary act.[108] Discovery begins with faith, in that those who seek to discover trust their abilities to identify the problem and its possible solutions, and devise means by which the correct solution may be distinguished from its alternatives. It is this aspect of Polanyi's thought which has been welcomed most widely within the theological community, particularly by those who wish to develop systematic critiques of the Enlightenment commitment to neutrality or detachment as a precondition for true knowledge.[109]

The reception of Polanyi's thought has been confused through the widely accepted assumption that Polanyi and Thomas S. Kuhn can be grouped together as representatives of a 'truth by consensus' ideal – that is, that truth is what most people believe to be true.[110] In fact, Polanyi must be distinguished from Kuhn in relation to this point: for Polanyi, 'truth in general, and in the natural sciences in particular, is understood to be a fundamentally correct insight into the *real*, as it is independent of

---

[107] Polanyi, *Personal Knowledge*, 266–7.

[108] See particularly Michael Polanyi, 'Faith and Reason', *Journal of Religion* 41 (1961), 237–47. In this article, Polanyi acknowledges his indebtedness to Paul Tillich for some of his ideas.

[109] See the very extensive use of Polanyi in Colin Gunton, *Enlightenment and Alienation: An Essay towards a Trinitarian Theology*. Basingstoke: Marshall, Morgan & Scott, 1985. See also Lesslie Newbigin, *The Gospel in a Pluralist Society*. London: SPCK, 1989, 29–32.

[110] See Imre Lakatos, 'Falsification and the Methodology of Scientific Research Programmes', in I. Lakatos and A. Musgrave (eds), *Criticism and the Growth of Knowledge*. Cambridge: Cambridge University Press, 1970, 91–196, especially 92 n. 2.

human thought processes'.[111] Indeed, it is this commitment to realism which constitutes one of the reasons for Torrance's respect for and use of Polanyi's ideas. Torrance, of course, was a theological realist long before he read Polanyi; nevertheless, his engagement with Polanyi offered him a means of refining the manner in which he conceived and expressed his realist convictions.

The point at which Polanyi may be regarded as having most stimulated Torrance's theological reflections concerned his hierarchical structuring of the world, and, in consequence, our knowledge of that world. Polanyi sets out a comprehensive vision of a 'universe of levels' or a 'hierarchical universe'.[112] The natural sciences reveal the universe to be multi-levelled, with successive levels inter-related by a 'principle of marginal control'. The laws and structures of higher levels are thus dependent upon those of lower levels, even though they cannot be reduced to them; furthermore, the higher level laws control the behaviour of the lower levels. The term 'marginal control' is used by Polanyi to refer to the manner in which the upper controls the lower level.[113] For example, someone might design a machine – such as a clock. The manner in which the clock functions is governed by the laws of physics. Yet those laws cannot illuminate the *purpose* for which the machine was designed. The laws of physics are put to different uses by different machines, with the result that these lower laws are being controlled (yet not abrogated) by the higher level (purpose). The lower level is thus regulated both by the laws of nature and the higher-level purpose which devised the clock in order to keep time. Polanyi discerns a series of levels (such as inanimate matter, physiology, intelligence and moral choice) within the universe, and argues for a complex inter-relatedness between them.

Space, time and incarnation

Torrance develops this model as he sets out his understanding of the universe as a multi-levelled yet unitary whole. It constitutes an integral element of his defence of the unity of the world against dualist approaches, and also offers him an important means of developing a natural theology.

> The universe that is steadily being disclosed to our various sciences is found to be characterised throughout time and space by an ascending gradient of meaning in richer and higher forms of order. Instead of levels of existence and

[111] Maben Walter Poirier, 'A Comment on Polanyi and Kuhn', *The Thomist* 53 (1989), 259–79.
[112] Alan Olding, 'Polanyi's Notion of Hierarchy', *Religious Studies* 16 (1980), 97–102; Weightman, *Theology in a Polanyian Universe*, 71–9.
[113] Polanyi offers the analogy of a machine to illuminate this point: *Personal Knowledge*, 328–32.

reality being explained reductionally from below in materialistic and mechanistic terms, the lower levels are found to be explained in terms of higher, invisible, intangible levels of reality. In this perspective, the divine splits become healed, constructive syntheses emerge, being and doing become conjoined, and integration of form takes place in the sciences and arts, the material and spiritual dimensions overlap, while knowledge of God and of his creation go hand in hand and bear constructively on one another.[114]

The point that Torrance is particularly concerned to emphasize is that Polanyi has created space for the 'spiritual' within the universe, by rejecting the reductionist position which asserts that all of nature is to be considered as existing at one level only.[115] This would, in Torrance's view, lead to everything being seen in a mechanistic manner – a form of materialism which leaves no place for the spiritual. It is this point which is encapsulated in Laplace's famous comment, made in relation to the idea of God as a sustainer of planetary motion: *nous n'avons pas besoin de cette hypothèse-là.* Polanyi explicitly critiques Laplace at this point, as he develops the idea of a multi-levelled rather than single-levelled universe;[116] Torrance, who voices similar criticisms of the French scientist, notes that Polanyi offers an integrated view of knowledge which eliminates segregation between disciplines, and opens the way to recognizing 'an inner semantic structure which coordinates and holds together all levels and areas of knowledge within the one universe of human inquiry'.[117]

It will be clear that this general approach is of importance in the rehabilitation of the 'spiritual' within the 'scientific'. Yet Torrance also suggests that the recognition of the 'multi-levelled structure of human knowledge' has particular relevance to individual aspects of Christian theology. Perhaps Torrance's most creative application of this point relates to the resurrection. Traditional discussions of the resurrection had proceeded along rather Humean lines, involving debate over whether God could violate the laws of nature through miraculous acts. Torrance argues that a multi-levelled approach to the question allows the distinctive nature of the resurrection to be appreciated, while avoiding reducing it to a 'spiritual' event (for example, purely in the experience of the disciples) or explaining it away on purely rational grounds.

---

[114] Torrance, *Reality and Scientific Theology*, ix.

[115] Torrance, *Ground and Grammar of Theology*, 13–14.

[116] Polanyi, *Personal Knowledge*, 139–40.

[117] Torrance, *Space, Time and Resurrection*, 189. It must, however, be noted that Torrance finds a recognition of the 'stratified structure' of the sciences in Einstein as much as in Polanyi, although he notes that each interprets this multiplicity in different manners. See, for example, *Space, Time and Resurrection*, 191–2.

> In fulfilment of his eternal design God has acted in the resurrection of Jesus Christ from the dead in such a way that, far from setting aside or infringing or interfering with the spatio-temporal order of the universe which he created (and which we try to formulate in what we call 'laws of nature'), he accepts and affirms its reality, but he introduces into the situation a transcendently new factor which brings about an utterly astonishing transformation of it which is quite inexplicable in terms of anything we are able to conceive merely within the intelligible structures of the world, or in accordance with our scientific formulations of them.[118]

This single sentence of more than one hundred words indicates Torrance's concern to interpret the resurrection 'according to its own distinctive nature' on the one hand; on the other, it clearly indicates his concern to avoid rationalist or spiritualist approaches to the issue – both of which he clearly regards as reductionist, failing to do justice to the phenomenon of the resurrection at every level of inquiry. It is one of Torrance's most distinctive emphases, and may be regarded as one of the core assumptions of his scientific theological method.

Conclusion

It will be clear that Torrance's general approach to the natural sciences bears a direct correspondence to his theological method in general. The term 'scientific theology' thus comes to possess, in Torrance's hands, rather different nuances than that found in the German phrase *die wissenschaftliche Theologie*. The German term implies only an intellectual coherence; the English-language associations of the word 'scientific' implies at least a degree of affinity with the natural sciences. Basing himself on the Christian understanding of the created order, including humanity itself, Torrance argues that it is to be expected that there will be significant degrees of convergence or consilience between the natural sciences and Christian theology, in that both rest upon and reflect the divine ordering of reality.[119]

 Yes.

The quintessence of Torrance's scientific theology may be argued to rest on the affirmation that every reality is to be investigated *kata physin* – that is, according to its own distinct nature – in an a posteriori manner.

> A genuine theology is distrustful of all speculative thinking or of all *a priori* thought. Theological thinking is essentially positive, keeping its feet on the

---

[118] Torrance, *Space, Time and Resurrection*, 190.
[119] The parallels and contrasts between Torrance's approach and that found in Edward O. Wilson, *Consilience: The Unity of Knowledge*. New York: Knopf, 1988, repay careful study.

ground of actuality; *a posteriori* thinking that follows and is obedient to the given and communicated Word and Act of God.[120]

Torrance's general approach to 'scientific theology' contains four central components:

1. a realist epistemology; theological and scientific statements are grounded in an objective reality independent of the observer
2. a rejection of a priori modes of thinking; scientific and theological thinking takes place a posteriori, after the actuality of knowledge
3. the recognition of the need to respond to each reality according to its own distinctive nature
4. the 'truth' of reality is multi-layered (the order which is uncovered by scientific or theological investigation proves to have many levels or layers).

It is of particular importance to note how Torrance interacts with Barth at this point. Torrance's 'kataphysical' approach to scientific method allows him to affirm a universal scientific (in the sense of *wissenschaftlich*) method while at the same time maintaining the distinctive place and approach of theology. Each science investigates reality *kata physin*, with the result that the method to be adopted is at least partly determined by the distinctive nature of the 'reality' under consideration. Torrance's approach thus allows for the affirmation of a universal scientific method on the one hand, and the particularity of theology on the other, avoiding the potential weaknesses of Barth's approach while maintaining the uniqueness of theology as an intellectual discipline.

We have already seen how this correlates with Torrance's thinking on the doctrine of the Trinity. If God is indeed to be considered *kata physin*, according to God's own nature rather than according to human preconceived notions of divinity, that knowledge of God turns out to be inextricably trinitarian. For Torrance, Barth had demonstrated beyond doubt that the doctrine of the Trinity must be considered

> to belong to the fundamental grammar of our knowledge of God. The closer our thought of God is coordinated with our experience of him in the fundamental datum of revelation, the more it is forced upon our understanding that to know God as he really is, is to know him as Father, Son and Holy Spirit.[121]

---

[120] *Theological Science*, 33.
[121] *Karl Barth: Biblical and Evangelical Theologian*, 19.

Torrance thus rejects any theological method which rests upon a priori conceptual systems, such as abstract or predetermined concepts of divinity. 'All unwarranted presuppositions and every preconceived framework' must be challenged and evaluated in the light of our actual knowledge of God.[122] As we have seen, these can be regarded as constituting 'natural theology' in the unacceptable sense of the word. Theology must be scientific, in that it faithfully and actually reflects the real knowledge of God which is given in and through Jesus Christ. It is, and can *only* be, a posteriori reflection – a reflection on something which has actually taken place, rather than a predetermination of what is permitted to happen. Torrance here faithfully reflects the theological concerns of writers such as Athanasius, Calvin and Barth, even if the vocabulary which he employs to express these concerns represents a development of (or even departure from) their characteristic modes of expression.

Perhaps one of Torrance's most signal achievements is to demonstrate that 'great-tradition Christianity' continues to have the intellectual energy and vitality to engage the agenda developed and pursued by the natural sciences. His greatest bequest to the next century may well be a theological foundation, widely acceptable within orthodox Christianity, on which to build for the future.

---

[122] *Karl Barth: Biblical and Evangelical Theologian*, 130.

Epilogue

TORRANCE retired from the Chair of Christian Dogmatics in Edinburgh in 1979. It was to prove to be a retirement only in the sense of being relieved from the burden of administrative and teaching responsibilities. Torrance's research, writing and public lecturing ministry continued relentlessly.[1] He found the time to enter into a new series of ecumenical discussions with the Orthodox Church. Perhaps most importantly, he was able to devote himself to writing the major works on the Trinity which had been a life-long ambition. As the Laureation Address on the occasion of his being awarded an honorary degree of Doctor of Divinity by Edinburgh University put it, Torrance's was 'a career of unequalled distinction in academy and church'.[2] There is no doubt that Torrance will be a major influence on Christian theological reflection in the next century.

Yet there is a danger that focusing on Torrance's substantial intellectual achievement will marginalize his personal concerns – concerns which the increased leisure of his retirement allowed him to develop. There is a danger that interest in the ideas Torrance developed may overshadow

---

[1] For example, he delivered major series of lectures at leading centres of theological education worldwide in the years following his retirement: the Queen's University Lectures on Theology, Belfast, 1980; Warfield Lectures, Princeton Theological Seminary, New Jersey, 1981; the Payton Lectures, Fuller Theological Seminary, Pasadena, California, 1981; the Didsbury Lectures, Nazarene College, Manchester, 1982.

[2] Laureation Address, University of Edinburgh, 6 July 1996. The address was delivered by David F. Wright.

more personal issues. Our story must therefore return to the subject with which it began – China.

Torrance left China as a boy of fourteen in 1927, as political instability swept the region and threatened the lives as much as the ministries of Christian missionaries and their families in the region. His father finally returned from Sichuan in 1934, to retire in Edinburgh. One of Torrance senior's major achievements had been to establish a church in Tong Men Wai. In 1935, news reached him that this church, along with others in the region, had been destroyed by Mao Zedong's army; its pastor and many leading Christians had been massacred. With the victory of Mao's forces, and particularly the later anti-religious measures of the 'Cultural Revolution', it seemed to some that Christianity might well be eradicated from China altogether.[3] The 'Cultural Revolution' is generally regarded as beginning on 16 May 1966 with a directive issued by the Central Committee of the Communist Party of China; it ended with the arrest of Jian Qing and other members of the 'Gang of Four' after Mao Zedong's death in 1976.[4] Its oppressive measures were designed to eliminate western influences and any lingering remnants of religious belief. Christianity thus found itself under a double burden, in that it was a religion which was considered to be western in origin. Its future seemed increasingly uncertain. As it was virtually impossible to obtain reliable information on the situation within China at this time, western Christians could only wait and wonder; the situation of their fellows within the Middle Kingdom was something about which they could not even obtain information, let alone hope to influence.

One of those who waited and wondered was Torrance, who never lost interest in the churches his father had left behind him on his retirement. By the time of Torrance's own retirement in 1979, there were indications that a more open period might lie ahead in China's history. Those intimations proved correct; it was possible for Torrance to return to the city of his birth, and discover the fate of the Xiang Christian church. It was to prove a momentous occasion, bringing back a flood of childhood memories.

---

[3] The mood of despondency within the missionary community after 1949 is well captured (and criticized) by Wayne Flynt, *Taking Christianity to China: Alabama Missionaries in the Middle Kingdom 1850–1950.* Tuscaloosa: Alabama University Press, 1997.

[4] The best study of this turbulent period in recent Chinese history is Roderick MacFarquhar, *The Origins of the Cultural Revolution.* 3 vols. Oxford: Oxford University Press, 1974–97. The origins of the Revolution were not, of course, religious, even though it would have important religious implications. The origins of the Revolution are probably best traced to struggles between the Peng Dehuai and Liu Deng factions within the Chinese Communist Party in the aftermath of the famine of 1959–61.

Torrance pictured with Xiang Christians during his 1994 visit to the region. Huang Tai Qing is fourth from the left in the back row. The photograph was taken on the roof of a Xiang home, close to the confluence of the Min and To rivers.

On Saturday 4 October 1984, Torrance arrived in Chengdu from Hong Kong.[5] He found that the city had changed considerably since his childhood; some landmarks, however, remained. Torrance's particular concern was to visit the Xiang people. Initially, he had to content himself with visiting Xiang villages in Wenchuan county, at the confluence of the To and Min rivers. Torrance's father's missionary work had taken him far up the Min and To valleys, to regions which were barred to foreigners. A special Alien's Travel Permit would be required to allow him to travel in these remote regions.

In an unexpected development, the Sichuan Security Authority decided to issue a permit to allow him to make the trip. So on 12 October, Torrance boarded a coach at Chengdu which would take him up the Min valley. In

---

[5] See the unpublished typescript 'The Visit by Thomas F. Torrance to Chengdu, the Capital of Sichuan, and to Weichou and Chiang Villages in Wenchuan County, the Upper Min Valley, Sichuan: October 4–18, 1986'.

five hours, the coach completed the journey which would once have taken Torrance and his father seven days on horseback. On his arrival in Weichou, Torrance explained his desire to visit the village of Tong Men Wai in the Prefecture of Long Qi Xiang, in which the first Xiang church had been established. The following morning, a minibus was made available to take Torrance to the upper reaches of the To valley. Finally, they reached the lateral valley which Torrance's father had called 'The Glen', at which the Tongmen stream flows into the To. It was here that Torrance's father had established the first Xiang church, which had been destroyed by Mao Zedong's forces in 1935.

The church still lay in ruins. All that remained were heaps of stones and the remnants of walls in a field of maize. Nevertheless, the Xiang Christian community remained alive and well. Torrance entered the village of Tong Men Wai, and was taken to the house of Huang Tai Qing, whose father had been killed by Mao Zedong's soldiers fifty-one years earlier. Torrance recalled the house vividly. It had been rented by his father as the first meeting place of the Christian community in Tong Men Wai. Torrance had brought with him the title deeds of the church, along with the copy of the New Testament that had been sent by Huang Tai Qing to his father in 1935 (see p. 28). The New Testament had been hidden in the aftermath of the communist massacre of Xiang Christians. Now, more than half a century afterwards, it had returned home. It was a deeply moving moment.

Torrance would return to Chengdu and Wenchuan in the late spring of 1994,[6] armed with financial support for local churches. His second visit allowed him to deepen his knowledge of the current state of Christianity among the Xiang people. The funds which he had been able to raise from a number of philanthropic foundations were used for the rebuilding of the Xiang church at Tong Men Wai, and for the training of Xiang pastors at Sichuan Theological Seminary in Chengdu. Yet perhaps most importantly of all, it allowed Torrance to discover that the work begun by his father had not been destroyed, despite all the adversities which the Xiang churches had been forced to endure. The churches in Chengdu, the original base of his father's missionary work, were full to overflowing. The years of oppression had, if anything, merely strengthened their determination to survive.

Perhaps this is a fitting note on which to end this account of the theological achievement of Thomas F. Torrance. His massive contributions

---

[6] Full details in unpublished typescript 'Journal of My Visit to Hong Kong, Chengdu and Wenchuan, April 22–June 3, 1994'.

to the discussion of the doctrine of the Trinity, to the development of the Reformed heritage, and to the dialogue between Christian theology and the natural sciences ensure that he will be a voice to be reckoned with in the next century. Yet perhaps Torrance himself might prefer to be remembered as one who both knew and proclaimed the faithfulness of God in the midst of the uncertainties and anxieties of this world, and saw the resurrection of the Chinese church as a symbol of that faithfulness.

Curriculum Vitae

BIRTH

> 30 August 1913, at Chengdu, Sichuan, China, eldest son of the Revd Thomas and Annie E. Torrance, Missionaries of the Gospel

SCHOOLING

> Chengdu Canadian Mission School, 1920–7
> Bellshill Academy, Scotland, 1927–31

UNIVERSITIES

> Edinburgh, 1931–7
> Basel, 1937–8
> Oxford, Oriel College, 1939–40
> Studied also in Jerusalem and Athens, 1936, Berlin, 1937, Basel, 1946

EARNED DEGREES

> MA, 1934: Classical Languages and Philosophy
>
> BD, 1937: Divinity, with specialization in Systematic Theology
>
> Dr.Theol., 1946: University of Basel, Doctoral Thesis: 'The Doctrine of Grace in the Apostolic Fathers'
>
> D.Litt., 1970: Edinburgh University, on submission of five published works on Theological Method

DEGREES, *honoris causa*

DD, 1950: Presbyterian College, Montreal

Dr.Theol., 1959: University of Geneva

D.Théol., 1959: Faculté Libre, Paris

DD, 1960: St Andrews University

Dr.Theol., 1961: Oslo University

D.Sc., 1983: Heriot-Watt University, Edinburgh

Dr.Th., 1988: Reformed College, Debrecen

DD, 1997: Edinburgh University

FELLOWSHIPS

Fellow of the Royal Society of Edinburgh, since 1979

Fellow of the British Academy, London, since 1982

HONOURS AND DISTINCTIONS

Member of the British Empire, 1944, as Church of Scotland Chaplain with the British Army

Collins Religious Book Prize, 1969

Cross of St Mark. Patriarchate of Alexandria, 1970

Protopresbyter of the Greek Orthodox Church. Patriarchate of Alexandria, 1973

Cross of Thyateira, 1977

Templeton Prize for Progress in Religion, 1978

ACADEMIC SOCIETIES

Scottish Church Theology Society. Founder, 1945

Church Service Society of the Church of Scotland. Member since 1946, President, 1970–1

Society for the Study of Theology. Founder, 1952; President, 1966–8

Société de l'Histoire du Protestantisme Français. Foreign Member, 1968

Société Internationale pour l'Étude de la Philosophie Médiévale. Member, 1968

Académie Internationale des Sciences Religieuses. Member, 1969; President, 1972–81

Institute of Religion and Theology of Great Britain and Ireland. Founder Member, 1973; President, 1976–7

Académie Internationale de Philosophie des Sciences, 1976

ACADEMIC INSTITUTIONS

Center of Theological Inquiry, Princeton, New Jersey. Member of Advisory Board, since 1980

Das Deutsche Institut für Bildung und Wissen, Berlin and Paderborn. Member of Kuratorium since 1983

Royal Society of Edinburgh. Committee member, 1985

Europäische Akademie für Umweltfragen, Tübingen. Member of Kuratorium since 1986

APPOINTMENTS

Assistant Professor of Systematic Theology, Auburn Theological Seminary, NY, USA, 1938–9

Ordained, 1940, Parish Minister at Alyth, Perthshire, Scotland, 1940–7; Chaplaincy Service with British Army, 1943–5

Minister of Beechgrove Parish Church, Aberdeen, 1947–50

Professor of Church History, Edinburgh University and New College, 1950–2

Professor of Christian Dogmatics, University of Edinburgh and New College, 1952–79

Convener of Church of Scotland Commission on Baptism, 1954–62

Moderator of the General Assembly of the Church of Scotland, 1976–7

LECTURESHIPS

Hewett Lectures, Union Theological Seminary, New York, and Andover Newton Theological School, Newton Center, Episcopal Theological School, Massachusetts, 1959

Harris Lectures, Queens University, Dundee, 1970

Anderson Lectures, Presbyterian College, Montreal, 1971

Taylor Lectures, Yale University, Connecticut, 1971

Keese Lecture, University of Tennessee, Chattanooga, 1971

Cummings Lecture, McGill University, Montreal, 1978

Richards Lectures, University of Virginia at Charlottesville, 1978

Staley Lectures, Davidson College, North Carolina, 1978

Queen's University Lectures on Theology, Belfast, 1980

Warfield Lectures, Princeton Theological Seminary, New Jersey, 1981

Payton Lectures, Fuller Theological Seminary, Passadena, California, 1981

Didsbury Lectures, Nazarene College, Manchester, 1982

Edmonton Lectures, University of Alberta, Canada, 1983

Staley Lectures, Regent College, Vancouver, Canada, 1983

Hellenic Societies Lecture, London, 1984

Donnell Lecture, Dubuque University, Iowa, 1988

John Chrysostom Lectures, Hellenic College, Brookline, MA, 1991

Throckmorton Lecture, Bangor, Maine, USA, 1991

Warburton Lecture, Lincoln's Inn, London, 1995

ECUMENICAL ACTIVITIES

Church of Scotland/Church of England Conversations, 1950–8

Faith and Order Conference of the World Council of Churches, World Council, Lund, Sweden, 1952

Faith and Order Commission on Christ and his Church, 1952–62

World Alliance of Reformed Churches, Princeton, New Jersey, 1954

World Council of Churches, Evanston, Illinois, 1954

Faith and Order Commission, Chicago, Illinois, 1954

Church Leaders Conference, British Council of Churches, Birmingham, 1972

Reformed/Roman Catholic Study Commission on the Eucharist, Woudschoten, Holland, 1974

Theological Dialogue between Orthodox and Reformed Churches, Istanbul and Geneva, 1979–83; Geneva and Leuenberg, 1986–8; Geneva–Minsk, 1988–90

'Agreed Statement on the Holy Trinity', Geneva, 1991

Reformed–Orthodox Consultations on the Doctrine of the Trinity: (1) 1979–83; (2) 1988–92

Unpublished Sources

This work has drawn extensively on unpublished sources relating to both the life and thought of Thomas F. Torrance. It is hoped that all of these will be published in the future, allowing general access to these papers.

LECTURE NOTES (MANUSCRIPT)

'Dogmatics', notes on lectures by Hugh Ross Mackintosh, delivered at New College, Edinburgh, 1935–6.

TEXT OF LECTURES

1. Auburn Theological Seminary, 1938–9
   The Doctrine of Christ
   The Christian Doctrine of God
   The Christian Doctrine of Revelation
   Science and Theology

2. New College, Edinburgh, 1952–78
   The Doctrine of Christ
   The Doctrine of Church, Ministry and Sacraments

AUTOBIOGRAPHICAL WRITINGS

'Itinerarium mentis in Deum: T. F. Torrance – My Theological Development'

'Journal of My Visit to Hong Kong, Chengdu and Wenchuan, April 22–June 3, 1994'

'Memoir of Visit to Palestine and the Middle East in the Spring of 1936'

'Memories of Auburn, 1938–39'

'Student Years: Edinburgh to Basel, 1934–1938'

'My Parish Ministry: Alyth, 1940–3'

'The Visit by Thomas F. Torrance to Chengdu, the Capital of Sichuan, and to Weichou and Chiang Villages in Wenchuan County, the Upper Min Valley, Sichuan: October 4–18, 1986'

'War Service: Middle East and Italy, 1943–45'

SERMONS AND OTHER PAPERS

Sermon series at Alyth and Beechgrove Churches, 1940–50

Notes for Bible Study Groups, 1940–50

Moot Paper (1941), 'Christian Thinking Today'. John Baillie Collection, New College Library, Edinburgh

James Clerk Maxwell memorial sermons, preached on 4 November 1979 at Corsock Parish Church, and on 11 June 1989 at Parton Kirk, Kirkcudbrightshire

A Complete Bibliography of the Writings of Thomas F. Torrance
1941–

THE material presented in this Bibliography represents a complete bibliography of all published works written, translated or edited by Thomas Forsyth Torrance, as an aid to researchers working in this field. Two earlier valuable bibliographies should be noted:

Bryan Gray, 'Bibliography of the Published Writings of Thomas F. Torrance (1941–75)', in R. W. A. McKinney (ed.), *Creation, Christ and Culture: Studies in Honour of T. F. Torrance*. Edinburgh: T&T Clark, 1976, 307–21

Iain R. Torrance, 'A Bibliography of the Writings of Thomas F. Torrance, 1941–1989', *Scottish Journal of Theology* 43 (1990), 225–62

Due to the lack of general agreement concerning the abbreviations to be used for journals and other standard works, all references in this bibliography have avoided abbreviated forms of any kind, to facilitate their easy identification and location.

The following arrangement of material has been adopted. Publications are grouped according to year of publication. Within each yearly section, publications are grouped, in alphabetical order, as follows: books or pamphlets published as individual items; edited, coedited or translated works; reviews; articles.

Note that some of Torrance's writings remain unpublished; those that have been used in the writing of the present work are identified at pp. 247–8.

It is intended to update this bibliography in successive reprints of the present volume, to allow for further works, including reprints. The present bibliography is believed to be complete, and has been rigorously checked; the author welcomes notification of any errors which have been undetected, or typographical errors which passed unnoticed at proofreading. Such corrections will be entered in subsequent printings of this volume.

1941

1. *The Modern Theological Debate*, pamphlet issued for private circulation by the Theological Students' Prayer Union of the Inter-Varsity Fellowship of Evangelical Unions, London, 1941.

2. Review of Norman Kemp Smith, *The Philosophy of David Hume*, in *The British Weekly* (15 May 1941), 48.

3. Review of *Thomas Reid's Essays on the Intellectual Powers of Man*, in *The British Weekly* (18 December 1941), 142.

4. 'The Importance of Fences in Religion', *The British Weekly* (30 January 1941), 179–80.

5. 'Predestination in Christ', *The Evangelical Quarterly* 13 (1941), 108–41.

6. 'Theology and the Common Man', *Life and Work* (Edinburgh, 1940), 177–8.

7. 'We Need a Decisive Theology before We Can Restate the Creed', *The British Weekly* (15 May 1941), 48.

1942

8. *The Place and Function of the Church in the World*, pamphlet. Foreword by D. F. Mackenzie, Moderator of Meigle Presbytery. Alyth Printing Works, 1942.

9. 'Reason in Christian Theology', *Evangelical Theology* 14 (1942), 22–41.

1943

10. 'Kierkegaard on the Knowledge of God', *The Presbyter* 1, no. 3 (1943), 4–7.

11. Review of Leonard Hodgson, *Towards a Christian Philosophy*, in *The Evangelical Quarterly* 15 (1943), 237–9.

1945

12. 'In hoc signo vinces', *The Presbyter* 3, no. 2 (1945), 13–20.

1946

13. *The Doctrine of Grace in the Apostolic Fathers*, limited paperback edition of doctoral thesis for Basel University. Edinburgh: Oliver & Boyd, 1946.

1947

14. Review of Emil Brunner, *Revelation and Reason*, in *The Record* (7 November 1947), 681.

15. Review of C. van Til, *The New Modernism: An Appraisal of the Theology of Barth and Brunner*, in *The Evangelical Quarterly* 19 (1947), 144–9.

16. 'The Word of God and the Nature of Man', in F. W. Camfield (ed.), *Reformation Old and New: Festschrift for Karl Barth*. London: Lutterworth Press, 1947, 121–41.

1948

17. *The Doctrine of Grace in the Apostolic Fathers*. Edinburgh: Oliver & Boyd, 1948.

18. 'The Word of God and the Preaching of It: Jeremiah 7.2 and 2 Corinthians 5.20', sermon, *Beechgrove Church* (November 1948), 2–4.

19. Review of K. E. Kirk (ed.), *The Apostolic Ministry: Essays on the History and Doctrine of Episcopacy*, in *Scottish Journal of Theology* 1 (1948), 190–201.

20. Review of T. H. L. Parker, *The Oracles of God: An Introduction to the Preaching of John Calvin*, in *Scottish Journal of Theology* 1 (1948), 212–14.

21. 'The Doctrine of Grace in the Old Testament', *Scottish Journal of Theology* 1 (1948), 55–65.

1949

22. *Calvin's Doctrine of Man*. London: Lutterworth Press, 1949.

23. 'Except a Man Be Born Again, He Cannot See the Kingdom of God (John 3.3–7)', sermon, *Beechgrove Church* (June 1949), 2–5.

24. 'Jesus Christ the Same Yesterday, Today and For Ever (Hebrews 13.8)', sermon, *Beechgrove Church* (February 1949), 2–4.

25. 'Where Two or Three Are Gathered Together, There Am I in the Midst of Them (Matthew 18.20)', sermon, *Beechgrove Church* (April 1949), 2–4.

26. 'Ye Worship Ye Know Not What: We Know What We Worship, for Salvation Is of the Jews (John 4.22)', sermon, *Beechgrove Church* (November 1949), 2–5.

27. Review of the Report of a Church of England Study Group, *Catholicity: a study in the Conflict of the Christian Traditions in the West*', in *Scottish Journal of Theology* 2 (1949), 85–93.

28. Review of Denzil G. M. Patrick, *Pascal and Kierkegaard*, in *Church of England Newspaper* (23 September 1949), 10.

29. Review of Johannes Klevinghaus, *Die theologische Stellung der apostolischen Väter zur altestamentlichen Offenbarung*, in *Evangelical Quarterly* 21 (1949), 153–4.

30. Review of Rudolph Pfister (ed.), *Zwingli Hauptschriften* XI:3, *Zwingli der Theologe*, in *Scottish Journal of Theology* 2 (1949), 441–4.

31. 'Concerning Amsterdam. I. The Nature and Mission of the Church: a discussion of Volumes I and II of the Preparatory Studies', *Scottish Journal of Theology* 2 (1949), 241–70.

32. 'Faith and Philosophy', *The Hibbert Journal* 45 (1948–9), 237–46.

33. 'Universalism or Election?' *Scottish Journal of Theology* 2 (1949), 310–18.

1950

34. 'Minister's Letter on Call to the Chair of Church History, New College, Edinburgh (John 21.18–19)'. *Beechgrove Church* (April 1950), 1–3.

35. 'Salvation Is of the Jews', *The Evangelical Quarterly* 22 (1950), 164–73.

36. 'A Study in New Testament Communication', *Scottish Journal of Theology* 3 (1950), 298–313.

1951

37. *Calvins Lehre vom Menschen*, translation by F. Keienberg. Zürich: Evangelischer Verlag, 1951. German translation of (22).

38. Review of William Robertson, *The Biblical Doctrine of the Church*, in *Scottish Journal of Theology* 4 (1951), 433–7.

39. Review of Edmund Schlink (ed.), *Evangelisches Gutachten zur Dogmatisierung der leiblichen Himmelfahrt Mariens*, in *Scottish Journal of Theology* 4 (1951), 90–6.

40. Review of A. E. J. Rawlinson, *Problems of Reunion*, in *Scottish Journal of Theology* 4 (1951), 427–33.

41. 'Answer to God', *Biblical Theology* 2 (1951), 3–16.

42. 'History and Reformation', *Scottish Journal of Theology* 4 (1951), 279–91.

1952

43. Review of L. Nixon (trans.), *Calvin's Sermons*, vol. 2: *The Deity of Christ and Other Sermons*, in *Scottish Journal of Theology* 5 (1952), 424–7.

44. Review of Oscar Cullmann, *The Earliest Christian Confessions*, in *Scottish Journal of Theology* 5 (1952), 85–7.

45. Review of William Manson, *The Epistle to the Hebrews*, in *Scottish Journal of Theology* 5 (1952), 309–13.

46. Review of Adolph Hamel, *Kirche bei Hippolyt von Rom*, in *Scottish Journal of Theology* 5 (1952), 208–11.

47. Review of C. R. B. Shapland (trans.), *The Letters of St Athanasius concerning the Holy Spirit*, in *Scottish Journal of Theology* 5 (1952), 205–8.

48. Review of Gordon Rupp, *Luther's Progress to the Diet of Worms*, in *Scottish Journal of Theology* 5 (1952), 427–8.

49. Review of Heinrich Heppe, *Reformed Dogmatics, Set Out and Illustrated from the Sources*, in *Scottish Journal of Theology* 5 (1952), 81–5.

50. Review of Alan Richardson, *A Theological Word Book of the Bible*, in *Scottish Journal of Theology* 5 (1952), 319–20.

51. Review of J. S. McEwen, *Why We Are Christians*, in *Scottish Journal of Theology* 5 (1952), 316–19.

52. 'Eschatology and Eucharist', in D. M. Baillie and J. Marsh (eds), *Intercommunion*. London: SCM Press, 1952, 303–50.

53. Report of a Church of England Study Group, *The Fulness of Christ: The Church's Growth into Catholicity*, *Scottish Journal of Theology* 5 (1952), 90–100.

54. Correspondence with Professor Brand Blanshard over his attack on 'The Theology of Crisis' as reported in *The Scotsman*, Edinburgh (9 April 1952); Torrance on 'The Theology of Karl Barth' (14 April), 4; Blanshard's reply (16 April), 6; Torrance again (19 April), 6; Blanshard (22 April), 6; Torrance again (23 April), 6; Blanshard (30 April), 6.

1953

55. Coedited with J. K. S. Reid, G. A. F. Knight, *A Biblical Approach to the Doctrine of the Trinity* (Scottish Journal of Theology Occasional Papers, No. 1) Edinburgh: Oliver & Boyd, 1953.

56. Coedited with J. K. S. Reid and others, *Eschatology: Four Occasional Papers read to the Society for the Study of Theology* (Scottish Journal of Theology Occasional Papers, No. 2). Edinburgh: Oliver & Boyd, 1953.

57. Review of Otto A. Dillschneider, *Das Christliche Weltbild*, in *Scottish Journal of Theology* 6 (1953), 435–6.

58. Review of Leroy Edwin Froom, *The Prophetic Faith of our Fathers: The Historical Development of Prophetic Interpretation*, 3 vols, in *Scottish Journal of Theology* 6 (1953), 207–12.

59. Review of J. Robert Nelson, *The Realm of Redemption*, in *Scottish Journal of Theology* 6 (1953), 320–5.

60. Review of F. L. Cross, *St Cyril's Lectures on the Christian Sacraments*, in *Scottish Journal of Theology* 6 (1953), 90–2.

61. 'The Christian Doctrine of Marriage', *Theology* 56 (1953), 162–7.

62. 'The Eschatology of the Reformation', in *Eschatology*, 36–90. See (56) above.

63. 'Our Witness through Doctrine', *The Presbyterian World* 22 (1953), 314–26. See also (75).

64. 'Where Do We Go from Lund?', *Scottish Journal of Theology* 6 (1953), 53–64.

65. 'Wohin führt Lund?', *Evangelische Theologie* 12 (1952–3), 499–508. German translation of (64).

1954

66. Review of P. Barth and D. Scheuner (eds), *Calvini Opera Selecta*, vol. 2, in *Scottish Journal of Theology* 7 (1954), 320–1.

67. Review of B. B. Warfield, *The Inspiration and Authority of the Bible*, in *Scottish Journal of Theology* 7 (1954), 104–8.

68. Review of Tiburtius Gallus, *Interpretatio mariologica Protoevangelii posttridentina usque ad Definitionem Dogmaticam Immaculatae Conceptionis, pars prior*, in *Scottish Journal of Theology* 7 (1954), 97–9.

69. Review of T. Stupperich (ed.), *Melanchthons Werke*, vol. 1, in *Scottish Journal of Theology* 7 (1954), 319–20.

70. 'The Atonement and the Oneness of the Church', *Scottish Journal of Theology* 7 (1954), 245–69.

71. 'Die Eschatologie der Reformation', *Evangelische Theologie* 14 (1954), 334–58. German translation of (62).

72. Letter to *The Scotsman* on 'Intercommunion' (8 December 1954).

73. 'Liturgy and Apocalypse', *Church Service Society Annual* 24 (1954), 1–18.

74. 'Our Oneness in Christ and Our Disunity as Churches', *The British Weekly* (4 February 1954), 7.

75. 'Our Witness through Doctrine', in *Proceedings of the 17th General Council of the Alliance of Reformed Churches throughout the World holding the Presbyterian Order, Princeton, NJ, 1954*. Geneva, 1954, 133–45. See (63).

76. French version of 'Our Witness through Doctrine', *Verbum Caro* 8 (1954), 110–20.

77. 'Proselyte Baptism', *New Testament Studies* 1 (1954), 150–4.

78. 'Die Versöhnung und das Eine-Sein der Kirche', *Evangelische Theologie* 15 (1954), 1–22. German translation of (70).

79. 'The Way of Reunion', *The Christian Century* 71 (1954), 204–5.

1955

80. *Les reformateurs et le fin de temps*, translated by Roger Brandt. Neuchâtel: Delachaux et Niestlé, 1955. French translation of (62).

81. *Royal Priesthood* (*Scottish Journal of Theology Occasional Papers*, No. 3). Edinburgh: Oliver & Boyd, 1955.

82. *Le Sacerdoce Royal*, translated by Gérard Huni. Neuchâtel: Delachaux et Niestlé, 1955. French translation of (81).

83. Coedited with J. K. S. Reid, *The Biblical Doctrine of the Ministry* (*Scottish Journal of Theology Occasional Papers*, No. 4). Edinburgh: Oliver & Boyd, 1955.

84. *Interim Report of the Special Commission on Baptism*, prepared by T. F. Torrance, with others, for the General Assembly of the Church of Scotland, May 1955 Report, 'The New Testament Doctrine of Baptism', 1–54.

85. Review of F. L. Cross, *1 Peter, a Paschal Liturgy*, in *Scottish Journal of Theology* 8 (1955), 101–2.

86. 'Karl Barth', *Expository Times* 66 (1955), 205–9.

87. 'Kingdom and Church in the Thought of Martin Butzer', *Journal of Ecclesiastical History* 6 (1955), 48–59.

88. Foreword to H. Quistorp, *Calvin's Doctrine of the Last Things*. London: Lutterworth Press, 1955, 7–8.

1956

89. *Kingdom and Church: A Study in the Theology of the Reformation*, Edinburgh: Oliver & Boyd, 1956.

90. Coedited with G. W. Bromiley: Karl Barth, *Church Dogmatics* I/2, *The Doctrine of the Word of God. Prolegomena*, Part 2, translated by G. T. Thomson and H. Knight. Edinburgh: T&T Clark, 1956.

91. Coedited with G. W. Bromiley: Karl Barth, *Church Dogmatics* IV/1, *The Doctrine of Reconciliation*, Part 1, translated by G. W. Bromiley. Edinburgh: T&T Clark, 1956.

92. Coedited with J. K. S. Reid: Karl Barth, *Christ and Adam: Man and Humanity in Romans 5*, translated by T. A. Smail (*Scottish Journal of Theology Occasional Papers*, No. 5). Edinburgh: Oliver & Boyd, 1956.

93. Review of Ronald Selby Wright (ed.), *Asking Them Questions*, in *Scottish Journal of Theology* 9 (1956), 112.

94. Review of *Martini Buceri Opera Latina* XV: *De Regno Christi: Libri Duo 1550*, & *Du Royaume de Jesus-Christ: édition critique de la traduction française de 1558*, edited by François Wendel, Paris: Presses Universitaires de France, 1955, in *Journal of Ecclesiastical History* 5 (1956), 143.

95. Review of F. C. Schmitt (ed.), *S. Anselmi Opera Omnia*, in *Scottish Journal of Theology* 9 (1956), 88–90.

96. Review of Ernst Staehelin, *Die Verkündigung des Reiches Gottes in der Kirche Jesu Christi: Zeugnisse aus allen Jahrhunderten und allen Konfessionen*, vols 1–2; in *Scottish Journal of Theology* 9 (1956), 290–2.

97. *1956 Interim Report of the Special Commission on Baptism*, prepared for the General Assembly of the Church of Scotland by T. F. Torrance, with others.

98. 'Baptism in the Early Church', *1956 Interim Report of the Special Commission on Baptism*, 1–42. See (97).

99. 'Israel and the Incarnation', *Interpretation* 10 (1956), 3–10.

100. 'Karl Barth: Appreciation and Tribute in Honour of His Seventieth Birthday', *Expository Times* 67 (1956), 261–3.

101. 'Karl Barth', *Union Seminary Quarterly Review* 12 (1956), No. 1 (November 1956), 21–31; reprinted from *Crossroads* (June, July, September, 1956).

102. 'The Meaning of Baptism', *Canadian Journal of Theology* 2 (1956), 129–32.

103. 'Le Mystère du Royaume', *Verbum Caro* 10 (1956), 1–10.

104. 'The Place of Christology in Biblical and Dogmatic Theology', in T. H. L. Parker (ed.), *Essays in Christology for Karl Barth*. London: Lutterworth Press, 1956, 13–37.

105. 'The Place of the Humanity of Christ in the Sacramental Life of the Church', *Church Service Society Annual* 26 (1956), 129–34.

106. 'A Sermon on the Trinity', *Biblical Theology* 6 (1956), 40–4.

107. 'Ein vernachlässigter Gesichtspunkt der Tauflehre', *Evangelische Theologie* 16 (1956), 433–57, 481–92.

1957

108. Japanese edition of *Calvin's Doctrine of Man*, translated by Sakae Izumeda. Tokyo: Japanese Association of Calvin Studies, 1957. See (22).

109. *When Christ Comes and Comes Again*. London: Hodder & Stoughton; and Grand Rapids, MI: Eerdmans, 1957.

110. Coedited with G. W. Bromiley: Karl Barth, *Church Dogmatics* II/1, *The Doctrine of God*, translated by T. H. L. Parker, W. B. Johnston, H. Knight and J. L. M. Haire. Edinburgh: T&T Clark, 1957.

111. Coedited with G. W. Bromiley: Karl Barth, *Church Dogmatics* II/2, *The Doctrine of God*, translated by G. W. Bromiley, J. C. Campbell, I. Wilson, J. Strathearn McNab, H. Knight and R. A. Stewart. Edinburgh: T&T Clark, 1957.

112. Coedited with J. K. S. Reid: N. Q. Hamilton, *The Holy Spirit and Eschatology in St Paul* (*Scottish Journal of Theology Occasional Papers*, No. 6). Edinburgh: Oliver & Boyd, 1957.

113. *1957 Interim Report of the Special Commission on Baptism*, prepared for the General Assembly of the Church of Scotland by T. F. Torrance, with others.

114. 'Abendmahlsgemeinschaft und Vereinigung der Kirchen', *Kerygma und Dogma* 3 (1957), 240–50.

115. 'Baptism in the Mediaeval Church', *1957 Interim Report of the Special Commission on Baptism*, 1–59. See (113).

116. 'Israel and the Incarnation', *Judaica* 13 (1957), 1–18. Reprint of (99).

117. Letter to *The Scotsman*, on 'The Impossibility of Seeking Unity with the Roman Church' (22 October 1957).

118. French version of 'Liturgy and Apocalypse', *Verbum Caro* 11 (1957), 28–40. See (73).

119. 'A New Approach: Presbyterian and Anglican Conversations', *The Presbyterian Record*, Toronto (July–August 1957), 19, 36–7. Also printed in *Biblical Theology* 8 (1957), 26–36.

120. 'One Aspect of the Biblical Conception of Faith', *Expository Times* 68 (1957), 111–14, 221–2.

1958

121. Translated and edited, *The Mystery of the Lord's Supper: Sermons on the Sacrament Preached in the Kirk of Edinburgh in A.D. 1589 by Robert Bruce*. London: James Clarke, 1958.

122. Introduction and Historical Notes to *Tracts and Treatises on the Reformation by John Calvin*, translated by H. Beveridge, 3 vols. Edinburgh: Oliver & Boyd; Grand Rapids, MI: Eerdmans, 1958.

123. Coedited with G. W. Bromiley: Karl Barth, *Church Dogmatics* III/1, *The Doctrine of Creation*, Part 1, translated by J. W. Edwards, O. Bussey and H. Knight. Edinburgh: T&T Clark, 1958.

124. Coedited with G. W. Bromiley: Karl Barth, *Church Dogmatics* IV/2, Part 2, *The Doctrine of Reconciliation*, translated by G. W. Bromiley. Edinburgh: T&T Clark, 1958.

125. Coedited with J. K. S. Reid: Arnold Ehrhardt, *The Apostolic Ministry* (*Scottish Journal of Theology Occasional Papers*, No. 7). Edinburgh: Oliver & Boyd, 1958.

126. *1958 Interim Report of the Special Commission on Baptism*, prepared for the General Assembly of the Church of Scotland by T. F. Torrance, with others.

127. Review of K. E. Skydsgaard, *One in Christ*, in *Scottish Journal of Theology* 11 (1958), 330–3.

128. Review of F. L. Cross (ed.), *The Oxford Dictionary of the Christian Church*, in *Scottish Journal of Theology* 11 (1958), 320–1.

129. Review of Kurt Galling (ed.), *Die Religion in Geschichte und Gegenwart* I, in *Scottish Journal of Theology* 11 (1958), 322–3.

130. 'Aspects of Baptism in the New Testament', *Theologische Zeitschrift* 14 (1958), 241–60.

131. 'Baptism in the Church of Scotland', in *1958 Interim Report of the Special Commission on Baptism*, 1–78. See (126).

132. 'Consecration and Ordination', *Scottish Journal of Theology* 11 (1958) 225–52.

133. 'La doctrine de l'ordre', *Revue d'Histoire et de Philosophie Religieuses* 38 (1958), 129–42.

134. 'Karl Barth', in G. L. Hunt (ed.), *Ten Makers of Modern Protestant Thought*, New York: Association Press, 1958, 58–68; reprinted from *Crossroads*, 1956.

135. 'The Mission of Anglicanism', in D. M. Paton (ed.), *Anglican Self-Criticism*. London: SCM Press, 1958, 194–208.

136. 'The Origins of Baptism', *Scottish Journal of Theology* 9 (1958), 158–71.

137. 'What is the Church?' *The Ecumenical Review* 11 (1958), 6–21.

1959

138. *The Apocalypse Today*. Grand Rapids, MI: Eerdmans, 1959. Abbreviated version of text of (154).

139. *Conflict and Agreement in the Church*, I: *Order and Disorder*. London: Lutterworth Press, 1959.

140. *The School of Faith: The Catechisms of the Reformed Church*, translated and edited with an introduction. London: James Clarke; New York: Harper & Row, 1959.

141. Coedited with J. K. S. Reid: Karl Barth, *God, Grace and the Gospel*, translated by J. Strathearn McNab (*Scottish Journal of Theology Occasional Papers*, No. 8). Edinburgh: Oliver & Boyd, 1959.

142. Coedited with D. W. Torrance, *Calvin's Commentaries, The Gospel According to St John, 1–10*, translated by T. H. L. Parker. Edinburgh: Oliver & Boyd; Grand Rapids, MI: Eerdmans, 1959.

143. *1959 Interim Report of the Special Commission on Baptism*, prepared for the General Assembly of the Church of Scotland by T. F. Torrance, with others.

144. Review of Joachim Beckmann, *Quellen zur Geschichte des christlichen Gottesdienstes*, in *Scottish Journal of Theology* 12 (1959), 108–9.

145. Review of Paul F. Palmer, *Sacraments and Worship*, in *Scottish Journal of Theology* 12 (1959), 109–10.

146. Review of M. F. Toal (ed.), *The Sunday Sermons of the Great Fathers*, in *Scottish Journal of Theology* 12 (1959), 109–11.

147. 'Baptism in the Church of Scotland, 1843–1959', in *1959 Interim Report of the Special Commission on Baptism*, 1–34. See (143).

148. 'Calvins Lehre von der Taufe', in Jürgen Moltmann (ed.), *Calvinstudien*. Neukirchen: Neukirchener Verlag, 1959, 95–129.

149. 'L'enseignement baptismal chez Calvin', *Revue de Théologie et de Philosophie* 2 (1959), 141–52. French translation of (148).

150. 'The Meaning of Order', *Church Quarterly Review* 160 (1959), 21–36. English translation of (133).

151. 'Uppfattningen om försoningen i urkyrkan. Kristi ämbete (Conceptions of Atonement in the Early Church: The Office of Christ), translated by L. G. Rignell, *Svensk Teologisk Kvartalskrift* 25 (1959), 73–100.

152. 'What Is the Reformed Church?', *Biblical Theology* 9 (1959), 51–62.

153. Contribution to *Special Number on John Calvin*, Tokyo, 1959, 46, *Fukuin to Sekai – Gospel and World* (August 1959). Shinkyo Shuppansha (Protestant Publishing Co. Ltd), Shin-Ogawa-machi, Shinjuku-ku, Tokyo.

1960

154. *The Apocalypse Today*. London: James Clarke, 1960. Full version of (138).

155. *Conflict and Agreement in the Church*, II: *The Ministry and the Sacraments of the Gospel*. London: Lutterworth Press, 1960.

156. Coedited with G.W. Bromiley: Karl Barth, *Church Dogmatics* III/2, *The Doctrine of Creation*, Part 2, translated by H. Knight, J. K. S. Reid, G. W. Bromiley and R. H. Fuller. Edinburgh: T&T Clark, 1960.

157. Coedited with G.W. Bromiley: Karl Barth, *Church Dogmatics* III/3, *The Doctrine of Creation*, Part 3, translated by G. W. Bromiley and R. Ehrlich. Edinburgh: T&T Clark, 1960.

158. Coedited with D. W. Torrance: *Calvin's Commentaries, The First Epistle of Paul the Apostle to the Corinthians*, translated by J.W. Fraser. Edinburgh: Oliver & Boyd; Grand Rapids, MI: Eerdmans, 1960.

159. Revised and edited with Ronald Selby Wright, *A Manual of Church Doctrine according to the Church of Scotland*, by H. J. Wotherspoon and J. M. Kirkpatrick. London: Oxford University Press, 1960.

160. *1960 Report of the Special Commission on Baptism*, prepared for the General Assembly of the Church of Scotland by T. F. Torrance, with others.

161. Review of Kurt Galling (ed.), *Die Religion in Geschichte und Gegenwart*, vols 2–3, in *Scottish Journal of Theology* 13 (1960), 217–19.

162. Review of Otto Karrer (ed.), *Neues Testament*, in *Scottish Journal of Theology* 13 (1960), 222.

163. 'Die Arnoldshainer Abendmahlsthesen', *Ökumenische Rundschau* 9 (1960), 131–50.

164. 'Justification: Its Radical Nature and Place in Reformed Doctrine and Life', *Scottish Journal of Theology* 13 (1960), 225–46.

165. 'The Ministry of Men and Women in the Kirk: Brief Theses', *Manse Mail* (May 1960), 11–13.

166. 'Report', in *1960 Report of the Special Commission on Baptism*, 1–16. See (160).

1961

167. Coedited with G.W. Bromiley: Karl Barth, *Church Dogmatics* III/4, *The Doctrine of Creation*, translated by A. T. Mackay, T. H. L. Parker, H. Knight, H. A. Kennedy and J. Marks. Edinburgh: T&T Clark, 1961.

168. Coedited with G. W. Bromiley: Karl Barth, *Church Dogmatics* IV/3, *The Doctrine of Reconciliation*, Part 3, vols 1 and 2, translated by G.W. Bromiley. Edinburgh: T&T Clark, 1961–2.

169. Coedited with J. K. S. Reid: Markus Barth, *Was Christ's Death a Sacrifice?* (*Scottish Journal of Theology Occasional Papers*, No. 9). Edinburgh: Oliver & Boyd, 1961.

170. Coedited with D. W. Torrance, *Calvin's Commentaries, The Gospel according to St John 11–12 and the First Epistle of John*, translated by T. H. L. Parker. Edinburgh: Oliver & Boyd; Grand Rapids, MI: Eerdmans, 1961.

171. Coedited with D. W. Torrance, *Calvin's Commentaries, The Epistles of St Paul to the Romans and to the Thessalonians*, translated by Ross MacKenzie. Edinburgh: Oliver & Boyd; Grand Rapids, MI: Eerdmans, 1961.

172. *1961 Report of the Special Commission on Baptism*, prepared for the General Assembly by T. F. Torrance, with others.

173. Letter to the Editor on 'Catholicity and the Reformed Tradition', *Bulletin of the Department of Theology*, World Alliance of Reformed Churches, 2, no. 1, Geneva (1961), 4–8.

174. 'The Doctrine of Baptism', in *1961 Report of the Special Commission on Baptism*, 1–16. See (172).

175. 'A Living Sacrifice: In Memoriam John Baillie, 1886–1960', *Religion and Life* 30 (1961), 329–33.

176. 'Reconciliation in Christ and in His Church', *Biblical Theology* 12 (1961), 26–35.

1962

177. *Karl Barth: An Introduction to His Early Theology, 1910–1931*. London: SCM Press; New York: Harper & Row, 1962.

178. *1962 Report of the Special Commission on Baptism*, prepared for the General Assembly of the Church of Scotland by T. F. Torrance, with others.

179. Review of John Calvin, *Concerning the Eternal Predestination of God*, translated by J. K. S. Reid, in *Scottish Journal of Theology* 15 (1962), 108–10.

180. Review of John Alexander Lamb (ed.), *Fasti Ecclesiae Scoticanae. The Succession of Ministers in the Church of Scotland from the Reformation*, vol. 9, in *Scottish Journal of Theology* 15 (1962), 90–1.

181. Review of Kurt Galling (ed.), *Die Religion in Geschichte und Gegenwart*, vols 4–5, in *Scottish Journal of Theology* 15 (1962), 84–5.

182. 'Barth. Equal to Athanasius?' *The British Weekly* (21 June, 1962), 2.

183. 'Doctrinal Consensus on Holy Communion: The Arnoldshain Theses', *Scottish Journal of Theology* 15 (1962), 1–35.

184. 'Gnade und Natur: Der Einfluss der reformatorischen Theologie auf die Entwicklung der wissenschaftlichen Methode', *Theologische Zeitschrift* 18 (1962), 341–56.

185. 'Introduction' to Karl Barth, *Theology and Church, Shorter Writings 1920–1928*. London: SCM Press, 1962, 7–54.

186. 'The Kirk and the Church of Rome', *The Scotsman* (12 April 1962), 6, cols 3–5.

187. 'Le Problème des relations entre Anglicains et Presbytériens en Grande-Bretagne', *Église & Théologie* 75 (1962), 15–39.

188. 'Report, with Appendix on the Doctrine of Baptism', *Assembly Reports* (1962), 613–24; Supplementary Report, 1–3. See (178).

189. 'Scientific Hermeneutics according to St Thomas Aquinas', *Journal of Theological Studies* 13 (1962), 259–89.

190. 'Die Wahrheit, Wie Sie in Jesus ist', in Kurt Scharf, *Vom Herrengeheimnis der Wahrheit: Festschrift für Heinrich Vogel*. Berlin: Lettner Verlag, 1962, 254–76.

1963

191. Coedited with J. K. S. Reid: John D. Godsey, *Karl Barth's Table Talk* (*Scottish Journal of Theology Occasional Papers*, No. 10). Edinburgh: Oliver & Boyd, 1963.

192. Coedited with D. W. Torrance, *Calvin's Commentaries, The Epistle of Paul the Apostle to the Hebrews; and the First and Second Epistles of St Peter*, translated by W. B. Johnston. Edinburgh: Oliver & Boyd; Grand Rapids, MI: Eerdmans, 1963.

193. Review of Y. H. Krikorian and A. Edel (eds), *Contemporary Philosophic Problems: Selected Readings*, in *Scottish Journal of Theology* 16 (1963), 302–3.

194. Review of Heinrich Scholz, *Mathesis Universalis: Abhandlungen zur Philosophie als strenger Wissenschaft*, in *Scottish Journal of Theology* 16 (1963), 212–14.

195. Review of G. A. Abernethy and T. A. Langford (eds), *Philosophy of Religion: A Book of Readings*, in *Scottish Journal of Theology* 16 (1963), 302–3.

196. Review of Bernard Lambert, *Le Problème Oecumenique*, in *Scottish Journal of Theology* 16 (1963), 101–5.

197. 'Anglican–Methodist Reconciliation', *The British Weekly* (28 February 1963), 7.

198. 'Foreword' to Jacques de Senarclens, *Heirs of the Reformation*, translated by G. W. Bromiley. London: SCM Press, 1963.

199. 'The Foundation of the Church', *Scottish Journal of Theology* 16 (1963), 113–31.

200. 'The Influence of Reformed Theology on the Development of Scientific Method', *Dialog* 2 (1963), 40–9.

201. 'Introduction' to William F. Keesecker (ed.), *A Calvin Treasury: Selections from the Institutes of the Christian Religion*, translated by F. L. Battles. London: SCM Press, 1963, v–xiii.

202. 'Jesus the Servant Today', in A. Reeves (ed.), *Christ's Call to Service Now*, report of the Student Christian Conference, Bristol, 1963. London: SCM Press, 1963, 11–21.

203. 'La Portée de la doctrine du Saint-Esprit pour la théologie oecumenique', *Verbum Caro* 17 (1963), 166–76.

204. German version of (203): *Ökumenische Rundschau* 12 (1963), 122–31.

205. 'Das Problem der theologischen Aussage Heute', *Theologische Zeitschrift* 19 (1963), 318–37.

1964

206. Coedited with D. W. Torrance, *Calvin's Commentaries, The Second Epistle of Paul the Apostle to the Corinthians*, translated by T. A. Smail. Edinburgh: Oliver & Boyd; Grand Rapids, MI: Eerdmans, 1964.

207. Review of Martin Heidegger, *Being and Time*, translated by John Macquarrie and Edward Robinson, in *Journal of Theological Studies* 15 (1964), 471–86.

208. Review of W. A. Whitehouse and others, *A Declaration of Faith*, in *The British Weekly* (18 June 1964), 4.

209. Review of J. B. Phillips, *Good News for Modern Man*, in *Scottish Journal of Theology* 17 (1964), 351–3.

210. 'Calvin on the Knowledge of God', *The Christian Century* 81 (1964), 696–9.

211. 'Changed Outlook of Christians on Unity', *The Scotsman* (29 January 1964), 8, cols 3–5.

212. 'A Comment on the New Morality', *Common Factor* 2 (1964), 17–20.

213. 'John Calvin's Values for Today', *Common Factor* 2 (1964), 24–5.

214. 'Knowledge of God and Speech about Him according to John Calvin', *Revue d'Histoire et de Philosophie Religieuses* 44 (1964), 402–22.

215. 'The Ministry of Men and Women in the Kirk' (Brief Theses. Second Series). *Manse Mail* (February 1964), 17–20.

216. 'A New Reformation?' *The London Holborn and Quarterly Review* 189 (1964), 275–94.

217. 'The Roman Doctrine of Grace from the Point of View of Reformed Theology', *The Eastern Churches Quarterly* 16 (1964), 290–312.

218. 'Science, Theology and Unity', *Theology Today* 21 (1964), 149–54.

219. 'Sermon on Exodus 20:1–14', *Monkton Combe Society*, Monkton Combe School, Somerset (April 1964), 13–18.

220. 'Theological Education Today', *New College Bulletin* 1 (1964), 18–30.

221. 'Theology and Science: Dogmatics, the Key to Church Unity', *The Scotsman* (10 February, 1964), 6, cols 3–5.

222. 'Women in the Ministry. Reply to Dr Lillie', *Manse Mail* (May 1964), 9–11.

1965

223. *Theology in Reconstruction*. London: SCM Press, 1965.

224. Coedited with J. K. S. Reid: C. E. B. Cranfield, *A Commentary on Romans 12–13* (*Scottish Journal of Theology Occasional Papers*, No. 12). Edinburgh: Oliver & Boyd, 1965.

225. Coedited with J. K. S. Reid: Emmanuel Amand de Mendieta, *Apostolic Traditions in the Theological Thought of St Basil of Caesarea* (*Scottish Journal of Theology Occasional Papers*, No. 13). Edinburgh: Oliver & Boyd, 1965.

226. Coedited with J. K. S. Reid: Paul Ramsey, *Deeds and Rules in Christian Ethics* (*Scottish Journal of Theology Occasional Papers*, No. 11). Edinburgh: Oliver & Boyd, 1965.

227. Coedited with D. W. Torrance, *Calvin's Commentaries, The Acts of the Apostles 1–13*, translated by W. J. G. McDonald and J. W. Fraser. Edinburgh: Oliver & Boyd; Grand Rapids, MI: Eerdmans, 1965.

228. Coedited with D. W. Torrance, *Calvin's Commentaries, The Epistles of Paul the Apostle to the Galatians, Ephesians, Philippians and Colossians*, translated by T. H. L. Parker. Edinburgh: Oliver & Boyd; Grand Rapids, MI: Eerdmans, 1965.

229. Revised and edited with Ronald Selby Wright, *A Manual of Church Doctrine according to the Church of Scotland*, by H. J. Wotherspoon and J. M. Kirkpatrick, 2nd edn, with corrections. London: Oxford University Press, 1965.

230. 'The Epistemological Relevance of the Holy Spirit' in R. Schippers, and others, *Ex Auditu Verbi: Theologische Opstellen Aangeboden aan Prof. Dr. G.C. Berkhouwer*. Kampen: Kok, 1965.

231. 'Komm Schöpfer Geist!', *Theologische Zeitschrift* 21 (1965), 116–36. German translation of (235).

232. 'Obituary' for Dr Albert Schweitzer, OM, *The Times* (6 September 1965), 10, cols 4–5.

233. 'The Scientific Character of Theological Statements', *Dialog* 4 (1965), 112–17.

234. 'A Tribute to Dr John Alexander Lamb', *New College Bulletin* 2 (1965), 5–6.

235. 'Viens, Esprit Createur, pour renouveau du culte et du témoinage', *Revue d'Histoire et de Philosophie Religieuses* 45 (1965), 193–211.

1966

236. *The Doctrine of Baptism: An Interpretation of the Biblical and Reformed Doctrine of Baptism*. Statement for the Special Commission on Baptism (1953–62) of the Church of Scotland. Edinburgh: Saint Andrew Press, 1966.

237. Coedited with D. W. Torrance, *Calvin's Commentaries, The Acts of the Apostles 14–26*, translated by J. W. Fraser. Edinburgh: Oliver & Boyd; Grand Rapids, MI: Eerdmans, 1966.

238. Review of Willis A. Shotwell, *The Biblical Exegesis of Justin Martyr*, in *Scottish Journal of Theology* 19 (1966), 229–31.

239. Review of Heinz Brunotte and Otto Weber (eds), *Evangelisches Kirchenlexikon, Kirchlich-theologisches Handwörterbuch*, in *Scottish Journal of Theology* 19 (1966), 226–7.

240. 'Bonhoeffer's Christology', *The Scotsman* (28 May 1966), 3, cols 1–3.

241. 'The Christian Doctrine of Marriage', in J. M. Morrison, *Honesty and God*. Edinburgh: Saint Andrew Press, 1966, 155–62.

242. 'Diakonie in Jesus Christus', *Die Innere Mission* 56, no. 5. Berlin (1966), 201–15. German translation of (246).

243. 'The Mission of the Church', *Scottish Journal of Theology* 19 (1966), 129–43.

244. 'La Mission de l'Église', *Verbum Caro* 20 (1966), 1–16. French translation of (243).

245. 'Queries to the General Assembly', *The Scotsman* (27 May 1966).

246. 'Service in Jesus Christ', in J. I. McCord and T. H. L. Parker (eds), *Service in Christ: Essays Presented to Karl Barth on his 80th Birthday*, London: Epworth Press, 1966, 1–16.

1967

247. Edited with an Introduction, William Manson, *Jesus and the Christian*. London: James Clarke; Grand Rapids, MI: Eerdmans, 1967.

248. 'The Eclipse of God', *The Baptist Quarterly* 22 (1967), 194–214.

249. 'The Implications of Oikonomia for Knowledge and Speech of God in Early Christian Theology', in Felix Christ (ed.), *Oikonomia: Heilsgeschichte als Thema der Theologie: Oscar Cullmann zum 65 Geburtstag gewidmet*. Hamburg: Herbert Reich, 1967, 223–38.

250. 'Reformed Dogmatics Not Dogmatism', *Theology* 70 (1967), 152–6.

251. 'Thomas Ayton's "The Original Constitution of the Church"', in Duncan Shaw (ed.), *Reformation and Revolution. Essays presented to the Very Rev. Principal Emeritus Hugh Watt, D.D., D.Litt. on the Sixtieth Anniversary of His Ordination*. Edinburgh: Saint Andrew Press, 1967, 273–97.

1968

252. Coedited with J. K. S. Reid: James D. Hester, *Paul's Concept of Inheritance* (*Scottish Journal of Theology Occasional Papers*, No. 14). Oliver & Boyd, Edinburgh, 1968.

253. Coedited with D. W. Torrance, *Calvin's Commentaries, A Harmony of the Gospels: Matthew, Mark and Luke*, 3 vols. Vols 1 and 3 translated by A. W. Morrison and vol. 2 translated by T. H. L. Parker. Edinburgh: Saint Andrew Press, 1972; Grand Rapids, MI: Eerdmans, 1968.

254. Review of Edward Schillebeeckx, *Revelation and Theology*, in *New Blackfriars* 49 (1968), 490–2.

255. 'Cheap and Costly Grace', *The Baptist Quarterly* 22 (1968), 290–311.

256. 'The Ethical Implications of Anselm's *De Veritate*', *Theologische Zeitschrift* 24 (1968), 309–19.

257. 'Hermeneutics according to Schleiermacher', *Scottish Journal of Theology* 21 (1968), 257–67.

258. 'Intuitive and Abstractive Knowledge from Duns Scotus to John Calvin', *De doctrina Ioannis Duns Scoti. Acta tertii Congressus Scotistici Internationalis. Studia Scholastico-Scotistica 5.* Rome: Societas Internationalis Scotistica, 1968, 291–305.

259. 'Obituary' for Karl Barth, *The Times* (11 December 1968), 10, cols 6–9.

260. 'Theological Persuasion', *Common Factor* 5 (1968), 41–57.

261. 'Theological Persuasion', in McDowell Richards (ed.), *Soli Deo Gloria.* Richmond, VA: John Knox Press, 1968, 125–36. Reprint of (260).

1969

262. *Space, Time and Incarnation*, London: Oxford University Press, 1969.

263. *Theological Science*, London: Oxford University Press, 1969.

264. Coedited with G. W. Bromiley: Karl Barth, *Church Dogmatics IV/4 The Doctrine of Reconciliation*, Part 4 (Fragment), translated by G. W. Bromiley. Edinburgh: T&T Clark, 1969.

265. Coedited with J. K. S. Reid: A. J. B. Higgins, *The Tradition about Jesus (Scottish Journal of Theology Occasional Papers*, No. 15). Edinburgh: Oliver & Boyd, 1969.

266. Review of Carolo Bali (ed.), *Joannis Duns Scoti Opera Omnia*, vols 1–6, 14–17, in *Scottish Journal of Theology* 22 (1969), 479–81.

267. Review of Karl Rahner, with Cornelius Ernst and Kevin Smyth, *Sacramentum Mundi. An Encyclopedia of Theology*, vols 1–3, in *Scottish Journal of Theology* 22 (1969), 481–4.

268. 'Ecumenism and Science', in F. W. Kantzenbach and Vilmos Vajta (eds), *Oecumenica: Jahrbuch für ökumenische Forschung*, 1969. Gütersloh: Gütersloher Verlagshaus Gerd Mohn; Minneapolis: Augsburg Publishing House; Neuchâtel: Éditions Delachaux et Niestlé; Paris: Éditions du Cerf, 1969, 321–38.

269. '1469–1969. La Philosophie et la Théologie de Jean Mair ou Major (1469–1550)', *Archives de Philosophie* 32 (1969), 531–47. Concluded with (284).

270. 'Karl Barth', *Scottish Journal of Theology* 22 (1969), 1–9.

271. 'Karl Barth: In Homage', *High Point College Review of Theology and Philosophy* (April 1969), 5–12.

272. 'La mission de l'Église', in S. Dockx (ed.), *L'Esprit saint et l'Élise. Catholiques, orthodoxes et protestants de divers pays confrontent leur science, leur foi et leur tradition: l'avenir de l'Église et de l'oecumenisme.* Paris: Fayard, 1969, 275–94.

273. 'The Roman Doctrine of Grace from the Point of View of Reformed Theology', in Piet Fransen, *Intelligent Theology*. London: Darton, Longman & Todd, 1969, vol. 3, 46–77. Reprint of (217).

274. 'Spiritus Creator', in Lukas Vischer (ed.), *Le Traité sur le Saint-Esprit de Saint Basile*, Taizé: Presses de Taizé, 1969.

275. 'Spiritus Creator', *Verbum Caro* 23 (1969), 63–85. Reprint of (274).

276. 'La teologia nell'età della scienza', *Renovatio* 4 Genoa (1969), 545–64.

277. 'The Word of God and the Response of Man', *Bijdragen* 30 (1969), 172–83.

1970

278. *Calvin's Doctrine of Man*, new Japanese edition by Sakae Izumida. Tokyo: Meigen Shobo Publishing Co., 1980.

279. *The Relevance of Orthodoxy*, edited with Introduction by John B. Logan. Stirling: The Drummond Press, for The Fellowship of St Andrew, 1970.

280. Review of E. D. Willis, *Calvin's Catholic Christology*, in *Scottish Journal of Theology* 23 (1970), 92–4.

281. Review of Karl Rahner, with Cornelius Ernst and Kevin Smyth, *Sacramentum Mundi. An Encyclopedia of Theology*, vol. 4, in *Scottish Journal of Theology* 23 (1970), 94.

282. 'Alexandrian Theology', *Ekklesiastikos Pharos* 52 (1970), 185–9.

283. 'Foreword' to *'Secular Christianity' and God Who Acts*, by Robert J. Blaikie. London: Hodder & Stoughton, 1970.

284. '1469–1969. La Philosophie et la Théologie de Jean Mair ou Major (1469–1550)', *Archives de Philosophie* 33 (1970), 261–94. Conclusion to (269).

285. 'The Hermeneutics of St Athanasius', *Ekklesiastikos Pharos* 52 (1970), 46–68, 89–106, 237–49.

286. 'The Problem of Natural Theology in the Thought of Karl Barth', *Religious Studies* 6 (1970), 121–35.

287. 'Professor Daniel L. Deegan', *New College Bulletin* 5 (1970), 121–35.

288. 'Sermon on Acts 2:41–47', *Ekklesiastikos Pharos* 52 (1970), 191–9.

289. 'Theological Rationality', in E. Descamps (ed.), *Ecclesia a Spiritu Sancto edocta, Lumen Gentium, Mélanges théologiques. Hommage à Mgr. G. Philips*. Gembloux: Duculot, 1970, 455–73.

1971

290. *God and Rationality*. London: Oxford University Press, 1971.

291. 'The Breaking of Bread', *Liturgical Studies* 1 (1971), 8–26.

292. 'Die eine Taufe, die Christus und seiner Kirche gemeinsam ist', *Kerygma und Dogma* 17 (1971), 188–208.

293. 'The Hermeneutics of St Athanasius', *Ekklesiastikos Pharos* 53 (1971), 133–49.

294. 'Karl Barth', in G. L. Hunt (ed.), *Ten Makers of Modern Protestant Thought*, revised edn. New York: Association Press, 1971, 47–54.

295. 'Newton, Einstein and Scientific Theology', *Eighth Annual Keese Lecture*, The University of Tennessee at Chattanooga, 1971.

296. 'The Place of Word and Truth in Theological Inquiry according to St Anselm', in R. Zavalloni (ed.), *Studia medievalia et mariologica: P. Carolo Balic OFM septuagesimum explenti annum dicata*. Rome: Editrice Antonianum, 1971, 131–60.

1972

297. Coedited with J. K. S. Reid: H. Martin Rumscheidt, *Revelation and Theology. An Analysis of the Barth–Harnack Correspondence of 1923 (Monograph Supplements to the Scottish Journal of Theology*, No. 1). Cambridge: Cambridge University Press, 1972.

298. Review of Alastair McKinnon, *Falsification and Belief*, in *Scottish Journal of Theology* 25 (1972), 435–53.

299. Review of S. Brown and G. Gall (eds), William of Ockham, *Opera philosophica et theologica. Opera theologica*, 2, in *Scottish Journal of Theology* 25 (1972), 459–60.

300. Review of G. Etzkorn and I. Brady (eds), Roger Marston, *Quodlibeta quattuor ad fidem codicum nunc primum edita*, in *Scottish Journal of Theology* 25 (1972), 461–2.

301. 'Doctrine', bibliographical contribution to *A Theological Book List*, edited by A. Marcus Ward. London: Theological Education Fund, 1972, 20–3.

302. 'Newton, Einstein and Scientific Theology', *Religious Studies* 8 (1971), 233–50. Reprint of (295).

303. 'Truth and Authority: Theses on Truth', *Irish Theological Quarterly* 39 (1972), 215–42.

304. 'Where is God?', in Ronald Selby Wright (ed.), *Asking Them Questions*. New Series. London: Oxford University Press, 1972, 17–26.

1973

305. Review of J. B. Bauer (ed.), *Bauer Encyclopaedia of Biblical Theology*, in *Scottish Journal of Theology* 26 (1973), 229–31.

306. Review of M. Schmaus, A. Grillmeier and L. Scheffczyk (eds), *Handbuch der Dogmengeschichte*, in *Scottish Journal of Theology* 26 (1973), 229–31.

307. Review of Alaster McKinnon (ed.), *The Kierkegaard Indices*, vol. 2, in *Scottish Journal of Theology* 26 (1973), 106–8.

308. Review of Thomas Aquinas, *Opera Omnia iussu Leonis XIII P. M. edita*, vols 40 and 48, in *Scottish Journal of Theology* 26 (1973), 350–2.

309. Review of Peter Lombard, *Sententiae in IV Libris Distinctae. Editio tertia. Ad fidem Codicum Antiquiorum restituta*, vols 1 and 2, parts 1 and 2, edited by fathers of the College of St Bonaventure, in *Scottish Journal of Theology* 26 (1973), 488–90.

310. 'The Church in an Era of Scientific Change', *The Month* (April 1973), 136–42, and (May 1973), 176–80.

311. 'The Church in an Era of Scientific Change', *New College Bulletin* 7 (1973), 19–31. Reprint of (310).

312. 'The Integration of Form in Natural and Theological Science', *Science, Medicine and Man* 1 (1973), 143–72.

313.   'The Relation of the Incarnation to Space in Nicene Theology', in Andrew Blane (ed.), *The Ecumenical World of Orthodox Civilisation. III. Russia and Orthodoxy: Essays in Honor of Georges Florovsky*. The Hague: Mouton, 1973, 43–70.

314.   'Vérité et Autorité: Thèses sur la Vérité', *Istina*, 18, Paris (1973), 44–7.

1974

315.   Coedited with J. K. S. Reid: Robin H. S. Boyd, *India and the Latin Captivity of the Church* (*Monograph Supplements to the Scottish Journal of Theology*, No. 3). Cambridge: Cambridge University Press, 1974.

316.   Coedited with J. K. S. Reid: Horton Harris, *David Friedrich Strauss and His Theology* (*Monograph Supplements to the Scottish Journal of Theology*, No. 2). Cambridge: Cambridge University Press, 1974.

317.   'Athanasius: A Reassessment of His Theology', *Abba Salama* 5 (1974), 171–87.

318.   'The Contribution of the Greek Community in Alexandria to the Intelligent Understanding of the Christian Gospel and Its Communication in the World of Science and Culture', *Abba Salama* 5 (1974), 188–92.

319.   'Une contribution aux recherches de Foi et Constitution sur le ministère ordonné', *Istina* 19 (1974), 429–34.

320.   'The Evangelical Significance of the Homoousion. Sermon on John 5:17', *Abba Salama* 5 (1974), 165–8.

321.   'Science and Philosophy in the Era of Cosmological Revolution', *Abba Salama* 5 (1974), 168–70.

1975

322.   *Theology in Reconciliation: Essays towards Evangelical and Catholic Unity in East and West.* London: Geoffrey Chapman, 1975.

323.   Coedited with G. W. Bromiley: Karl Barth, *Church Dogmatics* I/1, *The Doctrine of the Word of God*, Prolegomena, Part 1, translated by G. W. Bromiley. Edinburgh: T&T Clark, 1975.

324.   Coedited with J. K. S. Reid: Eberhard Jüngel, *The Trinity: God's Being is in Becoming*, translated by Horton Harris (*Monograph Supplements to the Scottish Journal of Theology*, No. 4). Cambridge: Cambridge University Press, 1975.

325. 'Ecumenismo', in *Enciclopedia del Novecento come lessico del massimi problemi*. Rome: Instituto dell' Enciclopedia Italiana – Ricordi, 1975, 294–313.

326. 'The Function of Inner and Outer Word in Lonergan's Theological Method', in Patrick Corcoran (ed.), *Looking at Lonergan's Method*. Dublin: The Talbot Press, 1975, 101–26.

327. 'Hermeneutics, or the Interpretation of Biblical and Theological Statements, according to Hilary of Poitiers', *Abba Salama* 6 (1975), 37–69.

328. 'Le Mystère pascal du Christ et l'Eucharistie', *Istina* 20 (1975), 404–34.

329. 'Toward an Ecumenical Consensus on the Trinity', *Theologische Zeitschrift* 31 (1975), 337–50.

1976

330. *The Centrality of Christ: Devotions and Addresses*: General Assembly of the Church of Scotland; Edinburgh: Saint Andrew Press, 1976.

331. *Space, Time and Resurrection*. Edinburgh: Handsel Press, 1976.

332. Translator, *The Catechism of Geneva*, in *The Proposed Book of Confessions of the Presbyterian Church of the United States*, Atlanta, Georgia: Materials Distribution Service, 11–43.

333. Review of Gordon Leff, *William of Ockham: The Metamorphosis of Scholastic Discourse*, in *Scottish Journal of Theology* 29 (1976), 271–4.

334. 'Christian Theology in the Context of Scientific Revolution', in Yves Congar and others (eds), *Pluralisme et Oecumenisme en Recherches Théologiques*, Mélanges offerts au R. P. Dockx, O.P., *Bibliotheca Ephemeridum Theologicarum Lovaniensium* 43, Paris-Gembloux: Éditions Duculot, 1976, 295–311.

335. 'Dietetic Deficiencies the Church Can Cure'; reprint of 'The Centrality of Christ', Address to the General Assembly, Edinburgh, 1976, *Christianity Today*, 20, no. 24, Washington, DC (September 1976), 10–13. Original in (330).

336. 'The First-Born of All Creation', *Life and Work*, Edinburgh (December 1976), 12–14.

337. 'I am Full of Hope', *The Church Herald*, Grand Rapids, MI (November 1976), 10–12. Reprint of (335).

338. 'The Pascal Mystery and the Eucharist: General Theses', *Liturgical Review* 6 (1976), 6–12.

339. 'Sermon on St John 17:17–19', preached at the Consecration of Dr Alastair Haggart as Bishop of Edinburgh, 5 December 1975, *Ekklesiastikos Pharos* 8 (1976), 226–31.

1977

340. Japanese Edition of *Karl Barth. An Introduction to His Early Theology, 1910–1931*. Tokyo: Shinkyo Shuppansha Publishing Co., 1977.

341. 'Foreword' to James Bulloch, *The Church of Scotland*, Exeter: Religious Education Press, 1976/7.

342. 'Foreword' to *Spotlight* 18. Edinburgh: The Woman's Guild (Spring 1977), 1.

343. 'God, Destiny and Suffering', *The Healing Hand, Journal of the Edinburgh Medical Missionary Society* (Summer/Autumn 1977), 8–15.

344. 'If I Were Starting Again', *Presbyterian Outlook, New Pulpit Digest*, Jackson, Mississippi (March/April 1977), 64.

345. 'Message of the Moderator', *Punchbole*, Magazine of Colvend and Southwick Parish, Dumfriess-shire, 4 (November 1976).

346. 'Moderatorial Tours', *Reports of the General Assembly of the Church of Scotland*, 1977, 374–5.

347. 'The Pre-eminence of Christ', Sermon to the General Assembly of the Church of Scotland before HM the Queen, *Expository Times* 89 (1977), 54–5.

348. 'Violence in Society: An Examination of the Destructive Forces Inherent in Modern-day Society'. *Independent Broadcasting* 13 (September 1977), 15–18.

349. 'The Whole Universe Revolves Round Christ', *Life and Work*, Edinburgh (April 1977), 12–14.

350. 'Why I'd Turn the Kirk Upside Down', *The Scotsman* (17 May 1977), 13.

1978

351. *Space, Time and Incarnation*. New York and Oxford: Oxford University Press, 1978. Galaxy book edition of (262).

352. *Theological Science.* New York and Oxford: Oxford University Press, 1978. Galaxy book edition of (263).

353. 'Determinism and Free Creation according to the Theologians', in *Communications of the New York Symposium*, July 1977, *Institut International des Sciences Théoriques*, Bruxelles, reprint from *Abba Salama* 9, Addis Ababa (1978).

354. 'Man the Priest of Creation', address on receiving the Templeton Prize, *The Templeton Prize 1978*, Dublin: The Lismore Press, 1978.

355. 'The New Lecturer – Alan Lewis'. *New College Bulletin* (February 1978), 7–8.

1979

356. 'Acceptance Address for the Templeton Prize for 1978', *Journal of the American Scientific Affiliation* 31 (1979), 102–6.

357. 'Determinismus und Freie Schöpfung aus der Sicht der Theologie', *Das Deutsches Institut für Bildung und Wissen*, Paderborn (December 1979), 1–20.

358. 'Foreword' to George C. Cameron, *The Scots Kirk in London*. Oxford: Becket Publications, 1979, vii-viii.

359. 'God and the Contingent World', *Zygon* 14 (1979), 329–48.

360. 'Israel: People of God – God, Destiny and Suffering', *Theological Renewal* 13, Esher, Surrey (October 1979), 2–14.

361. 'Memorandum on Orthodox/Reformed Relations', *The Reformed World* 35 (1979), 337–45.

362. 'The Open Universe and the Free Society', *Ethics in Science and Medicine*, 6, no. 3, Oxford: Pergamon Press (November 1979), 145–53.

363. 'The Rev. Matthew James Cameron Dinwoodie', *Scottish Journal of Theology* 32 (1979), 301–2.

364. 'A Serious Call for a Return to a Devout and Holy Life', *Life and Work* (July 1979), 14–15.

365. 'We Have Broken Free from a Closed Universe' – Interview with Brian Cooper, *The British Weekly & Christian World* (21 September 1979), 7.

366. Reprint of selected articles in Ray S. Anderson, *Theological Foundations for Ministry: Selected Readings for a Theology of the Church and Ministry.* Edinburgh: T&T Clark; Grand Rapids, MI: Eerdmans, 1979:

> 'The Word of God and the Response of Man', 111–34 (= 277)
>
> 'The Foundation of the Church', 199–215 (= 199)
>
> 'Come, Creator Spirit, for the Renewal of Worship and Witness', 370–89 (= 235)
>
> 'The Ministry', 390–429 (= 150)
>
> 'Service in Jesus Christ', 714–33 (= 246)
>
> 'The Church in the New Era of Scientific and Cosmological Change', 752–76 (= 322, pp. 267–93)

1980

367. *Calvin's Doctrine of Man*, new translation into Japanese by Sakae Izumida. Tokyo: Meige Shobo Publishing Company Ltd, 1980.

368. *Christian Theology and Scientific Culture.* Belfast: Christian Journals; New York: Oxford University Press, 1980.

369. *The Ground and Grammar of Theology.* Charlottesville, VA: The University of Virginia Press; Belfast: Christian Journals, 1980.

370. Editor and contributor: *Belief in Science and in Christian Life. The Relevance of Michael Polanyi's Thought for Christian Faith and Life.* Edinburgh: Handsel Press, 1980.

371. *Christ's Words.* An Address given for The Order of Christian Unity. Jedburgh: The Unity Press, 1980.

372. 'Der Mensch, Priester der Schöpfung', *Das Deutsches Institut für Bildung und Wissen* 9, Paderborn (18 September 1980), 123–5.

373. 'Foreword' to *Christ's Words*, edited by Emily Astor. London: The Bible Societies and William Collins, 1980.

374. 'The Framework of Belief', in *Belief in Science and in Christian Life*, 1–27. See (370).

375. 'God and the Contingent World', *Epistemologia* 3 (1980) (*Numero Speciale*), 161–94.

376. 'Incarnation: Myth or Reality', *Scottish Church Society Report*, 1972–80, 12.

377. 'Introduction' to Ian Clark, *Reservoirs of Power*. London and Glasgow: Pickering & Inglis, 1980.

378. 'Introduction', *Belief in Science and in Christian Life*. See (370).

379. 'Memoranda A & B, on Orthodox/Reformed Relations', *Ekklesia kai Theologia* 1, Thyateira House, London (1980), No. 1, 197–205; No. 2, 337–45.

380. 'A New Vision of Wholeness', Interview with Mary Doyle Morgan, *Presbyterian Survey* (December 1980), Atlanta, Georgia, 21–3.

381. 'Notes and Comments', *Belief in Science and in Christian Life*, 133–47. See (370).

382. 'The Place of Michael Polanyi in the Modern Philosophy of Science', *Ethics in Science and Medicine* 7 (1980), 57–95.

383. 'Ultimate Beliefs and the Scientific Revolution', *Cross Currents* 30 (1980), 129–49.

1981

384. *Christian Theology and Scientific Culture*, vol. 1 of series, *Theology and Scientific Culture*, edited with General Foreword by Torrance. New edition. Belfast: Christian Journals; New York: Oxford University Press, 1981.

385. *Divine and Contingent Order*. Oxford and New York: Oxford University Press, 1981.

386. *The Incarnation: Ecumenical Studies in the Nicene-Constantinopolitan Creed A.D. 381*. edited with Introduction. Edinburgh: Handsel Press, 1981, xi–xxii.

387. Editor: *Theology and Science in Mutual Modification*, by Harold B. Nebelsick (*Theology and Scientific Culture*, No. 2). Belfast: Christian Journals; New York: Oxford University Press, 1981.

388. Review of Ivan Tolstoy, *James Clerk Maxwell: A Biography*. Edinburgh: Canongate, 1981, in *Life and Work*, Edinburgh (December 1981), 42.

389. 'Croyances Fondamentales et Revolution Scientifique', *Revue d'Histoire et de Philosophie Religieuses* 61 (1981), 43–66.

390. 'Foreword' to W. A. Whitehouse, *The Authority of Grace: Essays in Response to Karl Barth*. Edinburgh: T&T Clark, 1981, xix–xx.

391. 'Immortality and Light', The Drew Lecture on Immortality, November 1980. *Religious Studies* 17 (1981), 147–61.

392. 'The Nicene Creed: Its Emergence in History – The Nicene-Constantinopolitan Creed, 381 A.D.', *Scottish Church Theology Society Bulletin* (1981).

393. 'Putting First Things First', *Presbyterian Survey*, Atlanta, Georgia (October 1981), 10–12.

394. 'A Right-About Turn for the Kirk', *Life and Work*, Edinburgh (April 1981), 20–1.

395. 'A Right-About Turn for the Kirk', *The Presbyterian Record*, Ontario, Canada: Don Mills (November 1981), 30–2. Reprint of (394).

1982

396. *Juridical Law and Physical Law: Toward a Realist Foundation for Human Law.* Edinburgh: Scottish Academic Press, 1982.

397. *Reality and Evangelical Theology.* The 1981 Payton Lectures. Philadelphia: Westminster Press, 1982.

398. Editor: John B. Carnes, *Axiomatics and Dogmatics* (*Theology and Scientific Culture*, No. 4). Belfast: Christian Journals; New York: Oxford University Press, 1981.

399. Edited with Preface and Introduction: James Clerk Maxwell, *A Dynamical Theory of the Electromagnetic Field.* Edinburgh: Scottish Academic Press, 1982.

400. Editor: Iain Paul, *Science, Theology and Einstein* (*Theology and Scientific Culture*, No. 3). Belfast: Christian Journals; New York: Oxford University Press, 1981.

401. Review of Russell Stannard, *Science and Christian Belief*, in *Life and Work*, Edinburgh (December 1982), 42.

402. 'The Bible's Guide on Baptism: Acts 2:14–39', *Life and Work*, Edinburgh (September 1982), 16–17.

403. 'Charge Without Foundation', reply to Neil McCallum, 'Retraction sought', *Glasgow Herald* (29 June 1982).

404. 'Christian/Jewish Dialogue: Report of the Overseas Council of the Church of Scotland', in D. W. Torrance (ed.), *The Witness of the Jews to God*, Edinburgh: Handsel Press, 1982, 139–50.

405. Contribution to Seminar on *Das Problem der Zeit*, edited by Reinhard Wegner, Paderborn: Das Deutsches Institut für Bildung und Wissen, 1981, 7–16.

406. 'A "Dark Whirlpool" of Error', *Life and Work*, Edinburgh (July 1982), 18–19.

407. 'Divine and Contingent Order', in A. R. Peacocke, *The Sciences and Theology in the Twentieth Century*. Notre Dame, IN: University of Notre Dame Press, 1981, 81–97, 302–3.

408. 'The Divine Vocation and Destiny of Israel in World History', in D. W. Torrance (ed.), *The Witness of the Jews to God*. Edinburgh: Handsel Press, 1982, 85–104.

409. 'Not against S[cottish] N[ational] P[arty]', Reply to Mr Neil McCallum's letter in *The Scotsman*, 24 May, regarding his misrepresentation of my remarks in the General Assembly about anti-semitism and an unnamed Scottish nationalist, *The Scotsman* (1 June 1982).

410. 'Ökumene und Rom', in *Ökumene. Möglighkeiten und Grenzen heute*, edited by Karlfried Froelich. Tübingen: J. C. B. Mohr (Paul Siebeck), 1982, 40–9.

411. 'The Orthodox Church in Great Britain', *The Greek Review* 22 (18 December 1982), 22–4.

412. 'Reply: Infant Baptism – The Debate Continues', in *Ministers' Forum* 48, Edinburgh (December 1982), 4–5.

413. 'Theological Realism', in *The Philosophical Frontiers of Christian Theology. Essays Presented to D. M. MacKinnon*, edited by B. Hebblethwaite and S. Sutherland. Cambridge: Cambridge University Press, 1982, 169–96.

414. 'Transformation in the Frame of Knowledge', *Science and Public Policy*, Journal of the Science Policy Foundation, London, 9, no. 2 (April 1982), 97–100.

415. 'Über die Änderung des wissenschaftlichen Denkrahmens', *Evangelium und Wissenschaft* 7 (1982), 13–19.

416. 'Das Verhältnis zwischen christlichen Glauben und moderner Naturwissenschaft. Die geistesgeschichtliche Bedeutung von James Clerk Maxwell', *Das Deutsche Institut für Bildung und Wissen*, Paderborn (1982), 1–24.

417. 'What is "the Substance of the Faith"?' *Life and Work*, Edinburgh (November 1982), 16–17.

1983

418. *The Mediation of Christ* (The Didsbury Lectures). Exeter: Paternoster Press, 1983.

419. Editor: Peter E. Hodgson, *Our Nuclear Future?* (*Theology and Scientific Culture*, No. 5). Belfast: Christian Journals, 1983.

420. Review of Peter Lombard: *Sententiae in IV Libris Distinctae. Edit. Tertia. Ad Fidem Codicum Antiquorum restituta.* Tomus II, Liber III et IV. Roma, Grottaferrata, Editiones Collegii S. Bonaventurae ad Claras Aquas, in *Scottish Journal of Theology* 36 (1983), 129–31.

421. 'Comments on Eucharistic Practice in the Church of Scotland Today', *Church Service Society Record* 5 (Summer 1983), 17–18.

422. 'The Concept of Order in Theology and Science', *The Month*, Second New Series 16 (1983), 401–4.

423. 'The Deposit of Faith', *Scottish Journal of Theology* 36 (1983), 1–28.

424. 'Homoousion', *Evangelische Theologie* 43 (1983), 16–26.

425. 'John Philoponos of Alexandria, Sixth Century Christian Physicist', *Texts and Studies* vol. 2. London: Thyateira House, 1983, 261–5.

426. 'The Orthodox Church in Great Britain', *Texts and Studies* vol. 2. London: Thyateira House, 1983, 253–9.

427. 'Reply to Correspondence regarding Baptism', *Life and Work*, Edinburgh (January 1983), 32.

428. '"The Substance of the Faith": A Clarification of the Concept in the Church of Scotland', *Scottish Journal of Theology* 36 (1983), 327–38.

429. 'The Substance of the Faith', *The Monthly Record of the Free Church of Scotland* 2 (1983), 261–5. Condensed version of (428).

1984

430. *The Christian Doctrine of Marriage*, pamphlet. Edinburgh: Handsel Press, 1984.

431. *The Eldership in the Reformed Church*, pamphlet. Edinburgh: Handsel Press, 1984.

432. *Test-Tube Babies: Morals, Science, and the Law*, pamphlet. Edinburgh: Scottish Academic Press, 1984.

433. *Transformation and Convergence in the Frame of Knowledge. Explorations in the Interrelations of Scientific and Theological Enterprise.* Belfast: Christian Journals; Grand Rapids, MI: Eerdmans, 1984.

434. Review of Robert Grosseteste, *Hexaemeron*, edited with an Introduction by Richard C. Dales and Servus Gibben, in *Scottish Journal of Theology* 37 (1984), 408–10.

435. Review of Colin E. Gunton, *Yesterday and Today: A Study of Continuities in Christology*, in *Kings' Theological Review* 7 (1984), 29–30.

436. 'Der Begriff der Ordnung in der Theologie und in der Wissenschaft. Neue Fragen erfordern neue Zusammenarbeit', *Das Deutsches Institut für Bildung und Wissen* 22, Jahrgang (June 1984), 81–6. See (422).

437. 'Christ's Human Nature', letter to the Editor. *The Monthly Record of the Free Church of Scotland* (May 1984), 114.

438. 'The Concept of Order in Theology and Science', *The Princeton Seminary Bulletin* 5 (1984), 130–9. See (422).

439. 'Le concept d'ordre, en théologie et dans la science', in *Resurrection*, 73 *Cahiers Théologiques*, edited by Jerome de Gramont. Paris, 1984, 65–72. See (422).

440. 'Ecumenism and Rome', *Scottish Journal of Theology* 37 (1984), 59–64.

441. 'The Eldership in the Reformed Church', *Scottish Journal of Theology* 37 (1984), 503–18.

442. '"The Historical Jesus": From the Perspective of a Theologian', *The New Testament Age: Essays in Honor of Bo Reicke*, edited by William C. Weinrich. Macon, GA: Mercer University Press, 1984, vol. 2, 511–26.

443. 'A Pilgrimage in the School of Faith – An Interview With T. F. Torrance', by John I. Hesselink, *Reformed Review* 38 (1984), 49–64: see also *Thomas F. Torrance: Reformed Theologian*, Michigan: Holland, 1984, 2–68.

444. 'Ho Sebasmiotatos Archiepiskopos Thyateiron kai Megales Bretannias Kurios Methodios', Rotary Club International, District 247, Rotary Club of Athens 1928 (18 October 1984), 28–34.

445. 'The Three Hierarchs and the Greek Christian Mind', *Texts and Studies* vol. 3. London: Thyateira House, 1984, 87–96.

446. 'The Tide Has Turned', *Life and Work*, Edinburgh (March 1984), 14–15.

447. 'Transformation in the Frame of Knowledge', contribution to *In Necessariis Unitas. Mélanges offerts à Jean-Louis Leuba*, edited by Richard Stauffer. Paris: Editions du Cerf, 1984, 397–484. See (414).

448. 'To triadologikon themelion kai o triadologikos charakter tes pisteos kai tes authentias en te ekklesia', *Ekklesia kai Theologia*, vol. 5, London (1984), 11–57.

1985

449. *The Christian Frame of Mind*. Edinburgh: Handsel Press, 1985.

450. *Reality and Scientific Theology*, The Margaret Harris Lectures, Dundee, 1970 (*Theology and Science at the Frontiers of Knowledge*, vol. 1). Edinburgh: Scottish Academic Press, 1985.

451. *Space, Time and Resurrection*, Japanese edition, translated by Nobuo Kosaka. Tokyo: Otaku, 1985.

452. Editor: Harold P. Nebelsick, *Circles of God. Theology and Science from the Greeks to Copernicus* (*Theology and Science at the Frontiers of Knowledge*, vol. 2). Edinburgh: Scottish Academic Press, 1985.

453. Editor, *Theological Dialogue between Orthodox and Reformed Churches*. Edinburgh: Scottish Academic Press, 1985.

454. Review of J. Wreford Watson, *The Wounds of Love*, in *Life and Work*, Edinburgh (August 1985), 36.

455. 'The Eschatology of Faith: Martin Luther', in *Luther: Theologian for Catholics and Protestants*, edited by George Yule. Edinburgh: T&T Clark, 1985, 145–213.

456. 'God Did IT!' *Decision*, British Edition, 25, no. 9, London (September 1985), 16–17. Abbreviated version of (422).

457. 'Grundlegende Aufgaben in Theologie und Wissenschaft', *Evangelium und Wissenschaft* 13 (1985), 4–22.

458. 'Introduction' to George Dion, *St. Athanasius Contra Apollinarem*. Athens: Dragas, 1985, 1–2.

459. 'Memoranda on Orthodox/Reformed Relations', in *Theological Dialogue between Orthodox and Reformed Churches*, 3–18. See (453).

460. 'The Open Texture of "Faith" and "Godliness" in the Church's Confession', in Dr George Dion Dragas (General Editor), *Aksum – Thyateira, A Festschrift for Archbishop Methodios of Thyateira and Great Britain*. Athens, 1985, 143–58.

461. 'Sur le dialogue du juif et du chrétien', *Communio: Revue Catholique Internationale* 10 (1985), 140–52. See (404).

462. 'Theological and Scientific Inquiry', *Dedication Addresses. The Center of Theological Inquiry*. Reports from the Center, No. 2, Princeton, 1985, 7–21.

463. 'Theologische und Wissenschaftliche Forschung', *Das Deutsches Institut für Bildung und Wissen* 23 No. 7 (July/August 1985), 3–16.

464. 'The Trinitarian Foundation and Character of Faith and Authority in the Church', *Theological Dialogue between Orthodox and Reformed Churches*, 79–120. English version of (448). See also (453).

1986

465. Editor: Iain Paul, *Science and Theology in Einstein's Perspective* (*Theology and Science at the Frontiers of Knowledge*, vol. 3). Edinburgh: Scottish Academic Press, 1986.

466. Review of Karl Barth, *Witness to the Word: A Commentary on John 1*, in *Life and Work*, Edinburgh (November 1986), 42–3.

467. 'Answer to Prosch on Polanyi's Convictions about God', letter to the Editor, *Tradition and Discovery: The Polanyi Society Periodical* 14, no. 1 (1986–7), 30.

468. 'Jesus is God and Man in One Person . . . and Will Come Again', *Life and Work*, Edinburgh (March 1986), 16–17.

469. 'Karl Barth: 1886–1986', *TSF Bulletin* 10, no. 1 (1986), 4–5.

470. 'Karl Barth and the Latin Heresy', *Scottish Journal of Theology* 39 (1986), 461–82.

471. 'Karl Barth and Patristic Theology', in *Theology beyond Christendom: Essays on the Centenary of the Birth of Karl Barth*, edited by John Thomson. Allison Park, PA: Pickwick Publications, 1986, 215–39.

472. 'The Legacy of Karl Barth (1886–1986)', *Scottish Journal of Theology* 39 (1986), 289–308.

473. 'My Interaction with Karl Barth', in *How Karl Barth Changed My Mind*, edited by Donald K. McKim. Grand Rapids, MI: Eerdmans, 1986, 52–64.

474. 'Theological and Scientific Inquiry: Conjoint Research between Theology and Science at Points of Their Deepest Convergence', in *Journal of the American Scientific Affiliation* 38, no. 1 (March 1986), 2–10.

475. 'Time in Scientific and Historical Research', in *Gottes Zukunft – Zukunft der Welt: Festschrift für Jürgen Moltmann zum 60. Geburtstag*, Herausgegeben von Hermann Deuser, Gerhard Marcel Martin, Konrad Stock und Michael Welker. Munich: Chr. Kaiser Verlag, 1986, 292–7.

476. 'Why Karl Barth Still Matters So Much', *Life and Work*, Edinburgh (June 1986), 16.

1987

477. Editor: Carver T. Yu, *Being and Relation: A Theological Critique of Western Dualism and Individualism* (*Theology and Science at the Frontiers of Knowledge*, vol. 8). Edinburgh: Scottish Academic Press, 1987.

478. Editor: Ralph G. Mitchell, *Einstein and Christ: A New Approach to the Defence of the Christian Religion* (*Theology and Science at the Frontiers of Knowledge*, vol. 5). Edinburgh: Scottish Academic Press, 1987.

479. Editor: John C. Puddefoot, *Logic and Affirmation – Perspectives in Mathematics and Theology* (*Theology and Science at the Frontiers of Knowledge*, vol. 9). Edinburgh: Scottish Academic Press, 1987.

480. Editor: Victor Fiddes, *Science and the Gospel* (*Theology and Science at the Frontiers of Knowledge*, vol. 7). Edinburgh: Scottish Academic Press, 1987.

481. Editor: Alexander Thomson, *Tradition and Authority in Science and Theology* (*Theology and Science at the Frontiers of Knowledge*, vol. 4). Edinburgh: Scottish Academic Press, 1987.

482. Editor: W. G. Pollard, *Transcendence and Providence, Reflections of a Physicist and Priest* (*Theology and Science at the Frontiers of Knowledge*, vol. 6). Edinburgh: Scottish Academic Press, 1987.

483. Review of *Cyril of Alexandria: Select Letters*. Edited and translated by Lionel R. Wickham. Oxford: Clarendon Press, 1983; *Peter of Callinicum: Anti-Tritheist Dossier*, edited by R. Y. Ebied, A. Van Roey and L. R. Wickham, in *Scottish Journal of Theology* 40 (1987), 317–19.

484. 'The Hermeneutics of John Reuchlin, 1455–1522', in *Church, Word and Spirit. Historical and Theological Essays in Honor of Geoffrey W. Bromiley*, edited by James E. Bradley and Richard A. Muller. Grand Rapids, MI: Eerdmans, 1987, 107–21.

485. 'Hugh Ross Mackintosh: Theologian of the Cross', *Scottish Bulletin of Evangelical Theology* 5 (1987), 160–73.

486. 'The Reconciliation of Mind', *TSF Bulletin* 10, no. 3 (1987), 4–7.

487. 'Time in Scientific and Historical Research', *Epistemologia* 10 (1987), 73–80. Reprint of (475).

1988

488. *The Hermeneutics of John Calvin* (*Monograph Supplements to Scottish Journal of Theology*, edited by A. I. C. Heron and I. R. Torrance). Edinburgh: Scottish Academic Press, 1988.

489. *The Trinitarian Faith: The Evangelical Theology of the Ancient Catholic Church*. Edinburgh: T&T Clark, 1988.

490. Edited with Introduction and Bibliography, new edition of Thomas Torrance, *China's First Missionaries, 'Ancient Israelites'*. Chicago: Daniel Shaw Co., 1988.

491. Editor: W. P. Garvin, *Creation and Scientific Explanation* (*Theology and Science at the Frontiers of Knowledge*, vol. 10). Edinburgh, Scottish Academic Press, 1988.

492. 'The Apocalypse Now 1: On the Book of Revelation', *Life and Work*, Edinburgh (October 1988), 19–20.

493. 'The Apocalypse Now 2: The Gospel Depends on the Cross', *Life and Work*, Edinburgh (November 1988), 20–1.

494. 'The Apocalypse Now 3. Babylon – Symbol of Worldly Power . . . an Imitation of the Kingdom of God', *Life and Work*, Edinburgh (December 1988), 16–17.

495. 'Early Patristic Interpretation of the Holy Scriptures', *Ekklesia kai Theologia* 9 (1988), 137–70.

496. 'Foreword' to *Words of Jesus Christ*, revised on behalf of the Order of Christian Unity. Oxford: Oxford University Press, 1988, iii–iv.

497. 'Fundamentale Ergebnisse in Theologie und Wissenschaft', *Das Deutsches Institut für Bildung und Wissen*, 1 (January 1988), 11–21.

498. 'The Goodness and Dignity of Man in the Christian Tradition', *Modern Theology* 4 (1988), 309–22.

499. 'The Hermeneutics of Clement of Alexandria', *Texts and Studies. A Review for Hellenism in the Diaspora* 7 (1988), 61–105.

500.   'Interview with Professor Thomas F. Torrance', in *Different Gospels*, edited by Dr Andrew Walker. London: Hodder & Stoughton, 1988, 42–54.

501.   'The Light of the World', sermon, *The Reformed Journal* 38, no. 12 (December 1988).

502.   '*Physikos kai Theologikos Logos:* St Paul and Athenagoras at Athens', *Scottish Journal of Theology* 41 (1988), 11–26.

503.   'Realism and Openness in Scientific Inquiry', in *La Mystique*, edited by Jean-Marie Van Cangh, *Relais Etudes* 4, Paris: Desclée, 1988, 231–41. See also (504).

504.   'Realism and Openness in Scientific Inquiry', *Zygon* 23 (1988), 159–69. See also (503).

1989

505.   *The Christian Frame of Mind: Reason, Order, and Openness in Theology and Natural Science.* Colorado Springs, CO: Helmers & Howard, 1989. New and enlarged edition of (449).

506.   Editor: Russell Stannard, *Grounds for Reasonable Belief* (*Theology and Science at the Frontiers of Knowledge*, vol. 12). Edinburgh: Scottish Academic Press, 1989.

507.   Editor: J. E. Ambrose, *The Mirror of Creation* (*Theology and Science at the Frontiers of Knowledge*, vol. 11). Edinburgh: Scottish Academic Press, 1989.

508.   'The Apocalypse Now 4: The Voice of Jesus Breaks through, *Life and Work*, Edinburgh (January 1989), 19–20.

509.   'A Centenary with Implications' (Alfred Edward Edersheim), *Life and Work*, Edinburgh (April 1989), 17–18.

510.   'The Doctrine of the Holy Trinity according to St Athanasius', *Anglican Theological Review* (1987), 395–405.

511.   'The Goodness and Dignity of Man in the Christian Tradition', in *Christ in Our Place. The Humanity of God in Christ for the Reconciliation of the World*, essays presented to Professor James Torrance, edited by Trevor A. Hart and Daniel P. Thimell (Princeton Theological Monograph Series 25). Exeter: Paternoster Press; Allison Park, PA: Pickwick Publications, 1989, 369–87. Reprint of (498).

512. 'The Hermeneutics of Erasmus', in *Probing the Reformed Tradition. Historical Studies in Honor of Edward A. Dowey, Jr.*, edited by Elsie Anne McKee and Brian G. Armstrong. Louisville, KY: Westminster/ John Knox Press, 1989, 48–76.

513. 'An Open Letter to the Church and Nation Committee' (Tom Torrance and the 'Claim of Right'), *Life and Work*, Edinburgh (September 1989), 39.

514. 'The Soul and Person in Theological Perspective', in *Religion, Reason and the Self: Essays in Honour of Hywel D. Lewis*, edited by Stewart R. Sutherland and T. A. Roberts. Cardiff: University of Wales Press, 1989, 103–18.

515. 'Tom Torrance's Reply on Israel', *Life and Work*, Edinburgh (July 1989), 33–4. (Response to 'Mission to the Jews', letters by Colin Morton and Chris Wigglesworth in *Life and Work* [June 1989], 7.)

516. 'Where is the Church of Scotland Going?', *Life and Work*, Edinburgh (May 1989), 25–6.

1990

517. *Karl Barth: Biblical and Evangelical Theologian.* Edinburgh: T&T Clark, 1990.

518. *Science Théologique.* Paris: Presses Universitaires de France, 1990. French translation of (263), with a new preface by Torrance.

519. 'Calvin's Doctrine of the Trinity', *Calvin Theological Journal* 25 (1990), 165–93.

520. 'The Distinctive Character of the Reformed Tradition', in *Incarnational Ministry. The Presence of Christ in Church, Society, and Family*, edited by Christian D. Kettler and Todd H. Speidell. Colorado Springs, CO: Helmers & Howard, 1990, 2–15.

521. 'The Doctrine of the Holy Trinity – Gregory Nazianzen and John Calvin'. The Nicholas Zernov Lecture, Oxford, 1989. *Sobornost* 12 (1990) 7–24.

522. 'The Doctrine of the Holy Trinity – Gregory Nazianzen and John Calvin', in *Calvin Studies* 5, edited by John H. Leith and W. Stacy Johnson, Richmond, VA: Union Theological Seminary, 1990, 7–19.

523. 'Foreword' to Gordon Martin, *St Paul's Table Talk and Other Papers.* Braunton, Devon: Merlin Books, 1990, 5.

524. 'Fundamental Issues in Theology and Science', in *Science and Religion: One world – Changing Perspectives on Reality*, edited by Jan Fennema and Iain Paul. Dordrecht: Kluwer Academic Publishers, 1990.

525. 'The Message of Pope John Paul II to Theologians and Scientists Commemorating the Third Centenary of Sir Isaac Newton's *Philosophiae Naturalis Principia Mathematica*', in *John Paul II On Science and Religion: Reflections on the New View from Rome*, edited by Robert John Russell, William R. Stoeger, S.J., and George V. Coyne, S.J. Vatican City: Vatican Observatory Publications, 1990, 105–12.

526. 'Nachruf auf Harold P. Nebelsick', *Glaube und Denken* 3 (1990), 11–19.

527   'The Real Crises, Part 1 – The Kirk's Crisis of Faith', *Life and Work*, Edinburgh (October 1990), 15–16.

528. 'The Real Crises, Part 2 – The Crisis of Morality', *Life and Work*, Edinburgh (November 1990), 15–16.

529. 'The Real Crises, Part 3 – The Crisis of Community', *Life and Work*, Edinburgh (December 1990), 16–17.

530. 'Thomas Torrance', interview in Michael Bauman, *Roundtable Conversations with European Theologians*. Grand Rapids, MI: Baker Book House, 1990, 111–18.

531. Tribute to J. S. Stewart, *Life and Work*, Edinburgh (August 1990), 29.

1991

532. 'The Enlightenment Reviewed' – Review of Alexander Broadie, *The Tradition of Scottish Philosophy: A New Perspective on the Enlightenment*, Edinburgh: Polygon, 1990, in *Chapman: Scotland's Quality Literary Magazine*, Edinburgh (1991), 86–8.

533. 'Another View of Scripture', letter on Baptism, *Minister's Forum*, no. 139 (December 1991), 2.

534   'Archbishop Methodios Fouyas', *Ekklesia kai Theologia* 10 (1989–91), 11–15.

535. 'Crisis in the Church', *Theological Digest and Outlook* 6, no. 2, Burlington, Ontario (July 1991). Reprint of (527) (528) and (529).

536. 'Donor Insemination for the Single Woman: The Animalisation of the Human Race', *Ethics and Medicine* 7 (1991).

537. 'Historic Agreement by Reformed and Orthodox on the Doctrine of the Holy Trinity', *Minister's Forum*, edited by John Sim, no. 138, Edinburgh: Church of Scotland (November 1991).

538. 'Light from the East, Personal Experiences of Eastern Christianity: Report of the The Order of Christian Unity – Scottish Branch', with Lady Lothian: 'Light for East and West. The Historic Agreement by Reformed and Orthodox Churches on the Doctrine of the Holy Trinity – an Event of Unique Significance'. Kelso Graphics, 1991, 11–16.

539. 'Mission Scotland 1991 with Billy Graham', letter to *Life and Work*, Edinburgh (August 1991), 31.

540. 'The Transcendental Role of Wisdom in Science', *Science et sagesse: Entretiens de l'Académie Internationale de Philosophie des Sciences, 1990*, edited by Evandro Agazzi. Fribourg: Éditions Universitaires Fribourg Suisse – Universitätsverlag Freiburg Schweiz, 1991, 63–80.

1992

541. *Divine Meaning. Studies in Greek Patristic Hermeneutics*. Edinburgh: T&T Clark, 1992.

542. *The Mediation of Christ: Evangelical Theology and Scientific Culture*. Edinburgh: T&T Clark, 1992. New enlarged edition of (418).

543. *The Ministry of Women*, pamphlet. Edinburgh: Handsel Press, 1992. Reprinted in *Touchstone* (Fall 1992), 5–12.

544. *Senso del divino e Scienza moderna*. Vatican City: Libreria Editrice Vaticana, 1992.

545. *Trinitarian Perspectives: Toward Doctrinal Agreement*. Edinburgh: T&T Clark, 1992.

546. Editor, *Theological Dialogue between Orthodox and Reformed Churches*. Edinburgh: Scottish Academic Press, 1992.

547. 'Bad Taste' – Protest over anti-Jewish Cartoon in *Life and Work* for October, in *The Scotsman* (20 October 1992), 14.

548. 'The Christian Apprehension of God the Father', in *Speaking the Christian God: The Holy Trinity and the Challenge of Feminism*, edited by Alvin F. Kimel, Jr. Grand Rapids, MI: Eerdmans, 1992, 120–43.

549. 'Christian Theology and Scientific Culture. The Way Ahead', in *The Future Agenda. A Festschrift in honour of John Templeton, on his 80th Birthday, November 29th, 1992*. Edinburgh: Hanover Press, 1992, 39–53.

550. 'Crisis in the Kirk', in *St Andrews Rock: The State of the Church in Scotland*, edited by Stewart Lamont, London: Bellew Publishing Company, 1992, 13–23.

551. 'Dramatic Proclamation of the Gospel: Homily on the Passion of Melito of Sardis', *The Greek Orthodox Theological Review* 37 (1992), 147–63.

552. 'Finding Common Ground on the Doctrine of the Trinity: An Introduction & Commentary on a Historic Agreement between Reformed and Orthodox Churches on the Doctrine of the Holy Trinity'. *Touchstone. A Journal of Ecumenical Orthodoxy*, Chicago, 5, no. 1 (Winter 1992), 20–7.

553. 'Finding Common Ground on the Doctrine of the Trinity': An Introduction & Commentary on a Historic Agreement between Reformed and Orthodox Churches on the Doctrine of the Holy Trinity, *Theological Digest & Outlook* 7, no. 2, Burlington, Ontario (July 1992), 13–16.

554. 'The Greek Conception of Space in the Background of Early Christian Theology', *Ekklesia kai Theologia* 11 (1992), 245–94.

555. 'Historic Agreement by Reformed and Orthodox on the Doctrine of the Holy Trinity', republished in *E.C.N.L.: The Journal of the Anglican and Eastern Churches Association*, New Series no. 34 (Spring 1992), 30–2.

556. 'Incarnation and Atonement: Theosis and Henosis in the Light of Modern Scientific Rejection of Dualism'. *Society of Ordained Scientists*, Bulletin no. 7, Edgware, Middlesex (Spring 1992), 8–20.

557. 'Kerygmatic Proclamation of the Gospel: The Demonstration of Apostolic Preaching of Irenaeus of Lyons', *The Greek Orthodox Theological Review* 37 (1992), 105–21.

558. 'More Kirk Teachers Needed for Divinity Faculties', *The Scotsman*, Edinburgh (27 May 1992), 12.

559. 'The Spiritual Relevance of Angels', *Alive to God, Studies in Spirituality Presented to James Houston*, edited by J. I. Packer and Loren Wilkinson. Downers Grove, IL: InterVarsity Press, 1992, 121–39.

560. 'Unchristian Illustration' – Protest over anti-Jewish Cartoon in *Life and Work* for October, *Life and Work*, Edinburgh (November 1992), 4. See (547).

1993

561. *Royal Priesthood: A Theology of the Ordained Ministry.* Edinburgh: T&T Clark, 1993. New edition of (81).

562. 'Anti-Semitism' – Reply to the letter of the Rev. Margaret Forrester, Convener of the Board of World Mission and Unity, *Life and Work*, Edinburgh (March 1993), 41.

563. 'Athanasius Approved of Women Priests?', reply to correspondence, *Touchstone* 6, no. 2 (Spring 1993), 5.

564. 'The Atonement. The Singularity of Christ and the Finality of the Cross: The Atonement and the Moral Order', in *Universalism and the Doctrine of Hell*, edited by Nigel M. de S. Cameron. Exeter: Paternoster Press, 1992; Grand Rapids: Baker Book House, 1993, 225–56.

565. 'The Catholic and Apostolic Church' ('A Machine Grinding Out Its Dogmas'), *Church Times* (21 May 1993), 10.

566. 'In Reply to Henry Reardon' regarding Athanasius, *De Virginitate*, *Touchstone* 6, no. 3 (Summer 1993), 3.

567. 'Israel and Palestine. The Covenant of God with Abraham and his Descendants', reply to letter by Hugh Erskine Fraser, *Life and Work*, Edinburgh (October 1993), 41.

568. 'John Baillie at Prayer', in *Christ, Church, and Society: Essays on John Baillie and Donald Baillie*, edited by David Fergusson. Edinburgh: T&T Clark, 1993, 253–61.

569. 'Preaching Christ Risen Today', *Ministers' Forum*, no. 155 (June 1993), 2.

570. With D. W. Torrance, 'To the Jew First – An Urgent Call', *Life and Work*, Edinburgh (May 1993), 17.

1994

571. *Preaching Christ Today: The Gospel and Scientific Thinking.* Grand Rapids, MI: Eerdmans, 1994.

572. *Preaching Christ Today*, pamphlet. Edinburgh: Handsel Press, 1994.

573. *Trinitarian Perspectives: Toward Doctrinal Agreement.* Edinburgh: T&T Clark, 1994.

574. 'Christ's People in a Secular World', *Life and Work*, Edinburgh (April 1994), 14–15.

575. 'Church Finance and Mission', letter, *Ministers' Forum*, Edinburgh (April 1994), 2.

576. 'The Doctrine of the Virgin Birth', *Scottish Bulletin of Evangelical Theology* 12, no. 1 (1994), 9.

577. 'Foreword' to Iain Mackenzie, *The Anachronism of Time: A Theological Study into the Nature of Time.* Norwich: The Canterbury Press, 1994, ix–xi.

578. 'Foreword' to Fraser McLuskey, *The Cloud and the Fire. His Path For Me.* Edinburgh, Cambridge and Durham: The Pentland Press, 1994, ix–xi.

579. 'The Ought and the Is: Moral Law and Natural Law', *Insight: A Journal of the Faculty of Austin Seminary – A Festschrift in Honor of George Stuart Heyer, Jr.* (Spring 1994), 49–59.

580. 'Prescription et description: Loi morale et loi naturelle', *Ethique: La vie en question* 13, Paris: Éditions Universitaires (1994), 101–9.

581. 'Professor Alan Lewis', obituary, *The Scotsman*, Edinburgh (1 March 1994), 14.

582. 'Professor Donald Mackinnon', *Church Times* (18 March 1994), 4.

583. 'Reaffirming the Cornerstone of Faith', *The Scotsman*, Edinburgh (3 January 1994), 4.

584. 'The Transfinite Significance of Beauty in Science and Theology', in *L'art, la science et la métaphysique: études offerts à André Mercier*, edited by Luz Garcia. New York/Berne: Peter Lang, 1993, 393–418.

585. 'The Truth of the Virgin Birth', *The Herald*, Glasgow (14 January 1994), 11.

586. 'The Truth of the Virgin Birth Is Not about "Immaculate Conception"', letter, *The Herald*, Glasgow (17 January 1994).

587. 'What He Meant by Heresy', a Defence of George Carey, Archbishop of Canterbury, against the Editor (Review, 13 March), *The Sunday Telegraph*, 1712 (27 March 1994), 32.

1995

588. *Divine Meaning: Studies in Patristic Hermeneutics.* Edinburgh: T&T Clark, 1995.

589. *The Uniqueness of Divine Revelation and the Authority of the Scriptures*, pamphlet. Edinburgh: Rutherford House, 1995.

590. 'Incarnation et rachat: Theôsis et hénôsis à la lumière du refus moderne et scientifique du dualisme', in *Le Salut Chrétien*, Académie internationale des sciences religieuses, sous la direction de Jean-Louis Leuba, Paris: Desclée, 1995, 231–50.

591. 'J. R. Porter's "Erroneous and Strange Doctrine"', in *Faith and Worship*. London: The Prayer Book Society, 1995, 24–5.

592. 'The Qiang Church', *Friends of the Church in China*, Newsletter, 29 (Spring 1995).

593. 'The Swamp of Secularism', *Ministers' Forum* 173 (April 1995).

594. 'The Uniqueness of Divine Revelation and the Authority of the Scriptures: The Creed Association Statement', *Scottish Bulletin of Evangelical Theology* 13 (1995), 97–101.

1996

595. *The Christian Doctrine of God: One Being Three Persons*. Edinburgh: T&T Clark, 1996.

596 *The Doctrine of Grace in the Apostolic Fathers*. Eugene, OR: Wipf & Stock, 1996. Reprint of (17).

597. *Kingdom and Church: A Study in the Theology of the Reformation*. Eugene, OR: Wipf & Stock, 1996. Reprint of (89).

598. *Scottish Theology, From John Knox to John McLeod Campbell*. Edinburgh: T&T Clark, 1996. Expanded version of (603).

599. *Theological Science*. Edinburgh: T&T Clark, 1996. New edition of (263).

600. *When Christ Comes and Comes Again*. Eugene, OR: Wipf & Stock, 1996. Reprint of (109).

601. Editor, *The Scottish Order of Christian Unity: Memorandum of Foundation, Charter, Structure, Constititution, Rules*. Edinburgh: Scottish Order of Christian Unity, 1996.

602. Review of Leanne Van Dyk, *The Desire of Divine Love. John McLeod Campbell's Doctrine of the Atonement*, in *Scottish Journal of Theology* 49 (1996), 125–7.

603. 'From John Knox to John McLeod Campbell: A Reading of Scottish Theology', in *Disruption to Diversity: Edinburgh Divinity 1846–1996*, edited by David F. Wright and Gary D. Badcock. Edinburgh: T&T Clark, 1996, 1–28.

604. 'The Ministry of Women', in *The Call to Serve. Biblical and Theological Perspectives on Ministry in Honour of Bishop Penny Jamieson*, edited by Douglas A. Campbell, Sheffield: Academic Press, 1996, 269–84. Reprint of (543).

605. 'Revelation, Creation and Law', The Warburton Lecture, *The Heythrop Journal* 37 (1996), 273–83.

606. 'The Transcendental Role of Wisdom in Science', in *Facets of Faith and Science*, vol. 1: *Historiography and Modes of Interaction*, edited by Jitse van der Meer. Lanham, MD: University Press of America; New York: Pascal Centre for Advanced Studies in Faith and Science, 1996, 131–49. Revised version of (540).

607. 'The Trinitarian Theology of Nicolas Nissiotis', in *Nikos A. Nissiotis: Religion, Philosophy and Sport in Dialogue. In Memoriam*, edited by Marina N. Nissiotis. Athens: Dragas, 1994, 170–3.

608. 'Ultimate and Penultimate Beliefs in Science', in *Facets of Faith and Science*, vol. 1: *Historiography and Modes of Interaction*, edited by Jitse van der Meer. Lanham, MD: University Press of America; New York: Pascal Centre for Advanced Studies in Faith and Science, 1996, 151–76.

1997

609. Edited with Preface and Introduction: James Clerk Maxwell, *A Dynamical Theory of the Electromagnetic Field*. Eugene, OR: Wipf & Stock, 1997. Reprint of (399).

610. *Conflict and Agreement in the Church*, vols. 1 and 2, Eugene, OR: Wipf & Stock, 1997. Reprint of (139) and (155).

611. *God and Rationality*. Edinburgh: T&T Clark, 1997. Reprint of (290).

612. *The School of Faith*. Eugene, OR: Wipf & Stock, 1997. Reprint of (140).

613. *Space, Time and Incarnation*. Edinburgh: T&T Clark, 1997. Reprint of (263).

614. *Theological Science*, Chinese Edition of (262). Tao Fong Shan, Shatin, NT, Hong Kong: Institute of Sino-Christian Studies, 1997.

615. *Theology in Reconciliation: Essays towards Evangelical and Catholic Unity in East and West*. Eugene, OR: Wipf & Stock, 1997. Reprint of (322).

616. *Theology in Reconstruction*. Eugene, OR: Wipf & Stock, 1997. Reprint of (223).

617. 'Figure Who Was Greatly Appreciated – R. S. V. Wright', *The Scotsman*, Edinburgh (30 June 1997), 16.

618. Foreword to *God, Family and Sexuality*, edited by David W. Torrance. Carberry: Handsel Press, 1997, iv–v.

619. Foreword to Henry Drummond, *The Greatest Thing in the World and Other Essays*. Guildford: Eagle, Inter Publishing Service, 1997, 1–3.

620. 'Legal and Evangelical Priests: The Holy Ministry as reflected in Calvin's Prayers', in *Calvin's Books: Festschrift for Peter de Klerk*, edited by W. H. Neuser, H. J. Selderhuis and W. van't Spijker. Heerenveen: Uitgeverij J. J. Groen en Zoon, 1997, 63–74.

621. 'The Transcendental Role of Wisdom on Science', reprinted in *From Polanyi to the 21st Century*, Proceedings of a Centenial Conference, Kent State University, 11–13 April 1991, edited by Richard Gelwick. The Polanyi Society, 1997, 2–18. Reprint of (606).

622. 'When Does a Personal Being Begin?' Supplementary Paper to *Building Healthy Babies: The Importance of the Pre-Natal Period*. Jedburgh: Women and Children's Welfare Fund, 1997, 13–18.

1998

623. *Divine and Contingent Order*. Edinburgh: T&T Clark, 1998. Reprint of (385).

624. Review of David Fergusson, 'The Cosmos and the Creator', in *Scottish Journal of Theology* 51 (1998), 507–8.

625. 'The Christian Charter: The Soul and Person of the Unborn Child', *Theological Digest and Outlook*, Burlington, ON (March 1998), 5–8.

626. 'Einstein and God', *Reflections* 1, Princeton, NJ: Center for Theological Inquiry (Spring 1998), 2–15.

627. 'The Federalist Principle', letter to the Editor, *Peace and Truth: The Magazine of the Sovereign Grace Union* 1 (1998), 28–9.

628. 'Ronald William Vernon Selby Wright', *Year Book of the Royal Society of Edinburgh*. Edinburgh: Royal Society of Edinburgh, 1998, 153–6.

629. 'Science and Access to God: Epistemological Perspectives', *Jian Dao* 10 (1998), 43–58.

630. 'Die Substanz des Glaubens', in *Zukunft der Reformierten Theologie: Aufgaben – Themen – Traditionen*, edited by Michael Welker and David Willis. Neukirchen: Neukirchener Verlag, 1998, 205–18. German translation of (423).

631. 'Torrance, David Watt', in *Biographical Dictionary of Christian Missions*, edited by Gerald H. Anderson. New York: Macmillan, 1998, 675.

632. 'Torrance, Thomas', in *Biographical Dictionary of Christian Missions*, edited by Gerald H. Anderson. New York: Macmillan, 1998, 675.

1999

633. *The Soul and the Person of the Unborn Child.* Edinburgh: Handsel Press, 1999.

Index

21656450R00167

Made in the USA
Lexington, KY
22 March 2013